# EDUCATION STRATEGY IN THE DEVELOPING WORLD: REVISING THE WORLD BANK'S EDUCATION POLICY

# INTERNATIONAL PERSPECTIVES ON EDUCATION AND SOCIETY

## Series Editor Volumes 1–4: Abraham Yogev

Volume 1: International Perspectives on Education and Society

Volume 2: Schooling and Status Attainment: Social Origins and Institutional Determinants

Volume 3: Education and Social Change

Volume 4: Educational Reform in International Perspective

## Series Editor from Volume 5: David P. Baker

Volume 5: New Paradigms and Recurring Paradoxes in Education for Citizenship: An International Comparison

Volume 6: Global Trends in Educational Policy

Volume 7: The Impact of Comparative Education Research on Istitutional Theory

Volume 8: Education For All

Volume 9: The Worldwide Transformation of Higher Education

Volume 10: Gender, Equality and Education from International and Comparative Perspectives

## Series Editor from Volume 11: Alexander W. Wiseman

Volume 11: Educational Leadership: Global Contexts and International Comparisons

Volume 12: International Educational Governance

Volume 13: The Impact of International Achievement Studies on National Education Policymaking

Volume 14: Post-Socialism Is Not Dead: (Re)Reading the Global in Comparative Education

Volume 15: The Impact and Transformation of Education Policy in China

INTERNATIONAL PERSPECTIVES ON EDUCATION AND SOCIETY VOLUME 16

# EDUCATION STRATEGY IN THE DEVELOPING WORLD: REVISING THE WORLD BANK'S EDUCATION POLICY

EDITED BY


CHRISTOPHER S. COLLINS

*University of Hawaii at Mānoa*

ALEXANDER W. WISEMAN

*Lehigh University*



Emerald

United Kingdom – North America – Japan
India – Malaysia – China

Emerald Group Publishing Limited
Howard House, Wagon Lane, Bingley BD16 1WA, UK

First edition 2012



**British Library Cataloguing in Publication Data**
A catalogue record for this book is available from the British Library

ISBN: 978-1-78052-276-0
ISSN: 1479-3679 (Series)

Printed and bound by CPI Group (UK) Ltd, Croydon, CR0 4YY

# CONTENTS

# LIST OF CONTRIBUTORS


| | |
|---|---|
| *Richard Allington* | University of Tennessee, Knoxville, TN, USA |
| *Robert F. Arnove* | Indiana University, Bloomington, IN, USA |
| *Supriya Baily* | George Mason University, Manassas, VA, USA |
| *Sarah Beardmore* | RESULTS Educational Fund, Washington, DC, USA |
| *Tammy Boyd* | University of Central Florida, Orlando, FL, USA |
| *Christopher S. Collins* | University of Hawaii at Mānoa, Honolulu, HI, USA |
| *Chijioke J. Evoh* | New York City Department of Education, New York, NY, USA |
| *D. Brent Edwards, Jr.* | University of Maryland, College Park, MD, USA |
| *Rachael Gabriel* | University of Connecticut, CT, USA |
| *Stephen P. Heyneman* | Vanderbilt University, Nashville, TN, USA |
| *Devin Joshi* | University of Denver, Denver, CO, USA |
| *Steven J. Klees* | University of Maryland, College Park, MD, USA |
| *Owen G. McGrath* | University of California (UC) Berkeley, Berkeley, CA, USA |
| *Francine Menashy* | University of Toronto, Toronto, ON, Canada |

| | |
|---|---|
| *John Middleton* | Education Consultant, Arlington, VA, USA |
| *Karen Mundy* | University of Toronto, Toronto, ON, Canada |
| *Tom Owens* | University of Central Florida, Orlando, FL, USA |
| *Victor J. Sensenig* | Penn State University, University Park, PA, USA |
| *M. Najeeb Shafiq* | University of Pittsburgh, Pittsburgh, PA, USA |
| *William Smith* | Penn State University, Bellefonte, PA, USA |
| *Nelly P. Stromquist* | University of Maryland, College Park, MD, USA |
| *Donna C. Tonini* | Teachers College, Columbia University, New York, NY, USA |
| *Athena Vongalis-Macrow* | Deakin University, Burwood, Australia |
| *Alexander W. Wiseman* | Lehigh University, Bethlehem, PA, USA |

# PREFACE

This volume of the International Perspectives on Education and Society series examines the development of the World Bank's *Education Strategy 2020*[1] (http://www.worldbank.org/educationstrategy2020). The Executive Summary of this strategy is reprinted in this volume for easy reference. Prior to the release of the *Education Strategy 2020*, a World Bank concept note was developed and consultations about the new strategy took place around the world. To document and analyze this process of education strategy development by the World Bank, this volume brings together a diverse array of voices and responses to the Bank's strategy for education in the developing world. As discussed in the introductory chapter, this volume primarily focuses on the World Bank's strategy development, and attempts to bridge the dichotomy between critics and advocates by providing relevant scholarship to influence both the World Bank's practice and the research and critiques that focus on the Bank's education strategies, policies and activities. The unique character of this volume is that it follows a significant shift in the World Bank's education policy as it was taking place and immediately following its development by using the unique approach of simultaneously documenting and analyzing the *Education Strategy 2020* development.

This volume is anchored by several chapters from recognized World Bank scholars and experts, yet still consists largely of chapters from a variety of perspectives and methodologies. For example, chapters in this volume include (a) historical overviews of Bank education strategies and impact, (b) evaluations and analyses of the Bank's call for input and response to the new strategy, as well as the voices represented in the actual process of development, (c) research on the current work of the Bank in education, and (d) implications of the *Education Strategy 2020*.

In summary, the chapters in this volume tie together the themes of education strategy development, economic development, and educational reform that gives both an overview as well as detailed analyses of both the predicted and observed impact of these changes. When the chapters in this volume are taken as a whole, this approach provides a framework for understanding the process and potential impact of the World Bank's

*Education Strategy 2020* development as well as for providing a framework for policymakers and comparative education researchers alike to investigate both the Bank's policymaking process and impact.

Many chapters were received and reviewed for potential inclusion, and the editors of the volume would like to especially thank the external reviewers who gave their time and expertise to make significant comments, suggestions for improvement, and recommendations regarding both content and contributions of the chapters published here. These scholars and external reviewers are:

Arvil V. Adams (World Bank)
Said Assar (Telecom Business School, France)
Felipe Barrera-Osario (World Bank)
Robin Broad (American University)
Brendan Cantwell (University of Georgia)
Timothy Chester (University of Georgia)
Brian Cooksey (University of Minnesota)
H.P.M. (Bert) Creemers (University of Groningen)
Jake Gross (Azuza Pacific University)
Lynn Ilon (Seoul National University)
Jae-Eun Jon (Korea University)
Alexander Jun (Azuza Pacific University)
David Kamens (George Mason University)
Krishna Kumar (World Bank)
Jon Lauglo (University of Oslo)
Amy Liu (University of California, Los Angeles)
Megan Madden (University of Toronto)
Lisa Millora (University of California, Los Angeles)
Russel Potter (University of Arizona)
Nitya Rao (University of East Anglia)
Robert Rhoads (University of California, Los Angeles)
Val Rust (University of California, Los Angeles)
Karen Sutton (Ventura County Community College District)
Kati Szelenyi (University of Massachusetts, Boston)
Fran Vavrus (University of Minnesota)
Richard T. Watson (University of Georgia)

Again, we extend a sincere and heartfelt thank you to the many supporters who made this volume possible, and who contributed to enhancing the quality and rigor of each chapter. The development of the World Bank's *Education Strategy 2020* is not only important to the developing world, but to the whole world. It serves as both an example and in some cases a model for how multilateral educational policy development occurs as well as how it is interpreted.

## NOTE

1. The publisher acknowledges the use of two different terms when referring to the World Bank's *Education Strategy 2020* in this book. These (*Education Sector Strategy* and *Education Strategy*) are the result of historical inconsistencies in the naming of the World Bank's Strategies in the past.

Alexander W. Wiseman
*Series Editor & Volume Co-Editor*

Christopher S. Collins
*Volume Co-Editor*

# PART I
# INTRODUCTION

# EDUCATION, DEVELOPMENT, AND POVERTY: AN INTRODUCTION TO RESEARCH ON THE WORLD BANK'S EDUCATION POLICY AND REVISION PROCESS

Christopher S. Collins and Alexander W. Wiseman

## ABSTRACT

*The World Bank's Education Strategy 2020 is the latest in a line of education-related strategies focused on supporting economic development in countries worldwide through systematic and targeted educational reform. Yet, the Bank has many critics and a history of developing educational policies that do as much to create inequality in education as to develop it. This chapter introduces the theme of the volume by focusing on the link between the World Bank's education strategy development and poverty reduction. The key emphasis of this volume is the development of the Bank's Education Strategy 2020 and how it is shaped by empirical evidence, contextualized by national and regional variations in education and the economy, and the legacy of World Bank educational involvement.*

**Education Strategy in the Developing World: Revising the World Bank's Education Policy**
**International Perspectives on Education and Society, Volume 16, 3–18**

**ISSN: 1479-3679/doi:10.1108/S1479-3679(2012)0000016004**

*This introductory chapter concludes by summarizing the ways in which each of the volume's chapters contribute to this theme, and suggests how the debates related to the Bank's education strategies and policies can move forward and contribute to educational improvement, economic development, and poverty reduction worldwide.*

The World Bank is arguably the most-discussed multinational organization in both empirical and policy research coming out of the field of comparative and international education. Most of the published research related to the World Bank and education presents the Bank's work as neoliberal in agenda and activity (Colclough, 1996; Goldman 2005, Hinchcliffe, 1993; Mamdani, 2007; Peet, 2003), but there is also a large literature that addresses the World Bank's involvement in education indirectly – from the Bank's perspective – and its impact on economic development in particular countries, regions or cross-nationally (Psacharopoulos & Patrinos, 2004; Yusuf, 2009). Among the topics frequently debated in the literature are the impact of World Bank education policy and activity by gender, race, and ethnicity, and national economic status (Benavot, 1989; King & Hill, 1997; Peppin Vaughan, 2010). There is also work that focuses on the Bank's impact on higher or tertiary education, secondary education, primary education, and early childhood education (Archer, 2006; Barrett, 2011; Heyneman, 2003; Rhoads & Torres, 2007).

Throughout all of the empirical and policy research focused on the World Bank, there is one common thread, which is the implied impact that the Bank's education policies and activities have on either the reduction or exacerbation of poverty and economic inequality, especially in developing countries and regions worldwide. In other words, while the research and policy work written from the Bank's perspective often talks about the impact of education on economic *development*, the critical approach to the Bank's education impact looks at economic *inequality* and overtly seeks to identify neoliberal agendas in the education-related policies and activities of the World Bank (Colclough, 1996; Goldman 2005; Hinchcliffe, 1993; Mamdani, 2007; Peet, 2003). Even a cursory review of the literature investigating education and the World Bank, reveals that the Bank is not the only multinational organization to be the subject of this kind of debate.

Regardless of the focus of the published research, in the background of conversations about the role of the Bank and other large development organizations like the OECD, is the need to understand mechanisms of poverty reduction and increasing equity. Over one billion people in the world live in extreme poverty, defined as less than 1.25 USD per day (Chen & Ravallion, 2008). While this is an often-used statistic, there are a variety of opinions about how to interpret the pervasive degree of the global population living in economic crisis. Furthermore, there is great disagreement about how to alleviate the problems. Microfinance innovator and founder of the Grameen Bank, Muhammad Yunus (2003, p. 35), asserts:

> Brilliant theorists of economics do not find it worthwhile to spend time discussing issues of poverty and hunger. They believe that these will be resolved when general economic prosperity increases. These economists spend all their talents detailing the processes of development and prosperity, but rarely reflect on the origin and development of poverty and hunger. As a result, poverty continues.

The search for root cause or causes of poverty continue, but there is no clear solution.

Although Yunus couples poverty and hunger together, others have maintained that while hunger is a problem related to drought and other natural causes, it does not have a primary role in solving the one billion in extreme poverty statistic. Abhijit V. Banerjee and Esther Duflo (2011) note that other than the 2004 tsunami and the 2010 Haiti earthquake, the announcement from the United Nations Food and Agriculture Organization in June 2009 that a billion people are suffering from hunger grabbed headlines in a way that the Bank's estimates about living under a dollar a day never did. While associations about poverty and hunger are common (see the UN Millennium Development Goals), Banerjee and Duflo reference evidence that most adults, even the most poor, exist outside of a nutrition and poverty trap. They do this in order to demonstrate that poverty-reduction policy is perhaps too focused on the idea that the poor need cheap grain. Instead, they advocate for a focus on nutrition for women and children, policies that avoid political quagmires, and educational reform.

Even the World Bank incorporates "fighting poverty with passion and professionalism" into the mission of the institution (World Bank, n.d.). Subsequently, the World Bank's *Education Sector Strategy 2020* identifies that education is fundamental to development and growth, which is related to access to education as a basic human right (as noted in the Universal Declaration of Human Rights and the United Nations Convention on the Rights of the Child). However, the Bank takes a formulaic approach in linking economic growth to poverty reduction. In other words, the World Bank's assumption that accompanies this approach is that as long as education can be tied to economic growth, it is indirectly tied to reducing poverty. In the Education Strategy 2020, there is a concerted effort to highlight a notion that acquired skills are a component of economic growth – not the number of years spent in a classroom. This suggests a significant shift in the way that the World Bank addresses the role of education in poverty reduction because it emphasizes educational content and its application rather than simply educational enrollment and attainment.

Traditional notions of development through economic growth are not always linked to poverty reduction. For example, Bank officials readily note examples of economic growth coupled with rising inequality (Collins & Rhoads, 2010). Even the most powerful and wealthy countries, in some cases, exhibit higher rates of poverty than other industrialized nations. These stratifications are noted in the United Nations Human Development Report (2010). Probing further, if the most powerful countries exhibit signs of inequality, what are the true markers of development? What is the goal? These are key questions for evaluating a strategy connecting education and poverty reduction. For example, the "Convention on the Rights of a Child" was signed by 192 nations. Two of the nations refusing to sign include the United States and Somalia, a highly developed and extremely poor nation (UNICEF, 2005). The fact that these countries on either end of the development spectrum connect in their resistance to a fundamental rights declaration suggests that development and poverty reduction may not be as directly connected as much as the World Bank's education-related policies suggest.

Many of the previous criticisms of the World Bank's education policies have evolved from the assumption that the contribution of education to economic development (and poverty reduction by proxy) is a zero-sum equation. In other words, it was argued for many decades that increased educational attainment was accompanied by increased economic productivity – at least for specific educational levels (e.g., primary education in Latin America in the 1980s) (Becker, 1993; Psacharopoulos & Woodhall, 1985). Yet, the development of communities' economic productivity has been shown to not equal the amount of inputs into the education system in every case. And, these zero-sum assumptions become even less likely as education becomes massified (Wiseman, 2010), meaning that the outcomes of education are neither consistent nor productivity related in all cases when education is institutionalized throughout national systems worldwide.

The relationship between education and poverty is an ongoing debate to which the Bank's Education Strategy 2020 adds direction. One way to think about this is to debate the roles that market-versus-government factors impact the ways that education can or cannot ameliorate poverty. From a specifically US perspective, David Berliner (2007, p. 489) writes:

> Perhaps we are not doing well enough because our vision of school reform is impoverished. It is impoverished because of our collective views about the proper and improper roles of government in ameliorating the problems that confront us in our schools; our beliefs about the ways in which a market economy is supposed to work; our concerns about what constitutes appropriate tax rates for the nation; our religious views about the elect and the damned; our peculiar American ethos of individualism; and our almost absurd belief that schooling is the cure for whatever ails society.

Berliner's comments suggest that the key concern may be more social and cultural than situated in a purely market-versus-government struggle. As mentioned previously, there is debate about the connection between education and poverty reduction. In some cases, the idea that schools cannot alleviate poverty may communicate a lack of confidence in education.

On the other hand when investments do not produce the desired results, education is questioned as a viable strategy. Some place economic problems as the primary component that needs to be solved prior to focusing on educational inequality (Traub, 2000) while others link educational inequality to biological inequality (Herrnstein & Murray, 1994). Yet, others still find fault with the fact that economic questions are being addressed rather than more specifically cultural or more overtly social justice issues (Kazamias, 2001). Similar to discussions about globalization and its impact on education, the debate about the World Bank's policies becomes embroiled in a debate that has more factors and threads than can be addressed at once. This often leads to strong criticisms of the World Bank, which may be highly appropriate, but are poorly communicated because of their overly complex nature or unarticulated presentation.

One such question, which often follows or accompanies these complex criticisms asks: what is the impact of globalization on social change, national development, the betterment of individuals in regions around the world and how education and learning might impact those processes? But, globalization alarms often result in misleading, overarching, or reductionist critiques that miss the crucial question about whether poverty reduction can be accomplished through educational reform and development. The difficulty in connecting the two comes from the fact that poverty-reduction strategies are often associated with reducing corruption, creating jobs, providing malaria nets, and other functions that show immediate results (Collins, 2011). Educational development as a means to advance learning, which then contributes to poverty-reduction, is much more complicated, much less direct, and requires additional work to understand the relationship between learning and development. When the links between learning or education and development attempt to be clarified there needs to be debate to produce more refined knowledge and understanding. This kind of reflective debate – rather than proclamations about which educational development model does or does not "work" – is what leads to change.

The Bank's Education Strategy 2020 is an attempt at clarification, albeit a particularly developed and presented attempt. This volume is, therefore, a venue for reflective debate that can provide a foundation for change in how the World Bank strategically positions education as a tool for economic development and how poverty reduction relative to educational reform can occur in countries worldwide. The chapters in this volume present a series of perspectives to create deeper understanding of the Bank's attempt at clarification, and how it is situated both in the history of the Bank's own education-related activity worldwide as well as the legacy of those actions as they relate to any and all future activity of the Bank in the realm of education for development.

## EVALUATING A "STRATEGY"

The finalized Strategy has become a policy statement of the Bank. Policy, however, carries a variety of meanings. In Bank publications there are (a) formal policy statements (approved by the World Bank Board and labeled as official policy), (b) policies that guide the actions of World Bank staff (which is not limited to official policy papers and may depart from them), and (c) policies as discerned from lending practices (which in education has often differed from formally stated policy). Although these categories make World Bank policy a complex notion, the Education Sector Strategy 2020 carries the weight of official policy with the World Bank listed as the author. This suggests that the Strategy has been vetted and approved by the World Bank and its agents as the defining statement related to the Bank's education policies and activities in countries around the world for the foreseeable future.

As mentioned in the previous section, the published empirical and policy research that focuses on the World Bank is plentiful, and often takes a critical stance. A closer investigation of the literature on the Bank's education policies and activities suggests that there are two expanding literatures that address how the World Bank impacts economic development through education. One focuses directly on the World Bank itself and includes attention to both organizational behavior and the Bank's global political role (Colclough, 1996; Goldman, 2005; Heyneman, 2003). The second focuses on aid and the aid process, and ranges from efforts to improve aid effectiveness to calls for dismantling the aid system entirely (Easterly, 2003, 2006; Peet, 2003; Sachs, 2005).

The chapters organized in this volume play a role in both the organizational and political category as well as the aid and effectiveness category – from both an historical perspective and with a focus on the future. Understanding and evaluating the consultation and strategy development process over time requires not only a review of calls for consultations and varied inputs, but also a careful comparison between inputs received and changes (or lack of change) in position and policy papers, from initial drafts to final versions. Chapters in this volume capture this consultation process and the development of the strategy from multiple angles.

In a follow up to his presentation at the annual meeting of the Comparative and International Education Society in Montreal in 2011 (also included in Chapter 4 of this volume), Stephen P. Heyneman notes that in the 1995 strategy, the World Bank was the author of 12 percent of the citations compared to 26.5 percent of the citations in the new strategy. Citations from other agencies (as opposed to independent authors) also increased from 5 percent to 29 percent from the 1995 to the 2011 strategy. Heyneman asserts that "the insularity of the Bank has gotten worse, not better." Building on the criticism of insularity, Heyneman also composed a list of questions that should be answered by the Bank (using the pronoun "you" to indicate a direct question to the World Bank and its staff):

1. Are you still recommending that public finances shift from higher to primary education?
2. Are you able to work outside of government ministries of education to assist the development of the private sector?
3. Are you prepared to confront the fact the greatest threat to the quality of education is from within the system itself in terms of corruption?
4. Are you prepared to stop lending to a country which steals your assistance?
5. Are you prepared to sanction staff who propose conditionalities which later prove to be professionally incorrect?
6. Are you prepared to equip low-income countries with policy advisors so they might negotiate loan conditionalities with more equity?
7. Are you willing to confront the fact that education constitutes only a tiny percent of the development agenda?

These questions, although not answered in the Strategy, represent criticisms of the Bank that are likely to guide future work of the World Bank in the education sector. Furthermore, the questions represent an examination of both the underlying motivations behind the strategy as well as the implications. While the Bank works with policy and developing knowledge, most of any Bank's work surrounds money, including both direct lending and grants. Many commentators see the various policy and policy-related papers, including periodic strategies, as largely inconsequential and not particularly indicative of what the World Bank does. However, the following chapters connect the Bank's education strategy and impact in meaningful ways by addressing both the organizational and political role of the Bank worldwide, but also by investigating the aid and effectiveness of the Bank, especially related to educational development and poverty reduction.

## PIECING THE PUZZLE TOGETHER

Like many good ideas, the spark that ignited this volume came about through a coincidence between existing interests and an opportunity to develop them further. It started in May 2010, during the Comparative International Education Society (CIES) Annual Conference held in Chicago, IL, USA. As a predominantly academic conference, it is typical for university faculty members and graduate students to attend the conference to present and listen to the latest research in the field. Given the topic of international education, practitioners in the field of international education development are also often present. These practitioners include people from agencies who are working in developing countries with a specific purpose of reducing poverty, raising capacities, or some combination of both. This combination of scholars and development practitioners is the spark that put this volume in motion.

At the May 2010 CIES conference, the World Bank had a larger presence than in previous years. For example, the exhibit hall featured a booth that promoted a concept paper for the new education strategy. This concept paper was widely distributed by Bank staff that were working at the booth and attending sessions. In addition, Elizabeth M. King, Director of Education in the Human Development Network of the World Bank, was slated to make a formal presentation about the strategy. In this position, Dr. King is the World Bank's senior spokesperson for global policy and strategic education issues in developing countries. The session was scheduled in a typical hotel conference room, but even 10 minutes before the time the session was supposed to begin, the room was filled past capacity. The president of CIES announced that the session was to be relocated to the grand ballroom of the hotel. Dr. King made a presentation about the strategy, and three scholars on the panel offered a brief response to the concept paper before the floor was opened to questions from a larger than usual audience. Questions varied in nature, but some well-known scholars from CIES asked directed questions including, "How do you explain the fact that poverty has increased on your watch?" and "Why does the World Bank not pay attention to scholarly research that should influence their practices?" These poignant questions were large in scope and consequently difficult to answer in a brief session, but Dr. King addressed the topics, albeit without providing a direct answer.

The session on the World Bank's new concept paper brought up some key questions about the relationship between a scholarly society and large agencies that enact policies and measures that have great impact on the developing world both through and on education. For example, is a scholarly society truly an audience for a large organization like the World Bank, and in turn, is the Bank utilizing research that emerges from scholarship in places like CIES? Questions like these and a desire to create a framework for evaluating the work of the new strategy provided the motivation to compose a volume focused on the World Bank's Education Sector Strategy 2020. Although it is unclear why CIES was on the list of places to host a consultation about the concept paper, it is clear that it was one consultation of many. A more constructed dialogue was held at the Brookings Institute (as documented in the chapter by Robert F. Arnove in this volume) and a majority of the consultations were held around the world with representatives from national ministries of education.

In the summer of 2010, this volume was in development as potential authors eagerly awaited the draft document of the strategy, which emerged in November 2010. Initial chapters were composed based on the draft as we waited for the final version to be published (this was expected in January 2011 according to the Bank website). However, since these strategies carry more weight than other Bank papers and publications, the Education Sector Strategy 2020 went through a series of approvals that took several months. Significant changes were made between the draft in November 2010 and the final and approved version that emerged in May 2011, just in time for the CIES Annual Conference in Montreal, Canada. The Bank had a much smaller presence at the 2011 conference, with just a handful of staff members passing out a printed copy of the "Executive Summary" of the Strategy (featured in this volume in Chapter 2). At the CIES 2011 conference, at least three scholarly panels were convened to discuss the draft strategy, which each presented different perspectives and angles about the work and potential impact of the Bank on education and development worldwide.

Although there will likely never be a response directly from the Bank regarding these scholarly evaluations, we as editors believe that this volume is an appropriate way to engage these types of global strategy documents. Our intended audience includes scholars who are building knowledge about the work of powerful development agencies, constituencies like ministries of education and educators who are considering the impact and application of strategy statements like this, and development agencies like the World Bank who are weighing the best ways to engage key problems related to development and education in many countries around the world.

## THE LANDSCAPE OF THE DISCUSSION

To evaluate the strategy, this volume has been organized into three main sections. The first section, Strategy Development, includes chapters that evaluate the consultations and the process of putting the document together. M. Najeeb Shafiq's Chapter 3, "Six Questions about The World Bank's 2020 Education Sector Strategy" outlines and answers issues using information directly obtained from Bank staff, including: What is the ESS 2020? What is it not? How is the ESS 2020 different from past Strategies in terms of preparation? How is the ESS 2020 different from past Strategies in terms of policy recommendations? Does the ESS 2020 fit in with the World Bank's broader development strategy? And finally, Does the ESS 2020 matter? This chapter provides a brief but important set of background information necessary to understand the strategy and the following chapters. Former Bank administrator and now professor at Vanderbilt, Stephen P. Heyneman offers a valuable historical perspective in Chapter 4, "When Models become Monopolies: The Making of Education Policy at the World Bank." The historical perspective is also a personal experience from working at the Bank, and this serves as a precursor to Heyneman's analysis of the new Strategy. The model that became a monopoly concerns the evolution of measuring the value of education. From this, Heyneman details organizational struggles for a strategy that is comprehensible, feasible, and compelling in its justification. However, whenever a strategy becomes common wisdom it takes on the form of dogma. Another salient point is that organizations need to be challenged in order to grow and improve, but when an organization silences the challenges, it creates problems for the organization and the stakeholders. This story of how the monopoly occurred in the Bank is a valuable precursor to understanding the development of strategy.

In Chapter 5, Robert F. Arnove's "The World Bank's "Education Strategy 2020": A Personal Account" discusses the Brookings Institute consultation in detail. As a participant in that consultation, his summary is a result of participant observation followed by a reflection on the Bank's response to the input it received as well as to subsequent iterations of its education strategy. Tammy Boyd and Tom Owens' Chapter 6, "Education Sector Strategy 2020 and Popular Participation: Parallels and Pitfalls" identifies the consultative process as a notable departure from standard Bank practices for setting a policy agenda. From their perspective, great potential exists for this new consultative process to produce substantive change in the way the World Bank supports educational efforts in less developed countries. Risk is present as well, depending on whose voice is present in the consolation. This chapter traces the consultative process used by the World Bank in developing ESS 2020. The consultative process and the documents produced by it are critically examined through the lens of post-structuralism, and early indicators of potential problems are discussed.

The next section of the volume, Critical Issues and Perspectives, includes a variety of research and perspectives on topics within the strategy. Chapter 7, "The World Bank, the International Finance Corporation, and Private Sector Participation in Basic Education: Examining the *Education Sector Strategy 2020*" by Karen Mundy and Francine Menashy evaluates the discourse on private engagement as well as the International Finance Corporation, in the particular context of the recent sector strategy. With policy development and advocacy and operations of the IFC as a background, the authors use research on the IFC to contribute to an understanding of the strategy document itself. In Chapter 8, "Theory and Ideology in the Gender Proposals of the World Bank's Educational Sector 2020," Nelly P. Stromquist focuses on two concepts: development and gender, examining how they have been defined and applied to educational policy by the World Bank. The chapter discusses the rationale and evidence presented by the Bank to substantiate its new policies and the extent to which these policies reflect current social science research theory as well as empirical findings concerning educational strategies to create both economic growth and social inclusion.

Steven J. Klees offers three directed critiques about the strategy in Chapter 9, "World Bank and Education: Ideological Premises and

Ideological Conclusions." According to Klees, the strategy is more about testing than learning, the emphasis on a "systems approach" is not substantiated with any evidence about how this may help productivity, and the focus on privatization ignores that education is a public good. Similarly, "Education and Inequality: Implications of the World Bank's Education Strategy 2020" by Devin Joshi and William Smith assesses the likely impact of the Strategy on issues of inequality. This analysis helps to expose both the underlying ideological orientation of World Bank education policy and its linkages to a political economy agenda that continues to emphasize economic growth and private sector schooling over educational equality and human rights.

"Constructing and Measuring Teacher Effectiveness in Global Education Reform" by Rachael Gabriel and Richard Allington builds upon the growing body of research that suggests teacher effectiveness ought to be the primary goal of educational reform efforts across the globe. Given the contingent and constructive nature of what is considered effective teaching, the ways in which effectiveness is measured will have a direct impact on the potential of any reform policy to positively influence the overall effectiveness of a teaching force and therefore the achievement of its students. The authors promote local adaptations of global policies for encouraging and measuring effective teaching. Athena Vongalis-Macrow continues the focus on teaching in Chapter 12, "Deliberative Educational Planning: Including Teachers' Deliberations in Educational Policy Making." This chapter makes a case for the need to include teachers and professional educators in the policy making and implementation processes. The exclusion of teachers' perspectives and teacher demands in World Bank education policies and planning has been an ongoing issue and, according to Vongalis-Macrow, limits the full potential of policy implementation.

In Chapter 13, "The Approach of the World Bank to Participation in Development and Education Governance: Trajectories, Frameworks, Results," D. Brent Edwards, Jr. explores Bank documents to (a) trace the emergence and unpack the theory of the SPF generally, (b) assess where and how within the Bank the SPF is adopted, (c) ascertain the extent to which these conceptions of participation are funded in practice, and (d) determine the effects of related Bank projects on both discrete outcomes as well as the capacity of communities and local governments to foster and support participation more broadly. The last chapter in this section, "ICT, the Education Sector, and Open e-Learning: A Unique Opportunity for the Decade Ahead" by Owen G. McGrath presents the growing education populations as a potential space crisis that can be addressed with using information and communications technologies (ICT). ICTs have reached a stage where virtual schools and distance learning can be employed at scale to meet such challenges. The purpose of the chapter is to draw attention to a specific opportunity that the World Bank has to shape and guide the many ICT-based virtual school projects that will be undertaken in the coming decade. The crucially important opportunity is one for which the World Bank is uniquely suited: to seed and grow an open e-learning movement based on open source, open educational resources, and open pedagogy for secondary and tertiary education in the developing world.

The final section of this volume is a set of "Regional Evaluations" that integrate perspectives from around the globe. Chapter 15, "What doesn't the Education Sector Strategy Say? How the Fast Track Initiative and Multi Sector Operations are Changing the Landscape of World Bank Education Financing" is written by Sarah Beardmore and John Middleton. This chapter identifies the distribution of World Bank-managed education financing programmed by the Bank's education sector, by other Bank sectors, and by the Education for All-Fast Track Initiative. One component of the chapter looks at the proportion of education financing for sub-Saharan Africa managed by other sectors, and reviews twenty education sector and multi-sector operations in the region to determine the presence of education objectives in the project design. Of this lending, a small but indicative sample of 10 operations showed that only half were linked to education objectives, indicators, and national education development goals. Chijioke J. Evoh focuses on the same continent in Chapter 16, "Taming the Youth Bulge in Africa: Rethinking the World Bank's Policy on Technical and Vocational Education for Disadvantaged Youth in the Knowledge Economy." NairoBits Digital Design School in Kenya is presented as a model of a vocational and training school that uses ICTs to improve skill formation among disadvantaged youths in informal settlements in urban Africa. Evoh advocates that meeting the objectives of an ICT-based training and employment generation program for underprivileged youth in Africa would benefit from strong regulatory frameworks and contributions from the World Bank.

In Chapter 17, "Framing the World Bank Education Strategy 2020 to the Indian Context – Alignments, Challenges and Opportunities," Supriya Baily offers a theoretical exploration of the relevance, challenges, and points of consideration to be taken into account as India prepares for the next stage of educational development. This chapter utilizes media reports, government documents, and in-country research to highlight how ES 2020 applies, falls short, or altogether misses the Indian context. Victor J. Sensenig's Chapter 18, "The World Bank and Educational Reform in Indonesia" analyzes two educational reforms that the World Bank has promoted in Indonesia in the last 10 years (one advancing vocational education and one decentralization) and examines how these priorities have been affected by local context and demands and shifts in the global discourse on education. Sensenig concludes that the World Bank's role in the diffusion of education reform is best understood from a world culture perspective but that its interests are advanced in particularly opportune moments like democratic transitions.

The final chapter of the volume by Donna C. Tonini, "Increasing the Flow of Students, Washing out Quality: World Bank Policy Effects in Tanzanian Secondary Schools," highlights the dichotomous nature of World Bank educational goals and examines how enrollment growth became prioritized over quality in Tanzania. Nestled within the theoretical framework of developmental discourse, the chapter evaluates the new World Bank 2020 educational strategy using the Tanzanian context to draw attention to policy strengths and weaknesses.

## MOVING THE DEBATE FORWARD

In general, this volume takes the approach that the language of policy documents matter. The way in which seminal documents include and exclude certain voices is a key factor when it comes to executing ideas or strategies. Clearly the Bank also matters. The sheer amount of World Bank money that goes into education lending each year is enough to make a significant impact. Furthermore, when the Bank lends or grants money, it is not detached from knowledge or requirements. Funding is only part of the equation to execute a particular view on global education. Policy certainly matters. Decisions on where the best investments take place, how effectiveness is measured, and where the priorities lie have historically shaped the work of the Bank. Based on the work of the authors in the following chapters, it is clear that the new Strategy is at the intersection of language, funding, and policy, and will likely play an important role in the way the Bank executes new ideas related to learning. The impact will only be seen in the future, but scholarly engagement and attention to strategy provides a framework for evaluating the impact of ideas.

## REFERENCES

Archer, D. (2006). The impact of the World Bank and IMF on education rights. *Convergence, 39*(2/3), 7–18.

Banerjee, A. V., & Duflo, E. (2011). *Poor economics: A radical rethinking of the way to fight global poverty*. New York, NY: Public Affairs.

Barrett, A. M. (2011). A millennium learning goal for education post-2015: A question of outcomes or processes. *Comparative Education, 47*(1), 119–133.

Becker, G. S. (1993). *Human capital*. Chicago, IL: University of Chicago Press.

Benavot, A. (1989). Education, gender, and economic development: A cross-national study. *Sociology of Education, 62*(1), 14–32.

Berliner, D. C. (2007). Our impoverished view of education reform. In A. R. Sadovnik (Ed.), *Sociology of education: A critical reader*. New York, NY: Routledge.

Chen, S., & Ravallion, M. (2008). *The developing world is poorer than we thought, but no less successful in the fight against poverty*. Washington, DC: Development Research Group, World Bank.

Colclough, C. (1996). Education and the market: Which parts of the neo-liberal solution are correct? *World Development, 24*, 589–610.

Collins, C. S. (2011). *Higher education and global poverty: University partnerships and the World Bank in developing countries*. Amherst, NY: Cambria Press.

Collins, C. S., & Rhoads, R. A. (2010). The World Bank, support for universities, and asymmetrical power relations in international development. *Higher Education: The International Journal of Higher Education and Educational Planning, 59*(2), 181–205.

Easterly, W. (2003). What did structural adjustment adjust? The association of policies and growth with repeated IMF and World Bank adjustment loans. *Journal of Development Economics, 76*(1), 1–22.

Easterly, W. (2006). *The white man's burden: Why the West's efforts to aid the rest have done so much ill and so little good*. New York, NY: Penguin Press.

Goldman, M. (2005). *Imperial nature: The World Bank and struggles for social justice in the age of globalization*. New Haven, CT: Yale University Press.

Herrnstein, R. J., & Murray, C. (1994). *The bell curve: Intelligence and class structure in American life*. New York, NY: The Free Press.

Heyneman, S. P. (2003). The history and problems in the making of education policy at the World Bank, 1960–2000. *International Journal of Educational Development, 23*(3), 315–337.

Hinchcliffe, K. (1993). Neo-liberal prescriptions for education finance: Unfortunately necessary or inherently desirable? *International Journal of Educational Development, 13*, 183–187.

Kazamias, A. M. (2001). Re-Inventing the historical in comparative education: Reflections on a protean episteme by a contemporary player. *Comparative Education, 37*(4), 439–449.

King, E. M., & Hill, M. A. (1997). *Women's education in developing countries: Barriers, benefits, and policies*. Washington, DC: World Bank.

Mamdani, M. (2007). *Scholars in the marketplace: The dilemmas of neo-liberal reform at Makerere Univeristy: 1989–2005*. Kampala, Uganda: Fountain Publishers.

Peet, R. (2003). *Unholy trinity: The IMF, World Bank and WTO*. London: Zed.

Peppin Vaughan, R. (2010). Girls' and Women's Education within UNESCO and the World Bank, 1945–2000. *Compare: A Journal of Comparative and International Education, 40*(4), 405–423.

Psacharopoulos, G., & Patrinos, H. A. (2004). Returns to investment in education: A further update. *Education Economics*, *12*(2), 111–134.

Psacharopoulos, G., & Woodhall, M. (1985). *Education for development: An analysis of investment choices*. New York, NY: Oxford University Press.

Rhoads, R. A., & Torres, C. A. (Eds.). (2007). *The university, state, and market: The political economy of globalization in the Americas*. Stanford, CA: Stanford University Press.

Sachs, J. D. (2005). *The end of poverty: Economic possibilities of our time*. New York, NY: Penguin Books.

Traub, J. (2000). What no school can do. *New York Times Magazine*.

United Nations Human Development Report. (2010). *The real wealth of nations: Pathways to human development*. New York, NY: United Nations.

UNICEF. (2005). Child poverty in rich countries, 2005. Innocenti Report Card No. 5. Florence, Italy: UNICEF Innocenti Research Center.

Wiseman, A. W. (2010). The uses of evidence for educational policymaking: Global contexts and international trends. In A. Luke, G. J. Kelly & J. Green (Eds.), *Review of research in education* (Vol. 34, pp. 1–24). Washington, DC: American Educational Research Association.

World Bank. (n.d.). "About us." Washington DC: World Bank. Retrieved from http://go.worldbank.org/3QT2P1GNH0. Accessed on October 15, 2011.

Yunus, M. (2003). *Banker to the poor*. New York, NY: Public Affairs.

Yusuf, S. (2009). *Development economics through the decades: A critical look at 30 years of the world development report*. Washington, DC: World Bank.

# WORLD BANK GROUP EDUCATION STRATEGY 2020☆

# LEARNING FOR ALL: INVESTING IN PEOPLE'S KNOWLEDGE AND SKILLS TO PROMOTE DEVELOPMENT

## EXECUTIVE SUMMARY[1]

**Education is fundamental to development and growth.** Access to education, which is a basic human right enshrined in the Universal Declaration of Human Rights and the United Nations Convention on the Rights of the Child, is also a strategic development investment. The human mind makes possible all other development achievements, from health advances and agricultural innovation to infrastructure construction and private sector growth. For developing countries to reap these benefits fully—both by learning from the stock of global ideas and through innovation—they need to unleash the potential of the human mind. And there is no better tool for doing so than education.

**The Education Sector Strategy 2020 lays out the World Bank Group's agenda for achieving "Learning for All" in the developing world over the next decade.** The overarching goal is not just schooling, but learning. Getting millions more children into school has been a great achievement. The World Bank Group is committed to building on this progress and stepping up its support to help all countries achieve Education for All (EFA) and the education Millennium Development Goals (MDGs). The driver of

☆Reprinted from: World Bank. (2011). *Learning for All: Investing in People's Knowledge and Skills to Promote Development, Executive Summary* (pp. 1–10). Washington, DC: The International Bank for Reconstruction and Development/World Bank Group. Available online at: http://www.worldbank.org/educationstrategy2020

development will, however, ultimately be what individuals learn, both in and out of school, from preschool through the labor market. The Bank's new 10-year strategy seeks to achieve this broader "Learning for All" objective by promoting country-level reforms of education systems and building a global knowledge base powerful enough to guide those reforms.

### *Why a New Strategy?*

**The Bank Group has made substantial contributions to educational development around the world over the past 49 years.** Since launching a project to build secondary schools in Tunisia in 1962, the Bank has invested $69 billion globally in education via more than 1,500 projects. The Bank's financial support for education has risen over the decade since the MDGs were established, surging to more than $5 billion in 2010. Since 2001, when the International Finance Corporation (IFC) started to focus on the education sector, it has invested $500 million in 46 private education projects.

**This period has seen great educational advances, particularly in enrolling children in school and keeping them there, and in improving gender equality.** Compared to a decade ago, far fewer children in developing countries are now out of school, thanks to more effective education and development policies and sustained national investments. The number of out-of-school children of primary school age fell from 106 million in 1999 to 68 million in 2008. Even in the poorest countries, average enrollment rates at the primary level have surged above 80 percent and completion rates, above 60 percent. And between 1991 and 2007, the ratio of girls to boys in primary and secondary education in the developing world improved from 84 to 96 percent, with even larger gains in the Middle East and North Africa and in South Asia. Governments, civil society organizations (CSOs), communities, and private enterprises have contributed to this progress by building more schools and classrooms and recruiting teachers at unprecedented levels. The World Bank Group has supported these efforts—not only with financing and technical assistance, but also with ideas.

**But that success has bred new challenges at a time when conditions in the world have changed.** With tens of millions of children still out of school and substantial gender gaps remaining, efforts to achieve the education MDGs must continue. Gains in access have also turned attention to the challenge of improving the quality of education and accelerating learning. In addition, the global environment for education is changing. One set of changes is demographic: lower fertility rates are shifting population profiles from the very young populations typical of many low-income countries to "youth bulges" more typical of middle-income countries, increasingly concentrated in urban areas. At the same time, the stunning rise of new middle-income countries has intensified the desire of many nations to increase their competitiveness by building more skilled and agile workforces. Another set of changes is technological: incredible advances in information and communications technology (ICT) and other technologies are changing job profiles and skills demanded by labor markets, while also offering possibilities for accelerated learning and improved management of education systems.

**These developments call for a new World Bank Group education strategy for the next decade.** To be sure, the Bank Group has not stood still since it adopted its last strategy in 2000. It has moved closer to client countries by decentralizing its operations, with 40 percent of staff now in country offices. It has improved its results measurement and orientation, and also invested in better evaluation of program impacts, with the education sector helping to lead the way. It has also innovated financially through greater use of sectorwide financing, pooled funding, performance-based instruments, and other approaches. And it recognized the growing role of the private sector in education by creating a health and education department at IFC. This new education strategy aims to build on these changes by setting out a new objective, together with strategic directions and instruments for implementing them. This education strategy supports and implements key Bank Group priorities—targeting the poor and vulnerable, creating opportunities for growth, promoting global collective action, and strengthening governance—laid out in its recent post-crisis directions strategy.

### *Objective: Learning For All, Beyond Schooling*

**The new strategy focuses on learning for a simple reason: growth, development, and poverty reduction depend on the knowledge and skills that people acquire, not the number of years that they sit in a classroom.** At the individual level, while a diploma may open doors to employment, it is a worker's skills that determine his or her productivity and ability to adapt to new technologies and opportunities. Knowledge and skills also contribute to an individual's ability to have a healthy and educated family and engage in civic life. At the societal level, recent research shows that the level of skills in a workforce—as measured by performance on international student assessments such as the Programme for International Student Assessment (PISA) and the Trends in International Mathematics and Science Study (TIMSS)—predicts economic growth rates far better than do average schooling levels. For example, an increase of one standard deviation in student reading and math scores (roughly equivalent to improving a country's performance ranking from the median to the top 15 percent) is associated with a very large increase of 2 percentage points in annual GDP per capita growth.

**Learning levels that have been measured in many developing countries are alarmingly low, especially among disadvantaged populations.** Of course, even in poor learning environments, most students acquire some skills from school. But too often these skills are rudimentary at best. In some countries, recent studies show that a quarter to a half of youth who have graduated from primary school cannot read a single sentence. International student assessments also reveal wide knowledge gaps between most developing countries and members of the Organization for Economic Co-operation and Development (OECD). Despite the impressive performance of Shanghai-China in the recently released PISA 2009 results, the scores of almost every other low- and middle-income country or region were in the bottom half of results, with many lagging far behind the OECD average.

**Learning needs to be encouraged early and continuously, both within and outside of the formal schooling system.** The emerging science of brain development shows that to develop properly, a child's growing brain needs nurturing long before formal schooling starts at age 6 or 7. Investments in prenatal health and early childhood development programs that include education and health are essential to realize this potential. In the primary years, quality teaching is critical for giving students the foundational literacy and numeracy on which lifelong learning depends. Adolescence is another fertile period for learning, but also a time when many students leave school to marry (especially in the case of girls) or to work full-time. Second-chance and nonformal learning opportunities are thus essential to ensure that all youth can acquire skills for the labor market.

**The Learning for All strategy promotes the equity goals that underlie the education MDGs.** In adopting the objective of learning for all, the new strategy elevates the education MDGs by linking them to the universally shared objective of accelerating learning. Major challenges of access remain for disadvantaged populations (especially girls and women) at the primary, secondary, and tertiary levels, with demand for the latter two levels of education having grown sharply as primary completion has increased. Without confronting these challenges, it will be impossible to achieve the objective of learning for all. Children and youth cannot develop the skills and values that they need without the foundational education provided by schools. Indeed, the latest (2009) PISA results reinforce the lesson that the countries that are most successful overall in promoting learning are those with the narrowest gaps in learning achievement among students.

**The bottom line of the Bank Group's education strategy is: Invest early. Invest smartly. Invest for all.** First, foundational skills acquired early in childhood make possible a lifetime of learning; hence the traditional view of education as starting in primary school takes up the challenge too late. Second, getting value for the education dollar requires smart investments—that is, investments that have proven to contribute to learning. Quality needs to be the focus of education investments, with learning gains as a key metric of quality. Third, learning for all means ensuring that all students, not just the most privileged or gifted, acquire the knowledge and skills that they need. This goal will require lowering the barriers that keep girls, people with disabilities, and ethnolinguistic minorities from attaining as much education as other population groups.

**To achieve learning for all, the World Bank Group will channel its efforts in education in two strategic directions: reforming education systems at the country level and building a high-quality knowledge base for education reforms at the global level.**

### *System Reform, Beyond Inputs*

**At the country level, the Bank Group will focus on supporting reforms of education systems.** The term "education system" typically refers to the public schools, universities, and training programs that provide education services. In this strategy, "education system" includes the full range of learning opportunities available in a country, whether they are provided or financed by the public or private sector (including religious, nonprofit, and for-profit organizations). It includes formal and nonformal programs, plus the full range of beneficiaries of and stakeholders in these programs—teachers, trainers, administrators, employees, students and their families, and employers. It also includes the rules, policies, and accountability mechanisms that bind an education system together, as well as the resources and financing mechanisms that sustain it. This more inclusive concept of the education system allows the Bank Group and its partner countries to seize opportunities and address barriers that lie outside the bounds of the system as it is traditionally defined.

**Improving education systems means moving beyond simply providing inputs.** There is no question that providing adequate levels of schooling inputs—whether these are school buildings, trained teachers, or textbooks—is crucial to a nation's educational progress. Indeed, the increase in inputs in recent years has made it possible to enroll millions more children in school; this effort must continue wherever levels of inputs remain inadequate. But improving systems also requires ensuring that inputs are used more effectively to accelerate learning. While past strategies have recognized this goal, the new strategy gives it more emphasis, setting it in a context of education system assessment and reform.

**The education system approach of the new strategy focuses on increasing accountability and results as a complement to providing inputs.** Strengthening education systems means aligning their governance, management of schools and teachers, financing rules, and incentive mechanisms with the goal of learning for all. This entails reforming relationships of accountability among the various actors and participants in an education system so that these relationships are clear, consistent with functions, measured, monitored, and supported. It also means establishing a clear feedback cycle between financing (including international aid) and results. Because failures of governance and accountability typically have their severest effects on schools serving disadvantaged groups, this system approach promotes educational equity as well as efficiency.

**Operationally, the Bank will increasingly focus its financial and technical aid on system reforms that promote learning outcomes.** To achieve this, the Bank will focus on helping partner countries build the national capacity to govern and manage education systems, implement quality and equity standards, measure system performance against national education goals, and support evidence-based policy making and innovations. While this agenda sounds challenging, the system approach does not require reforming all policy domains at once. Detailed system analysis and investment in knowledge and data will allow the Bank and policymakers to "analyze globally and act locally"—that is, to assess the quality and effectiveness of multiple policy domains, but focus action on the areas where improvements can have the highest payoff in terms of schooling and learning outcomes. Internally, the Bank Group will work to improve project outcomes by strengthening the results framework for projects, improving portfolio monitoring, and selecting the right operational instruments.

### *Building The Knowledge Base*

**At the regional and global level, the Bank will help develop a high-quality knowledge base on education reform.** Analytical work, practical evidence, and know-how related to education programs and policies are critical to improving the performance of education systems around the world. By investing in system assessments, impact evaluations, and assessments of learning and skills, the Bank will help its partner countries answer the key questions that shape educational reform: Where are the strengths of our system? Where are the weaknesses? What interventions have proven most effective in addressing them? Are learning opportunities reaching the most disadvantaged groups? What are the key roles of public and private sector in service delivery? Are children and youth acquiring the knowledge and skills that they need?

**The Bank is developing new knowledge approaches to help guide education reform.** New tools for system assessment and benchmarking ("system tools") will provide detailed analysis of country capacities in a wide array of education policy domains, from early childhood development (ECD), student assessment, and teacher policy to equity and inclusion, tertiary education, and skills development, among others. In each policy domain, the system tools will analyze the "missing middle" of intermediate outcomes, illuminating the part of the results chain that lies between inputs and learning outcomes. This vital information will allow policymakers and civil society organizations to make better-informed decisions about education reforms and interventions by determining where the results chain is breaking down. And by benchmarking progress against international best practices, the tool will highlight areas of strength and weakness as well as identify successful reformers whose experience can inform education policy and practices in other countries.

**Better knowledge of the strengths and weaknesses of particular education systems will enable the Bank Group to respond more effectively to the needs of its partner countries.** Countries at different levels of educational development face different challenges, and priorities for assistance and knowledge sharing should vary accordingly. The new strategy therefore supplements the Bank Group's usual regional groupings with developmental groupings based on whether a country is middle-income, low-income, or fragile, and sets out distinct priorities for each of these groups. For example, in middle-income countries, where a higher proportion of available jobs is likely to require higher-level skills, one priority is to improve quality assurance and financing for tertiary education and for workforce development. In many low-income countries and fragile states, striving to reach the MDGs remains a key priority.

**Careful analysis of each country's level of educational development, in addition to its overall development, allows for sharper and more operationally useful differentiation.** Some countries achieve much higher levels of educational performance, in terms of system operation as well as outcomes, than would be expected based on their incomes. Detailed and internationally comparable information about education systems helps identify these strong performers in specific areas—such as teacher professional development, student assessment, or university accreditation—while also flagging weaknesses in other areas. In addition to helping the Bank Group prioritize its assistance, this system information will facilitate more effective South-South learning, by enabling countries facing specific educational challenges to learn from the stronger performers.

### *From Strategy To Action*

**To implement the new strategy, the World Bank Group will focus on three areas: knowledge generation and exchange, technical and financial support, and strategic partnerships** (see figure 1). To generate knowledge about education reforms and interventions, the Bank will provide: system assessment and benchmarking tools, along with data, to assess the capacity of an education system to improve learning outcomes; assessments of student learning and achievement that cover the basic competencies of reading and numeracy, as well as other skills, including critical thinking, problem solving, and team skills; and impact evaluations and other

<table>
<tr><td>Bank's mission in education</td><td colspan="6">Learning for all</td></tr>
<tr><td>Strategic directions to achieve results</td><td colspan="3">Strengthen education systems</td><td colspan="3">Build a high-quality knowledge base</td></tr>
<tr><td>Implementation levers</td><td colspan="2">Knowledge<br>☐ System assessment and benchmarking tools<br>☐ Learning assessments<br>☐ Impact evaluations & analytical work</td><td colspan="2">Technical & financial support<br>☐ Technical support for system strengthening<br>☐ Results-oriented financing<br>☐ Multisectoral approach</td><td colspan="2">Strategic partnerships<br>(UN agencies, donor community, private sector, civil society organizations)</td></tr>
</table>

*Figure 1.* World Bank Strategic Priorities in Education 2020.

analytical work that can inform policies and interventions, together with knowledge exchange and debate that facilitate learning across partner countries and organizations.

**Knowledge generation and exchange is an essential tool for increasing the effectiveness of all spending in a country's education sector, not just financing from the Bank Group.** The Bank will use this knowledge to guide technical and financial support for countries, including: technical and operational support for system strengthening, prioritized according to its expected contribution to strengthening a country's education system and advancing learning goals; results-oriented financing; and a multisectoral approach to educational development that provides the right incentives, tools, and skills for staff to work across all sectors that influence education outcomes. Improving education outcomes depends heavily on links with the health and social protection sectors: these sectors influence whether students are healthy enough to learn well, whether the system offers families a strong enough safety net to protect education in times of crisis, and whether schooling reflects adequately the demand for skills in the labor market. Within the Bank Group, the World Bank and IFC will work together to improve knowledge about the private sector's role in education and to help countries create policy environments and regulatory structures that align the private sector's efforts with national education goals. Finally, the Bank will implement this strategy through strategic partnerships at both the international and country levels to improve education systems. It remains committed to supporting and strengthening the global partnership EFA Fast Track Initiative, which aims to help low-income countries achieve the education MDGs.

**To measure the success of the strategy, the Bank Group will use a number of performance, outcome, and impact indicators.** Given that accountability is a major emphasis of the system approach to education, the Bank is committed to tracking the effectiveness of its own strategy. The indicators (see Table 1) that it will use include: performance indicators for areas over which the Bank has direct control; outcome indicators for areas in which progress requires the efforts of both partner countries and the Bank; and impact indicators, which will monitor progress toward the ultimate goals of the education strategy.

**Achieving Learning for All will be challenging, but it is the right agenda for the next decade.** While countries can achieve rapid changes in enrollment rates from one school year to the next, it is much harder to make significant gains in learning outcomes. Learning gains typically require structural and behavioral shifts made possible by institutional changes, which the new strategy will support. It is not enough to get the technical details right;

***Table 1.*** Performance, Outcome, and Impact Indicators for the 2020 Education Strategy.

| Performance Indicators | Outcome Indicators | Impact Indicators |
|---|---|---|
| *Changes in Bank Group actions to support countries* | *Changes in policy and programs of countries receiving Bank Group support* | *Ultimate goals monitored in countries receiving Bank Group support* |
| 1. **Knowledge development to strengthen country education systems**<br>a. Number of education system tools developed and launched[a]<br>b. % use of Bank knowledge products that use system tools in the analysis<br>c. % of knowledge products that use learning outcomes in analyses of basic education | 1. % of (i) middle-income countries, (ii) low-income countries, (iii) fragile or conflict-affected states, (iv) Fast Track Initiative (FTI)-endorsed countries that have applied system tools and have collected and used system data<br>2. % of countries that have applied learning or skills (national or international) assessments[b] | 1. % of countries (or beneficiaries in countries) with increases in measured learning or skills since 2010 (or since the earliest available baseline)<br>2. % of countries that have reduced schooling or learning gaps for disadvantaged populations (e.g., income groups, gender, ethnolinguistic groups, disability) since 2010[c] |
| 2. **Organizational development to strengthen country education systems**<br>a. % of Education Sector staff who have completed a competency program on the education system approach and tools and on Monitoring and Evaluating (M&E) methods | 3. % of countries whose systems have improved in at least one policy domain as measured by the system assessment tools<br>4. % of countries furthest from reaching the education Millennium Development Goals (MDGs) that have taken new steps since 2010 to addressing the obstacles to attaining those goals | 3. % of countries furthest from reaching the education MDG in 2010 that progressed towards their attainment since 2010<br>4. % of countries with gains in the skills level of their labor forces since 2010 |
| 3. **Technical and financial support to strengthen country education systems**<br>a. % of education projects or programs that have learning- or skills-related key performance indicators (KPI)<br>b. % of education projects or programs that use education system tools in their design and/or their M&E approach | | |

c. % of education projects or programs that have a satisfactory M&E in their design and implementation
d. % of countries furthest from reaching the education Millennium Development Goals (MDGs) that have received increased support (lending and non-lending) from the Bank Group
e. % of education projects or programs that finance outputs/outcomes

*Note*: a. The World Bank is developing education system tools under the System Assessment and Benchmarking for Education Results (SABER) Program. One system tool, "Teacher Policies," has been launched as a prototype, together with the publication of the strategy. Other system tools to be launched during the first year of the strategy include "Student Assessment," "Early Childhood Development," and "Workforce Development." The online SABER database will be maintained by the World Bank on its externally accessible Education Web site.

b. Assessment application conducted on a regular basis and in a sustainable manner.

c. Beginning in 2010, the World Bank Group will commit US$750 million to those countries furthest from the education MDGs, with an emphasis on countries in Sub-Saharan Africa. The Bank Group will work closely with development partners, in particular through the Fast Track Initiative, to scale up results-based financing and to support innovative interventions in these countries. Lessons from some countries indicate that demand-side interventions such as girls' scholarships and conditional cash transfer programs, as well as school grants, can lower obstacles to school enrollment and increase attendance for disadvantaged populations, as well as in lagging areas. The Bank also commits to making the lessons from these innovations more widely accessible so they can inform future policies and investments.

reforms also require navigating the twin challenges of constraints on a nation's implementation capacity and its political economy. Reforms require buy-in from a large group of stakeholders, with teachers playing a special role. Progress on the outcome and impact indicators listed in Table 1 will therefore hinge on countries instituting real reforms and having the political will to follow through. The Bank Group's assistance will need to take these constraints into account, with support tailored to country circumstances and realistic targets set for learning outcomes. Yet all this effort will be worth it: when children and young people learn, lives improve and nations prosper.

## NOTE

1. All textual emphases (e.g., bold, italics), tables and figures are reproduced here as found in the original document.

# PART II
# STRATEGY DEVELOPMENT

# SIX QUESTIONS ABOUT THE WORLD BANK'S 2020 EDUCATION SECTOR STRATEGY

M. Najeeb Shafiq

## ABSTRACT

*This chapter presents the findings from a series of interviews with World Bank staff on the topic of the World Bank's Education Sector Strategy 2020. The six questions used in these interviews serve as the template for the information presented in this chapter. This chapter provides a brief but important set of background information necessary to understand the strategy and the following chapters because it provides a reflective voice to the World Bank staff involved in the development of the new strategy or familiar with the development process.*

## INTRODUCTION

In April 2011, the World Bank published a revised version of strategic plan for the work it will do in the education sector. This article presents findings from interviews with nine World Bank staff in April 2011 about the new World Bank Education Sector Strategy (henceforth referred to as ESS 2020).

**Education Strategy in the Developing World: Revising the World Bank's Education Policy**
**International Perspectives on Education and Society, Volume 16, 33–41**

**ISSN: 1479-3679/doi:10.1108/S1479-3679(2012)0000016006**

Using these interviews, this article answers six questions: What is the ESS 2020? What is it not? How was the development process of the ESS 2020 different from that of past Strategies? How are the policy recommendations of the ESS 2020 different from those of past Strategies? Does the ESS 2020 fit in with the World Bank's broader development strategy? And finally, does the ESS 2020 matter?

Each interviewee was asked a series of open-ended questions and follow-up questions. Initially, interviewees were asked, "How is the ESS 2020 different from previous ones?" and "What were some of the internal debates during the preparation of the ESS 2020?" They were assured that their identities would be protected. The interviewees consisted of six economists (three specializing in the economics of education), one education sociologist, one education psychologist, and one education comparativist. Eight of the nine interviewees were senior level staff.

## WHAT IS THE ESS 2020?

All the interviewees said that the target audience for the ESS 2020 consists of government ministers of education and other bureaucrats in the Bank's client countries. The secondary audience includes members of academia, NGOs, and international organizations. According to the interviewees, an understanding of the target audience is essential before directing criticism at the ESS 2020. The language and presentation of the ESS 2020 are designed to resonate with government bureaucrats. The interviewees said that clients are not interested in having statements about issues such as human rights and causal inference methodology in the ESS 2020.

The ESS 2020 reveals what the Bank believes will work in education. Client countries can choose to accept, modify, or reject the Bank's ESS recommendations. The Bank's beliefs in the ESS 2020 can be summed up in two words: "learning" and "systems." The new emphasis on "learning" is based on the difficult lesson that access to schools does not necessarily result in learning. Consequently, the ESS 2020 marks a shift in the Bank's position from "access for all" to "learning for all."

The "systems" emphasis has two components. The first component is that the document recognizes the importance of all levels of the education system, from early childhood to higher education. The emphasis on early childhood is new for the Bank and draws from the research on industrialized countries that provides evidence that early investment in high quality preschool contributes to cognitive development and better adult labor market outcomes. One interviewee attributed the focus on early childhood education to the scholarship of economics Nobel laureate James Heckman. The ESS 2020's emphasis on higher education is a change from the relatively secondary position it has in previous strategies.

The second component of the ESS 2020's systems approach is that for any level of education, careful attention needs to be paid to: the inputs, processes, and outcomes of education. For the Bank, the focus on the process stage is new and reflects the movement in industrialized countries to hold teachers, administrators, and parents accountable for using educational inputs appropriately to achieve at least minimally acceptable educational outcomes. The scientific basis for accountability been influenced by the growth of evaluation research in industrialized and developing countries, particularly randomized evaluations.[1]

## WHAT IS THE ESS 2020 NOT?

The interviewees argued that the ESS 2020 is not a literature review. They reemphasized that the key audience is clients, not those in academia. Of the 117 citations, there were only 3 citations to education journals and no citations to comparative education journals. At least 58 Bank documents or staff publications were cited. When asked if the approach made the Bank appear insular, several interviewees said that the cited Bank-authored documents were literature reviews. It was also claimed that clients have an easier time accessing Bank documents (often freely available on the Bank's website) than the original books, journal articles, and book chapters.[2]

The interviewees expressed the desire not to produce a "how-to guide" or "solutions manual." When asked for an explanation, the interviewees envisioned the establishment of data collection systems (such as the U.S. National Center for Education Statistics), monitoring systems (such as the U.S. Department of Education's "What Works Clearinghouse"), and rigorous evaluation procedures (such as the randomized evaluations conducted at MIT's Jameel Poverty Action Lab) that could be used to generate specific policy solutions appropriate for the context. With these resources in place, the interviewees believe that each client could design customized education policies, preferably based on the learning and systems approach.

## HOW WAS THE DEVELOPMENT PROCESS OF THE ESS 2020 DIFFERENT FROM THAT OF PAST STRATEGIES?

The ESS 2020 is different from past strategies in its development and content. Several interviewees admitted that past strategies were often developed behind closed doors by a small team of like-minded male economists. In contrast, the team behind the ESS 2020 included a larger share of women and noneconomists. The preparation of the ESS 2020 also involved a more inclusive process. The interviewees praised ESS 2020 leader and Bank Director of Education Elizabeth King's efforts in establishing a sense of collaboration and inclusiveness among the core team of educational specialists that developed the document.

Though preparation was inclusive, all interviewees acknowledged that there were disagreements among Bank personnel on some of the issues and positions included in the ESS 2020. Some felt that the ESS 2020 was not inclusive of some important topics. One interviewee, for example, wanted a section on the advances in education psychology that could be applied to developing country settings. A senior interviewee countered that Bank clients are not generally interested in such topics, and, for those who are, the Bank already provides free online access to a book on the topic (i.e., Abadzi, 2006). Another issue of disagreement was the future role of the private sector in education – with only one interviewee suggesting that the private sector was not emphasized enough in the ESS 2020. Most interviewees agreed that the modest emphasis on the private sector reflects an ideological change in the Bank. One interviewee noted that the newer staff showed a deeper awareness of evidence-based policymaking; another interviewee fondly discussed the healthy skepticism toward free-market ideology among newer staff.[3]

Another difference in preparation between the ESS 2020 and past strategies is the involvement of Bank clients and stakeholders. Comments were solicited at 24 sites and in virtual meetings in all client regions (Sub-Saharan Africa, South Asia, Latin America, the Caribbean, East and Southeast Asia, the Middle East, North Africa, and Eastern Europe). Clients and stakeholders were consulted on whether the contents of the ESS 2020 resonate with their concerns. According to the interviewees, the draft reports were well received at the meetings. The interviewees did not recall cases of significant opposition to the final draft of the ESS 2020.

## HOW ARE THE POLICY RECOMMENDATIONS OF THE ESS 2020 DIFFERENT FROM THOSE OF PAST STRATEGIES?

The ESS 2020 recommendations reflect the third phase of education policy thinking at the Bank (for discussions, see Heyneman, 2003; Mundy, 2002; Psacharopoulos, 2006). In the first phase (1980s), the strategy recommendations were inspired by the success of manpower planning in post-World War II Germany and Japan. The strategies during this period therefore recommended using vocational and higher education to prepare future workforces. After years of tracking client countries, the Bank eventually understood the ineffectiveness of manpower planning. As former staff education economist George Psacharapoulos (2006) quipped, "… trying to predict the number of people with given educational qualifications to meet production requirements was a vain exercise, often leading to forecast errors of 1000 percent."

In the second phase (late 1980s to mid-2000s), the Bank education strategies recommended school access for all children and the provision of school inputs at the primary and secondary education levels. Early in this second phase, the Bank hired architects to design and build schools in client countries. The second phase gained momentum after the hiring of economists and a few quantitative sociologists, who began investigating the effect of school inputs, such as per-pupil expenditure, teachers, and supplies in developing countries (e.g., Heyneman & Loxley, 1983). The Bank's research and policies that were related to school inputs were influenced by the increase in Western school input studies and the expanding of computing power that followed the Coleman Report in 1966.[4]

As discussed earlier, in the third and current phase, the ESS 2020's recommendations on learning and systematic approach encompasses all levels of education (from early childhood to higher education) and the stages of educational input, process, and output. Given the unprecedented breadth in content, the ESS 2020 is the Bank's most ambitious strategy to date.

## DOES THE ESS 2020 FIT IN WITH THE WORLD BANK'S BROADER DEVELOPMENT STRATEGY?

The World Development Report (WDR) records the World Bank's development strategy at various times. Several interviewees noted the influence of the 2004 and 2007 WDRs on the ESS 2020. *WDR 2004: Making Services Work for Poor People* reflected the broader anticorruption strategy under former Bank President James Wolfensohn (1995–2005). Regarding education, WDR 2004 argued that corrupt education systems compromise learning. In recent years, the Bank had accumulated anecdotal and empirical evidence of corruption in education, such as teacher absenteeism (e.g., Chaudhury, Hammer, Kremer, Muralidharan, & Rogers, 2006).

The ESS 2020's emphasis on learning was influenced by *WDR 2007: Development and the Next Generation*. In the WDR 2007, the Bank argued that skills development is essential for addressing development challenges like that of youth unemployment. The WDR 2007's focus reflected the fact that several developing regions had "youth bulges" – the demographic phenomenon of a disproportionately large share of youth relative to non-youth. Recent discoveries of youth involvement in extremist activities – including the tragic 9-11 attacks in New York – further motivated the youth theme of the WDR 2007. The ESS 2020 focus on learning (rather than just access) from preschool to higher education is aimed at preparing youth for jobs that benefit themselves, the economy, and society.

The focus on education data is consistent with the vision of current Bank President Robert Zoellick. From 2007 to 2011, *The New York Times* (2011) reports that he has overseen the release of over 7,000 data sets that were previously available only to governments and selected researchers; Zoellick also declared that, "the Bank's most valuable currency is no longer its money but its information."

## DOES THE ESS 2020 MATTER?

Will client countries adopt the "learning" and "systems" approach recommended in the ESS 2020? The interviewees were unsure. The predicament at the Bank is that it has presented its most ambitious strategy despite declining financial influence and staff size. (Several interviewees mentioned that the Bank would face sharper criticism if it had prepared a (simpler) ESS 2020 modeled after past strategies.) At the very least, the interviewees felt that the ESS 2020 resulted in improved perceptions about the Bank among client countries because of the inclusiveness in its development.

Some interviewees discussed another potential effect. If client countries are persuaded by the ESS 2020, the interviewees envisioned assisting clients in the collection, analysis, and dissemination of education data in a manner that parallels the *Living Standards Measurement Surveys* (*LSMS*) – household surveys that are collected by the Bank and client governments, which are then made available on the Bank's website. All interviewees hoped that domestic and international researchers would use such detailed data on teachers, administrators, and students. The Bank intends to add to its guidebooks on data analysis and impact evaluation (e.g., Deaton, 1997; Khandker, Koolwal, & Samad, 2010).

With more people investigating richer data, the interviewees foresaw evidence-based debates on the strengths and weaknesses of proposed education reforms (involving alternative learning and systems approaches) in client countries. As a model, one interviewee cited the evidence-based debates on poverty and inequality in India (Deaton & Kozel, 2005).

## NOTES

1. Such evaluation methods draw from medical research, where one group receives a treatment and another group is a control group that does not. Researchers then monitor the behavior of both groups, and after a certain point, compare outcomes. To initiate the culture of randomized evaluations, the Bank collaborated with leading social scientists. The Bank hired University of California – Berkeley economics professor Paul Gertler as its Chief Economist of the Human Development Network from 2004 to 2006. Bank staff and clients also engaged in frequent consultation with the Jameel Poverty Action Lab, including MIT economics professors Abhijit Banerjee and Esther Duflo and Harvard economics professor Michael Kremer.

2. Among the Bank produced literature reviews, the most exhaustive and recent is Bruns, Filmer, and Patrinos (2011).

3. Some of the ideological shift began with the hiring of Joseph Stiglitz as the Chief Economist of the World Bank in 1997. Stiglitz challenged much of the free-market ideology that had dominated World Bank development policy. As evidence of the changing ideologies within the Bank, one interviewee drew attention to an article by lead economist Halsey Rogers (2010) that said, "On the one hand, changed global circumstances and new awareness of vulnerability should lead to some policy changes, as developing countries take steps to reduce and buffer risks, including risks generated in developed countries. At the same time, the crisis should largely reinforce the Post-Washington Consensus on development that has emerged over the past decade – a world view that aims to achieve private sector-driven growth but sees a facilitating role for the state, promotes engaging with the global economy in ways that advance development, and values pragmatism, experimentation, and evidence-based policymaking over ideology."

4. For readers who lack familiarity with the Coleman Report: The prominent American education sociologist James Coleman and colleagues were commissioned by President Lyndon B. Johnson to investigate the relationship between school

resources and student outcomes. Coleman and colleagues concluded that family characteristics – not school characteristics – were the main determinants of student outcomes. The Coleman Report was subsequently challenged by numerous social scientists.

## ACKNOWLEDGMENTS

This article would not have been possible without the encouragement of Christopher Collins, Stephen Heyneman, Harry Patrinos, Alexander W. Wiseman, and the nine World Bank staff who generously and patiently participated in the interviews. I am also very grateful to Barry Bull for detailed comments on an earlier draft. Finally, I thank Mary Jane Alms, Robert Arnove, Shaista Baksh, Karen Mundy, Steven Klees, Ali Protik, Afra Rahman, and seminar participants at the 2011 Annual Meetings of the Comparative and International Education Society in Montreal. I alone am responsible for errors.

## REFERENCES

Abadzi, H. (2006). *Efficient learning for the poor: Insights from the frontier of cognitive neuroscience*. Washington, DC: World Bank.

Bruns, B., Filmer, D., & Patrinos, H. (2011). *Making schools work: New evidence on accountability reforms*. Human Development Perspectives. Washington, DC: World Bank.

Chaudhury, N., Hammer, J., Kremer, M., Muralidharan, K., & Rogers, F. (2006). Missing in action: Teacher and health worker absence in developing countries. *Journal of Economic Perspectives*, *20*, 91–116.

Deaton, A. (1997). *The analysis of household surveys*. Baltimore, MD: Johns Hopkins University Press.

Deaton, A., & Kozel, V. (2005). Data and dogma: The great India poverty debate. *World Bank Research Observer*, *20*, 177–199.

Heyneman, S. (2003). The history and problems in the making of education policy at the World Bank: 1960–2000. In D. P. Baker, A. W. Wiseman (Eds.), *Global trends in educational policy* (Vol. 6, pp. 23–58). International Perspectives on Education and Society Series. Oxford: Elsevier Science.

Heyneman, S., & Loxley, W. (1983). The effect of primary-school quality on academic achievement across twenty-nine high-and low-income countries. *American Journal of Sociology*, *88*, 1162–1194.

Khandker, S., Koolwal, G., & Samad, H. (2010). *Handbook of impact evaluation*. Washington, DC: World Bank.

Mundy, K. (2002). Retrospect and prospect: Education in a reforming World Bank. *International Journal of Educational Development*, *22*, 483–508.

*The New York Times*. (2011). World Bank is opening its treasure chest of data. Published online 2 July 2011. Retrieved from http://www.nytimes.com/2011/07/03/business/global/03world.html?pagewanted=all

Psacharopoulos, G. (2006). World Bank policy on education: A personal account. *International Journal of Educational Development, 26*, 329–338.

Rogers, H. (2010). *The global financial crisis and development thinking*. Policy Research Working Paper No. 5353, World Bank, Washington, DC.

# WHEN MODELS BECOME MONOPOLIES: THE MAKING OF EDUCATION POLICY AT THE WORLD BANK

Stephen P. Heyneman

## ABSTRACT

*To understand the World Bank's education sector strategy development, an historical perspective of where previous strategies have gone is essential. Rather than building schools the Education Strategy 2020 suggests that it will emphasize the efficiency of the education system and help reform its management, governance and finance. Rather than provide new curriculum, it will try to lay the foundations of an education knowledge base by supporting the use of assessments of academic achievement, both local and cross-national. Countries will be asked to measure their progress against statistical evidence. While none of these changes are entirely new, they all represent progress. In this chapter, the new strategy efforts of the World Bank are examined in relation to the contribution of education to social cohesion, education and corruption, education financing and educational quality and cognitive skills and economic development. This portion of the volume will emerge from a 22-year personal history of working with the World Bank on researching*

**Education Strategy in the Developing World: Revising the World Bank's Education Policy**
**International Perspectives on Education and Society, Volume 16, 43–62**

**ISSN: 1479-3679/doi:10.1108/S1479-3679(2012)0000016007**

*education quality, designing policies to support educational effectiveness and training senior officials worldwide in education policy-related lending strategy.*

## BACKGROUND: THE DILEMMA OF MANPOWER PLANNING

In April 1976, I was invited to join the Education Department of the World Bank.[1] Like the departments of Transport, Agriculture, Banking and Industry the Education Department was situated in the Central Project Staff (CPS). The purpose of CPS was to design policy, assess the effectiveness of current lending, support operations (on invitation from the operating divisions), design new policy and do 'quality control'. This latter was thought to be the most delicate in that one was asked to comment on all operations, and in very extreme circumstances, one might object to those thought to be inadequate (Fig. 1). On my first day I was assigned 16 countries to 'monitor', most were countries I knew little about, including India, Algeria and Nicaragua. On my second day I was told to attend a 'decision meeting' concerning a vocational education loan to Algeria.

The decision meeting was attended by 20 people, senior economists from the region, representatives of the department director, the legal department and the team of experts who had appraised the project. The meeting was chaired by the education division chief for the Europe, Middle East and North Africa region. The project intended to build new vocational schools and to modernize the existing schools. On educational grounds it was justified because current curriculum was 'overly academic'. On economic grounds it was justified because, according to a recent manpower forecast, the need for technical manpower was growing. The chair asked if there were any questions. I put up my hand to ask if we had any other economic evidence to justify the project other than a manpower plan. There was a moment of silence. The chair responded that in economics no other evidence existed. That is how the trouble began.

I had just completed a degree at the University of Chicago and was nurtured on the evidence described by Mary Jean Bowman as economic rates of return. I knew that in economics there was other evidence. I reported the essence of the meeting to my director, Mats Hultin, the ex-minister of education from Sweden. He told me to chat with the chief economist, Manuel Zymelman who carefully explained to me why economic

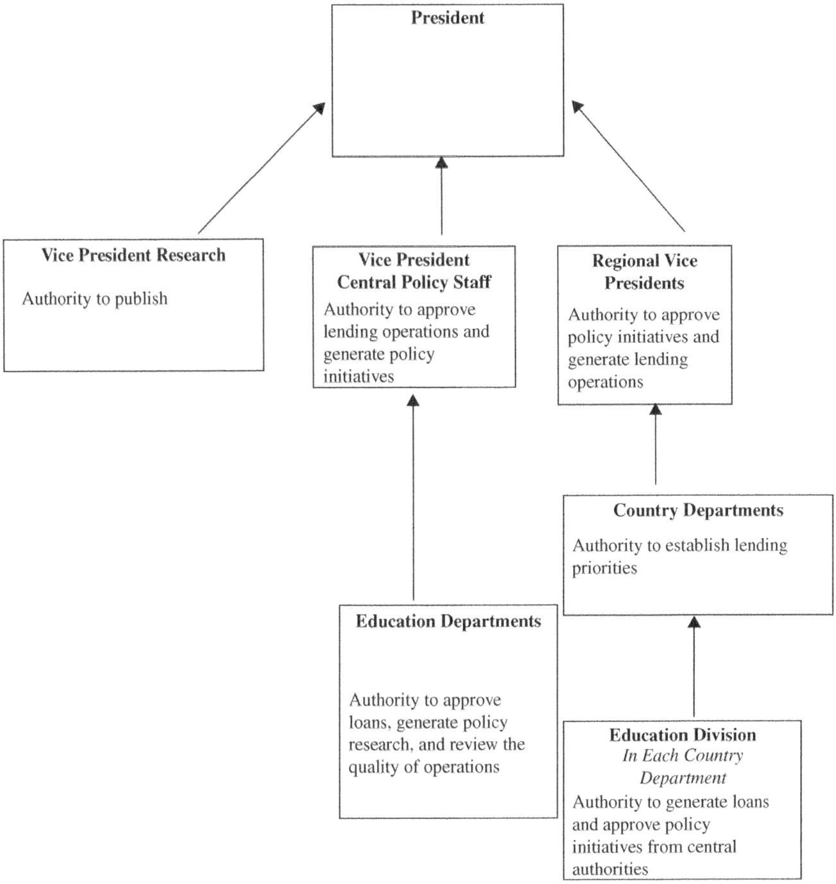


*Fig. 1.* World Bank Internal Processes – Early 1970s to Early 1980s. *Source*: Heyneman, 2005, p. 31.

rates of return were useless for planning development. Wage rates were a poor substitute for productivity. The evidence took years to collect and, while perhaps marginally useful for sector work, economic rates of return were completely impractical for deciding on a specific loan.

There were two problems with his explanation. Manpower planning could only justify the expansion of specific skill training. This left out any assistance to primary or general secondary education or higher education which was not engineering or one of the technical fields. Because only one type of evidence was acceptable, the bank could not respond to country requests for assistance to any other part of the education sector, in spite of the fact that, in many cases, the needs were desperate. The absence of prices in manpower forecasting allowed the Bank, in the effort to infuse skill training into general education, to design projects which were underutilized and distorted. For instance, every secondary school assisted by the Bank was required to build 'diversified' workshops in agriculture, metalwork, woodwork and domestic science (for girls). These increased the unit cost by 2.5 times and ended up being unused for their original purposes but turned into normal academic classrooms. It also meant that primary schools, when assisted, had to double as community centres. In one case it meant that the construction of a university library could only use the bank's support for books and materials related to engineering (Heyneman, 1985, 1987, 1999). When I tried to discuss the importance of primary education with the chief economist of the Africa region, he was quick to tell me that primary education could never be considered a priority for the Bank. It was too scattered in implementation; it was unrelated to a nation's manpower needs and it was the responsibility of local governments, not a development assistance agency.

The second problem had to do with the Bank's education sector staff. All were well versed in manpower planning; none had experience with any other kind of evidence. The monopoly of manpower planning implied a powerful vested interest within the staff which would be threatened if change were to occur. How could one break the monopoly of manpower planning when there was such a strong opposition to any analytic change?

As luck would have it, the answer came in the form of a new Education Director. Aklilu Habte was suggested by the president, Robert McNamara. He was the first Ethiopian to receive a PhD in education (Ohio State, 1952), professor of education, dean of education, and president of the University of Addis Ababa, minister of education, member of the United Nations Educational, Scientific and Cultural Organization (UNESCO) governing board; he was the first African director in the Bank.

The first move was to actually utilize rates of return in a Bank document. Since India was assigned to me to monitor I was asked to draft a desk study on the economics of education in India. This short paper relied on economic rates of return and challenged the common perception in the Bank that India was 'overeducated' (Heyneman, 1979). Fortunately the new vice president for South Asia, David Hopper, had been a friend of Aklilu for years. While the India paper was slowly making its way through the layers of bureaucracy for (mostly sceptical) comment, Aklilu sent it directly to David Hopper at his home address. The next day a memo came from the Vice President's office to me personally (an unprecedented event). It had one sentence: re: paper on India: 'Damn fine paper'. This effectively trumped the many layers between the vice president's office and me and helped to encourage an encouraging response from the India division.

A second opportunity occurred with the announcement that there was a tracer study in Malawi, another country on 'my watch'. This study had followed secondary school students into the labour market. Data existed for those who had left secondary school after two years as well as those who finished in four years. The questionnaire asked about earnings. This led to the first use of rate of return evidence to assess the economic viability of investments in secondary education in Eastern Africa (Heyneman, 1980).

In some ways having these two precedents helped make the point that other kinds of evidence were feasible. But the major thrust for change came from a decision of the president himself. To explore new education policies which Aklilu might wish to inaugurate the president appointed an external panel. Included on the external panel was Mary Jean Bowman from the University of Chicago. The panel's report (World Bank, 1978) was explicit in pointing out the likely distortions from manpower planning and called for a diversity of evidence. This led the way to the next question as to who we might invite to help us systematize alternative sources of economic evidence.

## ACT TWO: THE ACQUISITION OF GEORGE PSACHAROPOULOS

Over a lunch with Aklilu, I suggested that we approach George Psacharopoulos, an economics graduate of the University of Chicago, currently teaching at the London School of Economics. Arrangements were made for me to visit London and take him and his wife out to dinner. Over that dinner I proposed he consider joining the World Bank. The offer was accepted.

Psacharopoulos was not seen as being problem free. He had a reputation for being a strong advocate of the use of economic rates of return; the question was raised whether he was broader than that. I pointed out his work on equity. This was accepted as a sign of diversity of interest and he was hired by the Bank to manage a research unit within the Education Department. Immediately 'war' broke out with Manuel Zymelman. But this conflict was exactly what had been anticipated and the purpose behind his acquisition. We could not diversify our evidence if the current senior economist was opposed to it; he had to be 'neutralized'.

The combination of having a precedent for using economic rates of return in education sector work (Malawi and India), guidance from the external panel and an articulate advocate (Psacharopoulos) led to the explicit statements in the new Education Policy paper which called for diversity of evidence and, as importantly, diversity in the purposes of lending. Specifically mentioned were general primary and secondary education, higher education and education research. Under certain conditions, all were economically justified (World Bank, 1980).

## ACT THREE: THE MONOPOLY OF RATE OF RETURN EVIDENCE

While the use of economic rates of return opened the Bank to consider general, as opposed to vocational, education, problems quickly came with the data's interpretation. In a report published by Psacharopoulos and two colleagues (Psacharopoulos, Tan, & Jiminez, 1986), and later followed by additional evidence (Psacharopoulos, 1994). It was argued that public finance for higher education should be transferred to primary education and that higher education should be increasingly privately financed through tuition. Low-income students should be offered loans to help finance their university studies. Immediately there was a reaction from East Africa. Newspapers and radio commentators associated this line of argument with neocolonialism, and a way in which the Bank could be trying to keep Africa in a subordinate position. In response Psacharopoulos was sent to Nairobi to explain the paper's point of view. As I recall it was thought that the Kenyans simply needed to 'better understand economics' and the reasons why these policy recommendations were 'equity-enhancing'. He returned stunned by the response, which evidently was close to being violent. This was the first encounter with a line of argument not included in our regressions. It was, as I recall, dismissed as being 'just politics'.

In the 1980s, Psacharopoulos was transferred to the office of the Vice President in the Latin America region. The region was volatile. Flush with Middle Eastern capital from the oil embargo, banks had made extensive, often improper, investments. Crippled by bad loans in Brazil and Argentina, major banks in New York and London were in danger. New infusion of capital had to be quickly transferred to local authorities to refinance the otherwise faulty loans. This was the 'Baker Plan' named after the U.S. Secretary of the Treasury. At one of the meetings to implement this plan it was said that he commented about 'the absence' of the World Bank at the table. Until then the Bank was an institution operated on the basis of project-by-project development. Each project was geared to a five-year implementation cycle. While the International Monetary Fund (IMF) was supposed to be the 'fireman' which one calls in the case of a fiscal crisis, the bank had very different terms of reference. But to not be at the table when strategies are planned is not in the nature of any important institution, hence the birth of a new form of lending called structural adjustment. Instead of allocating monies to cover the cost of improvements to infrastructure, the Bank's Board of Directors approved the possibility of allocating resources on the basis of policy change. The resources were large, often in the hundreds of millions of dollars, and were implemented quickly, in some cases within a week of being approved.

When the Bank began loaning money in Latin America for structural adjustment, criticisms arose that the poor were adversely affected. Moreover, because reductions in public sector salaries (including teacher salaries) were sometimes part of the adjustment process, it was said that education in rural areas was suffering (UNICEF, 1987). The question became whether there might be a way to protect the poor through education within a structural adjustment loan. Psacharopoulos' response included the same 'short menu' of policy options proposed in his earlier paper (Psacharopoulos et al., 1986), namely to reduce public expenditures on higher education, transfer those expenditures to primary education and institute a program of educational loans to help finance the private higher education costs of those who could not afford the tuition. The difference in this case was that the policy menu was negotiated in the context of a structural adjustment loan, a loan usually to the Ministry of Finance; hence the education policy changes were agreed with the Ministers of Finance, sometimes over the objections of the Ministers of Education.

Policy-based lending became an important new sector in the Bank with active projects in Africa, Latin America and occasionally in other regions. And because policy-based loans were a hybrid between policy and lending operations, a new office was established above the vice presidents. This office was titled the Senior Vice President for Policy (see Fig. 2).

Psacharopoulos was transferred to this office in the late 1980s, thus raising visibility of rates of return and the short policy menu that had been proposed many times in Latin America and Africa. This new position gave the rate of return approach virtual monopoly over sector work, lending as well as policy development.

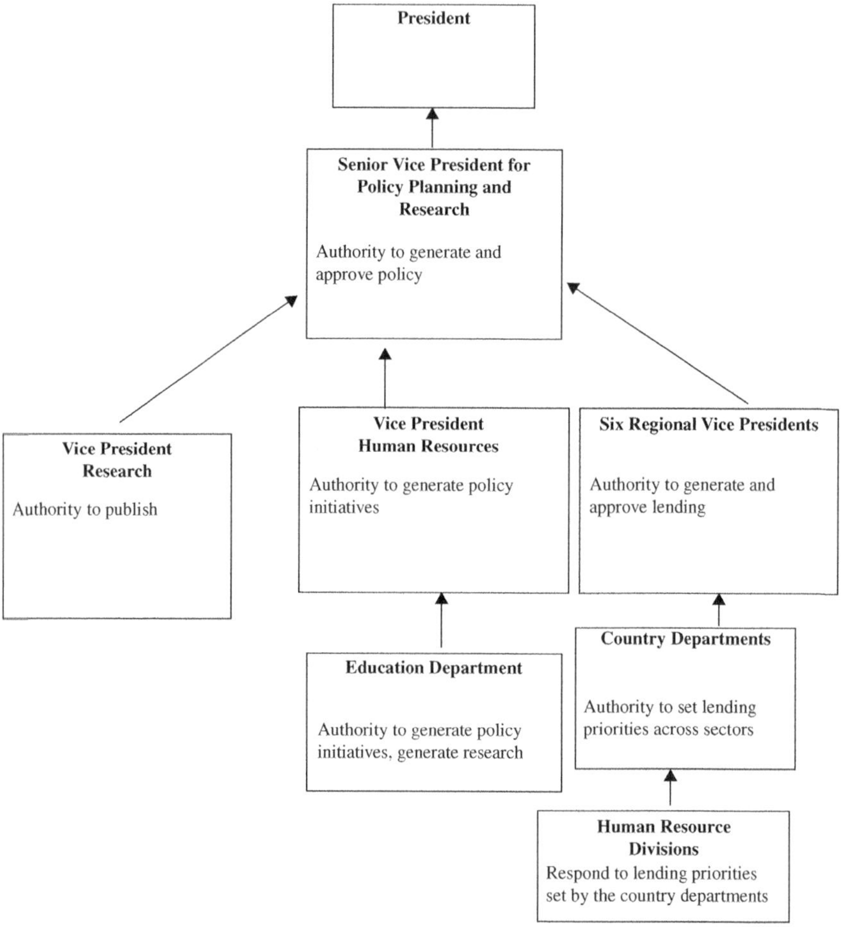


*Fig. 2.* World Bank Processes – Early 1980s to Early 1990s. *Source*: Heyneman, 2005, p. 35.

## ACT FOUR: THE STRUGGLE OVER HIGHER EDUCATION POLICY

The first sign of a problem occurred with the development of a new policy paper on higher education (World Bank, 1994). While the content of the paper was unobjectionable and approved by each of the regional division chiefs,[2] the published version contained a statement which had not been in the approved draft. It was

> Primary and secondary education will continue to be the highest priority subsectors in the Bank's education lending to countries that have not yet achieved universal literacy and adequate access, equity and quality at the primary and secondary levels. In these countries our involvement in higher education will continue to be mainly to make its financing more equitable and cost-effective, so that primary and secondary education can receive increased attention at the margin. (World Bank, 1994, p. 12)

The statement implied that expansion of higher education was not among the Bank's priorities and for most countries higher education constitutes a lower priority than other education levels. The paper quickly came in for criticism from the academic community (Buchert & King, 1995). King commented that the title was not conceived as a 'bank-bashing' exercise, but only to imply that the bank had not learned from its lessons (Morna, 1994).

What the academic community may not have realized is that the appearance of this statement without our clearance led many of us to suspect that an ideological battle had commenced in our sector over and above our authority. Our feelings that we were being circumvented were substantiated in the development of a new policy paper which discussed the sector from primary to graduate education designed to cover each of the six regions (World Bank, 1995). The problem, slow to be recognized, was that in the last few years the developing world had changed. Many of the staff had been exposed to problems of sub-Saharan Africa and south Asia, problems of extreme poverty where a lack of educational opportunity in primary education was among the most serious. But we were responsible for a completely new category of borrower: the Russian Federation, China, Indonesia, Brazil, South Africa, Chile and Malaysia, countries whose reference group came not from low-income countries but from the world's industrial democracies. Often, these countries had full enrolment in primary education, and whose primary priority was higher education access, quality and efficiency. In many instances, the concerns of the education sectors in these countries focused on the innovations prevalent in the Organisation for Economic Co-operation and Development (OECD) countries – merit pay, voucher systems, site-based management and performance standards. The professional experience of many Bank education staff did not include the educational debates in their own countries. Hence the Bank's education sector was the object of 'adjustment' of a kind not unlike their client countries (Heyneman, 1994). To suggest that resources should be shifted away from higher education would be political suicide in the Russian

Federation, for instance, yet this suggestion was again made in the draft of the new policy paper. In fact, one draft of the executive summary contained the statement that 'higher education can become or remain largely privately funded'. The response to this statement from the regions was unambiguous: 'take it out' (Heyneman, 1994).

In one note from the operational division chiefs to the paper's authors, criticism of was explicitly spelled out.

> The paper draws upon the same rate-of-return evidence to guide policy and future investment priorities, and that leads to catastrophe. The evidence is faulty; drawn from a few traditional borrowers; only provides a backward explanation of trends and only refers to the most simple of education categories – primary, secondary and higher education. Because the paper relies exclusively on rates of return, it excludes other possible justifications for the allocation of public finance: national interest, market failure, and equity. ... Though over one half of World Bank lending is devoted to post secondary education the paper is silent on the role of higher education. It is also silent on graduate education, adult education, pre-school education, and education research, educational technology, and education for the handicapped. All professional education is ignored, including medical education, engineering education, law education, public administration, and the social sciences. Every single country makes public investments in these areas and it would be irresponsible to treat them in a cavalier fashion. One division chief characterized the problem by saying that the paper takes us racing into the future with our face pressed firmly against the rear view mirror. (Internal note, 18 November 1994)

In spite of the dissent within the Bank, the text of the paper changed very little between drafts. The regional division chiefs felt that the education sector was in danger of becoming a source for 'cheap ideology'. The leaders of four of the six regions met once at night to discuss what to do. Their meeting took place in a park so as to ensure confidentiality. Each regional representative decided to draft a memorandum addressed to their vice president objecting to the paper. The memorandum was to be signed by each of the operational division chiefs within each region. Of the 26 division chiefs responsible for education, 20 signed the memorandum on 2 February 1995, asking that the paper not be sent to the Bank's Board. Two others agreed with the memorandum but refused to sign. One objected to the memorandum. Three others were travelling and could not be reached. For all intent and purposes, the Bank's education sector was in revolt.

The paper was eventually re-edited, but its thrust was unchanged. Even after an unprecedented level of internal protest the monopoly over the Bank's view from the position of the office of the senior vice president for policy was too powerful to overcome. Eventually, the publication led to many objections from the academic community and replies from the Bank

(Bennell, 1996; Burnett, 1996; Burnett & Patrinos, 1996; Jones, 2000, Lauglo, 1996; Samoff, 1996, 1999; Watson, 1996).

During this period, I often felt that the academic community misunderstood the Bank's staff. It was often assumed that they were subject to a unanimity of thinking. The internal struggles were not common knowledge. I felt that it might be important to raise some of the internal objections in a public forum. I summarized the arguments against using economic rates of return for making investment decisions and presented them to UNESCO. I was encouraged to publish them. However, were they to be published, given my position, would mean that I would probably be fired. One evening I gathered my children around the kitchen table and explained the situation. It might mean that we would have to sell the house; perhaps move to a different neighbourhood and change schools. One son, known even today for his commitment to good causes, replied: go get'em dad. His view was not enough to convince me. I had to make a Hobbes-like choice – loyalty to an institution which I dearly loved; or loyalty to my profession as educator, to which I had devoted my life. I had come to believe that the behaviour of the institution had come to be antithetical to the standards of my profession. I am sure that many others have found themselves in parallel circumstances. The choice is not easy.

The article titled 'Economics of Education: Disappointments and Potential' went to the head of the publication schedule and quickly appeared in *Prospects* (Heyneman, 1995). I sent each director and each division chief a copy with a cover note of explanation. My phone started ringing within a few minutes.

## THE FINAL ACT: THE BANK RIGHTS ITSELF

My personal story aside, however, the Bank began to realize that it had lost professional credibility with the education community and decided to make amends by sponsoring a new paper on higher education. Unlike previous papers though, the Bank chose to not use any World Bank staff. The paper was drafted entirely by external experts. These experts consisted of a panel chosen for their independence and unquestionable credibility. They included: Mamphela Ramphele (vice-chancellor, University of Cape Town), Henry Rosovsky (former dean of the Faculty of Arts and Sciences, Harvard University), Kenneth Prewitt (ex-Chairman, Social Science Research Council and current director, U.S. Census), Babar Ali (pro-chancellor, Lahore University of Management), Hanan Ashrawi (former minister of education, Palestine), Jose Joaquin Brunner (former minister of education,

Chile), Lone Dybkjaer (former Danish minister of the environment and current member of the European Parliament), Georges Haddad (professor, University of Paris), Motoo Kaji (vice president, University of the Air, Japan), Jajah Koswara (director of Research and Community Service Development, Directorate for Higher Education, Indonesia), Narciso Matos (secretary general, African Association of Universities), Manmohan Singh (former minister of finance and current member of parliament, India), Carl Tham (former minister of education and current secretary general of Palme International Center, Sweden), Kamal Ahmad (attorney, Fried, Frank, Harris, Shriver and Jacobson) and David E. Bloom (professor, Harvard University). Their report was published by the Bank in 2000 (Task Force on Higher Education and Society, 2000).

This report included extensive discussions of higher education and the public interest, the importance of higher education to science and technology and the importance of general education. In its coverage of the economics of higher education, the report has this to say:

> The Task Force believes that traditional economic arguments are based on a limited understanding of what higher education institutions contribute. Rate of return studies treat education people as a valuable only through their higher earnings and greater tax revenues extracted by society. But educated people clearly have many other effects on society: educated people are well positioned to be economic and social entrepreneurs, having a far-reaching impact on economic and social well being of their communities. They are also vital to creating an environment in which economic development is possible. Good governance, strong institutions, and a development infrastructure are all needed if business is to thrive – and none of these is possible without highly educated people. Finally, rate of return analyses entirely misses the impact of university based research on the economy – a far-reaching social benefit that is at the heart of any argument for developing strong higher education systems. (Task Force on Higher Education and Society, 2000, p. 39)

Several years later the *Comparative Education Review* sponsored a 'moderated discussion' of these issues (Task Force on Higher Education and Society: A Moderated Discussion, 2004). Psacharopoulos was asked to comment on the report. He begins by quoting a statement in the report, then says:

> At first sight, one might think that the (above) statements come from a term paper by a student in international education or an obscure mimeo found in the ERIC Database. However, they are from the 'main conclusion' … of the Task Force Report. What is even more astonishing is that such general statements resulted from intensive discussion and hearing over a 2-year period by a group of eminent task force members, two study directors from reputable institutions, dozens of task force supporters, nine generous international financiers, 10 in-kind contributors, and five international seminars. The

> report is clearly that of a committee. It offers nice-sounding statements but no specific advice about what developing countries should do regarding higher education or education in general. In this sense, it is disappointing that such a major effort will not have any real impact on the cause it was supposed to serve … When we adjust the private rates for the true resource cost of education, primary education exhibits a higher rate of return relative to the other levels. Hence, in a country where primary education is not universal, priority should be given at the margin to basic education. And the World Bank was absolutely right to have adopted such strategy in its lending program. … we know that the incidence of public spending on higher education is highly regressive. That is, in most countries the children of the poor receive less than do the children of the rich. Hence, any expansion of higher education should be linked to selective e student fees (equal to the full social cost for the rich but including stipends for the poor, with student loans available to all. … (in future) we will eliminate international seminars and divert the resources to finance research on the economics of education …. (Psacharopoulos, 2004, p. 76)

Bloom and Rosovsky were asked to respond. They did:

> In his brief communication, George Psacharopoulos has managed not only to insult every member of the task force … but also to ignore 90 percent of the report's content …. We are surprised that the editors of this review would print such intemperate and ill-founded communications … But we are not surprised by Psacharopoulos' evident agitation. Standard rate-of-return analysis … is increasingly being questioned in terms of its sufficiency for making investment decisions. And for good reason. … Standard rate-of-return estimates dominated investment priority decisions at influential organizations like the World Bank for many years. The apparent precision and rigor of these estimates crowded out alternative decisions frameworks … These analyses completely neglect externalities associated with education – at all levels. These range from the nutrition and health benefits that literate and numerate women confer on their families and communities to the benefits of university-based research and training on the pace and sustainability of national development. This line of thinking is certainly not unique to the Task Force Report. It is, indeed, a widely held view …. Our overarching point here is that, when rate of return analyses are based on incomplete models and imperfect data, they will yield estimates whose relation to true rates of return are not clear. More careful analyses might well lead to a reordering of social investment priorities … The Task Force does not contend that rate of return analyses are meaningless. But it does highlight the dangers embodied in excessive reliance on rate of return analyses insofar as they provide distorted and potentially misleading views of the case for higher education, to the peril of well-intentioned development policy makers. … as Nancy Birdsall wrote to us in a personal communication, 'unmeasured externalities dictate humility and deference to local realities, as opposed to preaching primarily on the (incorrect) grounds that social returns are highest at the primary level'. (Bloom & Rosovsky, 2004, pp. 85–86)

The Task Force Report, as the Education Sector Policy did in 1980, essentially liberated the Bank from its previous dogma. Since the Task Force Report, several new higher education policy papers, all of them carefully done and highly appreciated, have appeared (Salmi, 2009; World Bank, 2002; Yusuf & Nabeshima, 2007). Psacharopoulos himself seems to have dropped out of favour. In the 1995 policy paper, he is cited nine times; in the most recent policy paper (World Bank, 2011), he is not cited at all (Heyneman, 2011).

## IMPLICATIONS

From this story of how a model became a monopoly, one might draw two lessons. Every organization struggles for a strategy which is comprehensible, feasible and compelling in its justification. In this the Bank is typical. United Nations Children's Fund (UNICEF), UNESCO and Department for International Development (DFID) are no different. Dogma occurs whenever a strategy becomes common wisdom. The problem is that all organizations need to grow and improve, and none can do this unless what is taken to be common wisdom can be challenged. Whenever an organization silences those challenges, it will be in danger. This monopoly occurred in the Bank and it took a decade for it to recover.

But in addition to the lesson of monopoly is that of what to do when an organization, otherwise well-meaning, becomes a danger to one's profession and one's professional standards of honesty. Many parallels exist – in the military, in the pharmaceutical industry, power companies, banks and insurance companies. The question then becomes a matter of the final responsibility. In my case I felt that the responsibility was mine. I asked myself many times if it was a trivial issue on which I went to battle. A trivial issue would be pointless. In the end I felt that the issue was not trivial but essential to the making of public policy. In her book *Democratic Education*, Amy Gutmann (1987) argues that rates of return, or any economic model is only a guide to policy, not a road map to making investment decisions. In her view, as in mine, assessing the value of public goods and externalities, because it is not easily quantified, can only be made by the public at large. This is why a poor country may choose higher education over primary education, because what it values may be different and, for the most part, outside of our best models.

## HAS THE BANK LEARNED ITS LESSON: A BRIEF COMMENT ON THE EDUCATION PAPER OF 2011

The World Bank has a lot of publications on education. Some are authored and are the responsibility of that author. These may be circulated in a journal as a product of research or as a discussion series to generate debate. A policy paper is different. This is a paper which must be approved by the executive directors, and the World Bank is listed as the author.

From the beginning, policy papers have shared certain characteristics, this one included. None may contain a statement which would challenge long-standing convention. It may infer. It may suggest. But in the end, it must be approved by all the executive directors which represent the 185 members. No draft policy paper would be put to a vote of the executive directors if were to generate opposition or even controversy. Essentially a policy paper must represent a consensus.

Policy papers reiterate that it is the Bank which is the subject of its suggestions. Countries are autonomous and independent entities. If directives are included in the paper they are turned inward and suggest that the Bank will operate differently in one or another arena, or that the bank will place new criteria for its operations or that the Bank will respond warmly to new initiatives in the arenas under discussion.

In spite of these organizational restrictions, this paper pioneers new arenas for the Bank. It redefines the term 'education system'. The new definition includes learning wherever it occurs and can be organized. It places a heavy emphasis on early childhood education and adult literacy. It includes corporate training. It includes providers of all kinds, public, private, charitable and for-profit. It includes not only providers of education programs but also providers of education products and services. In fact it leaves out very little and other than early childhood education it places no priority anywhere.

But will it do things differently? Rather than building schools this new strategy suggests that it will emphasize the efficiency of the education system and help reform its management, governance and finance. Rather than provide new curriculum, it will try to lay the foundations of an education knowledge base by supporting the use of assessments of academic achievement, both local and cross-national. Countries will be asked to measure their progress against statistical evidence. The bank may also experiment with a reorganization of its education staff. Instead of them working on regions in isolation from one another, they will begin working on education systems divided by their stages of development. While none of these changes are entirely new, in my view, all represent progress.

Early childhood education is nice, but has the Bank made progress on the elements which were the subject of criticism in the past. One criticism was that it was ideological; on the basis of a narrow interpretation of economic rates of return that it advocated a 'short policy menu' demanding that

***Table 1.*** World Bank Education Policy Papers and George Psacharopoulos.

| | Number of Citations |
|---|---|
| 1995 | 9 |
| 2011 | 0 |

countries shift public resources from tertiary to primary education. The major proponent of this view was George Psacharopoulos. In the education policy paper of 1995, the one to which 20 division chiefs signed a memorandum of protest (Heyneman, 2005), Psacharopoulos was cited nine different times. However, in the policy paper of 2011, he was not cited at all (Table 1). There are some (perhaps including myself) who would interpret this as progress.

Another criticism of the World Bank in the past has been that it has been insular in its orientation and that it tended to cite only its own work and its own staff members. This implied that it saw development in a narrow way and ignored much of the analytic work done by the world outside itself. This was said to be parochial and counterproductive.

For instance, in the policy paper of 1995, over 13% of the references were other policy papers and 32% of the references were of its own staff members. If one includes the references to the reports from other agencies, the Bank only used sources outside the development community about 50% of time. That was 1995.

In 2011 the sources of references had changed dramatically, but in the wrong direction. Twenty-six percent of the references were derived from other policy papers; 16% from its own staff and 29% from other agencies. This latter figure is the result of James Wolfenson's efforts. The official rationale was to collaborate with other agencies as though development should be a team effort. But it also serves the Bank's needs for political coverage to protect itself from external criticism. It is more difficult to criticize the Bank when UNICEF and Save the Children and the Sierra Club are sitting on the podium. This is not an accident.

The problem is that the portion of the cited references from other sources has declined. In 1995 it was 50%. Today it is 28%.

One might counter with the suggestion that this is an accurate reflection of the insight and knowledge in the field of education and development. To explore this I looked at the sources for the report on basic education published by the U.S. National Academy of Sciences in 2006. This report cites the World Bank policy papers 2.2% of the time; they cite other academic sources 89% of the time. This suggests to me that the insularity of the Bank has gotten worse, not better (Table 2).

Another criticism of the Bank was that it did not consult enough; that it developed its policy papers in isolation from the opinions of 'stakeholders'. This paper goes a long way to convince the reader that its consultations were extensive. It lists a total of 69 meetings held to discuss the content of this paper, meetings across all regions and with all donors. It even lists the most frequently asked questions. Here they are in the order of importance:

1. What is the 'strategic' component of Education Sector Strategy (ESS) 2020?
2. How does ESS 2020 address the Millennium Development Goals (MDGs) and support countries to reach the two education MDGs?
3. How does ESS 2020 relate to the Education for All Fast Track Initiative (EFA FTI)?

This continues for 16 more questions.

My reaction to this list of questions from the consultation meetings is one of horror. If anyone needed a sign as to whether the Bank was out of touch with the world of education and development all they need to do is read through these questions. They constitute what the Soviets used to call a 'langue de bois', a wooden language. They have no importance to the scholars of development and they have no relationship to the real questions

***Table 2.*** Sources for References in Education Policy Papers: Percent of References in Each Category.

| | Other | | | | |
|---|---|---|---|---|---|
| | World Bank as author | WB Staff as author | Agencies as author | Other authors | (#) |
| World Bank (1995) | 11.9 | 28.5 | 4.8 | 45.2 | (270) |
| World Bank (2011) | 26.5 | 16.2 | 29.1 | 28 | (117) |
| U.S. National Academy of Sciences | 2.2 | 8.8 | 0 | 89 | (45) |

*Sources*: World Bank. (1995). *Priorities and strategies for education*. Washington, D.C.: The World Bank.

World Bank. (2011). *Learning for all: Investing in people's knowledge and skills to promote development*. Washington, D.C.: The World Bank.

Cohen, J. E., Bloom D. E., & Malin M. (2006). *Educating all children: A global agenda*. Cambridge, MA: National Academy of Sciences/MIT Press.

about the new policy paper. They reflect the fact that the Bank continues to listen to itself and to those in similar agencies.

What might be a frequently asked question about this policy paper? I would ask the Bank: Are you still recommending that public finances shift from higher to primary education? I would ask: Are you able to work outside of government ministries of education to assist the development of the private sector? I would ask: Are you prepared to confront the fact the greatest threat to the quality of education is from within the system itself in terms of corruption? I would ask: Are you prepared to stop lending to a country which steals our assistance? I would ask: Are you prepared to sanction staff who propose conditionalities which later prove to be professionally incorrect?[3] I would ask: Are you prepared to equip low-income countries with policy advisors so they might negotiate loan conditionalities with more equity? I would ask: Are you willing to confront the fact that education constitutes only a tiny percent of the development agenda? To these questions, and perhaps others, there is no response in this new policy paper.

## NOTES

1. It is assumed that the reader knows the purposes and mechanisms of the World Bank. If not, one might read Heyneman (2005).
2. I was division chief in the technical department of the new region titled: Europe and Central Asia responsible for the 27 countries in Eastern and Central Europe and the former Soviet Union.
3. Payment by results might apply to both borrower and lender.

## REFERENCES

Bennell, P. (1996). Using and abusing rates of return: A critique of the World Bank. *International Journal of Educational Development*, *16*(3), 235–248.

Bloom, D., & Rosovsky, H. (2004). Reply to Psacharopoulos. *Comparative Education Review*, *48*(1), 85–86.

Buchert, L., & King, K. (Eds.). (1995). *Learning from experience: Policy and practice in aid to higher education*. CESO Paperback No. 24, CESO, The Hague.

Burnett, N. (1996). Priorities and strategies for education: A World Bank review: The process and the key messages. *International Journal of Educational Development*, *16*, 215–220.

Burnett, N., & Patrinos, H. (1996). Response to critiques to priorities and strategies for education: A World Bank review. *International Journal of Educational Development*, *16*, 273–276.

Gutmann, A. (1987). *Democratic education*. Princeton, NJ: Princeton University Press.

Heyneman, S. P. (1979). *Investment in Indian education: Uneconomic?* World Bank Staff Working Paper (May) No. 327, World Bank, Washington, DC; Republished: *World Development* 1980, (4), 145–163.

Heyneman, S. P. (1980). *The evaluation of human capital in Malawi.* World Bank Staff Working Paper (October) No. 420, World Bank, Washington, DC; Republished: Heyneman, S. P. (1984). Educational investment and economic productivity: The evidence from Malawi. *International Journal of Education Development, 12*(1), 9–15.

Heyneman, S. P. (1985). Diversifying secondary school curricular in developing countries: An implementation history and some policy options. *International Journal of Education Development, 5*(4), 283–288.

Heyneman, S. P. (1987). Curriculum economics in secondary education: An emerging crisis in developing countries. *Prospects, 18*(1), 63–74.

Heyneman, S. P. (1994). *Heyneman to Burnett.* Private communication (October 25).

Heyneman, S. P. (1995). Economics of education: Disappointments and potential. *Prospects, XXV*(4), 559–583. Republished: T. Lakshmanasamy (Ed.). (1997). *The economics of human behavior.* Mumbai, India: Allied Publishers Ltd.

Heyneman, S. P. (1999). Development aid in education: A personal view. In K. King & L. Buchert (Eds.), *Changing international aid to education: Global patterns and national contexts* (pp. 132–146). Paris: UNESCO Publishing.

Heyneman, S. P. (2005). The history and problems in the making of education policy at the World Bank: 1960–2000. In D.P. Baker & A. W. Wiseman (Eds.), *Global trends in educational policy* (Vol. 6, pp. 23–58). International Perspectives on Education and Society Series. Oxford: Elsevier Science.

Heyneman, S. P. (2011). World Bank Policy Paper of 2011: A brief comment. *CIES Perspectives* (156), 10–11.

Jones, P. (2000). Increasing aid effectiveness in Africa? The World Bank and sector investment programs. In C. L. Gilbert & D. Vines (Eds.), *The World Bank: Structures and policies* (pp. 266–281). Cambridge: Cambridge University Press.

Lauglo, J. (1996). Banking on education and the uses of research: A critique of the World Bank priorities and strategies for education. *International Journal of Educational Development, 16*, 221–222.

Morna, C. L. (1994). World Bank's approach to education in Africa called narrow and inadequate. *Chronicle of Higher Education*, July 27.

Psacharopoulos, G. (1994). Returns to investment in education: A global update. *World Development, 22*(9), 1325–1343.

Psacharopoulos, G. (2004). The empirical basis of task force conclusions. *Comparative Education Review, 48*(1), 75–78.

Psacharopoulos, G., Tan, J. P., & Jiminez, E. (1986). *Financing education in developing countries: An exploration of policy options.* Washington, DC: The World Bank.

Task Force on Higher Education and Society. (2000). *Higher education in developing countries: Peril and promise.* Washington, DC: The World Bank.

Task Force on Higher Education and Society. (2004). Moderated discussion. *Comparative Education Review, 48*(1), 70–88.

Salmi, J. (2009). *The challenge of establishing world-class universities.* Washington, DC: The World Bank.

Samoff, J. (1999). Which priorities and strategies for education? *International Journal of Educational Development, 16*, 1–27.

UNICEF. (1987). *Adjustment with a human face*. New York: UNICEF.

Watson, K. (1996). Banking on key reforms for educational development: A critique of the World Bank review. *Mediterranean Journal of Educational Studies*, *1*, 41–61.

World Bank. (1978). *Report of the external advisory panel on education*. Washington, DC: The World Bank.

World Bank. (1980). *Education sector policy paper*. Washington, DC: The World Bank.

World Bank. (1994). *Higher education: Lessons of experience*. Washington, DC: The World Bank.

World Bank. (1995). *Priorities and strategies for education*. Washington, DC: The World Bank.

World Bank. (2002). *Constructing knowledge societies: New challenges for tertiary education*. Washington, DC: The World Bank.

World Bank. (2011). *Learning for all: Investing in people's knowledge and skills to promote development. Education sector strategy, 2020*. Washington, DC: The World Bank.

Yusuf, S., & Nabeshima, K. (Eds.). (2007). *How universities promote development*. Washington, DC: The World Bank.

# THE WORLD BANK'S "EDUCATION STRATEGY 2020": A PERSONAL ACCOUNT

Robert F. Arnove

## ABSTRACT

*This chapter recounts my involvement with one of the World Bank's consultations soliciting critical input into the draft of its Education Strategy 2020. Following a summary of the consultation that took place at the Brookings Institution, I reflect on the Bank's response to the input it received as well as to subsequent iterations of its education strategy. This chapter suggests how education has been narrowly conceptualized by the World Bank in past lending policies and how the Bank now conceptualizes it with regard to its intrinsic or external value to human and societal well-being. To elaborate upon these opening points, it will be pointed out how the language and circulating discourses of the World Bank, as well as those of other major international policy and funding actors, reflect and limit the vision of what the goals and purposes of an education system should be. In short, this chapter suggests that the language and discourses of the new World Bank Education Strategy 2020 (like previous World Bank education strategies) are narrowly framed in market and commercial terms focused on improving the competitive position of a country in the global economy, which does not maximize human development.*

**Education Strategy in the Developing World: Revising the World Bank's Education Policy**
**International Perspectives on Education and Society, Volume 16, 63–80**

**ISSN: 1479-3679/doi:10.1108/S1479-3679(2012)0000016008**

## PHASE I CONSULTATION AT THE BROOKINGS INSTITUTION

At the invitation of the Center for Universal Education of the Brookings Institution, I attended a May 13, 2010, afternoon private discussion with key staff of the World Bank's education sector. The invitation read as follows: "The consultative meeting will bring together a select group of progressive critical thinkers from diverse academic and professional backgrounds. The meeting will endeavor to analyze the World Bank's role as a leader in the global education sector and offer recommendations for ways in which this position can be strengthened to best deliver education worldwide."

Over the previous months, the Bank had been gathering input for its new education strategy paper from a variety of sources across the globe. Frequent criticism of the Bank's policies at past meetings of the Comparative and International Education Society (the last time being the March 2009 Chicago meeting of the Council for International Exchange of Scholars [CIES]) led to the specific invitation to the small group of educators attending the Brookings meeting.

The intimate meeting consisted of 10 "progressive critical thinkers" from both academia and nongovernmental organizations working in the field of international education;[1] three World Bank staff (Elizabeth King, director of education, and Robin Horn, education sector manager of the Human Development Network); three Brookings staff from the Center for Universal Education (including its co-director, Rebecca Winthrop); and David Edwards of the international division of the American Federation of Labor and Congress of Industrial Organizations (AFL-CIO). A set of broad questions were sent to the participants ahead of time. Briefly they were the following:

- What are the most important challenges facing the education sector over the next 10 years?
- What are concrete recommendations for infusing the global education field with innovative education? What changes in policy could affect education delivery in developing countries where the Bank is active?
- How should the Bank balance its support for foundation education and support for building skills for the labor market?
- What is the scope for private financing and provisioning of education?
- How should the Bank approach the apparent trade-off between quantity and quality? Should our next motto be "learning for all"? Can we afford "learning for all"?

- How should the Bank be approaching the challenge that a large population of out-of-school youth is also in need of education services?

Accompanying the questions was a very concise (10 single-spaced pages) "Concept Note for the World Bank Education Strategy 2020."

In the approximate four hours the group was together, not all of these questions were addressed. At the same time other education issues were raised, many of them arising from the Concept Note. For the most part, the atmosphere was congenial and conducive to raising hard questions about the Bank's proposed education strategy. The "progressive critical thinkers" – one participant objected to the term and preferred instead "leading scholars on development and education" – came with the intention of offering constructive suggestions in the hope that the Bank, with its enormous resources, would be able to make a positive contribution to more enlightened education policies and practices benefitting the societies where it worked.

A brief summary of the May 13 proceedings was sent to the participants. Before discussing my personal reactions to the subsequent draft of November 2010 "Education Strategy 2020" document, I will review the Bank summary of the consultation and the response of several of its participants.

## WORLD BANK SUMMARY OF THE CONSULTATION[2]

The summary reviewed the opening remarks by Elizabeth King about the Bank's new education strategy, which emphasizes the connection of education to the whole development agenda; better measurement of results and impact; the development of effective partnerships with governments, other organizations, and civil society groups; and education staff development to ensure education is well managed. The overall goal of Bank strategy, according to King, was to address the needs of the world's poorest in the changing context brought about by "greater globalization, explosion of ICT in schools and the marketplace, and progress on the Millennium Development Goals."

Following King's introductory remarks, the ensuing discussion immediately raised the issue of education as a human right. Many thought that the Bank did not sufficiently stress education as a human right and this was reflected in funding. King countered that although the Bank had competing demands from other development sectors such as health, water and sanitation, and justice, education funding had risen to unprecedented levels in the past two years.

There was general agreement with a whole-sector approach to education and integrating education program with other sectors. Similarly, there was support for the Bank strategically partnering with civil society organizations. The nongovernmental sector is increasingly important with respect to envisioning education systems in more comprehensive terms than just schooling – especially in light of a need to reach marginalized youth populations with low-level marketable skills.

With regard to the Bank serving as a source of knowledge on best practices in education, participants emphasized "the benefits of using country or regional researchers to undertake" more of the work, which would "add to existing capacity and knowledge about education, as well as reduce the cost of these activities." In addition to collaborating with United Nations Educational, Scientific and Cultural Organization (UNESCO)'s Institute of Statistics and the Organization for Economic Co-operation and Development (OECD) (e.g., Programme for International Student Assessment [PISA]), which the Bank does, newer data collection methods were recommended. They include qualitative studies at school and classroom levels to examine what factors affect the quality of teaching and learning as well as the study of "under-measured school outcomes such as citizenship, teamwork, and critical thinking." (More will be said about this later in my critique of the April 2011 Education Strategy 2020 paper that emerged from this and dozens of other consultations.)

The group discussed the need to examine obstacles to achieving more equitable education systems within the context of specific countries. South Africa illustrated the case of unequal school quality between urban and rural areas and subsequent differences in test scores. A main point here was the relationship between poverty and inequality, not only in schooling but in life chances for individuals who will be severely handicapped in "a knowledge economy."

As noted by King, the emphasis on the quality of instruction is especially important as the "World Bank moved from an 'Education for All' approach to a 'Learning for All' one." Integral to this approach is the achievement of gender parity, which requires breaking "intergenerational gender stereotypes with respect to education." An emphasis on learning also leads to student-centered pedagogies.

There was consensus that achieving a quality, equitable education for all involved "the incorporation of teachers into the education plan." Unlike past failed policies, a new direction for the Bank would require including "teacher preparation, motivation and other aspects as vital to learning." Although the Bank cannot support teacher salaries, a major issue in the recruitment and retention of quality teachers, it can explore potential "sustainable ways to help countries pay for teacher salaries."[3]

King closed the meeting by noting "the Bank's appreciation of external critiques of its education policy because they provide an opportunity for the Bank to examine its vision, sharpen its own thinking, and improve the practices and plans for the future." She affirmed that "all comments and ideas would be considered in the development and implementation of the new education strategy."

## PARTICIPANT RESPONSES TO THE WORLD BANK SUMMARY

A less than three-page, single-spaced summary of four hours of a spirited conversation necessarily fails to capture the richness of the different points articulated. One shared e-mail response to the summary noted that it failed to distinguish between "discussants" who were members of the World Bank and those who were labeled "critics." Points of disagreement and dissent tended to be "washed out." For example, the role of "knowledge bank" was hotly, albeit briefly, contested. Homogenizing the input negated what could be the most useful feedback with regard to reformulating or refining the concept paper. One participant thought that the tone of the summary seemed unnecessarily defensive and appeared to be aimed at "helping 'critics' to better understand the Bank's rationale for the new strategy."

Among other concerns expressed by non-Bank participants was how the summary distilled the discussion on the significance of teachers in education reform. To accord with the Bank's initiative to professionalize the knowledge base of teaching, it would be more appropriate to discuss teacher "education," not teacher "training." Dissatisfaction with the Bank's generally negative attitude toward teacher unions, an issue raised in the meeting, was not included in the summary, nor was the positive role that unions have played as advocates for universal, free education in countries around the world. Another point of contention was presenting quantity and quality as alternative funding priorities, rather than seeing them as inseparably related to achieving an excellent education for all. A further constructive suggestion involved the Bank giving substantial attention to strengthening local institutional capacity in a more comprehensive way.

This would involve contributing to the formation of research communities with support for various means of generating and sharing knowledge through professional associations and publications.

## MY RESPONSE TO THE CONCEPT PAPER AND BANK SUMMARY

Before attending the meeting, I drafted an initial response to the Concept Note. What troubled me the most about it was its narrow, instrumental concept of education and the language used to discuss the goals, processes, and outcomes of education systems. What surprised me the most, and most of my colleagues who attended the meeting, was the pedestrian and unimaginative nature of the Concept Note. It seemed to be offering the same tired nostrums that had failed to have a significant impact on remedying persistent problems of low-quality, inequitable education systems.

If this was so, how could the Bank represent itself as a leading force in bringing about education change or being a knowledge bank of best practices? Moreover, there is the abiding problem of any set of global actors entering countries and offering solutions that do not fit local contexts. As the World Bank is well aware, there is also the issue of creating dependencies that effectively hinder the ability of countries to resolve their own problems in sustainable ways.

I had prepared comments on how the Bank refused to mine its own rich source of data in its "Voices of the Poor Study." The 1999 study gathered the voices of over 60,000 poor men and women in 23 countries. The poor – the "true poverty experts" – narrated their perceptions of the good life and the bad life, and the quality of their interactions with the major institutions, both public and private, that had a major impact on their daily existence. Education was one of the key institutions that the survey respondents discussed. How they viewed education should have played a significant role in reformulating a new vision of the Bank's role in education and development. Insights garnered from the study would have helped efforts to contextualize the meanings of education and what external aid policies may have contributed to the empowerment of individuals and their communities to flourish (a point that will be discussed at greater length later). Yet, there was no mention of this study. This failure of a major international technical and financial assistance agency to draw upon and critically analyze its own past policies as well as the vast amount of data it collected and urged aid recipients to gather was typical of another set of transnational actors I had studied.

In previous writings, I had critiqued major philanthropic foundations (Ford, Rockefeller, and Carnegie), who played the role of international catalysts for social and educational change. I argued that these external actors offered elitist, technocratic approaches to the resolution of societal ills that required a political resolution. Against the top-down approaches of these foundations, as well as the World Bank and the International Monetary Fund (IMF), a bottom-up approach was essential for redistributing power and creating education systems that contributed to the well-being of all individuals in a society (Arnove, 1980/1982).

There were other, more specific, issues I had with the paper and the conversation that took place with Bank officials. They included the relative neglect of adult education and literacy programs, especially for those over specific age – usually 35 or 40. The Bank's setting of efficiency criteria – for example, a student–teacher ratio of 45:1 – contradicted laudable goals, such as constructivist, child-centered pedagogies.

In the consultation I raised several of these points, especially with regard to the Bank's narrow vision of education and its accompanying discourse expressed in the Concept Note and previous strategy papers. In my response to the summary of the meeting, they were reiterated, as the report failed to adequately capture them.

## PHASE II CONSULTATION ON THE BANK'S EDUCATION STRATEGY 2020

There was a follow-up Consultation II held at Brookings with Bank officials on the afternoon of October 13. The goal of the consultation was to "provide stakeholders with a new opportunity to provide feedback on the World Bank's approach to education development and specifically to respond to the draft Education Strategy, which was produced following the Phase I consultations." After incorporating this feedback and conducting internal reviews of the strategy in November and December, the final Education Strategy was to be presented to the World Bank Board of Directors in January 2011.[4]

I did not attend as funds were no longer available to pay travel and accommodation costs. Apparently, the first round of consultation with "progressive critical thinkers," many of whom came from outside the

Washington, DC area, had exhausted funds for this purpose. I found this shortage of funds to be incredible.

In October and then November, drafts of the "2020 Strategy" were made available on the World Bank's Web site. Although the World Bank officials were sincere in their expressions of appreciation for the feedback they received, it was obvious that many points just did not seem to register with them; or, if they did, they were not deemed acceptable to those higher up in the governance and administration of the Bank. The World Bank Education Strategy 2020 draft statement issued in November of 2010 certainly did not reflect the progressive educators' more penetrating criticisms. What follows is my response to the draft strategy and the final 2011 strategy paper.

## WORLD BANK GROUP'S EDUCATION STRATEGY 2020

### *Bank's Vision and Discourse*

As discussed previously, my principal criticism of the Bank relates to its limited vision of education. Throughout the document, the Bank make passing nods to education as having desirable outcomes other than preparing individuals for the market and enhancing the competitive position of a country in the global economy. For example, the opening sentence of the rationale for the strategy refers to education's role in development. While essentially a "human capital" approach to development, it does note education's contribution to other desirable goals:

> People are the real wealth of nations (UNDP, 2010) and education enables them to live healthier, happier, and more productive lives. There is broad agreement, backed by research findings, that education enhances people's ability to make informed decisions, sustain a livelihood, adopt new technologies, be better parents, cope with shocks, and be responsible citizens and effective stewards of the environment. Given that global economic growth remains sluggish despite signs of recovery from the recent economic crisis, the shortage of the "right skills" in the workforce has taken on a new urgency across the world. (World Bank, 2011, p. 1)

The reference to health, the economy, and polity accords with the Bank's interest in a whole-development approach that links the education sector to other sectors of a society. References are sprinkled throughout the text to goals other than preparing individuals for graduate employment with the necessary skills to be gainfully employed for the marketplace and contributing to economic growth and a country's competitiveness. Still, the main focus of the Bank's intervention strategies in education is poverty reduction – a noble goal – but certainly not the sole, or even main reason, why nation-states establish, fund, and regulate education systems; nor is poverty only a material state of being. Poverty has its psychological and social – you could also say its spiritual – costs as well. If we are to look at the contributions of education systems to individual as well as societal well-being, then education needs to be viewed more broadly, perhaps as human flourishing (Brighouse, 2006). What the "Voices of the Poor" study referred to as "the good life."

With the Bank's emphasis on benchmarking and assessing the learning outcomes of an education system and other performance outcomes related to the financing and management of education projects, it is critically important to define what education can and should be able to do. In various publications I have written, particularly with regard to countries that have viewed education systems as instruments for bringing about major, if not radical changes in social structures, I have argued that it is neither realistic nor desirable to view an education system as the one agency capable of creating a transformed economic model of capital accumulation or as a political socialization machine capable of producing a radically transformed "new person." It is possible, however, to envision education in terms of its past historical mission of contributing to the formation of active and inquiring citizens. Among laudable goals of an education system are developing and enhancing democratic sentiments, critical reasoning skills, ethical commitments, aesthetic sensibilities, tolerance of and respect for differences, and a sense of solidarity with others, both locally and globally – and, of course, contributing to personal self-fulfilment (Arnove, 2009) or what Noble Peace Laureate Amartya Sen (1999, p. 18) has called lives of people they "have reason to value."

Although the Bank mentions the contribution of education systems to social solidarity and informed citizens, it has difficulty in actually being able to give examples of how such desirable outcomes would be assessed. In the strategy paper, the Bank states that "The benefits from education extend well beyond productivity and growth to include better health, reduced fertility, an enhanced ability to adopt new technologies and/or to cope with economic shocks, more civic participation, and even more environmentally friendly behaviour" (pp. 2–3). It then proceeds to cite evidence for each one of these claims, with the exception of civic participation (p. 3).

Is this omission due to lack of evidence or less concern with the contributions of education to democratic practice?[5] While the omission is a likely outcome of any bank's investment policies, it is certainly one for the World Bank with a global mission to address poverty issues. At the same time, I believe this omission is also a reflection of the World Bank's limited systems analysis approach to studying education. As discussed below, a significant new focus of the Bank is on system outcomes and a context of better management.

### *Problems with a Focus on Performance-Based Outcomes*

Point 59 of the Education Strategy 2020 states:

> Elements of the previous strategies are still relevant in the new strategy but the new strategy offers a system framework for policy reform and investments. The centerpiece of the new education strategy is learning for all. This goal is to be attained not only through more investments in inputs (e.g., more trained teachers or university professors, a better curriculum, more learning materials), but also through greater attention to institutional changes in the education system. The new strategy emphasizes the importance of aligning governance arrangements, financing incentives, accountability mechanisms, and management tools with national educational goals.

While curriculum and learning materials are essential factors in a quality education, more needs to be said about the actual interactions that occur in an education system as teachers, students, and administrators engage with a curriculum and learning materials in a particular context. In other words, what is a glaring omission is the Bank's inability to address issues related to the processes of education. What we have is a listing of inputs and desirable outcomes.

Among the most important variables in any analysis of the internal workings of education systems are the quality of a teaching force and the conditions under which teachers work. In the Brookings consultation and in various Bank documents there are indications of a desire to professionalize the occupation. Yet, the vision and discourse that surrounds teaching are framed in terms of "managing them." For example, the 2020 strategy (on p. 17) refers to policy domains (financial allocation mechanisms; performance incentives, laws, rules, and regulations) that can be leveraged to determine how teachers are recruited, deployed, paid, and *managed* [emphasis mine] – with the goal of achieving desirable education reform.

The final 2020 Strategy, however, is a marked improvement over the November draft that discusses "improvements in teacher management procedures, establishment of a national certification board, development of a quality assurance process for universities" (p. 33). The document further states:

> The Bank will support the implementation of teacher reform programs through financing and analytical work. In particular, the Bank's knowledge agenda will: (i) build

> evident and develop best practice guidelines on teacher selection, management, incentives for performance, pedagogical practices, professional development, and alignment with the curriculum and assessment systems. (p. 34)

What accounts for this removal of almost any discussion of pre-and in-service teacher education from the 2011 final document merits further study. (Is it possible that the Bank responded to criticisms from teachers and their organizations?) What is noticeably missing from the 2020 Education Strategy is a discussion of policies that contribute to making teaching an attractive profession or that enhance the conditions under which teachers work. The overall tone is one of controlling teachers in accordance with what the draft document called the "political economy of education reform" (World Bank, 2010, p. 4).

Any ideal model of a profession would include the autonomy of practitioners (in this case, teachers) to determine how best to serve the well-being of their clients (students). Unfortunately, teacher autonomy is being greatly eroded by current incentive schemes, which the Bank appears to favor (as suggested by the education strategies bibliography), to reward teachers on the basis of how their students performance on high-stakes tests that measure a narrow range of knowledge and skills.[6] These schemes are necessarily punitive for teachers who work under difficult circumstances and with at-risk students. They also tend to be divisive, pitting teachers against one another, when only so many of them can be deemed meritorious.

Although absent from the April 2011 Education Strategy 2020, the draft strategy's reference to "development of a quality assurance process for universities" is indicative of past Bank and IMF conditionalities concerning investments in higher education. The conditionalities have generated conflict in a number of countries, where students and faculty have demonstrated, sometimes violently, against what they consider to be an assault on the historic autonomy of their higher education institutions. Tying Bank and IMF funds to cost recovery by charging tuition (where student fees were either very low or nonexistent) has been viewed as closing opportunities to students from historically disadvantaged backgrounds.

Not only are the poor placed at a disadvantage by current education emphases and assessment policies, but also, according to philosopher Martha Nussbaum (2010, p. 2), entire societies are placed at risk:

> Thirsty for national profit, nations and their systems of education are heedlessly discarding skills that are needed to keep democracy alive. If this trend continues, nations all over the world will soon be producing generations of useful machines, rather than complex citizens who can think for themselves, criticize tradition, and understand the significance of another person's sufferings and achievements.

Nussbaum is a strong advocate for instruction in the humanities, the liberal arts that enable and ennoble individuals but are precisely the subject areas that are downplayed in today's scramble to improve the competitive position of a country in the global economy.

### *Contextualizing System Interventions and Assessments*

My initial reaction to the Education Concept distributed to participants in the Brookings May 13 consultation was that the Bank had failed to take into account its own rich source of data on what education meant to individuals and their communities in specific national and subnational contexts. The Bank, as part of its Education Strategy 2020, advocates an approach to examining the impact of its policies by three large categories of countries: low-income, middle-income, and countries with fragile situations. In the Brookings consultation, I suggested adding further groupings of countries. Doing so would enable the Bank to identify what strategies made sense according to differing contexts. For example, the Bank might want to consider the data provided by the "Voices of the Poor" project to look at countries according to such issues as language policies where there were large blocks of ethnic groups that were effectively excluded from succeeding in schooling due to the use of an international or dominant group language. At the same time, there were countries (e.g., in the Andean region of Latin America) that were attempting to achieve intercultural, interethnic education that involved equal status relations and mutual respect between indigenous and nonindigenous populations, as well as between rural and urban dwellers.

Taking into account what languages were used in national, high-stakes tests would lead to more appropriate assessment processes and instruments. This is just one example of the need to contextualize education reform efforts. As noted by Samoff (2007, p. 60):

> Calls in many countries for global education standards have spawned a series of cross-national efforts to measure and compare achievement at different levels. Although they claim sensitivity to the unique characteristics of specific national and local settings, by design those assessments seek to use and thereby institutionalize internationally particular assumptions about both the content and the process of learning and teaching. The results of the assessment measures may contribute to improving the quality of education in some settings, but their more powerful role is to undermine the education philosophy that associates effective learning with education objectives and measures that are debated and decided locally.

### Neglect of Literacy for All

Literacy policy is one example of the Bank setting a standard followed by other countries. In this case, the Bank frames national investment strategies by what it fails to emphasize. While the Bank, rhetorically, notes the importance of literacy, funding for literacy consistently has represented less than 2 percent of the education sector budget. In fact, funding of literacy shrank from 1.3 percent in the 1996–2000 to 0.7 percent in 2006–2010 (World Bank, 2011, p. 31).[7] The Bank, according to Education Director Elizabeth King, depends on other agencies to address literacy needs;[8] and, when the Bank does support literacy programs, it does so almost exclusively for adults under 35 years of age. As a case in point, neoliberal governments in Nicaragua, in the 1990s, used the Bank's literacy policies to justify not investing adequately in adult education. Instead it depended on civil society organizations to reach over half a million illiterate adults with exceedingly limited funds (less than U.S. $50,000). The result was a systematic increase in illiteracy rates (Arnove, 1994, pp. 186–189).

At the 2001 CIES conference in Washington, DC, I raised contradictions in the Bank's literacy policies with its staff members serving on a panel. One of the staff pointed out the importance of parental education for the schooling success of their children. I pointed out that in Northeast Brazil, with the highest poverty and illiteracy rates in the country, the Bank was investing $100 million in basic education. Yet, the Bank, despite its focus on family background factors, was investing not a single penny in adult education. This point was reiterated to a member of that panel at the May 2010 Brookings consultation.

### Total Neglect of Language Policies

Perhaps the most shocking and significant omission is the lack of any systematic discussion of language of instruction with the exception of references in the 2011 Education Strategy document (p. 28) to groups benefitting from "the instructional use of their native languages" and in the November 2010 strategy draft to students from "ethno-linguistic minorities" being at a disadvantaged in school (p. 5), one endnote, and an oblique reference to the greater capacity for students to learn second and third languages [b]eyond the initial primary grades (pp. 14–15).[9] This omission stands in stark contrast to the stated emphasis of the Bank on "learning for all." As well documented by Birgit Brock-Utne, Desai, Qorro, and Pitman

(2010), Desai, Qoroo, and Brock-Utne (2010), and countless other language and literacy scholars (including my edited collection with Harvey Graff on the history of literacy campaigns), students consistently perform poorly when they take examinations not in their home language.[10] The result of teaching in unfamiliar languages (often those of the former colonizers) in the early grades systematically leads to grade repetition and school dropout.

### *Contradictions in Student-Centered Policies and Support*

One such example of a contradiction between policies pertains to the Bank's championing of more learner-centered pedagogies. To return to the case of Nicaragua, the Bank, in the early 1990s, set a student–teacher ratio of 45:1 as a benchmark for the efficient operation of schools. This standard was adopted by the ministry of education in the Chamorro administration as a cost-cutting measure. At the same time, the ministry, in accord with international trends and Bank initiatives, was promoting the notion of student-centered teaching and learning despite the lack of adequately prepared teachers and supporting curricular materials. The efficiency standard, if systematically applied, would have made achieving constructivist pedagogies even more difficult (Arnove, 1994, p. 106).

Problems involved in implementing child-centered education are evident in the case of the APRENDE (Learn) project of the late 1990s. APRENDE involved the Bank providing Nicaragua a U.S.$53 million loan that paid for the purchase of Colombian and Mexican constructivist teacher guides and learning materials for multigrade classrooms. The commitment of the Bank to the project, however, was haphazard as the loan did not fund publication of sufficient copies to cover the universe of multigrade schools. Moreover, the Bank staff didn't quite understand why there was a need for modular furniture. It did provide some modular tables for primary classrooms but also continued procuring and distributing old-fashioned individual desks with fixed writing surfaces, which made small-group, active learning much more difficult.

Then, there is the reverse situation of the Bank seeing a contradiction where there is none, at least according to the "critics" attending the May 2010 Brookings' consultation. The summary document suggested that increased attention to teacher education was "different from the student-focused strategies of recent years, which has failed to include teacher preparation, motivation and other aspects as vital to learning." In a shared e-mail message to the meeting rapporteur, one of the participants noted the "text suggests there is a tension between attention to teacher education and student-centered learning strategies." To the contrary, student-centered strategies in Africa and elsewhere necessarily emphasize teacher preparation.

## WRAPPING-UP THE ACCOUNT

Despite the holding of 24 consultation meetings in 69 countries with hundreds of representatives of different relevant constituencies, I found the final Education Strategy 2020 paper to be fundamentally the same as past Bank policy directions. Yes, there is more emphasis on a whole-development and intersector approach to education with a systematic effort to align education goals, financing, management, and assessment policies, while meeting the needs of out-of-school youth. But, the vision of what education can be and the discourse used to frame education policy continues to be too narrowly utilitarian and lacking in insights as to the very nature of the human interactions that constitute effective teaching and learning (see, e.g., Klees, 2009; Samoff, 2007).

The issue of external agencies shaping education agendas central to a society's processes of cultural transmission and socialization of individuals for adult roles raises concerns with regard to new forms of cultural imperialism. Problems I raised with regard to the role that philanthropic foundations (namely, Ford, Rockefeller, and Carnegie) played as catalysts for education and social change pertains to the role that the World Bank has now assumed as the repository of the best ideas on good education practice.

The constructive criticism offered by the education and development scholars attending the May 13, 2010, Brookings Institution consultation with the World Bank argued for a less hegemonic role for the Bank in grant and loan giving. If truly meaningful education reflects local sociocultural contexts and empowers individuals and their communities to live more fulfilling lives, then supporting the research capacities of regional, national, and local institutions as well as professional associations of individual scholars makes the most sense. Support for networking of institution and scholars, an initiative already on the Bank's agenda, should be a top priority, as would be investing in the creation of national/regional think tanks developing diverse paths to more desirable futures for their societies. Increasing opportunities for South–South cooperation, complemented by those for North–South, East–West exchanges, should contribute significantly to more appropriate and effective education policies and practices tied to poverty reduction and societal development. Ultimately and ideally, the Bank and other sources of external funding of education would be almost totally replaced by individual countries and the regional political/economic blocs to which they belong – which, for example, is occurring in Latin America.

Finally, my past research on major philanthropic foundations working in the fields of education, research, and development pointed out a serious blind spot in their operations. While they went about the world requiring institutions and programs to assess what they were doing, they systematically failed to evaluate critically their own workings and outcomes. The World Bank sits atop an enormous wealth of data gathered over the past 50 years. Yet, as is the case with "The Voices of the Poor" project, the Bank does not appear to have used this information to inform its policies in education and related fields. The Bank's best starting point for shaping a more meaningful and effective education strategy for the next 10 years is to learn from the successes and failures of its past policies.

## NOTES

1. In addition to me, the following critical educators were invited to the meeting: Sarah Beardmore (RESULTS Educational Fund), Mark Ginsburg (Academy for Educational Development), Amy Gray (Global Campaign for Education), Steven Klees (University of Maryland), Karen Monkman (DePaul University), Joel Samoff (Stanford University), Carol Anne Spreen (University of Virginia), Gita Steiner-Khamsi (Teachers College, Columbia University), and Fran Vavrus (University of Minnesota).

2. The summary includes not only the text provided by the World Bank but also my own interpretation of what was said and what occurred in the meeting.

3. As one of the "critics" noted, it was not clear what the Bank meant by "sustainable ways to help countries pay for teacher salaries."

4. Winthrop, R. "Brookings Invitation: Phase II Consultation on the World Bank Group's Education Strategy 2020 (October 21)," e-mail message sent to me on September 11, 2010.

5. Political socialization research over the past 50 years has indicated that civic education does contribute to more knowledgeable and active citizens, but the ideological orientation of that participation varies by sociocultural contexts and historical situations (Almond & Verba, 1989).

6. Moreover, many of the tests at state/provincial levels involve a "dumbing down" of test content so that schools and teachers are not penalized for poor performance. This "dumbing down" also is noted with regard to textbooks that are

designed to be "teacher proof" to guarantee that students' teachers are confined to covering what is required to succeed on these tests (see, e.g., Apple, 2004).

7. This reduction in literacy funding occurred, despite its citing an estimate by Hanushek and Woessman (2007) that "a one standard deviation increase in student scores on international assessments of literacy and mathematics competencies is associated with a 2-percent increase in annual growth rates of GDP per capita" (World Bank, 2011, p. 2).

8. With regard to the Bank's literacy policies, the summary of the May 13 Brookings reads the following: "She [Elizabeth King]noted that the Bank cannot be engaged in every aspect of education and training and that it is important for other international actors to lead efforts on other aspects of education, including adult literacy and lifelong learning" (p. 2).

9. End note of the strategy discusses the assessment of student learning in grade 2, which the Bank notes November 2000 draft "is a very early grade in which to test a student in a language [French] that is not his or her mother tongue." The November 2010 draft strategy, however, did, at least, discuss the deficit in the number of "trained teachers who can teach in a minority language" as one among various "multiple disadvantages," including gender, place of residence, and disability (p. 5).

10. See, for example, Arnove and Graff (1987).

## REFERENCES

Almond, G. A., & Verba, S. (1989). *The civic culture revisited.* Newbury Park, CA: Sage.

Apple, M. (2004). *Ideology and curriculum* (3rd ed.). New York, NY: Routledge Falmer.

Arnove, R. (2009). Who names the word with what consequences? In B. Brock-Utne & G. Garbo (Eds.), *Language and power: The implications of language for peace and development* (pp. 126–132). Dar es Salaam: Mkuki na Myota Publishers.

Arnove, R. F. (1980, 1982). *Philanthropy and cultural imperialism: The foundations at home and abroad.* GK Hall.

Arnove, R. F. (1994). *Education as contested terrain.* Boulder, CO: Westview.

Arnove, R. F., & Graff, H. J. (Eds.). (1987). *National literacy campaigns: Historical and comparative perspectives.* New York, NY: Plenum.

Brighouse, H. (2006). *On education.* New York, NY: Routledge.

Brock-Utne, B., Desai, Z., Qorro, M., & Pitman, A. (Eds.). (2010). *Language of instruction in Tanzania and South Africa – Highlights from a project.* Rotterdam: Sense Publishers.

Desai, Z., Qoroo, M., & Brock-Utne, B. (2010). *Educational challenges in multilingual societies.* Capetown: African Minds.

Hanushek, E., & Woessman, L. (2008). The role of cognitive skills in economic development. *Journal of Economic Literature, 46*(3), 607–668.

Klees, S. J. (2009). The language of education and development. In B. Brock-Utne & G. Garbo (Eds.), *Language and power: The implications of language for peace and development* (pp. 107–125). Dar es Salaam: Mkuki na Myota Publishers.

Nussbaum, M. C. (2010). *Not for profit: Why democracy needs the humanities.* Princeton, NJ: Princeton University Press.

Sen, A. (1999). *Development as freedom.* New York, NY: Alfred A. Knopf.

Samoff, J. (2007). Institutionalizing international influence. In R. Arnove & C. A. Torres (Eds.), *Comparative education: The dialectic of the global and the local* (3rd ed., pp. 47–77). Boulder, CO: Rowman & Littlefield.

World Bank. (November 2010a draft). *Learning for all: Investing in people's knowledge and skills to promote development*. Washington, DC: World Bank.

World Bank. (April 2011). *Learning for all: Investing in people's knowledge and skills to promote development*. Washington, DC: World Bank.

# EDUCATION SECTOR STRATEGY 2020 AND POPULAR PARTICIPATION: PARALLELS AND PITFALLS

Tammy Boyd and Tom Owens

## ABSTRACT

*This study compares the World Bank 2020 Education Strategy to research conducted a few years ago analyzing the effectiveness of the Bolivian Popular Participation law (1994) through policy study conducted from 2000 to 2004, including fieldwork in Cochabamba, Bolivia, in 2002. The policy research focused on Popular Participation and successive policy initiatives that modified or impacted public services, particularly public education. The fieldwork in Cochabamba focused on civil society and government interactions regarding public education. In studying the governance structures put in place by the Popular Participation law, particularly decentralizing authority and resources to the municipal level and creating mechanisms for civil society participation in governance, parallels to proposed Bank practices for the 2020 Education Strategy can been seen, as well as potential pitfalls. We cannot exam the World Bank 2020 Education Strategy development process in a vacuum – history, environment, and culture must be taken*

**Education Strategy in the Developing World: Revising the World Bank's Education Policy**
**International Perspectives on Education and Society, Volume 16, 81–109**

**ISSN: 1479-3679/doi:10.1108/S1479-3679(2012)0000016009**

*into account, as must the influence of particular stakeholder groups and established norms of behavior at the World Bank. The implementation of Popular Participation was problematic at best, and the response to features of Popular Participation that parallel the 2020 Education Strategy – in particular, the operating principles enumerated on pp. 7–8 of the 2020 Education Strategy Concept Note – have important implications for the proposed Bank strategy.*

## INTRODUCTION

The World Bank's consultative process for *Education Sector Strategy 2020* (ESS2020) represents a notable departure from standard Bank practices for setting a policy agenda. Tremendous potential exists for this new consultative process to produce substantive change in the way the World Bank supports educational efforts in less-developed countries – but abundant potential also exists for this process to quickly become enmeshed in traditional Bank/debtor-nation relations that sharply limit the interaction and impact of the new actors involved in the ESS2020 process.

This chapter traces the consultative process used by the World Bank in developing ESS2020. The consultative process and the documents produced by it are then critically examined through the lens of post-structuralism and early indicators of potential problems are discussed. Research conducted in Bolivia on the Law of Popular Participation is presented, and the findings from that research offer a sobering cautionary tale for the World Bank. The chapter concludes with recommendations for future actions to safeguard the autonomy and agency of member nations (and in particular, local actors) that is created by ESS2020.

## THEORETICAL FRAMEWORK

Poststructuralist critiques of the development discourse offer a useful framework for analyzing the World Bank's ESS2020 and the consultative process. While the field of post-structuralism is vast and varied, this analysis will focus on notions and expressions of power, drawing largely from Foucault's conceptualizations of power (see Foucault, 1970, 1971, 1972,

1977a, 1977b, 1979, 1980, 1988). In particular, this analysis explores disciplinary power, discursive power, and pastoral or governmental power.

Disciplinary power is defined as that power exercised by observing and measuring, as well as "the normalising judgements that are made as a result of these observations and measurements" (Ninnes & Burnett, 2003, p. 282). With respect to the World Bank, this power is exercised on nations as well as on individuals. Discursive power is defined as that power exercised through the control and/or use of particular discourses. According to Escobar (1995, 2000, p. 11), "[with] poststructuralist critiques ... development was shown to be a pervasive cultural discourse with profound consequences for the production of social reality in the so-called Third World." Finally, governmental power is defined as that power that emphasizes and/or manipulates free will as an object of power. Rahnema (1999) explains, "when A considers it essential for B to be empowered, A assumes not only that B has no power–or does not have the right kind of power–but also that A has the secret formula of a power to which B has to be initiated. In the current participatory ideology, this formula is, in fact, nothing but a revised version of state power" (p. 123).

Above and beyond specific types of power, Foucault in particular argued that power was ubiquitous – it is not only limiting but "also productive, creating certain ways of behaving or knowing" (Ziai, 2009, p. 185). More importantly, power can be exercised through the production of knowledge and through constituting specific avenues for action (Ziai, 2009); for example, the consultative process and resulting document, the *ESS2020*.

## METHODOLOGY

Guba (1983) states that policy is not defined in any uniform way and that most authors assume their audience shares their implicit definition of policy. This is problematic not only for communicative reasons but also because any particular definition of policy determines the questions asked, the data sources, methodology, and policy product. The definition of policy used herein is policy as *a strategy undertaken to solve or ameliorate some problem*. This definition dictates that the implementers of said policy be the main data source and qualitative inquiries such as interviews, observations, and *records analyses* be the methodology (Guba, 1983). Choosing another definition of policy would require different data sources and methodologies that would likely lead to different conclusions about the efficacy of the policy.

The overarching research question studied in this analysis was as follows:

- To what extent has the process and production of the *ESS2020* ameliorated the problem of member-nation marginalization?

As we were not participants in the consultative meetings or working sessions to draft *ESS2020*, interviews and observations were not practically feasible; therefore, the dominant methodology employed in this study was documentary analyses, focusing on policy documents. According to Jenny Ozga, "[u]sing policy texts as a research resource is one of the most accessible forms of research on education policy, and is to be commended not just for its accessibility, but because close reading of policy texts helps to generate critical, informed and independent responses to policy. Reading and interpreting texts can be an act of engagement with policy, for the researcher and those with whom she or he works" (2000, p. 107).

Coding of documents was done inductively, with the key terms and categories emerging from the documents themselves (Brent & Slusarz, 2003; Burck, 2005; Strauss & Corbin, 1990, 1998; White & Marsh, 2006); many of the World Bank documents provided coding schema in the document itself, created by the Bank as it analyzed – and categorized – input from members in consultative meetings. The initial analyses were quantitative, focusing on word frequencies – and word absences – in successive policy documents. A second, qualitative, analysis of the "tone" of the document was conducted. Critically reading and re-reading policy documents reveals key words and phrases that expose the assumptions of policymakers, while analyzing the tone of documents reveals how and when policymakers believe things should happen (Ozga, 2000). The qualitative analysis focused specifically on how ideas, suggested courses of action, and rationales provided for both could be understood as expressions of power, particularly power expressed by those entities (the World Bank and the Bolivian government, respectively) claiming that their new process was a way to share power.

The documents used to analyze ESS2020 include the consultative notes, member feedback, and successive draft copies of ESS2020, including the final version of ESS2020 released in April 2011. These documents were collected and analyzed from August 2010 to June 2011. The documents used to analyze *Popular Participation* include municipal plans and budgets, federal policies, and multinational polices, including those of the International Monetary Fund and the World Bank. These documents were collected and analyzed from 2000 to 2004.

## WORLD BANK CONSULTATIVE PROCESS FOR *EDUCATION SECTOR STRATEGY 2020*

### *Concept Note*

The first document (produced in advance of the consultative strategy) was the "Concept Note for the World Bank Education Strategy 2020." In the "Concept Note," the Bank described the role education has to play in development and provided a justification for writing a new education strategy. The justification revolved around the need to respond to substantial international contextual shifts, including globalization and the global financial crisis, lack of universal access to primary education, the growing need for support for secondary and tertiary education, the need to shift the focus from schooling to learning, and the impact of armed conflicts on education and society. There have also been changes in the Bank's internal environment, namely, decentralization of Bank staff and the growing demand for an evidence base for policy making. One of the explicitly stated objectives of the "Concept Note" was to discuss the Bank's future role and direction in education with "a broad set of partners and stakeholders" (World Bank, 2010a, p. 5, February 8). The "Concept Note" also suggested emerging themes for the new strategy, including focusing on learning and skills, and using the comparative advantage of a global institution. The document concluded with next steps for the consultative strategy and a timetable.

### *Report on Phase I External Consultations*

The World Bank held 34 meetings – 17 multi-stakeholder meetings and 17 targeted meetings – from March to June 2010; the meetings were held in 24 countries around the world and involved a total of 69 countries and over 1,100 participants (World Bank, 2010b, August 31). From June to August 2010, the Bank compiled the feedback collected through the face-to-face meetings, the web portal, and the dedicated e-mail address established for the consultative process and used that data to produce the "Report on Phase I External Consultations" dated August 31, 2010. The document reiterated the consultative process and reported the compilation of comments from participants. The discussions in the Phase I consultations were structured around a set of seven questions posed to participants by the World Bank, and questions were adapted as needed to the local context and/or the audience. The results of the consultations were presented according to theme and country type.

The themes, created by the World Bank and assigned to participants' comments, are access, context, curriculum, efficiency, finance, inputs, knowledge, learning & quality, monitoring & evaluation, management, politics, systems, TVET, teachers, and other. Each theme was broken down further into 69 subthemes. Furthermore, each theme's main points/discussion summary was presented broken down into country type. The four country types presented are low-income countries (LICs), middle-income countries (MICs), high-income countries (HICs), and countries in fragile situations (FSs). The World Bank noted, rightly, that countries in FSs are largely LICs, though they do face some unique challenges. The differences across themes identified by country type are illuminating.

Reporting detailed information about every theme by each country grouping is beyond the scope of this chapter. Nonetheless, a brief summary of differences needs to be presented. FS countries are still struggling with issues of equity, marginalization, and universal primary enrollment, particularly for girls. They would like support in serving out-of-school youth, including psychosocial rehabilitation services for victims of violence and former child soldiers. High-debt levels combined with a lack of infrastructure are especially problematic, as is the need to bridge the pullout of humanitarian aid and funding. Balancing immediate crisis needs and long-term development needs is a challenge as well as balancing the need for strengthening government capacities for education and facilitating local and civil society participation. Finally, FSs need best practice guidelines and data for evidence-based policy making.

LICs are also still struggling with equity of access, though their difficulties seem to revolve more around ethnic minorities and other excluded/marginalized populations. They also still need a focus on primary education, though they would also like to begin/expand work on tertiary education, adult education, and out-of-school youth. LICs in particular have noted the need to have more flexibility in funding and lending, particularly as they look at initiatives such as abolishing school fees. LICs also have infrastructure needs, though their needs tend more along the lines of curriculum and equipment as opposed to facilities. LICs would like education to be more closely linked to their citizenries' lived realities, in particular, climate change and work skills. They would like better accountability and local capacity as well as more south-south cooperation. One final point raised, that the LICs were quite adamant about, was that the World Bank needs to listen more.

MICs had a noticeably different set of needs than FSs and LICs. MICs feel they are in good shape with respect to primary education (though they do note some equity concerns with respect to girls, indigenous, and rural populations) and would like support to expand access to secondary and tertiary education. Their funding needs revolve around expanding capacity and access, and some MICs would like to see the World Bank provide more incentives for governments to invest in their own education while other MICs would like to see the World Bank reduce its lending to governments. Their largest infrastructure concerns seem to be information and communication technology (ICT), and most MICs would like support and training in monitoring and evaluation, including impact evaluation. Like the LICs, MICs would like to see more south-south exchanges. They are concerned with educational quality and skills for sustainable development, and they would like World Bank support to participate in international assessments like Trends in International Mathematics and Science Study (TIMSS). Finally, the MICs wanted it to be clear that they value the consultative process.

HICs had a set of concerns that were appreciably different from the other three country groupings, though there were points of overlap. HICs were concerned about life-long learning and the role of education in building peaceful societies and promoting sustainable growth. They were more concerned with affordability and regulatory frameworks than with funding flexibility or incentives, and they felt government should not have a monopoly on education provision. HICs were focused on the newest and best data collection methods, particularly with respect to reliable statistics, disaggregated data, and best practices. They recognized a need to build climate change, life skills, and international assessments into education as well as build management capacity. HICs felt that the World Bank should play an advocacy role for education and that it should include innovative finance tools like incentives. Their closing concern was that the ESS2020 have an implementation plan.

### *First ESS2020 Draft (October 2010)*

The first draft of the World Bank ESS2020 was published on the World Bank's web site on October 19, 2010. The draft is organized into three major sections. Part 1 provides a compelling rationale for supporting education and for focusing on learning as opposed to schooling. Part 2 begins to outline the Bank's education strategy. Part 3 considers implementation issues that could prove problematic as well as the first draft of performance and impact indicators for the proposed educational strategy.

This document largely presents what will become the final Educational Sector Strategy 2020; successive iterations enhanced, rather than substantively changed, the ideas presented here. This draft begins with presenting education's role in national development and argues for a conceptual shift from "education for all" to "learning for all." This shift is based on the premise that "for too many students, more schooling has not resulted in greater learning" (World Bank, 2010c, p. 5, October), and they cite data from international assessments like TIMSS and PISA to support their position. They go on to state that in addition to shifting the focus from education to learning, there needs to be an expanded definition of "education system." The definition of education system presented by the Bank encompasses all educational opportunities, including those provided by non-state providers; all beneficiaries and stakeholders, including communities and employers; and all the rules, regulations and policies regarding education. And an expanded definition of education system calls for a robust international knowledge base that will supply "(i) reliable and comparable statistics to measure learning outcomes and monitor aspects of the performance of education systems, and (ii) analytical and practical evidence and know-how about programs and policies that can improve the workings of education systems" (p. 16) (Fig. 1).

The World Bank can best meet the needs of the international community with respect to the shifted focus on learning and the expanded conception of education through three "implementation levers" – knowledge generation and policy debate; financial and technical support to countries; and

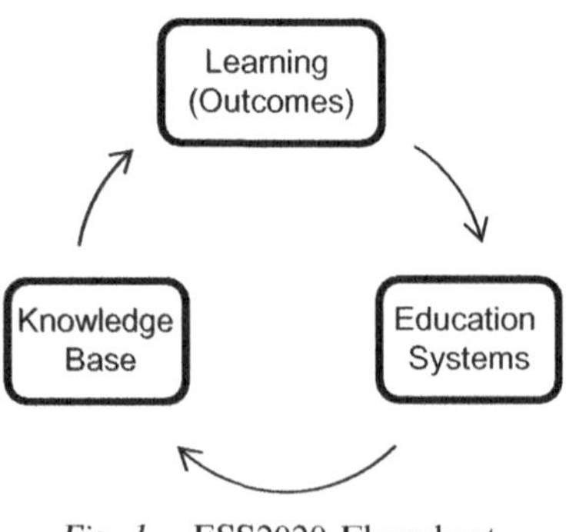


*Fig. 1.* ESS2020 Flowchart.

partnerships (p. 28). To that end, the Bank will engage in activities such as follows:

- Systems diagnostics, results measurement, and benchmarking
- Increasing learning assessments and other educational data
- Analytical and evaluative research
- Financing for results (results- or outcomes-based financing)
- Multisectoral approach (not addressing education in a vacuum, but considering the interrelatedness of sectors such as health, transport, agriculture, and environment)
- Strategic partnerships (multilateral and bilateral agencies, private donors, and civil society organizations)

Priorities within these activities will be differentiated for countries based on the country's need and capacity. The Bank's performance will be evaluated using a set of eight (8) performance and five (5) impact indicators focused on diagnostic tools, policies, and interventions using a systems approach, Bank staff development, loans/credits that use results-based financing, and progress on Millennium Development Goals (MDGs).

### *Second ESS2020 Draft (December 2010)*

The data from the Phase I consultations and the feedback on the first draft were used to guide the Phase II consultations, a briefer, more highly focused set of internal consultations supplemented by online and blended (online and face-to-face) discussions with external audiences. The result of the second round of consultations was the second draft of ESS2020.

The second draft of the World Bank ESS2020 was released on 3 December 2010. This draft did not substantially change the tone of the first draft; the focus is still on learning for all, education systems, and knowledge base. What this draft did provide that was new was the introduction of a multiyear testing program, the Systems Assessment and Benchmarking Education for Results (SABER), and expanded indicators, including performance, outcome, and impact indicators. There is more information provided in support of the Bank's proposed education strategy, and the Bank's focus on educational systems and the international knowledge base have now been pulled out and highlighted as "priorities" for the education strategy: (1) strengthening education systems and (2) building a high-quality knowledge base for education reforms

(World Bank, 2010d, December 3). The discussion of differentiating priorities is expanded, with specific examples of previous Bank activities presented, as is the discussion of the three implementation levers. The new indicators are briefly discussed at the end of the document, with minimal attention devoted to what the new indicators are or how the existing indicators were changed. The indicators in this document focus on diagnostic and measurement tools, inclusion of impact evaluation in Bank operations, Bank staff development, meeting MDG goals, adequate education finance data, and reduced gaps for disadvantaged populations.

### *Final ESS2020 Document (April 2011)*

The plan initially was to prepare the final version of ESS2020 in time for the January World Bank Board of Executive Directors meeting and to publish it by March 2011. However, the final version was not ready for Board review until the April meeting, when it was approved, and the final World Bank ESS2020 was published on April 12, 2011.

This strategy provided the most thoroughly integrated and comprehensive argument yet for the Bank's proposed strategy, with even more data and examples presented. However, with the exception of new indicators, the basic tone and proposed strategy was unchanged. The focus is still on learning, increased learning is still best accomplished through an expanded notion of education systems, and the best way to both measure learning outcomes and provide useful data to systems for policy initiatives is with expansive assessment and evaluation to inform a comprehensive knowledge base. The implementation levers are still knowledge generation and policy, financial and technical support, and partnerships (World Bank, 2011).

The main difference between this document and the first two drafts is the expanded discussion of indicators and the creation of a few new indicators. ESS2020 now has nine (9) performance indicators, four (4) outcome indicators, and four (4) impact indicators. While some details have changed, the indicators are largely still focused on tools (though they are now called system tools rather than diagnostic tools), Bank staff professional development, the inclusion of learning- or skills-related indicators and monitoring and evaluation (M&E) in projects and programs, progress toward MDGs, outputs/outcomes-based financing, application of learning or skills assessments, reducing gaps for disadvantaged populations and gains in labor force skills.

## POSTSTRUCTURALIST CRITIQUES OF THE DEVELOPMENT DISCOURSE EMBEDDED IN *EDUCATION STRATEGY 2020*

First and foremost, the World Bank is to be applauded for the level of engagement and participation they have sought from member nations during the consultative process for *Education Strategy 2020*. They have sought a wide range of voices from member nations who are the intended recipients of these policies, the so-called target population. Furthermore, they seem to have made a genuine effort to allow for differential assistance that countries might need based on location, level of development/income, and the possibility of instability/fragility. However, the World Bank has undertaken all these initiatives as an alternative way *to approach* development, rather than an alternative *to* development – and this capitulation to the development discourse already suggests that the implementation of ESS2020 will follow traditional Bank/debtor nation relations, including ways in which the World Bank exercises power.

The first problem was the creation of the Concept Note, which was a clear case of the Bank exercising discursive power. The Concept Note was created by World Bank staff and set out "key areas to be explored" (World Bank, 2010b, p. 4, August) in developing a new education strategy. Furthermore, the Concept Note was examined and approved by the World Bank's Committee on Development Effectiveness (CODE) before being released for the consultative process. This document was used to guide the Phase I Consultation Meetings, as were Discussion Questions that were also created by the World Bank. Bank staff scheduled and facilitated the meetings, and conducted the data analysis, by theme and subtheme that were apparently created by the Bank. In short, the World Bank set the parameters for, and tightly controlled the discourse on, ESS2020 from the outset.

The consultation meetings and electronic feedback portals were another problem, one that continued the discourse dominance of the World Bank. The consultative process required a fair amount of travel to country capitols, at a minimum, if not international travel. For those who were unwilling or unable (or not invited) to travel to the consultation meetings, documents were made available online for review and mechanisms for submitting comments/feedback via a web-based form or a dedicated e-mail address were put in place. Unfortunately, billions of people, most of whom are the target of the World Bank's education strategy (and other initiatives), cannot leave work long enough to travel to a consultative meeting – assuming they could afford to travel – nor do they have access to reliable telephone and/or electric service, not to mention a computer, which makes providing electronic feedback extremely difficult at best. While there were undoubtedly some individuals who were able to participate in Bank activities for the first time as a result of the consultative process, too many people were excluded from what was meant to be a participatory process, and they were largely individuals who already exist at the margins.

There were at least 1,100 people who were able to participate in the consultation meetings, and their input was collected and analyzed, as was the input received electronically. The Bank did seem to report the data they received faithfully, though the Bank was still fully in control of the discourse, and they did divide the data into several groupings based on a country's income level – and there were noticeable differences in the groups' responses. With a bit of oversimplification, the data can roughly be divided between FSs and LICs on the one hand and MICs and HICs on the other. The very act of dividing countries by income and then categorizing them was a clear, early indicator of the World Bank exercising disciplinary power. Much of what was important to FSs and LICs did not make it into any ESS2020 draft; what was important to MICs and HICs was better represented in the ESS2020 documents. Most importantly, what was important to the World Bank, including the main features of the World Bank's upcoming education strategy (learning for all, education systems and knowledge base), was immediately presented in the first draft of ESS2020 and was constant across all three drafts.

An examination of word frequency across the Report of the Phase I Consultations and all three drafts of ESS2020 starkly demonstrates this trend. While word frequencies may fail to obtain precision that is comparable educational production functions, they are nonetheless important and serve to give a general feel for the tone and trend of the documents. We selected terms from Table 4 in the "Report of the Phase I External Consultations" and from all three drafts of the ESS2020. Given that the final document was much longer than the initial report, it was necessary to compensate for this difference. To do this, we averaged the changes in the tracked terms across all reports to develop some notion of the center of the distribution controlling for a skewed distribution by constraining (eliminating) outliers at both ends of the curve. Once we were able to see which words were used more or less than the core group, we made an effort to analyze which words were more closely associated with the various groups of participants. The main goal was to see if the words that figured prominently in the LICs and FS countries formed part of the final document.

In general, there was considerable overlap between varying countries across different documents. This we expected for two reasons: (1) the conversation focused on schools, learning, systems, and development and (2) the questions in the concept document and in the first consultative report constrained discussion to those variables on which the World Bank intended the discourse to focus. However, despite these boundaries, there is evidence that the transition from consultation to final document was firmly controlled by the World Bank through the use of discursive and disciplinary power.

We selected a group of terms that included effectiveness, information, teacher, indicator, data, quality, knowledge, assessment, skill, school, learning, development and system. We then considered the extent to which these words occurred in Table 4 of the Phase 1 Consultation Report by income or situation groups. For example, common terms such as system, development, school and teacher were frequently used across all four groupings and show similarly frequent use in the final document. Other terms showed significant variation in usage when comparing the middle- and high-income (MHI) countries to the low-income and fragile (LIF) groups. Such variation should be anticipated as the needs and corresponding desires differ across contexts. Consequently, one would expect to see in the final document these differences would be reflected in the text. What we noticed was with the exception of the term "Indicator," the selected terms for analysis were much more prevalent in the comments of the MHI countries than the low-income and fragile situation countries.

Data, quality, assessment, knowledge, skill, learning and information were terms that have very high frequency in the final document with relatively low use by LIF countries in the consultation phase. The comparison in Table 1 summarizes that the term "quality" was used 14 times by the MHI and only 4 times by the LIF in the Consultation Notes.

***Table 1.*** High-Use Word Frequency Distribution.

| Term | LIF Term use in Table 4 | MHI Term use in Table 4 | Final Document |
|---|---|---|---|
| Information | 2 | 6 | 70 |
| Data | 5 | 8 | 80 |
| Quality | 4 | 14 | 130 |
| Knowledge | 1 | 6 | 136 |
| Assessment | 0 | 2 | 137 |
| Skill | 8 | 13 | 151 |
| Learning | 5 | 13 | 272 |

In the final document, the term was used 130 times. Similarly, "Assessment" was not used at all by the LIF and only twice by the MHI, yet figured 137 times in the final document.

The problem is not simply with the use of the terms. It would be difficult to have a conversation about education with talking about knowledge or learning. The problem is the insertion of terms not generated by member nations, rampant overuse of terms touched on tangentially by member nations – particularly lower-income member nations – and the World Bank's heavy-handed insistence on pursuing specific topics in education that are much less important to member nations than they are to the World Bank. Topics such as "quality" and "assessment" that not only demonstrate the Bank's (ab)use of its discursive and disciplinary power, but also strongly suggest the World Bank is reluctant to relinquish its governmental power as well.

As stated above, the new educational strategy focuses on learning for all, facilitated by an expanded definition of educational systems and built on a knowledge base that is generated through expanded assessment and evaluation that is governed by the World Bank. And it is the educational strategy itself – a neat, self-sustaining, *closed* loop that is to be measured by indicators that largely focus on the percentage of member countries that apply assessment tools and/or have projects with results-based funding – that is the most problematic of all. Not only is this educational strategy at best tangentially related to the stated needs of member nations (particularly FSs and LICs), but it is a strategy that focuses on producing data as opposed to learning gains – and that only holds the World Bank responsible for facilitating data acquisition and evaluation, not for learning outcomes as the Bank itself has stated. The intended flow of activities and information, the willingness on the part of the World Bank to dictate when and how member nations interact with the Bank – and to a lesser extent, each other – that demonstrates the prodigious governmental power the Bank is deploying. The closest the World Bank gets to measuring actual learning is encouraging countries to participate in international assessments and reducing the percentage of countries who are furthest from meeting the MDGs.

The ESS2020 is undeniably ensnared in the development discourse; those who are currently without power are minimally represented – or considered – by the final educational strategy published in April 2011. Furthermore, ESS2020 shows abundant evidence of being World Bank-driven (and United States-driven), despite the consultative process; the focus on learning outcomes assessment and non-state providers of education very, very closely parallels high-stakes testing and charter school/voucher programs in the United States. Furthermore, this focus on data production and the development of a knowledge base is at least as important to the World Bank for the Bank's sake as it is for the member countries' sake. "[T]he Bank likes to think of itself as the 'knowledge bank,' and has aspirations to be a *generator* of new knowledge, not just a *synthesizer* of existing knowledge" (World Bank, 2010a, p. 25, October 19). And establishing indicators that measure the extent to which the Bank's assessment and data agenda is adopted by member nations but *not* actual learning outcomes makes it very difficult to fault either the Bank or the development discourse when learning gains do not occur. Despite the Bank's best intentions – and laudable initial efforts – the new educational strategy, in the end, does not alter the power relations between the Bank and member nations nor does it impact the development discourse. It is rather a frustrating extension of the World Bank's existing disciplinary, discursive, and governmental power, especially with respect to "target" (LIF) nations.

## POPULAR PARTICIPATION: A CAUTIONARY TALE

On April 20, 1994, Popular Participation was passed as *Ley 1551, La Ley de Participación Popular*. It was a sweeping decentralization law that devolved much of the central government's authority to 311 municipal governments, which were held accountable by specific civil society instruments, the Grassroots Territorial Organizations (*Organizaciones Territoriales de Base*, or *OTBs*) and a Vigilance, or Oversight, Committee (*Comité Vigilancia*). It also provided for revenue sharing funds from the National General Treasury (Bolivia, 1995). Its stated objective was "aimed at improving the quality of life of Bolivian women and men through a fairer distribution and better administration of public resources" (Miró i Pascual, 2000, p. 319). The purpose of Popular Participation was to address historical inequalities in Bolivia, specifically (a) an ongoing problem of government legitimacy, (b) pervasive government corruption, and (c) the stark disparity in money and other resources between rural and urban populations. To that end, Popular Participation established the provincial section as the territory and jurisdiction of the municipal governments and transferred "to them the physical infrastructure for education, health, sports, local roads, [and] micro-irrigation systems, along with the obligation to administer, maintain and renew them" (Miró i Pascual, 2000, p. 320).

Popular Participation, much like the consultative process for ESS2020, was a remarkable departure from "business as usual" for the government of Bolivia and was intended to move government closer to the people, where civil society could, through the OTBs and the Vigilance Committee, participate directly in their own governance. Unfortunately, the dismantling of Popular Participation began almost immediately, and in less than 10 years, the political space created for civil society was gone and government had regressed to operating as it had before Popular Participation.

The changes made to Popular Participation over time were subtle, but a comprehensive review of successive policy initiatives shows how thoroughly both the multinational organizations and the Bolivian government modified Popular Participation until civil society's ability to "participate" was reduced to approving policies and plans that were completed before civil society was allowed to provide any substantive input. While a detailed review of the nearly 40 policies that modified Popular Participation is beyond the scope of this chapter (for a more comprehensive discussion, see Boyd, 2005), an illustrative summary is provided below.

### *The International Monetary Fund and the World Bank*

From late 2000 to early 2004, Bolivia was funded under four major programs through the IMF and the World Bank: its third Enhanced Structural Adjustment Facility/Poverty Reduction and Growth Facility (ESAF/PRGF), the Enhanced Heavily Indebted Poor Countries Initiative (HIPC), and Bolivia's Poverty Reduction Strategy Paper (PRSP), which operationalized the World Bank's Comprehensive Development Framework (CDF). Additionally, under the auspices of these umbrella loan packages, multiple smaller loans were being made to fund various components. The majority of funding for projects specifically related to Popular Participation and education came from the IDB and the World Bank.

As you trace the development of multinational organizational initiatives through time, a subtle, but undeniable erosion of the space created for civil society participation is visible, particularly through the use of discursive power on the part of the multinational organizations, though disciplinary power and the emphasis on people with technical knowledge certainly contributed. In earlier documents such as the EASF/PRGF, explicit references to involving civil society in school management are made (IMF, 1998, August 21), but as you move through successive iterations of HIPC plans, a shift toward "increas[ing] the buy-in to the strategy both within and *outside* the government" (IMF and IDA, 2001, p. 9, May 21, emphasis added) rather than safeguarding authentic civil society participation can be seen. By the time you get to the CDF, and more importantly the PRSP, which was written by the Bolivian government, civil society oversight – as opposed to active participation – is firmly entrenched. In the section "Institutional Framework and Social Control of the BPRS [Bolivian Poverty Reduction Strategy]," Bolivian authorities acknowledge the "current weakness of the Bolivian State" (2001a, p. 14), intending to address it by increasing transparency, fighting corruption, promoting institutional strengthening, and recognizing explicit *social control* – not participation – mechanisms. The best civil society can do at this point is note problems; civil society no longer has any effective means of participating in governance.

At the request of the Bolivian Government, the IMF and the World Bank conducted a Joint Staff Assessment of the PRSP. One of their first comments acknowledged the document as a balanced treatment of poverty and named its strong points as the focus on fiscal decentralization, *the commitment to developing social monitoring* – again, not participation – and the National Dialogue. They noted further that the government's lack of capacity to implement the program constituted a major risk. To mitigate the risk, "the monitoring of the poverty reduction strategy will be enhanced by the planned social oversight of anti-poverty programs" (IMF and IDA, 2001, p. 6, May 10). Further, neighborhood oversight committees needed to be strengthened, in particular that "these groups [need] sufficient power if they are going to have an impact on spending choices" (IMF and IDA, 2001, p. 10, May 10). Finally, the assessment noted that anticorruption strategies were hampered by entrenched interests and that civil society buy-in remained limited.

Another important multinational actor for Bolivia is the IDB. Early programs, such as the Education Reform Program (1994), focused on supporting administrative reforms and incorporating community participation. Later programs, such as the Program for Fiscal Adjustment and Maintenance of Social Spending (1998), acknowledged:

> The possibility of **resistance to the program-supported social reforms** on the part of groups affected in the political and labor-union sphere is a risk that will be minimized, especially as regards reform actions involving potential conflicts, by establishing a climate of dialogue in which the *social ministries will exercise an important influence for promoting a sense of ownership of the reforms among those affected by them.* (p. 3, italics added)

And programs funded toward the end of the research period, like the Social Sector Program in Support of the Poverty Reduction Strategy (2001), explicitly limited civil society participation. This document lists potential benefits from the program to be gained through "promoting participation by civil society in decision-making, and supporting the establishment of social supervision and control mechanisms, [that] will help strengthen democracy and the sustainability of public policies" (p. 4). Although it mentions participation, the intent is much more passive and observational.

### *Bolivian Government*

In addition to the abundance of multinational policies, there were Popular Participation and its supporting policies to consider. Popular Participation was one of three policies instituted by then-President Gonzalo Sánchez de Lozada, known collectively as the Plan for All (*Plan de Todos*), in an effort to promote growth and development in Bolivia. However, national policies began dismantling Popular Participation in small, subtle ways almost immediately through the strategic wielding of governmental power. To begin with, the funds to support decentralization were not devolved to the municipal level until 1996, two years after Popular Participation was passed. And multiple Supreme Decrees (the Bolivian version of an Executive Order) began the creep from active participation to passive social oversight almost immediately; as early as 1997 Supreme Decree 216961 effectively gave veto power over civil society to the municipal government. It stated that government and public institutions "have the *obligation* to direct, carry, and manage sustainable development in their jurisdiction" (Arias Durán, 2001, p. 141, November, emphasis added). The municipal governments were to control project execution, assure technical compatibility, and be responsible for promoting social participation only in planning, not execution. Moreover, the OTBs were dependent on the Vigilance Committee to safeguard their right to participate.

Larger pieces of federal legislation also did their damage, particularly the 1999 Law of Municipalities and the 2000 National Dialogue Law.

#### *Law of Municipalities*

The October 1999 Law of Municipalities was a fairly comprehensive statement on the rights and obligations of municipal government as well as a roster of rules and regulations for carrying out those rights and obligations. The municipal government had the authority to generate, collect, and invest resources; to issue ordinances and resolutions determined by municipal policies and strategies; and responsibility for programming and execution of all management functions. The Municipal Council was the designated final authority for municipal government. It had tremendous oversight authority for the municipal government, and with respect to Popular Participation, it was charged with approving Municipal Development and Annual Operating Plans, and issuing ordinances to register OTBs. The Mayor was the final executive authority, and with respect to Popular Participation, he or she was required to keep the Vigilance Committee *informed* on the use of resources and economic activities (Arias Durán, 2001, November). The Mayor was not, however, directed to be particularly receptive or inclusive.

Both the Mayor and the Municipal Council – as well as the rest of municipal government – were repeatedly directed to "guarantee the integration and participation of citizens in planning and sustainable human development" (p. 275); "promote citizen participation" (p. 276); "solicit public help" (p. 288) to carry out duties; and ensure participative municipal planning was coordinated with civil society. For its part, civil society had the right to organize into OTBs, to demand proper functioning of municipal services, to bring problems to the attention of the Mayor and the Municipal Council, and to petition the municipal government. However, nowhere in this document was the people's active participation requested or ensured. The most powerful civil society group in this document was the Vigilance Committee, and even it was relegated to a supervisory role. The Vigilance Committee was responsible for facilitating citizen participation, supporting participative municipal planning and evaluating the performance of policies, plans, programs, and projects. The Law of Municipalities also created a Municipal Social Control Fund controlled by the Vigilance Committee, but its resources came from OTBs and community associations, foundation contributions, and co-participation funds equal to 0.25% of the municipality's share.

Finally, the law gave the municipal government a veto power of sorts over civil society, a clear use of governmental power, propped up by disciplinary power. While the government was charged with protecting participation (in this legislation, participation was relegated to an advisory role), it was also charged with ensuring that plans were executed "in accordance with state and national laws and technical criteria" (p. 276); "to supervise, in accordance with the regulation, the designation of authorities" (p. 277); and to supervise the use of resources by educational services. While adherence to technical criteria had been mentioned in some earlier policy documents, this is one of the first instances in which technical criteria and technocrats are given so much attention. It is important to note that this was the first major policy document to be written following IMF and World Bank board approval of the HIPC Initiative and James Wolfensohn's proposal of the CDF. Many laws, rules, and regulations, especially at the national level, are heavily influenced and/or outright mandated by conditionalities attached to loans used to fund these projects, hence the importance of "technical criteria." The municipal government continued to be responsible for educational infrastructure.

*National Dialogue*

The National Dialogue Law, repeatedly referred to by the multinational organizations, was passed on July 31, 2001. National Dialogue was the process by which civil society could bring government attention to the concerns of constituents through municipal roundtables. The information was then taken to departmental roundtables and finally to a national discussion. Among other things, this law "establish[ed] the scope and mechanisms for the exercise of *social control* over programs and strategies intended to reduce poverty, and to institute the National Dialogue as a permanent mechanism of *social participation in the design, continuation and adjustment of the policies* intended to reduce poverty" (Bolivia, 2001b, p. 1, July 31, emphasis added). At this point, participation as social control has been limited to poverty reduction programs and no political space has been provided for civil society to have any involvement in administration or evaluation.

With regard to education and citizen participation, the National Dialogue Law created a Common Municipal Fund for School Education and Public Health, jointly housed in the Ministry of Education, Culture and Sports, the Ministry of Health and the Ministry of Social Provision. The fund was intended to address the funding shortfall for education and health, approximately $27 million annually. Accompanying this fund for each municipality was a Local Selection Committee, made up of a municipal government representative, the Education Unit Director for the municipality, a representative from the District Education Directors and a representative from the respective school board(s). The school board representative was the only member of civil society who participated in the fund. This advisory committee was to nominate teachers for employment (actually forward their names for incorporation in the pay form of the Ministry) and abide by the rules and regulations of the Ministry for Education, Culture, and Sports.

The Dialogue Law also created the Special Dialogue 2000 Account, housed in the General Treasury and managed by the Finance Ministry. The account housed the funds from the Enhanced HIPC (see above), the funds dedicated to poverty reduction. The law further reconstituted the National Fund for Regional Development (FNDR) and the National Productive and Social Investment Fund (FPS), both built on earlier models, decentralizing them to the department level – not to the municipal level. Additionally, the law reordered these funds into the Sole Directorate of Funds (DUF). The DUF was to consist of the President of the DUF, assigned by the President of Bolivia; one representative each from the Ministries of the President, Sustainable Development and Planning, and Treasury Department, for a total of three; and three municipal government representatives, one from department capitals and cities of more than 200,000, one from cities between 20,000 and 200,000, and one from cities less than 20,000. There were also three non-voting members (*con voz y sin voto*); two Vigilance Committee representatives, one of whom must be a woman, and one other civil society representative to be designated at the national level.

The law put in place safeguards for social control, which by now has been emphatically removed from governance. Those exercising social control had "the right, as organizations and institutions of civil society, to know, supervise and evaluate *the results and impact of the public policies and participative processes for decision-making*, as well as access information and analysis of social control instruments" (Bolivia, 2001b, p. 9, July 31, emphasis added). At the municipal level, social control was concentrated in the hands of the Vigilance Committee, through which all other civil society organizations would work. The Vigilance Committee had the right to watch over and check all resources, or as stated by a government publication explaining National Dialogue:

> For the municipal level, a great advance is the right that the National Dialogue law gives to the Vigilance Committees to have social control of 100% of the municipal resources. That is to say, according to this law, not only control of Popular Participation funds, but also all the resources the municipal government manages, including their own resources and the monies to fight poverty. (Choque & Quispe Acarapi, 2002, p. 25, January)

This law constitutes the most comprehensive dismantling of Popular Participation structures yet very effectively accomplished through governance power. To begin with, participation as social control is firmly entrenched. Additionally, all the new administrative structures exist at the department or national level. Furthermore, what few civil society representatives outside of the Vigilance Committee that are present are chosen at the department or national level, not the municipal level – and these very few civil society members are non-voting members of advisory committees. Civil society has been left no mechanism by which they can be proactive.

Unfortunately, without civil society having any real input participation has been reduced to rubber-stamping government programs. Furthermore, the subjects of Popular Participation, the OTBs, are glaringly absent. The only other avenue of participation is the municipal roundtables which, according to the National Dialogue Law, must be held at least once every five years. By the time civil society's concerns have gone through all the necessary layers to reach the national roundtable, however, there is a very real chance they would be significantly modified or eliminated.

### *Discussion of Popular Participation*

Three problems were identified by Sánchez de Lozada that Popular Participation was intended to address: government legitimacy, corruption, and the rural/urban divide. Successive policy initiatives have steadily eroded multiple aspects of Popular Participation, thereby minimizing its potential and its effectiveness. Three distinct corresponding trends can be identified from the policy environment: normalization of relations between actors, increased bureaucratization, and passive observation as active participation, respectively. It is important to understand, though, that there is significant overlap between these three problems and these three trends. For the sake of clarity and readability, they are presented in three separate sections and appear to be three distinct issues, but in reality they are very closely intertwined.

#### *The Problem of Government Legitimacy and the Trend of Normalization of Relations between Actors*

The problem of government legitimacy was intended to be redressed by Popular Participation through creating a political space for nontraditional actors, namely, civil society and its representatives, in which they could advocate on their own behalf in the policy process. As was seen in many of the policies passed after Popular Participation, this space has been steadily eroded, particularly through the use of disciplinary power; whatever space has not been usurped outright has been placed under the tutelage of technocrats whose profession is "development."

#### *The Problem of Corruption and the Trend of Increased Bureaucratization*

Corruption was, and continues to be, arguably the most urgent problem for Bolivia. The solution envisioned by Sánchez de Lozada and Popular Participation was to move government closer to the people, reduce as many administrative and bureaucratic barriers as possible, then have the citizenry police the government – in effect, a dramatic disruption of governmental power. And even if corruption could not be completely halted, at least it would be closer to civil society, giving civil society more of a chance to access resources, particularly money. There have been multiple policy initiatives that have insidiously added new bureaucratic obstacles to civil society's participation, largely through the creation of new government offices or reordering existing ones. The vast majority of the bureaucratic hurdles have been put in place by the Bolivian government, which seems determined to keep and tightly control the governmental power it wields.

*The Problem of the Rural/Urban Divide and the Trend of Passive Observation as Active Participation*

Popular Participation was intended to address one other problem, the rural/urban divide. Generally speaking, those who were of European descent and/or not living in poverty and/or already in possession of some measure of political power lived in the major urban areas, concentrating wealth and power there. In attempting to redress the rural/urban divide, Popular Participation was effectively attempting to redress the grossly unequal distribution of wealth and power. This was to be accomplished through purposefully drawing municipalities to include rural as well as urban districts; creating the OTBs and Vigilance Committees as a way for civil society to participate in governance and requiring them to apply for juridical status; and providing OTBs the right to ask for the dismissal of any government authority that was being exclusionary or unresponsive, as well as charging them with the duty to defend their rights under Popular Participation. Unfortunately, policymakers began recasting the more active participation envisioned in Popular Participation as passive observation and "oversight" without any real authority almost immediately, effectively using discursive power to maintain the status quo.

## DISCUSSION OF ESS2020 AND POPULAR PARTICIPATION

Within the World Bank's ESS2020, the stage is being set for feverish data collection that will contribute to a knowledge base that will, hopefully someday, be a repository of best educational practices and evidence aplenty for data-based decision making and evidence-based policy making, but the focus is supposed to be learning. Research previously conducted on

Bolivia's Popular Participation Law suggests that the inability of ESS2020 to escape the development discourse will have disappointing, if not devastating, consequences for member nations; see Table 2 for a comparison of Popular Participation and ESS2020.

ESS2020's three main foci, the three driving forces that will provide its engine, are (1) learning (outcomes) for all, (2) education systems, and (3) knowledge base. These three drivers parallel the response to Popular Participation that was seen in Bolivia. The primary point is that neither the World Bank nor the Bolivian Government seems able to escape who they are and what role they play in the development discourse. Promising initiatives that have tremendous potential to redistribute power throughout the development enterprise are quickly, even involuntarily, co-opted through the strategic use of disciplinary, discursive, and/or governmental power.

"Education systems" bears a strong resemblance to the trend of recasting active participation as passive observation in Popular Participation, and there is an appreciable expression of discursive power in both. In ESS2020, there is a noticeable emphasis put on initiatives like School-Based Management and opening up education to all providers, including non-state educational providers, in order to be more responsive, foster competition and thereby provide better educational services. This approach poses two problems that jointly marginalize the impact of civic participation while appearing to increase the range of voices represent. First, in tying funding to meeting specific educational indicators that are not locally created and do not address local needs in any meaningful way, the World Bank is effectively removing local participation – even debtor-nation participation – by insisting on who, when, and how actors participate in the discourse on education in-country. Second, it should be noted that efficiency arguments in support of the private sector have the potential to substantially weaken support for public schooling, again by changing the local interaction dynamic. So what apparent gains might have accompanied School-Based Management might well be diminished by corresponding declines in the viability of public schooling.

"Knowledge base" is akin to the trend of normalization of relations in Popular Participation, both of which are accomplished through expansive use of disciplinary power. The Banks felt need for more and better information in order to make data-driven decisions, including data for international comparative statistics, drives an ever-increasing need for researchers, statisticians, and programmers who can create, evaluate, and interpret reams of statistical data. Given the exceptionally low likelihood

***Table 2.*** Comparison of Popular Participation and ESS2020.

| | Popular Participation | ESS2020 |
|---|---|---|
| Discursive power | Recasting active participation as passive observation<br>• Shifting the focus from "participation" to "social control"<br>• Concentrating more and more power in the hands of the Vigilance Committee<br>• Concentrating more and more power in the state and national rather than municipal level | Education systems<br>• Controlling the agenda and topics for the ESS2020 consultation, including introducing the education systems concept<br>• Insisting on additional local actors in education, including private education providers<br>• Marginalizing space for local and civil society |
| Disciplinary power | Normalization of relations between govt. and civil society<br>• Increasing emphasis on public employees who have technical knowledge<br>• Insistence that bureaucrats and/or elected officials have veto power over civil society | Knowledge base<br>• Near zealous commitment to quality, assessment and evaluation<br>• Insistence on data-driven decision making<br>• Exponentially expanding need for researchers, statisticians, etc. |
| Governmental power | Increased bureaucratization<br>• Gradual move away from civil society participation in governance, including steadily reducing the number of local actors who can participate<br>• Introduction of more and more levels of bureaucracy that need to be navigated<br>• Fewer and fewer opportunities for local actors to interact among themselves | Learning for all<br>• Reordering Bank offices and/or creating new ones<br>• Requirement for member nations to participate in SABER<br>• Need for layer of educational specialists to act as intermediaries between the Bank and member nations |
| In the end ... | Popular Participation was unable to escape the development discourse, and within 10 years of its passage governance and government/civil society relations had regressed to "business as usual" | Existing power relations and dynamics are unchanged, and nothing in ESS2020 seems able/willing to challenge them; inability of ESS2020 to escape the development discourse suggests a very high likelihood that ESS2020 will be "business as usual" |

that those specialists will be found in country for most debtor-nations who are the target of this strategy, relations between those nations and the World Bank will most likely quickly revert to a subordinate/superordinate dynamic. Data will likely become a tool of subjugation, not liberation.

More egregious yet is the notion that there is a knowledge base that can effectively serve across the broad spectrum of needs, beliefs, and values of those people groups that the Bank would purport to assist. That knowledge can exist devoid of contextual understanding (or power) is as vacuous as the assumption that because someone is of a particular nationality, ethnicity, or gender, their voice should be taken as representative for all those similarly positioned. Given the globalization of education, it seems far more likely that those participating in a meeting with Bank personnel would hold similar values, particularly with respect to the general beneficence of "experts," especially as opposed to local knowledge.

Finally, "learning for all" is very like the trend of increased bureaucratization in Popular Participation and is facilitated by the crafty use of governmental power. Already the World Bank is reordering old offices and creating new ones, not to mention new data collection and reporting mechanisms like SABER. Furthermore, the target nations themselves will have to create whole new industries to meet the Bank's demand for assessment (not to mention the demand for more and better information). Additionally, the indicators being proposed by the World Bank (and that must be satisfied for funding to be disbursed) deal almost exclusively with system tools, data collection, or data reporting – in other words, with the structure of meeting information needs, not the substance of educating a nation's youth and certainly not any discrete learning outcomes. The focus is on who interacts when, and in response to what data – in other words, interaction as is deemed appropriate by the World Bank. There is a growing cadre of technical and statistical specialists who are located between the Bank and target countries, and increasingly between educators and policymakers in the target nations, which has the positive side effect of using disciplinary power to substantiate governmental power.

While the value of appropriate and accurate data is undeniable, it is reasonable to question the value of indicators that do not recognize the beliefs of the intended beneficiaries. Jonas Yoder complained that the things that matter in life are neither sought nor taught in schools, yet he was able to help define education practices within the United States. One might imagine that there are many such individuals in the countries served by the World Bank whose needs simply will not be met by better data collection.

## RECOMMENDATIONS

But ESS2020 need not become more of the same from the World Bank or for member nations. There were FS and LIC stated needs that were included in the final strategy, and it should be noted that the Bank is trying to differentiate aid based on country income; they recognize that impact indicators in particular must be monitored continuously and that change will not occur overnight. And while most of the FS and LIC needs (like the need for local and civil society participation) have been put into service of the Bank's agenda, the Bank does have the option of stepping back and letting the member nations set the agenda. The World Bank can even step aside altogether and allow South-South interactions to take place without them. So there is guarded hope that the member nations will be able to insist on a structure that meets their needs rather than one that is imposed as emerging from consultation. There is room for the World Bank to lend increased substance to the apparent desire for consultation by engaging in activities that are more inclusive and participatory and less about the legitimation of a desired course of action. But, as Kipling (1935) warned the crew of Nakhoda,

> This new ship here, is fitted according to the reported increase of knowledge among mankind. Namely, she is cumbered, end to end, with bells and trumpets and clocks and wires which, it has been told to me, can call Voices out of the air or the waters to con the ship while her crew sleep. But sleep thou lightly, O *Nakhoda*! It has not yet been told to me that the Sea has ceased to be the Sea. (Foreword)

Similarly it has not been told to us that the Bank has ceased to be the Bank.

## REFERENCES

Arias Durán, H. I. (2001). *Legislación Municipal 2001*, November. La Paz, Bolivia: Ministerio de Desarrollo Sostenible y Planificación.

Bolivia. (1995). *Ley de Participación Popular y su reglamentación*. La Paz, Bolivia: Author.

Bolivia. (2001a). *Poverty reduction strategy*, March. La Paz, Bolivia: Author.

Bolivia. (2001b). *National dialogue*, 31 July. La Paz, Bolivia: Author.

Boyd, T. (2005). *Popular participation in Cochabamba, Bolivia as an ameliorative policy treatment affecting public education*. Retrieved from ProQuest. (UMI Number: 3163307).

Brent, E., & Slusarz, P. (2003). "Feeling the beat": Intelligent coding advice from metaknowledge in qualitative research. *Social Science Computer Review*, *21*(3), 281–303.

Burck, C. (2005). Comparing qualitative research methodologies for systemic research: The use of grounded theory, discourse analysis and narrative analysis. *Journal of Family Therapy*, *27*, 237–262.

Choque, R. M., & Quispe Acarapi, R. P. (2002). *Para entender la Ley del Diálogo*, January. La Paz, Bolivia: Ministerio de Desarrollo Sostenible y Planificación.
Escobar, A. (1995). *Encountering development: The making and unmaking of the Third World*. Princeton, NJ: Princeton University Press.
Escobar, A. (2000). Beyond the search for a paradigm? Post-development and beyond. *Development, 43*(4), 11–14.
Foucault, M. (1970). *The order of things: An archaeology of the human sciences*. New York, NY: Pantheon Books.
Foucault, M. (1971). *L'Ordre du Discours* [Orders of Discourse]. Paris: Gallimard.
Foucault, M. (1972). *The archaeology of knowledge*. London: Tavistock Publications.
Foucault, M. (1977a). *Discipline and punish: The birth of the prison*. London: Penguin.
Foucault, M. (1977b). *Language, counter memory, practice: Selected essays and interviews*. Oxford: Blackwell.
Foucault, M. (1979). Governmentality. *Ideology and Consciousness, 6*(1), 5–21.
Foucault, M. (1980). *Power/Knowledge: Selected interviews and other writings 1972–1977*. New York, NY: Pantheon.
Foucault, M. (1988). *Politics, philosophy, culture: Interviews and other writings 1977–1984*. New York, NY: Routledge.
Guba, E. (1983). The effect of definitions of *policy* on the nature and outcomes of policy analysis. *Educational Leadership, 42*(2), 63–70.
Inter-American Development Bank. (1994). Education reform program, November. Retrieved from http://www.iadb.org/en/projects/project,1303.html?id=BO0133
Inter-American Development Bank. (1998). Program for fiscal adjustment and maintenance of social spending, October. Retrieved from http://www.iadb.org/en/projects/project,1303.html?id=BO0173
Inter-American Development Bank. (2001). Social sector program in support of the poverty reduction strategy, December. Retrieved from http://www.iadb.org/en/projects/project,1303.html?id=BO0203
International Monetary Fund. (1998). Bolivia: Enhanced structural adjustment facility policy framework paper, 1998–2001, 25 August. Retrieved from http://www.imf.org/external/country/bol/index.htm
International Monetary Fund and the International Development Association. (2001). Completion point document for the enhanced heavily indebted poor countries (HIPC) initiative, 21 May. Retrieved from http://www.imf.org/external/country/bol/index.htm
Kipling, R. (1935). *A Kipling Pageant*. New York, NY: Doubleday.
Miró i Pascual, J. M. (2000). *Popular participation by law: Advancing state authority in Mizque, Bolivia*. Doctoral Dissertation, SUNY Binghamton.
Ninnes, P., & Burnett, G. (2003). Comparative education research: Poststructuralist possibilities. *Comparative Education, 39*(3), 279–297.
Ozga, J. (2000). *Policy research in educational settings: Contested terrain*. Philadelphia, PA: Open University Press.
Rahnema, M. (1999). Participation. In W. Sachs (Ed.), *The development dictionary: A guide to knowledge as power*. New York, NY: Zed Books Ltd.
Strauss, A., & Corbin, J. (1990). *Basics of qualitative research: Grounded theory procedures and techniques*. Newbury Park, CA: Sage.
Strauss, A., & Corbin, J. (1998). *Basics of qualitative research: Techniques and procedures for developing grounded theory* (2nd ed). Newbury Park, CA: Sage.

White, M., & Marsh, E. (2006). Content analysis: A flexible methodology. *Library Trends*, *55*(1), 22–45.

World Bank. (2010a). Concept note for the World Bank Education Strategy 2020, 8 February. Retrieved from http://siteresources.worldbank.org/EDUCATION/Resources/ESSU/Concept_Note_ESS2020_Feb8.pdf

World Bank. (2010b). Report on phase i external consultations, 31 August. Retrieved from http://siteresources.worldbank.org/EDUCATION/Resources/ESSU/Phase_I_consultation_Report_2010.08.31.pdf

World Bank. (2010c). Comment Draft: Learning for all: Investing in people's knowledge and skills to promote development, World Bank Education Strategy 2020, 19 October. Retrieved from http://siteresources.worldbank.org/EDUCATION/Resources/ESSU/Education_Sector_Strategy_draft_for_comment.pdf

World Bank. (2010d). Learning for all: Overview of world bank group education sector strategy 2020, 3 December. Retrieved from http://siteresources.worldbank.org/EDUCATION/Resources/ESSU/463292-1269917617150/6915424-1279137061297/Summary_of_Education_Strategy_with_Indicators.pdf

World Bank. (2011). Learning for all: investing in people's knowledge and skills to promote development: World Bank Group Education Strategy 2020, 12 April. Retrieved from http://siteresources.worldbank.org/EDUCATION/Resources/ESSU/Education_Strategy_4_12_2011.pdf

Ziai, A. (2009). "Development": Projects, power and a poststructuralist perspective. *Alternatives*, *34*, 183–201.

# PART III
# CRITICAL ISSUES AND PERSPECTIVES

# THE WORLD BANK, THE INTERNATIONAL FINANCE CORPORATION, AND PRIVATE SECTOR PARTICIPATION IN BASIC EDUCATION: EXAMINING THE *EDUCATION SECTOR STRATEGY 2020*☆

Karen Mundy and Francine Menashy

## ABSTRACT

*The World Bank's new Education Sector Strategy 2020 (2011) points to an important role for private actors in the development of high-quality, high-equity education systems that effectively address poverty alleviation in low and middle-income countries. This chapter asks whether this emphasis on private participation is new, focusing in particular on Bank policies, research, and operations in K-12 education. It also explores some*

☆Research for this chapter has benefited from funding from the Open Society Institute Education Support Programme, the Social Sciences and Humanities Research Council of Canada, and the Ontario Ministry of Research and Innovation.

**Education Strategy in the Developing World: Revising the World Bank's Education Policy**
**International Perspectives on Education and Society, Volume 16, 113–131**

**ISSN: 1479-3679/doi:10.1108/S1479-3679(2012)0000016010**

*surprising disjunctures between the World Bank Group's official policies promoting privatization and its operational practices. To do so, the chapter draws on a separate research project for which we completed a review of the Bank's current portfolio of projects in K-12 education and a series of interviews with World Bank staff. We also look at the expansion of Bank activities beyond its traditional arms – the International Bank for Reconstruction and Development (IBRD) and International Development Association (IDA) lending facilities – by including a brief a review of the educational activities of the International Finance Corporation (IFC), which directly supports the private sector in education.*

## INTRODUCTION

The World Bank Group[1] is the largest external provider of funds and expertise to education in the world. With approximately 5 billion US dollars in loans, credit, and grants to low- and middle-income countries in FY10, the Bank's education sector operations and research include varied issues such as early childhood education, teacher training and accountability, adult education and literacy, gender equity, and HIV/AIDS education programs, to name a few (Jones, 2007; Mundy, 2002; World Bank, 2011).

The Bank's central mandate is to increase the social and economic development of the world's poorest countries and populations. It does so directly, via the provision of financial resources, advice, research, and training, and indirectly, by acting as a leader in international poverty alleviation initiatives, coordinating various multi-donor activities and trust funds, and by helping to develop poverty reduction strategies at the country level (Jones, 2007; Marshall, 2008; Weaver, 2008). Apart from a few regional and thematic initiatives, almost all lending operations are conducted via country governments.

The Bank's new *Education Sector Strategy 2020* (2011) points to an important role for private actors in the development of high-quality, high-equity education systems that effectively address poverty alleviation in low- and middle-income countries. This chapter asks whether this emphasis on private participation is new, focusing in particular on Bank policies, research, and operations in K-12 education. It also explores some surprising disjunctures between the World Bank Group's official policies promoting privatization and its operational practices. To do so, the chapter draws on a separate research project for which we completed a review of the Bank's current portfolio of projects in K-12 education and a series of interviews with World Bank staff.[2] We also look at the expansion of Bank activities beyond its traditional arms – the International Bank for Reconstruction and Development (IBRD) and International Development Association (IDA) lending facilities – by including a brief a review of the educational activities of the International Finance Corporation (IFC), which directly supports the private sector in education (IFC, 2001, 2009).

## BACKGROUND: THE EVOLUTION OF BANK SUPPORT FOR PRIVATE ENGAGEMENT IN EDUCATION

Since the 1980s, the World Bank has held a strong interest in strengthening the private sector of developing nations. While the two main arms of the World Bank (IBRD and IDA) do not work directly with the private sector, scholars have argued forcefully that the Bank's work in the 1980s era of structural adjustment was shaped by "interlocking conditionalities" between Bank lending operations and the policies and prescriptions of the IMF. Together, the two institutions pushed governments to reduce expenditures and increase private sector involvement in the provision and financing of traditionally public sector activities (Mehrotra & Delamonica, 2005; Miller-Adams, 1999). During the 1980s, and well into the 1990s, the Bank remained responsive to pressure from the US government to expand its focus on the private sector and development, establishing a Private Sector Development Review Group in the late 1980s. This group designed and released the Private Sector Development Strategy in 2002, which endorsed the expansion of bank support for privately provided educational and other basic services (Alexander, 2001, p. 287; Kessler, 2003).

However, in education, the nature of Bank support for private sector roles shifted considerably between 1980 and 2000. In the 1980s, in the context of structural adjustment policies, the Bank focused on parental participation in the funding of schooling and on cost-recovery measures that could shift public finance from higher to lower levels of educational systems. This became what has been termed the Bank's "Edlib" era (Colclough, 2000), where the Bank argued for the inclusion of market mechanisms in schooling at all levels, and comfortably promoted the raising of resources through fees, in order to "improve economic efficiency as well as raise revenue" (World Bank, 1988a, 1988b, p. 131).

The most controversial aspect of the Edlib era was the Bank's approach to school fees or the private financing of education (Vavrus & Kwauk, 2011). Such fees were largely framed by the Bank as unfortunately necessary, because the State was seen as unable to meet demand. As late as the 1995 education sector policy paper *Priorities and Strategies in Education*, private, fee-charging K-12 schools were portrayed as freeing up resources for poor students, by diverting rich students away from the public sector (p. 54). Charging fees was also presented in many World Bank policy documents as inherently desirable because parental contributions increase their stake in schools and accountability (Hinchliffe, 1993). Specifically, the Bank advocated what it termed "community participation," by which it meant raising resources for schools from families. As described in the *World Development Report* of 1988: "In education … fees induce students, their parents, and administrators to scrutinize costs" (p. 136). Much of the emphasis on fee charging and private education during the 1980s and 1990s was in fact not on primary education but on higher education, where it was believed that private participation was crucial for innovation and could allow for more government funding to target basic education (Samoff & Carrol, 2004).

In the 1990s, the Bank gradually shifted its education policy emphasis from a focus on fees (private financing) to the potential of private delivery (private provision) to improve the efficiency of K-12 educational systems. In its 1986 *Financing Education in Developing Countries: An Exploration of Policy Options*, the Bank argues that "easing restrictions on private and community school operations, as well as channelling subsidies through parents and students, increases competition among schools. In turn, competition is argued to increase the numbers of educational services, lower costs, and give parents or students a wider choice of schools. Increased competition within the system means higher efficiency through greater managerial accountability" (p. 36). The role of choice and competition in improving quality of services was taken up even more forcefully in the Bank's 1995 policy paper *Priorities and Strategies in Education*, where these terms appear frequently (p. 122). In addition to arguing for increased roles for private actors in textbook production and school-level governance, the 1995 strategy argued strongly for the value of publicly financed but privately managed institutions, through vouchers or other forms of subsidy, and linked private provision to greater school autonomy and accountability for learning (p. 13).

The Bank's formal emphasis on private provision remained relatively stable in its policy documents and research products after the 1995 paper, despite the Wolfensohn presidency of the World Bank (1995–2005) during which the Bank became increasingly supportive of the rapid expansion of free primary education and the abolition of school fees (Chabbott, 2003; Jones, 2007; Vavrus & Kwauk, 2011; World Bank, 1999; World Bank & UNESCO, 2006). The Bank's 1999 *Education Sector Strategy*, for example, describes changing public/private roles as one of five key "drivers of change" (p. 2) in education and first used the term "partnering" to describe solutions that create more diversity and completion in K-12 education. It identified as viable partners "not-for-profit groups, community-level organizations, and corporations with public commitments" (p. 18). The 2005 *Education Sector Strategy Update* summed up the Bank's position on private participation in education as follows:

> Public provision of good-quality primary education at no cost to parents or children is the cornerstone for achieving the Millennium Development Goals, but there is room and need – in low- and middle-income countries alike – to promote increased private participation in education. (p. 34)

Alongside these sector strategies, over the past decade, the Bank has released a series of knowledge products – published by the World Bank press and authored by staff – which are evidence that a good deal of Bank intellectual resources have been channeled into private sector engagement in education. Such knowledge products published since 2000 include *Trends in Private Sector Development in World Bank Education Projects* (Sosale, 2000), *Enhancing Accountability in Schools: What can Choice and Contracting Contribute* (Patrinos & Laroque, 2007), *Public-Private Partnerships: Contracting Education in Latin America* (Patrinos, 2006), *Mobilizing the Private Sector for Public Education: A View from the Trenches* (Patrinos & Sosale, 2007), *The Role and Impact of Public-Private Partnerships in Education* (Patrinos, Barrera-Osorio, & Guaqueta, 2009), and *Emerging Evidence on Vouchers and Faith-Based Providers in Education* (Barrera-Osorio, Patrinos, & Wodon, 2009). The Bank's knowledge mobilization efforts have also included a series of biannual conferences on public-private partnerships (PPPs) in education. More recently, the Bank has sponsored new work on the role of private provision in expanding secondary education, particularly in Africa (Verspoor, 2008).

Several authors have noted how these knowledge products have promoted an expanded role for the private sector in education, for example, by invoking evidence of inherent problems with public schools; providing evidence that is biased toward cases where private provision can be shown to have improved education outcomes on standardized tests; and neglecting counterfactual evidence of positive outcomes from publicly provided services (Menashy, 2011; Verger, 2011). For instance, the widely disseminated report by Patrinos et al., *The Role and Impact of Public-Private Partnerships in Education*, proposes that "The private sector can compete for students with the public sector. In turn, the public sector has an incentive to react to this competition by increasing the quality of education that it provides ..." and goes on to argue that PPPs are "likely to increase efficiency in the delivery of services" (2009, p. 4). Even the Bank's claims that the private sector is expanding rapidly in the K-12 education space can be disputed (since there is significant evidence that in many countries, such as Brazil, the ratio of public to private provision is moving in the opposite direction, while in others, it has remained static for decades). In these documents, the Bank can be described as playing the role not of policy analyst, but of policy advocate.

Finally, it is worth noting one discernable rhetorical shift in the Bank's official policies for private participation in education since 2000, centering on increased use of the terms "partnering" and "partnership" (as opposed to the early use of the terminology of choice and competition). For instance, while the 1995 *Priorities and Strategies* only contained 4 instances of "partner" or "partnership," in the 1999 Strategy, the use of "partner" rose to 86 times, including a full chapter dedicated to "Partnering: A World of Opportunities." The 2005 *Update* continued this rhetorical trend with 98 instances of the term "partner," "partnering," or "partnership." Defined by the Bank as a means of joining together the public and private sectors so as to complement each sector's strengths in educational provision, the concept of partnership engenders a softer tone than that of privatization, allowing the greater emphasis on collaboration, not competition, and implying that private and public actors have shared values and goals (Draxler, forthcoming, 2012).

## PRIVATE SECTOR PARTICIPATION IN THE *EDUCATION SECTOR STRATEGY 2020*

The current *Education Sector Strategy 2020* (2011) replaces the Bank's 1999 *Education Sector Strategy* and its 2005 *Education Sector Strategy Update* as the premiere statement of the Bank's approach to aiding education in low- and middle-income countries. The new strategy trumpets two central shifts in the Bank's approach to education: a new focus on the achievement of learning for all and an emphasis on the Bank's central role in strengthening education systems. Presented as a novel departure for its education activities, the Bank's new systems approach includes a commitment to expanding the Bank's work on private participation in education.

To justify this expansion, early on, the new strategy points to the positive impact of private actors in education, noting that the past decade has seen "great educational advances" in access, and that "[g]overnments, civil society organizations, communities, and private enterprises have contributed to this progress" (2011, p. 2). The Bank also presents the growth of the private sector as "sparked by the limited ability of many governments to meet growing demand" (p. 24) and carefully documents the growth of private sector provision and the mounting diversity of providers in many educational systems. It notes that "nonstate provision of education services at all levels has increased dramatically across the world" (pp. 34–35). Furthermore,

> Although it is often assumed that the private sector serves mainly students who can afford to pay, private entities are important providers of education services to even the poorest communities, especially in areas that governments do not reach. In many countries, governments subsidize or contract nonstate organizations to provide education but cover much of the cost. (p. 35)

Building on its analyses of a growing role for private participation, the strategy then argues that the Bank has been too tightly focused on "formal schools that are funded and/or operated by governments," ignoring the significant learning opportunities in the nonstate sector. It calls for "a system approach [that] can broaden the potential agenda for action in education policy, enabling governments to take advantage of a greater number of service providers and delivery channels" (p. 34). Thus,

> At the country level, the Bank Group will focus on supporting reforms of education systems ... In this strategy, "education system" includes the full range of learning opportunities available in a country, whether they are provided or financed by the public or private sector (including religious, nonprofit, and for-profit organizations). It includes formal and nonformal programs, plus the full range of beneficiaries of and stakeholders in these programs – teachers, trainers, administrators, employees, students and their families, and employers. It also includes the rules, policies, and accountability mechanisms that bind an education system together, as well as the resources and financing mechanisms that sustain it. *This more inclusive concept of the education system allows the Bank Group and its partner countries to seize opportunities and address barriers that lie outside the bounds of the system as it is traditionally defined.* (p. 5, emphasis ours)

As a first plank in its new focus on education systems, the Bank promises to use its lending to help governments to carry out results-oriented, country-level system reform. The second plank in its systems approach is a commitment to building a more robust knowledge base for education systems reform. In both dimensions, there is significant attention to private participation. We are told, for example, that "better information about the private education market can help policy makers assess supply shortages and financing deficits, design appropriate expansion plans, and inform reforms of secondary or higher education levels where there are typically more private providers," and thus that the Bank is committed to "the expansion of the knowledge base through data collection, impact evaluation and the development of a system assessment and benchmarking tool for the private education policy framework" (p. 42). Private provision of education is still identified as one of seven core policy domains for Bank supported efforts to reform educational systems (p. 61); as a focal area for the development of SABER tools (System Assessment and Benchmarking for Education Results) (p. 73); and "leveraging the private sector" is also named as one of four focal areas for Bank funded impact evaluations. The strategy refers to programs involving private provision as examples to demonstrate how lending operations can become more results and innovation oriented. As well, there is a cautious nod to projects that utilize performance based contracting out to private providers.[3]

Despite claims to novelty, key tenets from previous World Bank thinking on the private sector are amply present in this document. First, the Bank argues that private providers are key to meeting system expansion needs (p. 42). Second, it emphasizes the role that private providers play in meeting the needs of the poor (p. 35). Third, it returns repeatedly to vouchers and scholarships for use at private institutions as preferred "demand side" interventions that produce higher levels of schooling for the most marginal populations. Thus, "vouchers that enable poor students to attend private educational institutions have been especially advantageous for raising girls' educational enrolment in rural areas" (p. 17). However, in this document, vouchers are primarily presented as a way of tackling major gaps in accountability in educational systems. Thus the strategy notes, "One aspect of this is the importance of greater autonomy at the provider level; together with competition for resources (e.g., through the use of performance incentives or vouchers), this autonomy can generate strong provider motivation to improve service delivery" (p. 29).

Nonetheless, this document shifts the Bank's framing of private provision in several ways. First, it gives new emphasis to governmental roles in regulating the quality of private education providers. Thus,

> Recognizing the value of private sector involvement does not mean abdicating government responsibility: governments typically have to pro-vide appropriate regulation and oversight to ensure the quality and relevance of privately provided services, as well as access for disadvantaged students. (p. 35)

The strategy also softens several aspects of the Bank's rhetorical advocacy for private provision, as compared both to earlier education strategies and to recent World Bank publications on public-private partnerships (Patrinos et al., 2009). Thus, the document generally avoids using the language of the market. References to the role of "competition" and parental "choice" in enhancing learning outcomes are virtually absent from the document (apart from the one short reference, mentioned above). The *ESS 2020* uses the term "nonstate actors" more frequently than earlier strategies and continues to elide nonprofit, religious organizations together with for-profit providers and employs the language of partnership.[4] Examples of areas where private participation is required are focused on private provision at secondary and postsecondary levels, not on the more controversial elementary level.

Most surprisingly, this strategy makes no strong claims made about the superiority of learning outcomes derived from private (rather than state) provision in K-12 education. Though private provision is (as noted above) framed as one of several mechanisms through which school-level autonomy and accountability might be expected to enhance learning, no evidence or strong statements about this advantage is included in the final strategy. Such arguments – made forcefully in the Patrinos et al.'s (2009) report and in previous sector strategies – are now only to be found in the draft background documents being prepared for the benchmarking and systems analyses tools being developed as part of the Bank's SABER initiative. Although the SABER Scale and Framework for engaging the private sector are intended to act as diagnostic tools to assist governments to better regulate private sector provision, they explicitly frame the Bank as an advocate for the expansion of private provision. Thus, the SABER scale presents a graduated framework for "maturity" in governmental approaches to private participation, treating as most evolved those systems that "reflect international best practice, or full engagement with the private sector" by way of liberalized markets for the entry of private providers (Lewis & Patrinos, 2011; World Bank, n/d). The SABER Private Sector Scale argues that "the private sector when engaged properly provides governments with an effective means to increase education quality and equity" and treats as a given the need for competitive markets in education.

To summarize, the *ESS 2020* pays considerable attention to the private sector in education, where nonstate actors are inextricably involved in the

Bank's education systems approach. The Bank claims to have broadened its definition of this system in an effort to include the private – a group of actors ranging from nonprofit, for-profit, faith-based to community organizations – who serve various functions. The private sector is argued by the Bank to have the potential to contribute to equity via increasing the inclusion of the poor and marginalized groups and increases in accountability, but is more cautious than in the past about arguing that private provision enhances educational quality. The *ESS 2020* is by no means the first education policy document by the World Bank that emphasizes the private sector's role in education: a simple word count suggests that the Bank's attention to private provision has been remarkably consistent over its last four education sector policies.[5] Yet, among the major changes in this strategy are a clear decision to soften direct advocacy for the expansion of private provision and a downgrading of references to the importance of competitive markets in education.

## ENTER THE INTERNATIONAL FINANCE CORPORATION

> Within the Bank Group, the World Bank and IFC will work together to improve knowledge about the private sector's role in education and to help countries create policy environments and regulatory structures that align the private sector's efforts with national education goals. (World Bank, 2011, p. 9)

> The main focus of the IFC's education strategy is to: finance larger network providers, who have the ability to invest across borders and go down-market to reach poorer populations ... [and to] provide financing for education to small and medium enterprises, which typically target poor populations .... (World Bank, 2011, p. 50)

In the *ESS 2020*, the work of the International Financial Corporation is presented as a central component of the Bank's overall strategy for achieving "learning for all." While the idea of enhancing the role of the IFC in education is not new to the Bank, a striking shift in the treatment of the IFC occurred during the drafting of the *ESS 2020*. This, as well as controversial claims about the IFC's contribution to the poverty mandate of the Bank's work in education, warrants further examination.

Formed in 1956, the IFC is the private sector financing arm of the World Bank Group. It has the task, distinct from the World Bank's other four branches, of supporting the private sector in emerging markets. IFC education sector activities have grown substantially from a few small initial projects in the mid-1990s to the adoption of education as one of the organization's five "strategic pillars" in 2004. Today, the IFC describes itself as the world's "largest multilateral investor in private health care and education in developing countries" (IFC, 2010, p. 23). IFC investments in education are varied, but can be subdivided into two main groupings: at the postsecondary level, the IFC provides direct financing for institutions, holds equity in individual companies, and also supports student loan facilities. In K-12 education, the IFC invests directly in private schools and school franchises and provides credit guarantees to local banks to encourage them to provide financing to private schools.[6] As of March 2011, the IFC reported cumulative investments of over $500 million to 63 education projects in 31 countries, with a total project value of $1.5 billion (IFC, 2011b).

Inclusion of the IFC was not initially a prominent feature of the Bank's *ESS 2020*: the December 2010 consultation draft of the strategy contained only 5 mentions of the IFC (World Bank, 2010). Attention to the IFC only came after direction from the most senior levels of Bank management: its Board of Directors and President (Interview #8, World Bank; Interview #1, IFC). From the perspective of the IFC, its inclusion in the sector strategy is beneficial, for it demonstrates Presidential approval for increasing collaborative operations between the two education departments: "The new education sector strategy gives us a lot of impetus by saying, look, it's now in the strategy, so now we have a strong impetus to get involved in things. So [Bank President] Zoellick and folks say we need to work more closely together" (Interview #1, IFC).

Only the final document (with 18 IFC mentions) promises to accelerate the complementarity between IBRD/IDA and IFC activities, bringing *ESS 2020* into line with pledges made in earlier Bank education sector strategies, which recognized "the growing understanding of the actual and potential roles of private sector involvement in education" and argued that "IFC support for private investment in education can complement the Bank's aim of having public monies targeted more on helping the poor gain access to quality basic education" (1999, p. 19).

Despite these claims, collaboration between the World Bank and the IFC over the past decade has been extremely uneven (Mundy & Menashy, 2011). On the one hand, there has been an active effort to develop a common "community of practice" between the two organizations since 1999. World Bank staff played an important role in framing and conceptualizing IFC work, the drafting the IFC's first education strategy, and preparation of the 2001 *Handbook on Public Private Partnerships* (EdInvest/IFC, 2001). After 2000, staff from the IFC and key figures in the

Economics of Education group in the World Bank launched biannual conferences on PPPs in education and the established the EdInvest web site (World Bank, 1999, p. 35). Subsequent joint activities included the publication of "The evolving regulatory context for private education in emerging economies" (Fielden & LaRoque, 2008; World Bank, 2009); a recent impact evaluation of the Africa Schools initiative in Kenya (Barrera-Osorio & Zable, 2011); and a new program on technical vocational education in the Middle East (IFC, 2011a; World Bank, 2011). Convergence of beliefs about the value and role of the private sector in education were reflected in routine references to IFC projects in Bank education publications promoting public-private partnerships (Patrinos et al., 2009, p. 58; World Bank, 2009, p. 8; World Bank & IMF, 2009, p. 103).

In practice, very little formal engagement has occurred at the country or regional levels between the IFC and the World Bank (Mundy & Menashy, 2011). Collaboration with the IFC is absent in virtually all World Bank education sector projects and could be described (in the words of one staffer) as still at a "very nascent stage" (Interview #8, World Bank). Although a conceptual division of labor was agreed between the IFC and the World Bank – with the IFC financing private providers and student loan schemes and the World Bank conducting policy research on private provision and assisting governments to improve the regulatory and legal environment for private sector delivery of educational services – this dovetailing of activities has not occurred (IFC, 2001, p. 8). One IFC staff described the IFC/Bank relationship at the country level in these terms: "Integrated certainly not. Coordinated only as required" (Interview #1, IFC).

While there are a variety of reasons for this lack of collaboration, certainly high among them is the lack of common procedural framework for tackling issues of poverty in education. The IFC is focused on investments in private sector ventures that are substantial in size and already scaled, through which it can make a commercial return on its investments. Unlike the Bank, its entry point is not the government, and beyond removal of regulatory barriers, it has limited interest in shifting government policies or overall educational systems to address a poverty agenda. Although the IFC claims that its education sector activities reach the bottom billion, an analysis of its education sector portfolio belies this claim. Geographically, IFC investments are increasingly concentrated on middle-income and higher-income countries. In K-12 education, the IFC primarily supports elite private schools; even its much touted Africa schools program (which provides equity finance for loans to low fee private schools) typically supports schools with average fees per term of $284 (elementary) and $275 (secondary) in Kenya (Barrera-Osorio & Zable, 2011, p. 10). IFC investments in higher education institutions and student loans appear to do somewhat better in supporting expanded educational opportunities for the poorest students. However, the organization does not formally track the distributional outcomes of these investments or monitor the economic impact on families and individuals of the educational loans offered by its partners (IEG, 2011b).

Collaboration between the IFC and the World Bank appears to have been pushed both by senior Bank management and by an epistemic community within the Bank. However, the absence of programmatic (country level) collaboration after 10 years of commitment to building this relationship, the neglect of IFC in early drafts of the new sector strategy, and the absence of a deep real poverty mandate in the IFC's education initiatives each raise questions about the purpose and likely contributions of the IFC to objectives of the World Bank Bank Group's new education sector strategy.

## A POLICY/PRACTICE DIVIDE IN BANK COMMITMENTS TO ENGAGING THE PRIVATE SECTOR?

One further puzzling feature of the new *ESS 2020* arises from the observation that despite almost two decades of policy pronouncements on the value of private provision of K-12 education, only a small fraction of the World Bank's operations in education include components to support the expansion of private provision.

More than a decade ago, a World Bank study found that roughly 15% of IBRD and IDA projects in education (all levels) during the period 1995–1997 contained notable private sector components (11 out of 70 projects) (Sosale, 2000). A 2004 report on Bank activities in East Asia and Pacific (2004, p. 1) showing a similar absence of private sector components concludes that there is "a disconnect between analytical work (and policy advice) and lending operations" (p. 19). More recently, the Bank's Independent Evaluation Group's review of the Bank's portfolio concludes that despite a slight increase, fewer than 25% of all Bank operations had a component supporting private sector provision (IEG, 2011a, p. x, 91).

Our own review of the Bank's K-12 projects corroborates this trend: objectives to enhance private sector involvement in K-12 education appeared in only 7 of 43 projects approved in fiscal years 2008, 2009, and 2010. Furthermore, while many project documents provide an overview of the respective country's private education sector, very few go on to depict any engagement on the part of the Bank with these nonstate actors, nor do they indicate that the Bank will advise national governments on fostering a stronger relationship or regulatory framework for engaging private providers. Most World Bank interventions in support of private sector provision in K-12 education occur in countries where there is a significant historically grant-aided private sector that predates Bank support. However, for many country contexts with a large private sector in K-12 education, recent Bank projects have no objective or component focusing on private provision or the engagement of the private sector.

Interviews with Bank staff suggest two possible reasons for this palpable "disconnect" between the Bank's policies and analytic work and its project activities. First is the simple fact that the World Bank's lending arms can only work directly with governments: if the government does not wish to strengthen private participation, the Bank cannot force such a policy measure. As described by one World Bank staff member, "We engage with the government, we don't engage with the private sector ... It's very difficult to engage the private sector in an operation" (Interview #5, World Bank). And as echoed by another staffer, "We cannot, much as this may be a surprise to the people on the outside, especially our NGO critics, we cannot push a loan down anyone's throat" (Interview #7, World Bank).

A second reason may be that a subset of Bank staff remains skeptical about private provision – raising both equity concerns and the fact that it is the public school sector that will do the heavy lifting when it comes to the poor (Interview #10, World Bank; Interview #11, World Bank; Interview #21, World Bank). There is a concern among this subset of staff that the Bank has overstepped its advocacy for private provision as a panacea for poverty-focused education reform.

## CONCLUSION

Over the past two decades, as made clear in its policy papers and sector strategies, there has been an evident push on the part of the Bank to provide an understanding of the role that the private sector can play to improve public education systems. In reference to private providers, previous policy papers have all cited the efficiency and quality benefits of choice and competition, the equity benefits of voucher schemes, increasing community involvement, and the notion of the private as a partner. It is clear that at the level of policy, the Bank has advocated an increasing engagement with the private sector, and in support of this, a strengthened relationship with the IFC.

The new *ESS 2020* suggests both continuity and divergence from previous Bank approaches to the private sector, particularly in K-12 education. It takes a softer rhetorical approach, arguing that the world-wide growth of private provision justifies greater World Bank attention; avoiding the language of markets and competition; and focusing on private participation at higher secondary and tertiary levels. Although still quite present in such background documents as the SABER tools for private sector engagement, the Bank's official advocacy of private provision has become more muted.

Furthermore, we have suggested that the Bank's rhetorical advocacy of private participation in education, including its emphasis on an enhanced role for the IFC in education, contrasts quite remarkably to the limited engagement with private provision in its operational practices. Surprisingly few Bank operations contain private sector participation as an objective or component, nor have its projects with strong components of private provision provided conclusive evidence of superior learning outcomes. Despite strong corporate pressures, collaboration between the IFC and the World Bank has not moved beyond the rhetorical, and there are reasons to be highly skeptical about the poverty focus of IFC educational initiatives and their ability to enhance opportunities for the "bottom billion."

Over the past two decades, the World Bank's policies have arguably overrated and oversold the contribution that private participation can make to equity in education (Hinchliffe, 1993; Klees, 2008; Verger, 2011; Verger & Bonal, forthcoming, 2012). Yet, few observers or critics have commented on the significant and surprising disjunctures between Bank advocacy for expanded private provision and its limited ability to translate this advocacy into its operational practices. The Bank does not appear to be able to harness its own private sector arm to achieve poverty alleviation – a worrying commentary on its broader promotion of private participation. In addition, a significant gulf has emerged between its policy promotion activities and its operational activities in the area of advancing private participation – another cautionary trend, suggestive of resistance from both governments and some of its own staff. Given such trends, we may well question whether the Bank is really capable of providing what is promised in the new *ESS 2020*: an objective knowledge base and an equity and results-oriented program of country-level support on the issue of private sector engagement in education.

## NOTES

1. The World Bank Group consists of five branches. Its lending arms are the International Bank for Reconstruction and Development (IBRD) – which lends to middle-income nations and creditworthy less-developed countries – and the International Development Association (IDA) – which focuses on the poorest nations, providing them with essentially interest-free loans. The IBRD, IDA, and IFC have educational programs. The other two branches are the Multilateral Investment Guarantee Agency (MIGA) and the International Centre for the Settlement of Investment Disputes (ICSID), neither of which deals directly in education.

2. This chapter draws on a research study conducted for the Open Society Institute's Private Education Research Initiative, which will be published in a forthcoming report. As part of this research, 25 interviews were conducted: 19 current World Bank staff, 2 retired World Bank staff, 3 current IFC staff, 1 retired IFC/World Bank staff. Interviews took place between April and June 2011, and all but two interviewees were located in Washington, DC. A portfolio analysis was conducted based on the 43 World Bank K-12 education projects for which complete Project Appraisal Documents were available in the period 2008–2010. An analysis of the IFC's complete education portfolio was conducted, based on data provided by IFC staff to authors in May, 2011.

3. Among the operations with private sector components highlighted in the study are the Punjab Foundation Assisted Schools Program, which is described as providing a performance-based subsidy to low-cost private schools, which has enhanced enrollment and school inputs (p. 69); an output-based subsidy program for semipublic and private higher secondary schools in Vietnam to increase access of the poor (p. 66); and two technical vocational projects (including an IFC initiative supporting private technical vocational education in the Middle East).

4. Where the 1999 Strategy did not contain the term "nonstate" and the 2005 Update only utilized it one time, the ESS 2020 contains 11 references.

5. As a simple illustration of this consistency, the term "private" is used in the 1999 document 80 times, in the 2005 Update 109 times, and in the 2011 Strategy 81 times.

6. The IFC also provides technical assistance to governments interested in piloting infrastructure PPPs in education and supports private education providers with advice and training related to marketing, planning, and business development.

## REFERENCES

Alexander, N. (2001). Paying for education: How the World Bank and the IMF influence education in developing countries. *Peabody Journal of Education*, *76*(3–4), 285–338.

Barrera-Osorio, F., Patrinos, H., & Wodon, Q. (2009). *Emerging evidence on vouchers and faith-based providers in education: Case studies from Africa, Latin America, and Asia.* Washington, DC: World Bank.

Barrera-Osorio, F., & Zable, I. (2011). A characterization of the Private Education Sector: The Kenya Private Schools Support Program. Draft paper. Received electronically from author, June 4, 2011.

Chabbott, C. (2003). *Constructing education for development: International organizations and education for all*. London: Routledge Falmer.

Colclough, C. (2000). Who should learn to pay? An assessment of neo-liberal approaches to education policy. In C. Colclough & J. Manor (Eds.), *States or markets? Neo-liberalism and the development policy debate*. Oxford: Clarendon Press.

Draxler, A. (forthcoming, 2012). International PPPs in education: New potential or privatizing public goods? In S. Robertson, K. Mundy, A. Verger, & F. Menashy (Eds.), *Public private partnerships and education: New actors and modes of governance in a globalising world*. London: Edward Elgar.

EdInvest/IFC. (2001). *Handbook on public private partnerships*. Washington, DC: International Financial Corporation.

Fielden, J., & LaRoque, N. (2008). *The evolving regulatory context for private education in emerging economies*. IFC Discussion Paper. IFC and the World Bank, Washington, DC.

Hinchliffe, K. (1993). Neo-liberal prescriptions for education finance: Unfortunately necessary or inherently desirable? *International Journal of Educational Development*, *13*(2), 183–187.

IEG (Independent Evaluation Group). (2011a). *A portfolio note: World Bank support to education since 2001*. Washington, DC: The World Bank Group.

IEG. (2011b). *Assessing IFC's poverty focus and results*. Washington, DC: World Bank.

IFC. (1999). *Draft education strategy*. Washington, DC: International Finance Corporation.

IFC. (2001). *Investing in private education: IFC's strategic directions*. Washington, DC: International Finance Corporation.

IFC. (2009). Private finance initiatives: How to ensure delivery of high-quality public services – without the mandate to do so. Retrieved from http://www.ifc.org/ifcext/psa.nsf/AttachmentsByTitle/Smartlessons_Scobie/$FILE/Smartlesson_Schools_TScobie.pdf. Accessed on June 15, 2011.

IFC. (2010). IFC road map FY11-13: Maximizing impact, unlocking our potential. Retrieved from http://www.ifc.org/ifcext/disclosure.nsf/AttachmentsByTitle/IFC_Road_Map_FY11-FY13/$FILE/FY11_13_IFC_Road_Map.pdf. Accessed on April 21, 2011.

IFC. (2011a). *Education for employment: Realizing Arab youth potential*. Washington, DC: International Finance Corporation.

IFC. (2011b). IFC in support of private education. Power point presentation [provided directly to authors by IFC staff].

Jones, P. W. (2007). *World Bank Financing of education: Lending, learning and development* (2nd ed.). London: Routledge.

Kessler, T. (2003). *Assessing the risks of the private provision of public services*. Discussion paper for G-24 Technical Group Geneva, Switzerland, September 15–16. Retrieved from http://www.g24.org/ResearchPaps/tkessgva.pdf. Accessed on September 12, 2011.

Klees, S. (2008). A quarter century of neoliberal thinking in education: Misleading analyses and failed policies. *Globalisation, Societies and Education*, *6*(4), 311–348.

Lewis, L., & Patrinos, H. (2011). *Framework for engaging the private sector in education*. SABER System Assessment and Benchmarking Education for Results. Washington, DC: The World Bank. Retrieved from http://web.worldbank.org/WBSITE/EXTER

NAL/TOPICS/EXTEDUCATION/0,,contentMDK:22856833~menuPK:282391~pagePK:148956~piPK:216618~theSitePK:282386,00.html. Accessed on September 8, 2011.

Marshall, K. (2008). *The World Bank: From reconstruction to development to equity*. London: Routledge.

Mehrotra, S., & Delamonica, E. (2005). The private sector and privatization in social services: Is the Washington consensus dead?. *Global Social Policy*, *5*(2), 141–174.

Menashy, F. (2011). *Education as a Private or a Global Public Good: Competing Conceptual Frameworks and their Power at the World Bank*. Unpublished PhD dissertation, University of Toronto.

Miller-Adams, M. (1999). *The World Bank: New agendas in a changing world*. London: Routledge.

Mundy, K. (2002). Retrospect and prospect: Education in a reforming World Bank. *International Journal of Educational Development*, *22*, 483–508.

Mundy, K., & Menashy, F. (2011). The role of the International Finance Corporation in the promotion of public private partnerships for educational development. In S. Robertson, K. Mundy, A. Verger, & F. Menashy (Eds.), *Public private partnerships in education: New actors and modes of governance in a globalising world*. London: Edward Elgar.

Patrinos, H. (2006). *Public-private partnerships: Contracting education in Latin America*. Washington, DC: World Bank.

Patrinos, H., Barrera-Osorio, F., & Guaqueta, J. (2009). *The role and impact of public-private partnerships in education*. Washington, DC: World Bank.

Patrinos, H. A., & LaRocque, N. (2007). *Enhancing accountability in schools: What can choice and contracting contribute*. Washington, DC: World Bank.

Patrinos, H., & Sosale, S. (Eds.). (2007). *Mobilizing the private sector for public education: A view from the trenches*. Washington, DC: World Bank.

Samoff, J., & Carrol, B. (2004). *From Manpower planning to the Knowledge Era. World Bank Policies on Higher Education in Africa*. Unesco Forum Occassional Paper. No. 2. Paris: UNESCO. Retrieved from http://unesdoc.unesco.org/images/0013/001347/134782eo.pdf. Accessed on April 2011.

Sosale, S. (2000). *Trends in private sector development in World Bank education projects, World Bank policy research working paper 2452*. Washington, DC: World Bank.

Vavrus, F., & Kwauk, C. (2011). The new abolitionists? The World Bank and the 'boldness' of global school fee elimination reforms. Draft paper under review.

Verger, A. (2011). Framing and selling global education policy: The promotion of public-private partnerships for education in low-income contexts. *Journal of Education Policy*, *27*(1), 109–130.

Verger, A., & Bonal, X. (forthcoming, 2012). "All things being equal"? Policy options, shortfall and absences in the World Bank Education Sector Strategy 2020. In S. Klees, J. Samoff, & N. Stromquist (Eds.), *World Bank and education: Critiques and alternatives*. Rotterdam: Sense Publishing.

Verspoor, A. (2008). *At the crossroads: Choices for secondary education in Sub-Saharan Africa*. Washington, DC: World Bank.

Weaver, C. E. (2008). *Hypocrisy trap: The World Bank and the poverty of reform*. Princeton: Princeton University Press.

World Bank. (n/d). SABER: Engaging the private sector scale. Retrieved from http://web.worldbank.org/WBSITE/EXTERNAL/TOPICS/EXTEDUCATION/0,,contentMDK:22856833~menuPK:282391~pagePK:148956~piPK:216618~theSitePK:282386,00.html. Accessed on September 8, 2011.

World Bank. (1986). *Financing education in developing countries: An exploration of policy options*. Washington, DC: World Bank.

World Bank. (1988a). *Education in sub-Saharan Africa: Policies for adjustment, revitalization and expansion*. Washington, DC: World Bank.

World Bank. (1988b). *World development report 1988*. New York, NY: World Bank/Oxford University Press.

World Bank. (1995). *Priorities and strategies for education: A World Bank review*. Washington, DC: World Bank.

World Bank. (1999). *Education sector strategy*. Washington, DC: World Bank.

World Bank. (2004). *Private sector involvement in education: A review of World Bank activities in East Asia and the Pacific*. Washington, DC: World Bank.

World Bank. (2005). *Education sector strategy update*. Washington, DC: World Bank.

World Bank. (2009). *Education year in review*. Washington, DC: World Bank.

World Bank. (2010). *Education sector strategy 2020 draft*. Washington, DC: World Bank.

World Bank. (2011). *Education sector strategy 2020*. Washington, DC: World Bank.

World Bank, & IMF. (2009). *Global monitoring report 2009: A development Emergency*. Washington, DC: World Bank.

World Bank, & UNESCO. (2006). *School Fee Abolition Initiative (SFAI) Workshop: Building on what we know and defining sustained support*. Nairobi, Kenya: World Bank and UNESCO.

# THEORY AND IDEOLOGY IN THE GENDER PROPOSALS OF THE WORLD BANK'S *EDUCATION STRATEGY 2020*

Nelly P. Stromquist

## ABSTRACT

*This chapter focuses on two concepts: development and gender, examining how they have been defined and applied to educational policy by the World Bank. To accomplish these two objectives, key documents developed by the Bank are reviewed, paying special attention to the educational policy documents produced by the Bank since 2000. The chapter discusses the rationale and evidence presented by the Bank to substantiate its new policies and the extent to which these policies reflect current social science research theory as well as empirical findings concerning educational strategies to create both economic growth and social inclusion.*

## INTRODUCTION

The educational strategy to be enforced for the next 8 years by the most powerful financial agency in the field of development is introduced in *World*

**Education Strategy in the Developing World: Revising the World Bank's Education Policy**
**International Perspectives on Education and Society, Volume 16, 133–149**

**ISSN: 1479-3679/doi:10.1108/S1479-3679(2012)0000016011**

*Bank Education Strategy 2020. Learning for All: Investing in People's Knowledge and Skills to Promote Development* (World Bank, 2011; hereafter *WBES 2020*). This chapter seeks to locate the educational strategies identified in *WBES 2020* against two referents: development and gender theories, examining the World Bank's proposed strategies in the context of its previous practices in the developing world. The chapter discusses the rationale and evidence presented by the Bank to substantiate its new policies and the extent to which these policies reflect current social science research theory as well as empirical findings concerning educational strategies to create both economic growth and social inclusion.

## A NOTE ON METHOD

*WBES 2020* is a document that treats education and cannot present a full consideration of gender and development, yet the document does provide, in various degrees of explicitness, some theoretical assumptions about how national development can be attained and what role education plays in it. As we read *WBES 2020*, we engage in its deconstruction, meaning a close reading of the text, with particular sensitivity to the assumptions it makes, to the issues it does not cover, to the ways claims are put forward. Deconstruction enables us to bring to the fore concealed hierarchies and hidden oppositions, inconsistencies, presuppositions, and contradictions in the assertions being made (Derrida, 1976; Gough, 2000; Rosenau, 1992).

As we analyze *WBES 2020*, it becomes especially relevant to consider major omissions in its discourse. It is also pertinent to see this document as part of a larger web of other World Bank publications, which convey mutually supportive messages. We can ask, therefore, what does this policy document say about gender and education? What does it conflate? What does it ignore?

## THE *WBES 2020* DISCOURSE ON GENDER

Gender is a term that appears 21 times in the document. Most of its references are to the need to increase the participation of girls and women in education and thus to narrow the schooling gap between females and males. It places the importance of gender in a list that includes place of residence, disability, ethnolinguistic background, poverty, and "other sources of disadvantage" (p. 5 and 13), thus failing to identify gender as a major social marker, with attributes of its own. *WBES 2020* also refers to gender to manifest its concern with sex gaps in learning outcomes (p. 50) and asserts that eliminating disparities in education is a way to "empower women" (p. 62). The discussion of gender is limited to issues of access (essentially primary education though some reference is also made to secondary schooling), implicitly treating schools as neutral institutions, free of gender ideologies enacted on a daily basis. Gender receives superficial treatment, grossly ignoring causes and effects that are so central to designing a means toward a reconstituted social order.

## THE WORLD BANK AND DEVELOPMENT THEORIES

A development theory can be explicit or implicit. In the latter form, it becomes recognizable through the arguments made regarding the set of structures to be activated, the set of actors identified as crucial, and the interactions to be fostered. In that respect, the World Bank relies on market forces as critical to economic growth and sees government action as a source of distortion to the assumed free interplay between demand and supply. The key actors are innovative entrepreneurs and government agencies. The transactions to be attended to are those of a government responsive to market needs for transparency, efficiency, and fair treatment. In practice, this translates to an endorsement of neoliberal principles by the World Bank, in which economic growth is synonymous with development and in which export-led growth is the only path to a more developed society.

Munck (1999) considers that beginning with its 1980 *World Development Report*, the World Bank framed development as "the extent of participation and integration with the world market" and redefined "reform" to erase any consideration of income distribution or agrarian reform. The path in education has been parallel, with solutions that have called for the decentralization of management of public education, the expansion of the private sector, and the application of cost recovery in higher education (Jones, 1997). Those educational prescriptions continue in *WBES 2020*.

In other circles, however, conceptions of national development are undergoing change. First, there is a critique of markets, with some observers declaring that market forces cannot provide the accelerated and well-coordinated comprehensive economic plans that emergent nation-states require (Koorus & Badeaux, 2007) and that the market itself is a "social institution" (Hoff & Stiglitz, 1999, p. 7). Second, today there is more discussion of democracy and participation, human rights, equality, and ecological sustainability (Acemoglu & Robinson, 2006; Broad, 1990–1991; Fine, 2002; Hoff & Stiglitz, 1999, 2005, 2010; Skarstein, 1997).

Important contributions to the notion of development look at the role of institutions and informal rules. Notable among these ideas are the writings of Acemoglu and Robinson (2006) and Hoff and Stiglitz (1999). Acemoglu and Robinson argue that to attain democracy (and thus attention to social needs), countries need to create solid political institutions that, through stable commitment, will work to reduce economic inequality and will protect the nation against negative impacts of globalization. They consider that colonial elites were bent on exploitation rather than the fostering of human rights and neglected the formation of impartial and efficient public institutions, so historical factors affect development. Hoff and Stiglitz (1999, p. 8) complement these ideas by calling for a "modern economic theory," which is more appreciative of noneconomic forces and locates the economy in an "ecosystem," one that is "more affected by biological than physical models." Stiglitz, in fact, maintains that it is "only under very special circumstances that the market [can] be shown to be efficient" (2002, p. 479) and calls for a greater understanding of the connection between market and nonmarket processes. In a number of works, the World Bank firmly believes in the positive role of social capital; this is indeed a recognition of the importance of networks in configuring and strengthening a society. Yet, Hoff & Stiglitz (1999) make the point that at the same time the World Bank disregards the role of history and institutions.

A further contribution to the understanding of national development is offered by Helmke and Levitsky (2006) through their discussion of informal institutions, which they define as the "rules and procedures created, communicated and enforced outside the officially sanctioned channels" (p. 1). In their view, informal institutions are often as important as their formal counterparts in setting the rules of the game and, while they can play either a positive or negative role, frequently they undermine institutional work. One concept that appears frequently in *WBES 2020* is poverty, and its reduction is highlighted as a primary goal. The concept of poverty is certainly receiving increased attention in theories of development, but *WBES 2020* approaches it from a particular perspective. The World Bank, along with other financial institutions, avoids considering poverty as a political problem. Poverty is framed as a problem of individuals not of structures; consequently, there is no need to speak of redistribution (Ferguson, 1990; Tarabini, 2010). In contrast, Sen has introduced a broader view of poverty by bringing the concepts of entitlement and capabilities (highlighted in Prugl & Lutsgarten, 2006), which pays attention to the channels by which the lack of wealth finds expression.

A few decades ago, inequality was seen as an unavoidable feature of creative capitalism. The argument was that talent was not equally distributed and that those with innovative and entrepreneurial skills deserved rewards that put them above the rest. The emergence of income differences in a society was not seen as negative; rather, such inequalities served to motivate others to emulate their more successful peers. That view has come under criticism today. Economists such as Milanovic (2003) consider that inequalities are extremely negative to any national development project for they increase social tensions and levels of alienation as groups of people perceive themselves as left behind by economic growth. They deplore the fact that inequality is on the rise: the Gini coefficient of the GDP per capita of all countries has risen from 46 in 1978 to 54 in 2003, an increase of 17% (Milanovic, 2003; Wade, 2004).

One academic analysis that has received wide acceptance in Europe is presented by Wilkinson and Pickett (2009). Although these authors focus only on industrialized nations and do not explain how inequalities may have made them wealthy in the first place, they do show that their current inequalities create negative consequences for a large number of social outcomes, including child mortality, longevity, depression, crime, drug use, and obesity. Their analysis shows that income inequality is associated negatively with women's status along political and economic lines (Wilkinson & Pickett, 2009). Translating this to education, it could be argued that if public and private schools are likely to generate social distinctions, this should be a matter of concern. *WBES 2020* strongly proposes private schooling because it will reduce public expenditures and "is a cost that even poor parents can afford." The repercussions of inequality on gender – particularly given the fact that in patrilineal societies (which are still a sizable number) women are seen as assets from which the husband's family will benefit – are unexplored in *WBES 2020*.

Another change occurring in theories of national development is the recognition of new social actors in the process of social change. Some consider that the presence of social movements is symptomatic of the crisis of development but at the same time these movements offer the seeds for new models of development (Munck, 1999). In my view, social movements are a necessary expression because the formal political system is often so centered on economic growth that social justice is neglected. Paying attention to nongovernmental actors also implies seeing development from a cultural perspective. Fagan (1999) notes that a cultural perspective implies asking questions about the meaning of development, about the production of knowledge, and about who decides and who has the greater use of resources, coercive, or persuasive, to make their version of reality stick (Fagan, 1999). The development literature is giving increased recognition to the multiple nongovernment institutions and civil society organizations that contribute to the formation of public policy "from below," raising issues not attended by the formal political system and closely monitoring the implementation of policies put in place to improve the situation of marginalized or disadvantaged groups. In the case of gender transformation, it is essential to count on the participation of women's organizations to bring about a stronger understanding of women's problems and the possibilities for their solution.

The World Bank's views on development are somewhat stagnant. They are clearly illustrated in *The Growth Report. Strategies for Sustained Growth and Inclusive Development* (Commission on Growth and Development, 2010), an effort of over 2 years with the participation of 19 "leaders" and two Nobel Prize winners in economics (Michael Spence and Robert Solow). A detailed analysis of this document is essential to understand how the World Bank sees development. The *Report* presents the views of an "independent commission," yet its membership, its production, and its dissemination reflect a strong selectivity and endorsement by the World Bank.

The report is based on 13 successful country economies that "have grown at an average GDP rate of 7% per year or more for 25 years or longer" (p. 1). This assertion, however, is not supported by the scant pertinent data provided in the report. First, a core table (Table 1.13, p. 20) shows much lower levels of GDP growth and the time periods involved often cover spans in which the countries were not involved in trade liberalization; another table (no title, Appendix, p. 111), reporting the GDP growth rates for 25 countries in the world, shows that the 13 selected countries actually have *smaller* rates of growth than several other countries. Second, assertions are made without specific evidence. In the text, references to the 13 countries are sporadic and mention is often made of India, although this country is not one of the exemplary 13. The *Growth Report* makes a strong case for participation in the open world economy since "the home market is usually too small to sustain growth for long" (Commission on Growth and Development, 2010, p. 2) and for relying on the allocation of markets as "there is no known, effective substitute" (p. 6). While the title of the *Growth Report* mentions "inclusion," the text makes concrete reference to it only twice, once to say that policies of inclusion should be followed and again to observe that equity and equality of opportunity are needed to achieve inclusion. The report identifies some measures for which the state is needed: macro-economic stability and investments in infrastructure, notably education and health, and the creation of "committed, credible, and capable governments" (Commission on Growth and Development, 2010, p. 20). The role of the state, however, is dwarfed by the attributes assigned to the market. Overall, this report pays no significant attention to social, cultural, and political issues affecting the national development process.

These observations about factors that impinge on development are most relevant to the understanding of gender in society and how gender ideologies may be challenged, particularly, in our case, for education. A solid consideration of nonmarket forces would mean that, in addition to economic growth considerations, the entire structure of formal and informal networks in a society would be the target of research and subsequent improvement efforts. In education, it would mean that, far beyond the current concentration on school access, questions of content would receive substantial attention. Issues such as the formation of civic values, respect for institutions, and an understanding of human rights and responsibilities would be essential parts of the school's curriculum. Nonformal and popular education would similarly be embraced as ways to attend to adult women and even men in their quest for a resocialization.

## EDUCATION AND THE WORLD BANK

In harmony with its framing of poverty as an individual problem, the World Bank is a firm endorser of human capital theories. These theories emphasize what individuals bring to the marketplace – education, attitudes, experiences, and values – and assume that the quantity and quality of these attributes create different occupational and income positions for men and women. Human capital theories do not consider institutional and structural determinants of labor outcomes (Jones, 1997). This particular assumption is quite detrimental to groups that experience significant disadvantage due to race and sex discrimination.

Education is tied to reduction of poverty because of a firm belief in knowledge as a means of improving one's understanding of and position in society. But from a critical perspective, education is also favored as a means because it does not require redistribution of wealth, much less when the privatization of education is being endorsed. Education has emerged since the 1990s as a worldwide priority strategy to fight poverty, yet neither EFA nor the MDGs include the need to reduce *inequality* as an explicit goal among their objectives (Tarabini, 2010). This is linked to the fact that several international agencies, including the World Bank, attend to the needs of the poor through targeting strategies as opposed to universal policies that seek to diminish inequality (Bonal, 2007). The effect of such policies contributes to create distinctions between "deserving poor" and "non-deserving poor" (Bonal, 2007).

*WBES 2020* proposes a multisectoral approach to education, considering the relevance of areas such as legal frameworks, health, agriculture, and infrastructure (p. 27). Such a sectoral approach has been widely recommended in the development literature and would be extremely helpful in increasing the participation of girls and women in education. But how will that multisectoral approach be carried out in the absence of a policy to support public education at all levels, or without the national resources to make long-term investments in social arenas, including education? Bonal (2007) reminds us that too often we concentrate on considering what education might do to reduce poverty but fail to consider what poverty does to education. Poor families seldom have the capacity to act as proponents of girls' education. What is being done to help them engage in progressive roles? *WBES 2020* identifies measures such as conditional cash transfers to help poor families offset income foregone for girls. These programs have had beneficial impacts on girls' access to and completion of schools. Their contribution is not to be minimized, but such efforts occur only in a few countries. Why is this the case? A serious consideration of conditional cash transfers should look at why they need to exist and more importantly to continue.

Apart from supporting educational access, the World Bank encourages educational reform. Among these measures, two are paramount: decentralization and privatization. *WBES 2020* mentions them sparingly; yet, it is clear that such strategies will continue. The consequences of such measures for women have not received sufficient attention. The empirical evidence suggests a number of negative consequences (Stromquist, forthcoming).

## GENDER THEORIES AND EDUCATION

As Moghadam (1990) concisely puts it, gender refers "not only to women and men but to a structural relationship between the sexes which is linked to the state, the economy, and other macro- and micro-processes and institutions" (p. 8). Gender theories have undergone considerable evolution in recent decades. The role of ideology in the form of patriarchy (a sense that men are superior to women and responsible for them) continues to be a major factor in the explanation of women's disadvantageous position in most societies. This ideology provides the basis for a sexual division of labor and a strong divide between private and public spheres, with women assigned identities as mothers and family carers and men as breadwinners and decision-makers.

The issues of power, conflict, and oppression are present in contemporary explanations of gender asymmetries. We have come to recognize the compounding impacts produced by additional forces such as race, ethnicity, and age, and thus of differential impacts of gender across time, space, and culture. There is now a sharper realization of the potential and limits of state action and the imperative of reliance on organizations of civil society to build up new identities and engage in both corrective and transformative action. The links between the private and the public spheres in constraining women's freedom are also recognized. Significant contributions to gender theories highlight the importance of undoing gender at micro levels through constant performance on a daily basis (Butler, 1990). Recent theoretical developments link gender to cultural, historical, and sociological contexts and issues of power in private, institutional, and public domains (Collard & Reynolds, 2003). Fraser's insights (1995) about the need to work simultaneously on issues of redistribution (a fair partition of the material wealth) and recognition (acceptance and valuing of differences between men and women) have further increased our understanding of gender as a complex and deeply rooted social phenomenon.

Mainstream economists believe that women need to be integrated into the economy. Feminist economists contend that women are not only already integrated but that they are a source of cheap and expendable labor in a context of unchanged social relations (Deere, Alvarado, & Twyman, 2010; Elson & Cagatay, 2000; Elson & Pearson, 1981; Fuentes & Ehrenreich, 1983; Nash & Fernandez-Kelly, 1983). They further argue that modern forms of capitalism have led to the marginalization and impoverishment of women (Brodie, 2008; Moghadam, 1990; Sen & Grown, 1987; Ward, 1984) and observe that since cultural and structural factors influence gender occupational segregation, models based on supply and demand do not capture these influences.

The World Bank strongly endorses the integration of women in the economy and equality of opportunity within an unregulated market context. Yet, empirical studies of successful participation of women in the economy make it evident that such an objective can be reached only through state intervention that addresses the traditional division of labor in the household and women's responsibilities of motherhood (Moghadam, 1990; Mutari, 2006). To achieve change, the state cannot be simply neutral but must engage in the provision of high-quality public childcare, along with maternity and parental leaves, paid leave to take care of sick children, and flexible terms of employment (Mandel, 2009) – otherwise the existing sexual division of labor will continue the disadvantage for women. While at first sight these policies might seem to reproduce gender distinctions, they serve the powerful purpose of ensuring greater access by women to the labor force, thus lessening their economic dependence on husbands and families. The evidence from Sweden, Norway, Denmark, and Finland is categorical in this respect (Mandel, 2009). If only equality of opportunity is offered to women, those who benefit are women of the higher classes who can buy private childcare services and who then face no competition with low-income women for the available positions.

The World Bank has shown concern for women's education since its Education Sector Working Paper of 1974, which noted gender disparities in primary and secondary enrollment in the poorest countries (Vaughan, 2010). Its interest in women's education has increased over time, but then, as now, the World Bank does not address issues of power and status in affecting gender outcomes, "leaving more complex aspects of educational participation unexplored" (Vaughan, 2010, p. 412). For example, a recent World Bank document explains women's disadvantage in education as follows: "Gender differential access to school is usually caused by poverty, adverse cultural practices, schooling quality and distance to school" (World Bank, 2010a). Such a list conflates causes and consequences and does not recognize power and conflict issues. And, because of the World Bank's commitment to human capital theory, *WBES 2020* endorses education for women exclusively on instrumental grounds.

Recent evidence, based on data for 134 countries, shows a strong correlation between gender equality and GDP per capita (Hausmann, Tyson, & Zahidi, 2010). Countries stand to gain from equalizing conditions between men and women, but patriarchal ideologies sustain a different logic. Hausmann et al. (2010) have developed the Gender Gap Index, a measurement that focuses on outcomes along four dimensions: economic participation and opportunity, educational attainment, health and survival, and political empowerment. This index shows that the gender gap has been successfully closed in health outcomes (in 96% of the countries) and in education (in 90% of the countries). However, gender gaps remain sizable in economic outcomes (closed in only 59% of the countries) and even greater in political outcomes (closed in only 18% of the countries). These differential outcomes must be taken as evidence that access to education does not by itself produce assertive women or changes in the relations of gender. Schooling does contribute to critical thinking but it does not necessarily promote gender critical thinking. Ideologies of masculinity and femininity are so deeply engrained in society that challenging them calls for explicit targeting rather than assuming they will automatically weaken as levels of education rise.

Extending unproblematically the theory of human capital to women, the World Bank sees education as a means to increase their productive capacities and to render more efficient their reproductive roles (as mothers and wives). The World Bank also assumes that women's occupational choices are individual decisions rather than social products. Through this narrow lens, *WBES 2020* proposes discrete interventions such as scholarships for girls, recruitment and training of women teachers, girl-friendly curricula, after-school tutoring, and more support for nonformal education (p. 26). These measures are very useful but they are presented piecemeal with no sense that World Bank's commitment to them could ever approach the levels of privatization and testing, for instance. Moreover, a clear intention to making educational authorities, administrators, and teachers understand the processes by which gender operates in society and school – and be prepared to modify them – is absent from the *WBES 2020* narrative.

To be sure, the World Bank does not speak with a single voice. A World Bank policy research report (King & Mason, 2001), now 10 years old, focused on disparities in enrollment rates and average years of schooling but went farther, recommending changing several social practices, including family law, gender-related violence, traditional or customary laws, land rights, and enacting regulations in the labor market to promote equal pay, affirmative action, family welfare, old-age support systems, and regulation of the informal sector. A subsequent report (World Bank, 2002) considered partnering "with active women's advocacy groups on women's and gender studies units in research or educational institutions" (p. 33), and even detailed gender responsibilities for each position in the World Bank, including its top administrators and regional vice presidents.

In contrast, the *WBES 2020* is shy in proposals to challenge gender in education. It must be observed that this document does not even make mention of gender mainstreaming, even though the Beijing Platform for Action (globally agreed upon in 1995) mandates that all development institutions incorporate a gender perspective in all policies and programs (Gutierrez, 2003). Is this perhaps because the World Bank is responding as a bank? Gender mainstreaming is not an easy task but this does not justify its abandonment.

## THE BANK AS AN INTERESTED PARTY

Involved as it is in the provision of loans (and secondarily, grants), the World Bank cannot be considered a neutral party. Loans are assessed on their potential for repayment, with interest, and thus have a primarily economic rationale. This is hardly congruent with a rationale based on social equity.

To play a major role in national development, the World Bank minimizes this contradiction by silencing inconvenient facts. After severe criticisms of its structural adjustment programs (SAPs), imposed jointly with the International Monetary Fund (IMF), the World Bank has shifted into poverty reduction strategy papers (PRSPs), particularly influential in sub-Saharan African countries. The current strategies have corrected the trend of SAPs to reduce investment in health and basic education but, as in the case of SAPs, they prioritize the privatization of government services (Brym & associates, 2005). PRSPs make it possible for the World Bank to impose conditions on developing countries, conditions that match World Bank strategies. Based on a sample of World Bank loans in 20 countries, Eurodad Report (2006) found an average of 67 conditions per loan. One can wonder how much room is there for comprehensive measures to address gender inequality. A partial answer can be found in a review of 18 PRSP plans approved in 2002 and conducted by two researchers at UNESCO's Institute for International Planning. They concluded that these planning efforts have given more attention to agriculture, infrastructure, employment, and industry than to education (Caillods & Hallak, 2004). The researchers also stated that "the lack of involvement, internalization, and ownership of the objectives of the PRSP by the education administration lead to a cumulative feeling of frustration and skepticism" (Caillods & Hallak, 2004, p. 51).

The World Bank uses an additional mechanism that constrains investment in education. This is its structural adjustment lending (SAL) – non-project lending to reduce balance-of-payment deficits. SALs represent a major instrument for the enforcement of conditionalities that cement neoliberal policies (Broad, 2006). In effect since 1979, SALs mandate liberalizing the economy and curtailing spending on social services. Broad (2006) notes that by FY 1999, SALs represented 63% of total IBRD and IDA lending; consequently, most lending by the World Bank requires conditions that affect the policies of developing countries. A pertinent question is, if less public investment is to occur in education, where are the resources coming from to address social and gender inequalities? Serious and persistent criticism to conditionalities imposed by the World Bank and the IMF have been voiced by multiple observers (among them, King, 2004; Marphatia & Archer, 2005; Subrahmanian, 2002; Zuckerman, 2007). The position these enormously influential organizations have is a matter of concern for many who have followed their work, both scholars and social activists. A recent report commissioned by the United Nations recommended that the World Bank and IMF should separate the provision of grants and loans from technical assistance and policy advice, as the latter are often used to restrict policy choices and reinforce conditions (Civil Society, 2009). *WBES 2020* makes no reference to the fact that PRSPs constrain and shape decisions in all areas of society, including education.

While *WBES 2020* asserts that "currently, many young people in developing countries are leaving school and entering the workforce without the knowledge, skills, and competencies necessary to thrive in a competitive global economy" (p. 28), the document does not discuss the implications of the ongoing globalization process for education. The connection between skills and the economy suggests a world totally engaged in knowledge production and a high contact with industrialized goods; yet, Barnet and Cavanagh (1998) estimate that about 80% of the world's population lives outside global consumer networks (cited in Gough, 2000). Avoided in in the World Bank's discussion of the knowledge economy are the impediments countries face in their attempt to generate the wealth needed to acquire science and technology. In this respect, issues such as fair trade and terms of trade are not touched.

Globalization rarely appears in mainstream economics, as issues of power and conflict are avoided (Fine, 2002). Globalization is relevant to a discussion of gender in the sense that a successful participation in the global economy may generate revenues for investment in social issues. Undoubtedly, there have been countries that have done well in the globalized world – China, India, South Korea, and Taiwan being the most successful. Several developing countries have seen their GNP rise because of increases in the price of their natural resources, but many of them face external debts (estimated to be about $2.3 trillion globally by Broad and Cavanagh, 2006) that significantly constrain their ability to invest in education.

*WBES 2020* repeatedly observes that we are moving into a knowledge-based economy. That discourse does not coincide with the fact that the current international division of labor places many developing countries in the mode of resource extraction as opposed to value-added production. A globalized world intensifies the international division of labor. How are these forces going to be countered in the absence of determined state intervention? As Sassen (2007) observes, we need new conceptual frameworks for explaining reality, frameworks that do not assume that the national is a closed or exclusive system. Thus, a critical location for gender to be addressed through development policies – including those in education – needs to be the global context.

## THE WORLD BANK AS PROTECTOR OF EQUITY?

It is clear that the World Bank relies on a single dimension of development (economics) and a single perspective of economic development (neoliberalism). This emphasis on the market to the exclusion of other factors such as income inequality, external dependence, and patriarchal hegemony has been described by Haque (1999) as theoretical parochialism.

To reduce the subordinate situation of women, three dynamics must be in place: working simultaneously with other societal institutions that affect women's economic conditions (the labor market, health, and welfare protection); working with the mainstream media to counter still prevalent and omnipresent sex stereotypes; and working beyond educational access in order to alter the content of the knowledge learned in schools and the nature of the experience in those settings. This means reexamining the curriculum as well as providing teacher and administrator training and retraining in gender issues. The demise of patriarchal ideologies will require the fostering and explicit development of empowerment of women. It requires also the assertiveness at individual and collective levels to contest the existing social order; consequently, attention to adult education emerges as an essential component of education to transform the gender status quo.

International development organizations can play a crucial role in these efforts. But can the World Bank play such a role? So far, it has given very little indication that it is a learning organization. It relies mostly on in-house research and makes no use of contradictory viewpoints and findings. The solutions it proposes, as evident in the *WBES 2020*, present no discussion of the dynamics or strategies in conflict and the potential negative collateral effects. Gender issues are complex, controversial, and deeply inimical to change. Proponents of change in the social relations of gender need to give serious recognition to the importance of human rights, to act in unison with other organizations, and to recognize multiple voices emanating from researchers and from the women themselves. These requirements simply do not qualify the World Bank for this transformative role.

## REFERENCES

Acemoglu, D., & Robinson, J. (2006). *Economic origins of dictatorship and democracy*. Cambridge: Cambridge University Press.

Bonal, X. (2007). On global absences: Reflections on the failings in the education and poverty relationship in Latin America. *International Journal of Educational Development*, *27*(1), 86–100.

Broad, R. (1990–1991). Development: The market is not enough. *Foreign Policy*, 81, 700–708.

Broad, R. (2006). Research, knowledge, and the art of "paradigm maintenance": The World Bank's Development Economics Vice-Presidency (DEC). *Review of International Political Economy*, *13*(3), 387–419.

Broad, R., & Cavanagh, J. (2006). The hijacking of the development debate. How Friedman and Sachs got it wrong. *World Policy Journal*, *23*(2), 21–30.

Brodie, J. (2008). Putting gender back In Women and social policy reform in Canada. In Y. Abu-Laban (Ed.), *Gendering the nation-state: Canadian and comparative perspectives* (pp. 165–184). Vancouver, BC: University of British Columbia Press.

Brym, R., Chung,, R., Dulmage, S., Farahat, C., Greenberg, M., Ho, M., & Wu, T. (2005). *The Canadian Journal of Sociology*, *30*(1), 95–111.

Butler, J. (1990). *Gender trouble: Feminism and the subversion of identity*. New York, NY: Routledge.

Caillods, F., & Hallak, J. (2004). *Education and PRSPs: A review of experiences*. Paris: International Institute for Educational Planning.

Civil Society Consultation on the Work of the President of the UN General Assembly's Commission of Experts on Reforms of the International Monetary and Financial System. (2009). A compilation report prepared by the UN Non-Governmental Liaison Service. New York, NY; Geneva: UN Non-Governmental Liaison Service, United Nations.

Collard, J., & Reynolds, C. (2003). Conclusions and implications: Towards emergent theoretical perspectives on leadership, gender and culture. In J. Collard & C. Reynolds (Eds.), *Leadership, gender & culture in education: Male and female perspectives* (pp. 195–204). Berkshire: Open University Press.

Commission on Growth and Development. (2010). *The growth report. Strategies for sustained growth and inclusive development*. Washington, DC: World Bank.

Deere, C. D., Alvarado, G., & Twyman, J. (2010). *Poverty, headship, and gender inequality in asset ownership in Latin America*. Working Paper 296, March. Gender, Development and Globalization Program, Center for Gender in Global Context, Michigan State University, Ann Arbor, MI.

Derrida, J. (1976). *Grammatology*. Baltimore, MD: The Johns Hopkins University Press.

Elson, D., & Cagatay, N. (2000). The social content of macroeconomic policies. *World Development*, *28*(7), 1347–1364.

Elson, D., & Pearson, R. (1981). Nimble fingers make cheap workers: An analysis of women's employment in Third World export manufacturing. *Feminist Review*, *7*(87), 107.

Eurodad Report. (2006). *World Bank and IMF conditionality: A development injustice*, June. European Network on Debt and Development, Brussels.
Fagan, G. H. (1999). Cultural politics and (post) development paradigms. In R. Munck & D. O'Hearn (Eds.), *Critical development theory: Contributions to a new paradigm* (pp. 178–195). London: Zed Books.
Ferguson, J. (1990). *The anti-politics machine. "Development," depoliticization, and bureaucratic power in Lesotho*. Cambridge: Cambridge University Press.
Fine, B. (2002). Economics imperialism and the new development economics as Kuhnian paradigm shift? *World Development*, *30*(12), 2057–2070.
Fraser, N. (1995). From distribution to recognition? Dilemmas of justice in a "post socialist" age. *New Left Review*, July/August, 218, pp. 68–93.
Fuentes, A., & Ehrenreich, B. (1983). *Women in the global factory*. New York, NY: Institute for New Communications.
Gough, N. (2000). Globalization and curriculum inquiry: locating, representing, and performing a transnational imaginary. In N. Stromquist & K. Monkman (Eds.), *Globalization and education: Integration and contestation across cultures* (pp. 77–98). Lanham, MD: Rowman & Littlefield.
Gutierrez, M. (Ed.). (2003). *Macro-economics: Making gender matter*. London: Zed Books.
Hausmann, R., Tyson, L., & Zahidi, S. (2010). *The global gender gap report 2010*. Geneva: World Economic Forum.
Haque, M. (1999). *Restructuring development theories and policies. A critical study*. Albany, NY: State University of New York Press.
Helmke, G., & Levitsky, S. (2006). Introduction. In G. Helmke & S. Levitsky (Eds.), *Informal institutions and democracy: Lessons from Latin America* (pp. 1–30). Baltimore, MD: The Johns Hopkins University Press.
Hoff, K., & Stiglitz, J. (1999). *Modern economic theory and development*, November. Washington, DC: World Bank, draft.
Hoff, K., & Stiglitz, J. (2005). *The creation of the rule of law and the legitimacy of property rights: The political and economic consequences of a corrupt privatization*. Policy Research Working Paper 3779. The World Bank, Washington, DC.
Hoff, K., & Stiglitz, J. (2010). *Equilibrium fictions. A cognitive approach to societal rigidity*. Policy Research Working Paper 5219. The World Bank, Washington, DC.
Jones, P. (1997). On World Bank education financing. *Comparative Education*, *33*(1), 117–129.
King, E., & Mason, A. (2001). *Engendering development through gender equality in rights, resources, and voice*. A World Policy Research Report, January. World Bank, Washington, DC.
King, K. (2004). Development knowledge and the global policy agenda. Whose knowledge? Whose policy? Paper prepared for the UNRISD Conference on Social Knowledge and International Policy Making: Explaining the Linkages, April, UN Research Institute for Social Development, Geneva.
Koorus, S., & Badeaux, L. (2007). Economic development planning models: A comparative assessment. *International Research Journal of Finance and Economics*, *7*, 120–139.
Mandel, H. (2009). Configurations of gender inequality: The consequences of ideology and public policy. *The British Journal of Sociology*, *60*(4), 693–719.
Marphatia, A., & Archer, D. (2005). *Contradictory commitments: How the achievement of education for all is being undermined by the International Monetary Fund*. London: ActionAid International and Global Campaign for Education.

Milanovic, B. (2003). The two faces of globalization. *World Development*, *31*(4), 667–683.

Moghadam, V. (1990). *Gender, development, and policy: Toward equity and empowerment*. Helsinki: World Institute for Development Economics Research of the United Nations University.

Munck, R. (1999). Desconstructing development discourses: Of impasses, alternatives and politics. In R. Munck & D. O'Hearn (Eds.), *Critical development theory: Contributions to a new paradigm* (pp. 196–210). London: Zed Books.

Mutari, E. (2006). A feminist view of the state. In S. Pressman (Ed.), *Alternative theories of the state* (pp. 139–163). New York, NY: Palgrave Macmillan.

Nash, J., & Fernandez-Kelly, M. P. (1983). *Women, men, and the international division of labor*. Albany, NY: State University of New York Press.

Prugl, E., & Lutsgarten, A. (2006). Mainstreaming gender in international organizations. In J. Jacquette & G. Summerfield (Eds.), *Women and gender equity in development theory and practice* (pp. 53–70). Durham: Duke University Press.

Rosenau, P. (1992). *Post-modernism and the social sciences: Insights, inroads, and intrusions*. Princeton, NJ: Princeton University Press.

Sassen, S. (2007). *A sociology of globalization*. New York, NY: W.W. Norton & Co.

Sen, G., & Grown, C. (1987). *Development, crisis, and alternative voices: Third World women's perspectives*. New York, NY: Monthly Review Press.

Skarstein, R. (1997). *Development theory: A guide to some unfashionable perspectives*. Delhi: Oxford University Press.

Stiglitz, J. (2002). Information and the change in the paradigm in economics. *American Economic Review*, *92*(3), 460–501.

Stromquist, N. (forthcoming). The gender dimension in the World Bank's education strategy: Assertions in need of a theory. In S. Klees, J. Samoff, & N. Stromquist (Eds.), *World Bank and education. Critiques and alternatives*. Rotterdam: Sense Publishers.

Subrahmanian, R. (2002). *Gender and education. A review of issues for social policy*, April. Social Policy and Development Program Paper No. 9. UN Research Institute for Social Development, Geneva.

Tarabini, A. (2010). Education and poverty in the global development agenda: Emergence, evolution and consolidation. *International Journal of Educational Development*, *30*(2), 204–212.

Vaughan, R. (2010). Girls' and women's education within UNESCO and the World Bank, 1944–2000. *Compare*, *40*(4), 405–423.

Wade, R. (2004). Is globalization reducing poverty and inequality? *World Development*, *32*(4), 576–589.

Ward, K. (1984). *Women in the world system: Its impact on status and fertility*. New York, NY: Praeger.

Wilkinson, R., & Pickett, K. (2009). *The spirit level: Why greater equality makes societies stronger*. New York, NY: Bloomsbury Press.

World Bank. (2002). *Integrating gender into the World Bank's work: A strategy for action*, January. Washington, DC: World Bank.

World Bank. (2011). *World Bank Education Strategy 2020. Learning for all: Investing in people's knowledge and skills to promote development*. Washington, DC: World Bank.

Zuckerman, E. (2007). Critique: Gender equality as smart economics: A World Bank Group Gender Action Plan (GAP) (Fiscal Years 2007–10), January. Washington, D.C.: Gender Action. Retrieved from http://www.genderaction.org/images/04.22.08_EZ-GAPlan Critique.pdf. Accessed on 4 March 2009.

# WORLD BANK AND EDUCATION: IDEOLOGICAL PREMISES AND IDEOLOGICAL CONCLUSIONS

Steven J. Klees

## ABSTRACT

*The World Bank has been the predominant institution for developing and enforcing a global education policy for over three decades, eclipsing UNESCO, UNICEF, and bilateral institutions. Every decade or so the Bank writes up their current version of global education policy in a strategy report. The most recent strategy continues past trends that offer little actual attention to education itself but instead focus on a particular, narrow, ideologically based approach to managing education. This chapter highlights three of these trends. First, the title of the strategy is misleading as the report has little to do with "Learning for All." More accurately, the approach should be known as "Testing for All," focusing on partial measures of just two of the many outcomes of education that are important. Second, the strategy emphasizes that the Bank will use a "system approach" to analyze and manage education around the world (continuing their infamous one-size-fits-all methodology), yet it offers no evidence to support the productivity of such an approach and ignores decades of criticism of its narrow and distorting nature. Third, the*

**Education Strategy in the Developing World: Revising the World Bank's Education Policy**
**International Perspectives on Education and Society, Volume 16, 151–171**

**ISSN: 1479-3679/doi:10.1108/S1479-3679(2012)0000016012**

*strategy emphasizes the benefits of the privatization of education, ignoring issues of education as a public good and the inequities associated with fee-for-service, especially for marginalized groups.*

## INTRODUCTION

The World Bank prides itself on being evidence- and research-based, but it is not. Its premises and conclusions are based on ideology, not evidence. The Bank selects and interprets the research that fits with its ideology. In this sense, it resembles right-wing ideological institutions like the Cato Institute or the Heritage Foundation. However, it differs in two important ways. First, everyone realizes Cato and Heritage are partisan. The Bank, on the other hand, makes a pretense of objectivity and inclusiveness. Second, Cato and Heritage are private institutions with limited influence. The Bank is a public institution, financed by taxes, which gives grants, loans, and advice around the world, yielding a vast global influence.

The Bank is a monopoly.[1] There is no other institution like it. It is not too strong to argue that the Bank is the architect of what has become a truly global education policy (Klees, 2008a, 2002; King, 2007). UNESCO used to have a more dominant role, but withdrawal of the U.S. and U.K. contributions for a number of years forced it to play a much more minor role, and the Bank became the true director of the Education for All (EFA) processes and more (Jones, 2007; Mundy, 2002). While the Bank pretends everyone – countries, bilaterals, multilaterals, civil society, and more – is in partnership with it, it is the Bank that takes the lead on education policy. With its periodic strategy reports and a virtual juggernaut of research done internal to the Bank or financed by it, it decides on the global directions for education policy, backed by grant and loan money that ensures countries follow those directions.

The ideology that dominates the Bank is neoliberal. I find it useful to divide the world of political economy into three broad paradigms: neoliberal, liberal, and progressive. Neoliberalism, which predominates today, focuses on market solutions, criticizing the efficiency and equity of government interventions. A liberal perspective offers greater recognition of the inefficiencies and inequities of markets and puts more faith in government. A progressive perspective focuses on the reproductive nature of both the market and the state under current world system structures like capitalism, patriarchy, and racism, and puts greater reliance on transformation from below through more participatory forms of democracy and collective action. It should be noted that these paradigms, rather than being mutually exclusive, do overlap to some extent, and there are significant variations within each. However, the differences between them are very important for public policy. Most particular to the subject here is that the Bank ignores or critiques research that does not support its ideological commitment to neoliberalism.

In this chapter, I examine some of the ideological premises and conclusions that serve as the basis for World Bank policy toward education. I will focus some attention on the new 2020 Strategy Report (World Bank, 2011b), but this Report is part and parcel of more than 30 years of the Bank's neoliberal strategy papers, research, policy, and practice. There is little new in the Report; antecedents can be found in the World Bank's (1995, 1999, 2005) strategy papers, as well as further back. Neoliberalism rose to global dominance in the 1980s as part of the consequences of political shifts to the right embodied in politicians like Ronald Reagan, Margaret Thatcher, and Helmut Kohl. While I will not specifically focus on the history of the Bank's stance on education policy, you can see a sharp transformation from its liberal perspective in the 1960s and 1970s to an increasingly strident neoliberal perspective since the early 1980s (Jones, 2007; Klees, 2002)

The new Strategy Report was initiated with much fanfare. The Bank is especially proud of its consultation phase where dozens of meetings were held around the world with over 1,000 participants from over 100 countries. In the spirit of cooperation, I helped organize a meeting with progressive Bank critics. But the result of all this consultation is still a thoroughly neoliberal view of education policy. While other views were obviously heard, none of them were listened to, none made it to the Report. I do believe that Bank staff are well intentioned, just hopelessly biased.

The new Strategy Report and past World Bank policy have been an educational disaster, harmful to children around the world, as discussed below. There are many, many people around the world who agree with me (e.g., the authors in this book), but you will not find any of their views expressed in Bank reports. Instead, we get the narrow, ideological premises, and conclusions that the Bank brings to education policy, as exemplified below.

## THE RIGHT TO EDUCATION

For the Bank, education is not a right. The Strategy Report (p. 1) says the opposite: "Access to education … is a basic human right …" But that is it. It is hardly mentioned again. The sentence does not even consider the key issue of quality. And most importantly, the right to education is not used in any way as a basis for Bank strategy. The one sentence reflects either ignorance or duplicity – ignorant because anyone with any knowledge of what education as a right means understands that it fundamentally changes your approach to education policy. Instead of the Bank's instrumentalist, human capital approach using rates of return to establish investment trade-offs, a human rights approach does not consider trade-offs as legitimate. Access and quality are a child's right, and education must be provided to fulfill that right. For example, a child has a right to a qualified teacher; providing a barely trained contract teacher, as the Bank has advocated, is not a legitimate substitute and violates a child's right to education (Right to Education Project, 2011; Tomasevski, 2003).

The Bank has reluctantly added a sentence or two to its reports over the years offering grudging support for the idea of the right to education, while other private and public international agencies (e.g., ActionAid, UNESCO and UNICEF) have transformed their entire programming to make rights central. For UNICEF (2011), its "ultimate aim ... is the realization of the rights of children," the right to education "guides our work in all sectors." For UNESCO (2011b), its "constitutional mission" is the "right to education." On the other hand, the Bank has not even been able to take a strong stand against user fees that directly violate the right to education by limiting access. In its neoliberal zeal, the Bank was actually the architect of expanded user fees in the 1980s – even for primary education. In the 1990s, it backed off a little, but it has not campaigned for the elimination of all school fees as have UNESCO, UNICEF, ActionAid, and many others (Klees, 2008a).

Most fundamentally, the World Bank is a bank and does not know what to do with a rights-based argument. Everything to the Bank is instrumental in terms of how it affects economic growth. And a basic problem for the Bank is that a rights-based approach doesn't stop at the right to education. What about a right to health? to food? to shelter? to a sustainable livelihood? to development itself? Such a perspective on development contradicts the economic logic of a bank and calls for more government intervention than a neoliberal can stomach. It is no wonder the Bank refuses to be serious about human rights.

## EDUCATION AND DEVELOPMENT

Development for the Bank mainly refers to economic growth, and the approach taken follows neoliberal ideology. The ethnocentrically named

Washington Consensus still prevails – cut and privatize government and deregulate and liberalize the private sector. This was and is a consensus only for neoliberals – liberal and progressive political economists see very different policies as necessary (Cornia, Jolly, & Stewart, 1987; MacEwan, 1999; Reich, 2007; Reinert, 2007). Even neoliberal economists had to admit that the Washington Consensus-inspired structural adjustment policies (SAPs) followed by the Bank, the IMF, and others in the 1980s and 1990s had devastating effects on poverty and inequality (Dollar & Pritchett, 1998). Liberal and neoliberal economists in the 1990s talked of searching for a modified approach to development, a post-Washington Consensus (Stiglitz, 2003). Very little has come of this. Current rhetoric about partnership and participation offers some different directions in theory, but in practice little has changed (Cornwall & Eade, 2010). The most visible change is the Poverty Reduction Strategy Paper (PRSP) process that now anchors the Bank and the IMF's work in developing countries, but, at the end of the day, the called-for participation by civil society is mostly a sham, and the results look an awful lot like SAPs (Dijkstra, 2005). What development means and how best to achieve it is widely contested (Alperovitz, 2004; Hahnel, 2005; Reinert, 2007; Rodrik, 2007; Stiglitz, 2003; Yates, 2003), yet what we get from the Bank is not a fair look at the evidence and debate but a continued commitment to a particular development ideology (World Bank, 2004).

Within this neoliberal view of development, education is extolled. The Report (p. 11) begins: "People are the real wealth of nations … and education enables them to live healthier, happier, and more productive lives." Earlier Bank reports sometimes made it sound like education was some sort of miracle cure: "All agree that the single most important key to development and poverty alleviation is education" (World Bank, 1999, p. iii). But this is far from agreed upon. A significant question is, given the decades of intense attention to education worldwide, why do development, poverty, and inequality continue to be so problematic? This comes as no surprise to liberals and progressives who have seen three decades of neglect of the public policies needed to change this state of affairs. In fact, the market fundamentalism promoted and practiced by neoliberals so constrains government action that one of the only things government is allowed to do is education (and even here privatization is pushed – see below). It is no wonder that neoliberals must expect a miracle out of education, because other than relying on the "miracle" of the market, education is about all they have.

The Bank has been very pleased with a spate of studies that support the argument that education contributes to GNP. Such empirical studies have been controversial since their inception (Blaug, 1970). The Bank especially likes the newer versions that argue that it is less the quantity of schooling and more the quality of schooling, as measured by test scores, that result in GNP growth (Report, pp. 12, 25; Hanushek & Woessmann, 2008). However, there are many problems with these studies. Test scores are a very inadequate measure of school quality. Our ability to model the many causes of GNP variation and growth is minimal. To get their results, Hanushek and Woessmann (2008) control for only two of the literally dozens of variables that they could have included, and these two variables reflected neoliberal development ideology (openness to trade and security of property rights). There's an old saw in economics: "If you torture the data long enough, nature will confess." And to top it off, the research was funded by the Bank.

## TESTING FOR ALL

The stated theme of the new Strategy Report (World Bank, 2011b) is "Learning for All." Unfortunately, in practice, the real theme is a much narrower, "Testing for All." In many ways, the new Strategy is an exported version of the U.S. failed strategy, No Child Left Behind, which offered narrow and extensive testing but little to improve schools (Au, 2009; Darling-Hammond, 2010; Ravitch, 2010). Under the new Strategy, all countries will be pushed to test their students in reading and math.[2] Now, of course, reading and math are important, but the tests used only offer partial and inadequate measures of reading and math and neglect the many other outcomes that we want to achieve through schools. The Bank briefly recognizes this and mentions that other outcomes are important, like critical thinking, problem-solving, and teamwork and says it will develop broader outcome measures (Report, p. 26). However, this same claim was made in their 2005 Education Sector Update (World Bank, 2005), and nothing has been done. Moreover, we need schools to foster many outcomes: critical and higher order thinking, problem-solving, creativity, curiosity, civic-mindedness, solidarity, self-discipline, self-efficacy, compassion, empathy, courage, conscientization, resilience, leadership, humility, peace, and more (Bracey, 2009). It is simply irrational and inefficient to base education policy on a partial measure of two outcomes when we want and need education to do so much more.

No Child Left Behind has shown that in a narrow testing regime, what is not tested gets de-emphasized or eliminated from the curriculum

(Au, 2009; Bracey, 2009; King & Zucker, 2005; Ravitch, 2010). Children in the United States get much less history, social science, art, music, physical education, and play than they used to get. And language, math, and science education become distorted toward the test. On top of this, there is no credible evidence that 10 years of this regime in the United States has actually improved test scores or narrowed inequalities (Au, 2009; Darling-Hammond, 2010; Institute of Education Sciences, 2009; Neal & Schanzenbach, 2010). There has been a notable increase in student and teacher anxiety and dissatisfaction (Ravitch, 2010), and the whole approach follows Freire's banking metaphor, with the job of education being to deposit knowledge in students' heads.

It is interesting to note that Finland that has been held up as an international exemplar due to its consistently high ranking on international achievement tests (Report, p. 19) follows a completely different educational path than the Bank usually recommends: there are no standardized tests in Finland, and grades are not even given until 5th grade; the curriculum is broad and balanced; students don't start school until age 7 and have 2 years fewer instructional hours than in the United States; a cooperative learning model is used, not a competitive one; teaching is a very attractive profession, well paid with 50% fewer instructional hours than in the United States; private schools are prohibited; teachers control curriculum implementation and their own professional evaluation; and teacher unions are true educational partners (Darling-Hammond, 2010; Sahlberg, 2011; Valijarvi, 2004). The Bank's "Learning for All" strategy is simply another expression of its neoliberal ideology, ignoring the logic and evidence of alternative educational approaches (see Hudson and Klees, forthcoming, for a discussion of alternative approaches).

## ADDITIONAL RESOURCES FOR EDUCATION

For the Bank, more resources for education are not that important. In most of its reports, there is only somewhere between a sentence and a paragraph concerned with resources, and most of those read something like "more resources are important, *but* the key issue is how to use existing resources better." After briefly saying that the Bank devotes the rest of each report to telling countries how it thinks existing resources should be used (World Bank, 1995, 1999, 2005). The new Strategy Report is no exception. In a rather bizarre paragraph (p. 15), the Bank poses a debate over how to improve education between three positions (this is really the only policy debate posed in the whole report). The first position, which they effectively dismiss, is that more resources are needed to supply education "inputs." The second position "places less emphasis on the quantity of resources allocated to an educational system and more emphasis on the system's ability to transform those resources into learning outcomes." However, the Bank seems doubtful that government is capable of doing this and seems to prefer their third position of restructuring education to increase school autonomy and competition. This is all pure neoliberal ideology talking. The Bank's long-term position on resources has been simply irresponsible.

Of course, spending wisely is important, but more money is desperately needed. We have almost 70 million children of primary school age out of school (UNESCO, 2011a). They need teachers, classrooms, and learning materials. Universal primary education and other EFA goals are estimated to require an additional $16 billion per year (UNESCO, 2010). The Fast Track Initiative (FTI), promised and touted by former Bank President James Wolfensohn as ensuring that countries could achieve EFA goals, has, until recently, only been supplying about $300 million per year. And the $16 billion per year is a considerable underestimate. For one, given the opportunity costs of sending children to primary school and the still prevalent fees, many families need scholarships to have their children attend school. Moreover, we need much more resources as we have many more millions of students in primary schools receiving a very low-quality education who need more and better educated teachers, improved facilities, and better learning materials. Then there is the huge secondary school coverage deficit and decades of cutting back on higher education. Within a neoliberal ideology of cutting government, these resource needs are not taken seriously. I attended a recent meeting with FTI staff who actually argued that we should reduce the $16 billion estimate to something more "reasonable," not necessarily because it was incorrect but because we are not going to be able to get donors to contribute with the bar set so high.[3] This is embarrassing. Although FTI has been separating itself from the Bank, it is still part and parcel of the same neoliberal reasoning. Having taken responsibility for global education improvement, it is simply irresponsible of the Bank to continually dismiss the dire need for vast additional resources and to pretend that problems can be solved cheaply by tinkering with education's governance structure.

## THE KNOWLEDGE BANK

Since, from the perspective of neoliberal ideology, resources are not that important, what is? A major answer for the Bank is knowledge, and the Bank has spent many years trying to position itself as the "Knowledge Bank." Its earlier strategy report (World Bank, 1999, p. 42) emphasized the importance of The Bank's Education Knowledge Management System that "creates, captures, distills, and disseminates relevant development knowledge on education. Its main goals are to document the corporate memory and to include the best development knowledge." The newest Strategy Report spends a lot of time on the need for the Bank to build "a global knowledge base powerful enough to guide" educational reform (p. 1) and its "aspirations to be both a generator of new knowledge and a synthesizer of existing knowledge" (p. 53). The new Report alludes to the Bank's latest initiative in this area, System Assessment and Benchmarking for Education Results (SABER), and makes major promises:

> This program will make it possible for stakeholders to obtain simple, objective, up-to-date snapshots of how their system is functioning, how well it is performing, and what concretely the system can do to achieve measurably better results. (p. 61)

> The Bank says SABER will do this by "benchmark[ing] education policies according to evidence-based global standards and best practices." (pp. 59–60)

This is absurd. The problems with this metaphor and practice are numerous and have been criticized previously (Samoff & Stromquist, 2001; Stromquist & Samoff, 2000). The idea of knowledge management was borrowed directly from the U.S. corporate sector, as have previous fads like total quality management, strategic planning, quality assurance, performance budgeting, and current ones like benchmarking. The Bank has tried to back off from the Orwellian specter of knowledge management, sometimes reframing the idea as "knowledge sharing" (Klees, 2002). But the "creates, captures, and distills" image connotes much more the idea of control than sharing. The Bank wants to be a clearinghouse for "best practice knowledge" from everywhere – its own and that of all its partners (World Bank, 1999, p. 42). Yet, the Bank has long been critiqued as almost completely focused on its own research or that of its consultants. (What better way to provide "evidence" for their own ideological commitments?) Some years back, when it felt especially stung by this self-referential critique the Bank actually hired the U.S. Comparative and International Education Society to add 400 references to the Bank's data base so it would look like they had a broader vision.

In the new Strategy Report, the Bank devotes some space to lauding its own contribution to the "global knowledge base" (p. 52). It talks of producing some 500 journal articles and another 500 books, book chapters, and working papers. It compares its publication record in the economics of education favorably with top universities – "only Harvard University comes close." (This should be no surprise since the Bank has many economists of education focused on doing research.) I found most interesting that between 2001 and 2010 the education sector at the Bank spent $49 million dollars on research and produced "about 280 pieces of research and other analytical work" (p. 52). If you do the math, that is costing about $175,000 per piece of research! In terms of productivity this is not very impressive, but it does indicate the incredible amount of resources lined up behind a juggernaut of neoliberal ideology in education (Broad, 2006).

The idea of a central repository of "best practice" is frightening. The Bank as that repository is more frightening still. This could never be done in the North. Imagine if, in the United States, Cato or Heritage said it was or wanted to be the central clearinghouse for distilling all ideas about educational or economic best practice. They would be laughed at. Given the diversity of views, for example, in think tanks and universities, no one would even consider having some such central knowledge manager or broker. Since the Bank pretends we are all partners, all in this together, and ignores conflict and debate, the idea is that it does not matter by whom or for whom this knowledge is generated. We can pool our knowledge and let the best ideas win out in the "free marketplace of ideas." This is never true in the real world where knowledge is contested, and power governs the outcome of that contestation (Klees, 2002).

There is no "Knowledge Bank," only an "Opinion Bank," and, worse still, an opinion bank with monopoly power. This Monopoly Opinion Bank (I cannot resist – it should be known as the MOB) may not be the only source of knowledge in education in developing countries, but it is the predominant producer and arbiter of what counts as knowledge. If there was applicable antitrust legislation, the MOB's research enterprise would be broken up. The MOB's defense is that they try to incorporate all knowledge from all their partners, including countries, other aid agencies, NGOs, other civil society organizations, indigenous people, and the poor of the world. This is neither possible nor sensible nor true in a world where knowledge is contested within and among all these groups. The MOB distills and disseminates the knowledge it wants to promulgate.

## UNDERSTANDING EDUCATION

Despite all this talk of knowledge and more than 50 years working in the area, education remains a black box to the Bank. Little attention is paid to what happens in classrooms. Instead, Bank ideology makes unwarranted assumptions: that teachers are the biggest problem with education, generally being ignorant and/or unmotivated; that teacher's unions work to subvert educational reform; that better governance is the key to reform; that teacher training has little payoff; that class size does not matter; that competition is more important than cooperation; and that privatization can increase efficiency and equity. The antipathy toward teachers and teacher unions is so strong that they have been portrayed as rioting in the streets (World Bank, 2004) or sleeping on the job (actually on the cover of Patrinos, Barrera-Osorio, & Guaqueta, 2009). Neoliberal principal-agent theory is used to argue that government generally does not pay attention to the public interest; therefore, government must be constrained or eliminated (World Bank, 2004).[4] The purpose and nature of education gets short shrift. The theories, practices, and even names of noted educators like Dewey, Freire, Montessori, Vygotsky are curiously absent from decades of Bank documents about education.

It could be argued that perhaps it is best that the Bank does not focus on the core of education because then education would be subjected to even more neoliberal ideological premises and conclusions. Unfortunately, however, the Bank has recently been venturing inside the classroom as a result of its attention to neuroscience. The Report mentions the need to heed the "science of brain development" (p. 4). While the Report does not elaborate much, the Bank has been very active in examining this literature and in designing and implementing programs based on their interpretation of it. Helen Abadzi, one of the few psychologists at the Bank, has become something of a guru to the Bank, USAID, and others in the international arena looking at what neuroscience offers education policy, especially in reading (Abadzi, 2006, 2010).[5] Her work is well known for concluding that neuroscience research implies that primary, if not exclusive, attention should be paid to reading fluency, and, most specifically, young children need to reach a level of reading 60 words/minute. There are dozens of reading interventions and assessments around the world based on these premises, many financed by the Bank and USAID.

However, these conclusions are debatable. Recent literature reviewing neuroscience implications for reading does not find reading fluency to be more important than other dimensions of reading such as comprehension, vocabulary, phonological awareness, and decoding (Stahl, 2004, p. 208; also see Howard-Jones, 2010; Hruby & Goswami, 2011; McCardle & Chhabra, 2004; Sousa, 2010, Wagner, forthcoming). And none of these studies offer a numerical target for fluency. In fact, most of these reviews are very cautious in suggesting that present neuroscience research has useful implications for education practice:

> I believe that expectations for neuroscience-based, easy-to-follow recipes for classroom practice are unrealistic … .The neuroscience studies reviewed in this chapter have not provided a recipe for practice or a prescription for a certain curriculum. [Coch, 2010, p. 139, 153]

> We believe that *much* more research on decoding processes in typically developing children is needed before profound implications [of neuroscience] for instruction can be expected. [emphasis added] [Hruby & Goswami, 2011, p. 156]

Abadzi (2006) is much less cautious. She says:

> What is the minimum amount of educational inputs that will teach basic skills to the majority of students in low-income countries rather than merely the gifted? Answers to this seemingly impossible question may be deduced from some branches of "hard" science. [p. 8]

Abadzi (2006) goes even further and uses her interpretation of neuroscience findings to examine policy issues like class size, constructivism, and teacher training. I do not wish to argue here whether Abadzi is right or wrong on these issues. I only wish to show that these uses of neuroscience, like all of the Bank's understandings of education, are debatable – and significant debate, with widespread participation of stakeholders, is absent from the Bank (Turner, 2011).[6]

## PRIVATIZATION

As mentioned above, for the most part, the Bank has paid little attention to what happens in the classroom, leaving education as a black box. What attention has been paid to is governance. And, most particularly, we have seen more than three decades of a continually increasing effort to promote the privatization of education by a global neoliberal political economy in general and by the Bank most particularly. By privatization I mean efforts to diminish public control and finance of education, thus including user fees, charters, vouchers, and other supports of private schooling (Klees, 2008a). Early on in this neoliberal era, the push toward privatization was much more tentative than now, often requiring elaborate rationales and appeals to supposed common sense and evidence (World Bank, 1995, 2004). Today, it is simply taken for granted. For the Bank, there is no longer any question of "whether" privatization; the questions are "when" and "how." The Report (pp. 34–35) argues that the "nonstate sector" is an integral part of offering "education services," serving "even the poorest communities," often subsidized or contracted by government.[7] The Bank, and others, often uses the term "partnership" as a way of avoiding the negative ethos of privatization. Partnership is a misleading term in a world of vastly unequal power.

Neoliberals argue that privatization in education has generally had positive effects (Patrinos et al., 2009), while progressive critics argue that it generally has not (Education International, 2009). Most of the research in this area has been done by those who share a neoliberal perspective, so it is not surprising that results favoring privatization dominate. However, even that favorable research does not show very impressive results, and the results themselves have major problems of validity (Center on Education Policy, 2011; Klees, 2010b).

Privatization is based on ideology, not evidence. Some years ago, I attended a meeting at the World Bank soliciting comments on a health-sector-oriented World Development Report. The Bank presenter pointed out how, in many poor countries, poor people chose to be treated at private health clinics for a fee instead of going to free public clinics. This was touted as evidence of the success and value of privatization. To the contrary, I pointed out that this is simply evidence of the success of 30 years of neoliberal ideology in which public clinics had been systematically decimated, ending up without doctors, nurses, or medicine. The same has happened in education. Privatization is supposed to help meet the growing education gap resulting from years of attack on the public sector, but all it does is replace an attempt to develop good public policy with the vagaries of charity or the single-mindedness of profit-making. It boggles the imagination how we have let neoliberal ideology run so rampant that we accept "low cost private schools for the poor" as good educational policy. What kind of world is it where we consider it legitimate to charge the poorest people in the world for basic education?

## A SYSTEMS APPROACH

One of the most problematic parts of the new Strategy Report is the framework the Bank proposes to bring to its analysis of educational policy and reform. The report spends a *lot* of time talking how everything the Bank will do in developing countries should be based on a "system approach." There is a lot of abstract talk of the "stages" of a system approach (p. 40), its need to be cross-sectoral (p. 45), or how it approaches reform (p. 52). Yet the approach is never defined or supported. In a Bank that is obsessed by evidence, there is no evidence offered that a system approach is productive. Yet it is touted as globally applicable, one-size-fits-all yet again.

While not defined, as described, the Bank's system approach is a resuscitated form of systems analysis that was popular in the 1960s and 1970s. Systems analysis took a simplistic view of a linear and mechanical connection between inputs, processes, and outputs (with perhaps a feedback loop included). However, it was strongly critiqued from its inception and is generally considered outmoded today. It is worth quoting an early major critic at length:

> Supposed to solve social problems, [systems analysis] has merely served to redefine them in a way amenable to ... technical treatment. Carried to logical extremes [as the Bank does], emphasis on quantification could so limit and bias perspectives as either to distort and violate the essential nature of social problems by forcing them into a tractable ... state or to institutionalize and legitimize neglect of ... their vital parts .... As an instrument of policy-making, techniques of systems analysis have encouraged emphasis on the wrong questions and provided answers the more dangerous for having been achieved through a "scientific" or "rational" means. The ultimate result is a systematic foreclosing of promising avenues towards possible improvement and reform. Contrary to being an instrument of innovation, systems analysis encourages systematic neglect of facets and variables which could be crucial in both their generation and amelioration. [Hoos, 1972, pp. 241–242]

The Bank's related promotion of what it has been calling Results-Based Finance (RBF) and SABER are carrying policy analysis to narrow and extreme limits. They ignore the many and repeated failures of similar efforts in the past: Program-Planning-Based-Budgeting Systems, Management by Objectives, Zero-Based Budgeting, Performance Budgeting, Performance Contracting, and Output-Based Aid – all of which relied on a narrow, mechanical, engineering version of systems analysis that inefficiently focused on narrow outcome measures and were incapable of relating cost and input measures even to the narrow outcomes chosen (Klees, 2008a).[8]

## EVIDENCE-BASED POLICY

Part of the reason that a mechanical systems approach cannot work is that the evidence that is used to inform it and on which it depends is limited, debatable, and ideological. Partly, this is an institutional issue as ideologues group together and develop powerful institutional bases like the Bank. But part of the problem is that our quantitative research methods are always and necessarily susceptible to researcher biases that make fair and "objective" research impossible.

I focus here on regression analysis, the set of statistical techniques (OLS, 2SLS, HLM, probit, logit, path analysis, etc.) for uncovering the causal impact of one variable on another. While some might see this as technical and esoteric, regression analysis is the dominant methodology for studying educational and social policy and practice, and it is important that all researchers and practitioners recognize their fundamental flaws. It is widely recognized that the main problem in the use of these techniques is misspecification. Proper model specification requires three conditions: that *all* variables that affect the dependent variable are included in the model; that all these variables are measured correctly; and that the mathematical relationship between independent and dependent variables be correctly specified. These stringent conditions never can hold in practice and so every literature becomes a debate over who has the better specification (Klees, 2008b).

For example, the privatization debate centers around what are called educational production functions (EPFs) or input–output functions, where the dependent variable most studied is student test score, and the type of school (public, private, voucher, charter, etc.) a student attends is the independent variable of primary interest. But there are literally dozens of other school and home variables that affect test score and need to be controlled for in the equation. Moreover, our ideas for how to measure most of these variables are very imprecise (e.g., SES or school climate) and their mathematical interrelationship is unknown, leaving most researchers to use an obviously incorrect linear model. Given the almost infinite varieties of model specification available, it is little wonder that the school choice debates come down to proponents using specifications that result in a positive impact of privatization and opponents using models that show the opposite. The almost complete indeterminacy of proper model specification is not restricted to EPFs but affects the study of most, if not all, dependent variables of interest such as earnings, voting behavior, GNP, or even agricultural production.

Some quantitative researchers, recognizing these problems, point to a "gold standard" for research methodology, namely randomization and experimental controls. But this is no gold standard for research for at least two reasons. First, experiments in areas of educational and social importance are difficult and even unethical as experimentation with people's lives is problematic, especially over the long term. Second, in practice, experimental methods are at least as flawed as any other. Educational and social experiments are never able to achieve randomization for many practical reasons (e.g., sample attrition). Therefore, they need to use the same regression analysis techniques used by survey researchers to control covariates. Thus, experimental research also turns into an issue of specification and differences in what variables are controlled for, and how they are controlled allow different researchers to come to opposite conclusions (Klees, 2008b).

I believe that this type of quantitative methodology is a dead end, no better than alchemy and phrenology, and someday people will look back in wonder at how so many intelligent people could convince themselves otherwise. This is not a problem that better modeling and data can fix. But I should say that I do not see the essence of the problem as quantification. Quantifying social phenomena clearly has its limits and, at best, yields approximations. But cross-tabulations and correlations are useful to suggest interrelationships. As is well known, however, any associations found may be spurious and have a myriad of alternative explanations. The problem is that the causal relations underlying such associations are so complex that the mechanical process of regression analysis has no hope of unpacking them. If we are interested in looking at quantitative data, I am afraid we are stuck with arguing from cross-tabulations and correlations. This is a dismal prospect for most quantitative researchers who have spent years becoming virtuosos at data analysis and see the implications of my argument as essentially abandoning the research enterprise. However, there are lots of alternative research methodologies that depart from qualitative and critical perspectives (Klees, 2008b; Mertens, 2010). While these alternatives have their own problems and will not yield the "objective truth" to feed naive visions of evidence-based policy, they can offer findings that illuminate and inform our policy debates.

## CONCLUSIONS

The Bank is not evil; as I said before, the people who work there are well intentioned. Yet, if you see the world as I do, as structured to yield poverty, inequality, and oppression through capitalist, patriarchal, racist and other structures, the Bank becomes a major player in their reproduction through its neoliberal ideology and resultant policies. Its ideology is so pervasive that even some of its own staff (and the IMF's) have referred to the internal "thought police" that force ideological conformity (Broad, 2006). Its ideology is so pervasive that when I did a report for the Bank on education in Nicaragua in 1990, they tried to get me to change my conclusions. After the U.S. embargo and U.S.-backed Contra War, Nicaraguan education was in such dire straits that more resources were desperately needed from primary education to the university. However, the Bank was only interested in charging user fees and privatizing. When I refused to go along, they simply had a more amenable analyst to redo the study. The same thing happened to a colleague studying development policies in Southern Africa. I am sure this is a common occurrence. Bank ideology brooks no opposition.

The best evidence for that is the almost complete lack of debate in Bank reports.[9] In a meeting about a World Development Report, I asked one of the Bank authors why it contained no debate. The answer I got was that debate would be too confusing. This should be considered shocking, embarrassing, and completely unacceptable. In a world where truth and best practice is in the eye of the beholder and all positions can marshal supporting evidence, all we have is debate. Key policy institutions, like the Bank, should build their legitimacy around broad, deep, and sustained participation of different stakeholders, especially those with the least power, and around processes that bring to the table the array of positions on any particular issue (Hudson & Klees, forthcoming). The Bank has not and probably cannot do this.

To conclude, the Bank is too one sided and one dimensional to be improved. Relying on the Bank for education policy is not in the interests of the world's children. The Bank needs to stop giving education advice. It probably should be replaced entirely (Klees, 2010a). At the very least, a bank has no business being the architect of global education policy.

## NOTES

1. For many low-income countries, the Bank is one of the few available sources of external financing for social investments, financing almost 20% of all development programs in International Development Association (IDA) countries. Even for countries with higher credit ratings and which are eligible for loans from other sources, the Bank's concessional loan rates make it an important source of external financing. With over $15 billion in concessional financing for development in low-income countries available annually, the Bank is therefore able to play a unique role at country level negotiating with ministries of finance on national development strategies and policies (World Bank, 2011a). The result is that the Bank has a monopoly position in determining the educational and other social policies that accompany its loans and grants.

2. There is an increasing push to give standardized tests to all students in a country. If testing is desired, there are many reasons to prefer a small sampling of students. Some facets of performance can be assessed without the monetary costs and educational dysfunctions of a census.

3. Actually, estimates for meeting EFA goals and needed secondary school improvements have been estimated at $25 billion (UNESCO, 2010), and this underestimates the need for quality improvements and ignores the need for scholarships.

4. Principal-agent theory argues, for example, that when a principal (e.g., a citizen) has an agent (e.g., government) to work for him or her, the agent may be motivated by self-interest or captured by other private interests and not work in the principal's interest. If principal-agent theory were true, it might explain how the Bank, itself a dreaded government monopoly, has been so captured by private interests and pays so little attention to the public interest.

5. Abadzi's (2006) book is one of the few Bank publications that does pay a little attention to noted educators like Montessori and Vygotsky.

6. Over the years, some Bank colleagues have told me that I don't know how much internal debate there is, but others say that substantive debate is minimal. The proof is in the pudding, and Bank reports and policies are uniformly neoliberal. If there is any significant debate, one side always wins.

7. A cross-country study by Woessman (2009) is cited to argue that not only are private schools better than public schools but that they are even better if they are publicly financed! This is an economist's neoliberal dream result but, unfortunately for them, the methodology is completely invalid (Klees, 2010b).

8. Systems analysis was, in many ways, superseded early on by systems theory, a collection of approaches that were more organic, holistic, and qualitative (Bateson, 1972; Laszlo, 1996).

9. Liberal or progressive economists in the Bank who have been vocal have left the Bank or been marginalized. It is not only the Bank that has been shaped strongly by neoliberal economists but universities, think tanks, bilateral aid agencies, and governments as well. It is telling that even in the liberal Obama administration, despite the serious current economic crisis, critical voices get excluded. Paul Krugman and Joseph Stiglitz, both Nobel Prize-winning economists, have not been part of White House efforts because "an entire economics perspective … a progressive-economist wing" has been excluded from policymaking (Krugman, 2009).

## ACKNOWLEDGMENTS

I would like to thank Anda Adams, Sarah Beardmore, Susanne Clawson, D. Brent Edwards, Mark Ginsburg, Wendi Ralaingita, Joel Samoff, Nelly Stromquist, and Justin W. van Fleet for comments on a draft of this chapter. This chapter is reprinted in S. Klees, J. Samoff, and N. Stromquist (Eds.), *World Bank and Education: Critiques and Alternatives*. Rotterdam: Sense, forthcoming.

# REFERENCES


Abadzi, H. (2006). *Efficient learning for the poor: Insights from the frontier of cognitive neuroscience*. Washington, DC: World Bank.

Abadzi, H. (2010). *Reading fluency measurements is FTI EFA partner countries: Outcomes and improvement prospects*. FTI EFA Working Paper Series. World Bank, Washington, DC.

Alperovitz, G. (2004). *America beyond capitalism: Reclaiming our wealth, our liberty, and our democracy*. New York, NY: Wiley.

Au, W. (2009). *Unequal by design: High-stakes testing and the standardization of inequality*. NY: Routledge.

Bateson, M. C. (1972). *Our own metaphor*. New York, NY: Knopf.

Blaug, M. (1970). *An introduction to the economics of education*. London: Penguin.

Bracey, G. W. (2009). *Education hell: Rhetoric vs. reality – Transforming the fire consuming America's schools*. Alexandria, VA: Educational Research Service.

Broad, R. (2006, August). Research, knowledge, and the art of "paradigm maintenance": The World Bank's development economics vice-presidency. *Review of International Political Economy*, *13*(3), 387–419.

Center on Education Policy. (2011). *Keeping informed about school vouchers: A review of major developments and research*. Washington, DC: Center on Education Policy.

Coch, D. (2010). Constructing a reading brain. In D. Sousa (Ed.), *Mind, brain, and education: Neuroscience implications for the classroom*. Bloomington, IN: Solution Tree Press.

Cornia, G., Jolly, R., & Stewart, F. (1987). *Adjustment with a human face*. Oxford: Clarendon Press.

Cornwall, A., & Eade, D. (2010). *Deconstructing development discourse: Buzzwords and fuzzwords*. Oxfam GB: Practical Action Publishing.

Darling-Hammond, L. (2010). *The flat world and education: How America's commitment to equity will determine our future*. NY: Teachers College Press.

Dijkstra, G. (2005). The PRSP approach and the illusion of improved aid effectiveness: Lessons from Bolivia, Honduras, and Nicaragua. *Development Policy Review*, *23*(4), 443–464.

Dollar, D., & Pritchett, L. (1998). *Assessing aid: What works, what doesn't and why*. New York, NY: Oxford University Press.

Education International. (2009). *Public private partnerships in education*. Brussels: Education International.

Hahnel, R. (2005). *Economic justice and democracy: From competition to cooperation*. New York, NY: Routledge.

Hanushek, E., & Woessmann, L. (2008). The role of cognitive skills in economic development. *Journal of Economic Literature*, *46*(3), 607–668.

Hoos, I. (1972). *Systems analysis in public policy: A critique*. Los Angeles, CA: University of California Press.

Howard-Jones, P. (2010). *Introducing neuroeducational research: Neuroscience, education, and the brain from contexts to practice*. New York, NY: Routledge.

Hruby, G., & Goswami, U. (2011). Neuroscience and reading: A review for reading education researchers. *Reading Research Quarterly*, *46*(2), 156–172.

Hudson, A., & Klees, S. (forthcoming). Alternatives to the World Bank's strategies for education and development. In S. Klees, J. Samoff, & N. Stromquist (Eds.), *World Bank and education: Critiques and alternatives*. Rotterdam: Sense.

Institute of Education Sciences. (2009). *Achievement Gap: How black and white students in public schools perform in mathematics and reading on the national assessment of educational progress*. Washington, DC: National Center for Education Statistics.

Jones, P. (2007). *World Bank financing of education: Lending, learning, and development* (2nd ed.). New York, NY: Routledge.

King, K. (2007). Multilateral agencies in the construction of the global agenda on education. *Comparative Education*, *43*(3), 377–391.

King, K., & Zucker, S. (2005). *Curriculum narrowing, policy report*. New York, NY: Pearson Education, Inc.

Klees, S. (2002). World Bank education policy: New rhetoric, old ideology. *International Journal of Educational Development*, *22*, 451–474.

Klees, S. (2008a). A quarter century of neoliberal thinking in education: Misleading analyses and failed policies. *Globalisation, Societies and Education*, *6*(4), 311–348.

Klees, S. (2008b). Reflections on theory, method, and practice in comparative and international education. *Comparative Education Review*, *52*(3), 301–328.

Klees, S. (2010a). Aid, development and education. *Current Issues in Comparative Education*, *13*(1), 7–27.

Klees, S. (2010b). Review of School choice international: Exploring public-private partnerships. In R. Chakrabarti & P. Peterson (Eds.), *Globalization, Societies, and Education* (8, 1, March), 159–166.

Krugman, P. (2009). Retrieved from http://www.huffingtonpost.com/2009/07/19/krugman-white-house-exclu_n_240032.html

Laszlo, E. (1996). *The systems view of the world: A holistic vision for our time*. Cresskill, NJ: Hampton.

MacEwan, A. (1999). *Neo-liberalism or democracy? Economic strategy, markets, and alternatives for the 21st century*. New York, NY: Zed.

McCardle, P., & Chhabra, V. (2004). *The voice of evidence in reading research*. Baltimore, MD: Paul Brookes Publishing.

Mertens, D. (2010). *Research methods in education and psychology: Integrating diversity with quantitative and qualitative approaches* (3rd ed.). Thousand Oaks, CA: Sage.

Mundy, K. (2002). Retrospect and prospect: Education in a reforming World Bank. *International Journal of Educational Development*, *22*, 483–508.

Neal, D., & Schanzenbach, D. (2010). Left behind by design: Proficiency counts and test-based accountability. *Review of Economics and Statistics*, *92*(2), 263–283.

Patrinos, H., Barrera-Osorio, F., & Guaqueta, J. (2009). *The role and impact of public-private partnerships in education*. Washington, DC: World Bank.

Ravitch, D. (2010). *The death and life of the great American school system: How testing and choice are undermining education*. NY: Basic.

Reich, R. (2007). *Supercapitalism: The transformation of business, democracy, and everyday life*. NY: Vintage.

Reinert, E. (2007). *How rich countries got rich … and why poor countries stay poor*. London: Constable and Robinson.

Right to Education Project. (2011). Retrieved from http://www.right-to-education.org/

Rodrik, D. (2007). *One economics, many recipes: Globalization, institutions, and economic growth*. Princeton, NJ: Princeton University Press.

Sahlberg, P. (2011). *Finnish lessons: What can the world learn from educational change in Finland*. New York, NY: Teachers College Press.

Samoff, J., & Stromquist, N. (2001). Managing knowledge and storing wisdom? New forms of foreign aid? *Development and Change*, *32*(4), 631–656.
Stahl, S. (2004). What do we know about fluency? Findings of the National Reading Panel. In P. McCardle & V. Chhabra (Eds.), *The voice of evidence in reading research*. Baltimore, MD: Paul Brookes Publishing.
Stiglitz, J. (2003). *Globalization and its discontents*. New York, NY: W.W. Norton.
Stromquist, N., & Samoff, J. (2000). Knowledge management systems: On the promise and actual forms of information technologies. *Compare*, *30*(3), 323–332.
Sousa, D. (Ed.). (2010). *Mind, brain, and education: Neuroscience implications for the classroom*. Bloomington, IN: Solution Tree Press.
Tomasevski, K. (2003). *Education denied: Costs and remedies*. London: Zed Books.
Turner, D. A. (2011). A manifesto for a dialogue between neuroscience and education, Paper presented at the annual meeting of the Comparative and International Education Society, Montreal, May 1–5, 2011.
UNESCO. (2010). *Global monitoring report: Reaching the marginalized*. Paris: UNESCO.
UNESCO. (2011a). *Global monitoring report: The hidden crisis: Armed conflict and education*. Paris: UNESCO.
UNESCO. (2011b). Retrieved from http://www.unesco.org/new/en/education/themes/leading-the-international-agenda/right-to-education/
UNICEF. (2011). Retrieved from http://www.unicefusa.org/work/education/
Valijarvi, J. (2004). The system and how does it work: Some curricular and pedagogical characteristics of the Finnish comprehensive school. *Education Journal*, *32*(1), 31–55.
Wagner, D. A. (forthcoming). *Smaller, quicker, cheaper: Improving learning assessments for developing countries*. Paris: IIEP.
Woessmann, L. (2009). Public–private partnerships and student achievement. In R. Chakrabarti & P. Peterson (Eds.), *School choice international: Exploring public-private partnerships*. Cambridge, MA: MIT.
World Bank. (1995). *Priorities and strategies for education*. Washington, DC: World Ban.
World Bank. (1999). *Education sector strategy*. Washington, DC: The World Bank. Human Development Network.
World Bank, X. (2004). *World development report 2004: Making services work for poor people*. Washington, DC: World Bank.
World Bank. (2005). *Education sector strategy update*. Washington, DC: World Bank.
World Bank. (2011a). *Addition to IDA resources: Sixteenth Replenishment – IDA16: Delivering development results*. Washington, DC: World Bank.
World Bank. (2011b). *Learning for all: Investing in people's knowledge and skills to promote development – World Bank Group Education sector strategy. (2020)*. Washington, DC: World Bank.
Yates, M. D. (2003). *Naming the system: Inequality and work in the global economy*. New York, NY: Monthly Review Press.

# EDUCATION AND INEQUALITY: IMPLICATIONS OF THE WORLD BANK'S EDUCATION STRATEGY 2020

Devin Joshi and William Smith

## ABSTRACT

*This chapter analyzes the World Bank's Education Strategy 2020 (WBES) to assess its likely impact on inequality. The chapter begins with a review of assessments of the Bank's past education policies. It then compares four different theoretical perspectives on education policy: social class equalization, public goods, human capital, and neoliberalism. Applying quantitative and qualitative content analysis to the WBES, we identify the World Bank's approach as promoting a neo-liberal capitalist development ideology emphasizing private sector schooling and nonformal education along with standardized testing. Our analysis predicts that this strategy will not lead to major increases in educational equality in the developing world, and may even increase inequality.*

The World Bank is the largest external financier of education in developing countries. Since the 1970s, World Bank spending on education increased

**Education Strategy in the Developing World: Revising the World Bank's Education Policy**
**International Perspectives on Education and Society, Volume 16, 173–202**

**ISSN: 1479-3679/doi:10.1108/S1479-3679(2012)0000016013**

substantially from $248 million per year to an estimated $5.0 billion in 2010 (Corrales, 2006; Heyneman, 2003; World Bank, 2011). Though the World Bank has a major influence on education policy through its lending and research capacities, it is not always clear whether its policies will be able to reduce widespread educational, economic, and status inequalities within developing countries.

To address this issue, we analyzed the World Bank's Education Strategy 2020 (WBES) to assess its likely impact on inequality. The chapter begins with a review of assessments of the Bank's past education policies. It then compares four different theoretical perspectives on education policy: social-class equalization, public goods, human capital, and neoliberalism. Applying quantitative and qualitative content analysis to the WBES, we identify the World Bank's approach as promoting a neo-liberal capitalist development ideology emphasizing private sector schooling and nonformal education along with standardized testing. Our analysis predicts that this strategy will not lead to major increases in educational equality in the developing world, and may even increase inequality.

## PAST ASSESSMENTS OF WORLD BANK EDUCATION POLICY

Scholars disagree on the extent to which the Bank's education policies reduce or exacerbate inequality. In her analysis of the 1999 World Bank Education Sector Strategy, Ilon (2002) claimed that the Bank disguises its goals of promoting foreign corporations and the private sector as strategies to reduce poverty. In particular, her analysis finds that the Bank focuses its development resources on countries that accept an open market philosophy, effectively discouraging alternative development strategies among countries seeking to obtain Bank financing.

Kane (2008) is likewise skeptical of World Bank declarations of objectivity, arguing it is a politically slanted institution dedicated to promoting the economic ideology of neo-liberal capitalism. For example, the Bank has supported private education to satisfy the demands of those with the ability to pay, while also claiming that privatization enhances social mobility. According to a report from the Bank's International Finance Corporation, "private education can indirectly benefit the lowest socio-economic groups by attracting families who can afford some level of fee away from the public system, thereby increasing capacity and per student spending for the students who remain in the public system" (as cited in Hill, Greaves, & Maisuria, 2008, p. 5).

Analyzing World Bank policy documents from 1993 to 1998, Vawda, Moock, Gittinger, and Patrinos (2001), however, find a strong correlation between the Bank's lending approach and the quality of education outcomes. An additional positive example regarding World Bank lending and the quality of education is found by Eginli (2010) who finds that the Bank's support has aided the Turkish education system's effectiveness, equity, and efficiency. Specifically, Basic Education Project 1 (BEP1) made progress in reducing class sizes and providing school supplies.

Much of the literature, however, suggests that in Latin America, World Bank education projects emphasizing privatization and decentralization have not met the same success. According to Bonal (2001), marketization of education in this region "conceals the social dualisation of public and private schools networks" (p. 661). Bonal (2002) likewise faults the World Bank for five negative impacts on education: (1) The reduction of educational expenditure. (2) The lowering of enrollment rates for secondary and tertiary education. (3) A shift in the balance between public and private education resulting in increased social segregation. (4) An increase in school and geographic inequalities due to decentralization. (5) Worsening working conditions for teachers in poor countries due to implementation of education evaluations.

For example, the Bank's education loans to Mexico increased from $61 million in 1990 to $218 million in 2004, but decision-making has shifted away from the government, transformed higher education into a commodity, and emphasized standardized proficiency exams to the detriment of other areas of the curriculum. In the 1990s, three World Bank loans financed the creation of 40 private institutions of higher education in Mexico, but this has arguably resulted in increased class conflict and brain drain (Delgado-Ramos & Saxe-Fernandez, 2005). Likewise, in Africa, Gonzales (1999) claims the limited cost–benefit cost-effectiveness approach of the World Bank is generally unsuccessful in predicting education project success.

In response to such criticisms, World Bank education policies have increased emphasis on consultation, community empowerment, and participatory planning (Coraggio, 1994). However, skepticism remains regarding whether changes in rhetoric are leading to visible policy shifts (Bonal, 2001; Kane, 2008). Studying 52 World Bank education projects implemented between 2002 and 2004, Lincove (2009) is optimistic about the direction of policy. She finds no evidence that the World Bank imposes a uniform approach to education reform. Studies by Bonal (2002) and Ilon

(2002), however, argue that the World Bank implemented essentially the same programs unilaterally regardless of the local country context.

As this review of the literature illustrates, past assessments of World Bank education policy are mixed, with scholars on the political left more critical than those on the political right. Therefore, in order to shed light on how the Bank's new education strategy may specifically impact inequality we believe it is fruitful to first compare theoretical expectations behind several different education policy approaches to distinguish between those which specifically aim to reduce inequality and those which do not.

## COMPARING EDUCATION POLICY APPROACHES

Among competing education policy approaches, we compare four influential strategies with relatively clear linkages to economic mobility. This selection criterion is appropriate given the World Bank's overriding emphasis on education as an economic input and as "an engine of economic progress" (World Bank, 2011, p. 25). Exploring the primary aims of each of these four approaches enables us to situate the WBES into a particular education policy paradigm and tease out the implications of that paradigm for inequality. We begin by discussing "social class equalization" and "public goods" as two policy approaches that aim for a relatively high degree of educational equality. We then discuss "human capital" and "neo-liberalism" as two policy approaches for which educational equality is not a primary goal.

### *Social Class Equalization Approach*

Approaching public policy from a social class framework allows one to investigate the impact of education on relative poverty reduction at the class level. In classical Marxist thought, the concept of class is essential in understanding inequity because it is the fundamental unit of production and reproduction of social relationships in a capitalist system (Hill et al., 2008). The power hierarchy in Marxist terms is often represented as the ruling class dominating the working class. However, Galtung (1971) presents a more complex image of this dyad whereby the periphery is in conflict with the center both between and within nations. In other words, the center of a country (the dominant class) benefits from the subjugation of the periphery of the country (the subordinate classes) just as powerful industrialized countries subordinate developing and post-colonial countries. Within this structure of international and intra-national imperialism, Galtung argues that the center controls the means of production, the means of destruction, and the means of creation or knowledge, while the periphery provides the raw labor and learns from the educational canon dictated by the center.

The distinction between center and periphery enables us to understand the incentives for elites to promote inequality in education. Johnson and Howard (2008) define educational inequality as "qualitatively distinctive educational experiences and processes that produce inequitable outcomes or identify disparities in access" (p. 446). For example, the United Nations' current emphasis on universal primary education (Millennium Development Goal #2) and gender equality in education (Millennium Development Goal #3) focuses on access to formal schooling in terms of enrollment rates. However, equality of access is only one of the several necessary steps to improve overall educational equality. Although the access gap between different groups may diminish, the relative distance between classes in output or outcome may persist (Farrell, 2003). Without each student receiving an equal quality education and equal access to life chances, social mobility between the center and periphery may be marginal at best.

Sociological analyses have likewise found that education has historically been a tool to both help and hinder social mobility (Buchmann & Hannum, 2001). Weiner (1991) found that countries where workers or labor unions held the reins of power were more prone to emphasize educational equality than in cases where land-owning aristocracies or racial elites have controlled the government. For example, during the Chinese Cultural Revolution egalitarian policy dominated education opening both education and economic access to rural residents and women (Zhou, Tuma, & Moen, 1996). By contrast, during *apartheid* in South Africa, education was a weapon to solidify class lines. Schools worked with other institutions to block the social mobility of the black majority (Seidman, 1999).

In Sorokin's (1927) classic analysis of social mobility, different social strata are separated by a membrane and the degree of social mobility in a country depends on the level of permeability in the line (membrane) separating social classes and ethnic groups. A solid demarcation line signifies no permeability and consequently no social mobility while a more porous line allows for greater movement between the center and periphery. Characteristics that strengthen permeability include not only efforts to equalize education, but also more equal housing programs, improved health care and nutrition, and greater income parity along with levels of meritocracy and democracy in a country (Apple, 1999; Ranis, Stewart, & Ramirez, 2000; Reimers, 1999). Since socio-economic class stratification in a country is closely tied to educational stratification, the largest gaps in education are found in countries with the greatest income inequality (Reimers, 1999). From a social class perspective, therefore, the great intentions of expanding access to schooling will only have a minimal impact in "the context of broader policies that do nothing to challenge the deeper social and cultural inequalities" (Whitty, 1997, p. 58).

### *Public Goods Approach*

The second approach we examine is the public goods approach. A public good is defined as "one where benefits are enjoyed by all members of the community, whether or not they actually contributed to the production of this good" (Labaree, 1997, p. 51). In other words, public goods can be distinguished from private goods by asking the questions; "Who contributes?" and "Who benefits?" Due to the perceived public benefit of education, and its contribution to both individual and general welfare, education is often viewed as a public good (Kaul, Grunberg, & Stern, 1999a). Kaul, Grunberg, and Stern (1999b) identify two primary attributes of public goods. First, these goods do not elicit rivalry in competition – the benefits enjoyed by some do not detract from the benefits experienced by others. Second, benefits cannot be exclusively held by a single group.

Because the total social gains incurred from public goods tend to exceed private individual gains, misalignment of incentives often leads to problems of undersupply resulting from what David Hume (1961) labeled the "free-rider problem." This problem is present when not everyone that benefits is required to contribute, therefore allowing some people to simply enjoy the "free-ride" while others work. Concern with education and the free-rider problem can be alleviated by community payment in the form of taxation (Kaul et al., 1999a; Stiglitz, 1999). Those who view education as a public good further emphasize the need for increasing public financing and provision of education to reap its larger social and economic benefits.

In their work on the perception of education, Kohlrausch and Leuze (2007) emphasize that public goods should be equally available to all, that the pricing mechanism should not occlude individuals from the good and that their benefits accrue to both the individual and society. Education fails to be a public good when it does not meet these three measures. Due to the individualistic character of private market actors, strong state support for education is generally a prerequisite for it to be adequately supplied. As Stiglitz (1999) notes, "the central public policy implication of public goods is that the state must play some role in the provision of such goods; otherwise they will be undersupplied" (p. 311). In support of this approach, studies from several world regions have found a clear and direct relation between public education spending and school enrollment (Bing, 2008; Bonal, 2001; Poot, 2000).

The initiation of tuition charges however signals the shift from a public to private good. In Great Britain, the argument that education brings mainly private benefits is used to justify tuition increases (Kohlrausch & Leuze, 2007). However, tuition increases are also likely to expand the gap between the center and the periphery. Education as a private good reclassifies students as clients (Mok, 1999) and turns education into a private commodity. Ball and Youdell (2007) recognize that the movement from a public to private good includes a "conceptual shift from education as an intrinsically valuable shared resource which the state owes to its citizens to a consumer product for which the individual must take first responsibility" (p. 53). Taking on this responsibility is often difficult for low-income families. Their freedom of choice may be limited by high costs of transportation and communication that price them out of participating (Lincove, 2009). In summary, Table 1 adapted from Ball and Youdell (2007) contrasts the values and expectations of education when treated as a public versus private good.

***Table 1.*** Comparing Public Good and Private Good Approaches to Education.

| Education as a Public Good | Education as a Private Good |
|---|---|
| • Focus on individual need | • Focus on individual performance |
| • Serves community needs | • Attracts clients or customers |
| • Emphasis on resource allocation to those with the greatest learning need | • Emphasis on resource allocation to those considered most able |
| • Cooperation between schools and students | • Competition between schools and students |
| • The education of all children is held to be intrinsically of equal worth | • The education of children is valued in relation to costs and outcomes |

*Source*: Adapted from Ball and Youdell (2007).

### *Human Capital Approach*

Originating in the 1950s, human capital theory (HCT) frames education as an investment opportunity whereby education is valued primarily as a capital good to meet the ends of economic and social transformation (Olaniyan & Okemakinde, 2008). Based on this logic, "increasing the availability of education would produce net social benefits, increasing the amount of total wealth in a society and improving its distribution" (Farrell, 2003, p. 147). Howard Becker (2002), a proponent of HCT, maintains that the degree to which individuals invest in skills, ideas, and knowledge determines the success of an economy. As human capital increases it is supposed to enhance both collective capacity and individual production (Olaniyan & Okemakinde, 2008; Ranis et al., 2000; Sen, 2003). The belief that education drives economic growth can also be found in developing countries where "education is … commonly regarded as the most direct avenue to rescue a substantial number of people out of poverty" (Babatunde & Adefabi, 2005, p. 3).

In order to maximize the efficiency of investments, HCT holds that "resources in education should be expanded to the point where the value of the streams of returns on marginal investment is greater or equal than the marginal costs" (Olaniyan & Okemakinde, 2008, p. 161). Following neo-classical economic theory, the greatest economic benefit to society is assumed to occur when the supply of an object – associated with the expected return on investment – equals its demand – associated with the perceived costs. For education, this occurs by matching demand in the economy for skilled work with the appropriate number of qualified workers. The supply of qualified workers can shift over time as a function of the price of education. If, for instance, there is a shortage of qualified accountants, the price of the corresponding education required to become an accountant can decrease to encourage more individuals to move into that occupation. In the case of surplus, education prices can increase until an equilibrium is reached.

Based on the framework of human capital theory, global education expansion should lead to an increase in national economic growth, individual prosperity through education attainment, and a reduction in social inequalities due to the promotion of meritocracy (Hannum & Buchmann, 2006). Human capital theory, therefore, has been used to justify investment in education as a catalyst for growth (Fagerlind & Saha, 1997). Numerous studies have linked the expansion of schooling to increases in economic production. In a sample of 46 countries, Cooray (2009) concluded that enrollment ratios at all levels of education had a significant impact on economic growth. Similar findings are seen in the work of Mankiw, Romer, and Weil (1992) and Gemmel (1996). School enrollment also appears to spur output per worker (Babatunde & Adefabi, 2005) and job creation (Ayeni, 2003).

Educational attainment has likewise been identified as a crucial source of economic prosperity in the United States (Denison, 1967) and East Asia (Krugman, 1994). These links have been supported by a cross-national study completed by Garba (2002). Estimates based on the 2004 Current Population Study reveal that for every additional year of schooling a person completes, the individual can expect an 11% increase in their earnings (Rouse, 2007). Barro (2002) also found a one year increase in education by the general public to result in a 0.44% increase in GDP growth.

The literature also contains some results that contradict human capital theory. Negative or insignificant connections between education enrollment and growth are seen in the work of Devarajan, Swaroop, and Zou (1996), Landau (1986), and Levine and Renelt (1992). In a large, cross-national study done for the World Bank, Pritchett (1996) showed that increasing education actually produced a negative impact on the rate of growth of output per worker. However, in explaining his findings, Pritchett, justifying a human capital orientation, laid the blame on schools for not creating any human capital and bureaucratic mechanisms for wasting human capital.

One limitation of HCT is that increasing school enrollment rates can mask increases in economic stratification. Although there may be some absolute economic gain in the community, the relative earnings gap can remain stagnant or increase (Hannum & Buchmann, 2006). Studies done on Jamacia (Strudwick & Foster, 1991), Latin America (Bonal, 2001; Reimers, 1999), and China (Bing, 2008) reveal that increased enrollment has not always resulted in greater social mobility. Bonal (2001) suggests that rather than fighting poverty, increasing education in Latin America simply made poverty more visible. Explanations given for the inability of education expansion to reduce economic inequality in many societies include emphasis on the quantity rather than quality of education as well as cultural and structural impediments (Barro, 2002; Hannum & Buchmann, 2006).

### *Neo-Liberal Approach*

Neo-liberalism is an ideology of advanced capitalism that promotes private property, free trade, and free markets (Harvey, 2005). It relies on several core assumptions rarely met in practice. First, all producers and consumers in the market must have accurate and complete information. Second, all individuals are expected to act rationally to maximize their own profits. Third, it is assumed that private provision and competition among producers leads to greater efficiency and quality of goods and services than those provided by the state (Jolly, 2003).

In the past three decades, corporations have been at the forefront of a movement in the United States and the United Kingdom promoting the ideology of neo-liberalism while lobbying to privatize the education sector (Beder, 2009). They argue that competition between private schools will improve school quality and performance (Apple, 1999) and "inefficient schools will lose students and be forced to improve or shut down" (Lincove, 2009, p. 20). Based on the belief that increased quantity of school choices spurs quality improvements, the neo-liberal paradigm promotes policies to privatize formerly publicly owned services and deregulate or decentralize existing infrastructure (Hill, 2006). Although neo-liberals have been unable to find strong empirical evidence to support their claims, their policy prescriptions have nevertheless been influential as they claim their policy proposals follow "common sense" (Apple, 1999).

Privatization, decentralization, and the expansion of a competitive testing culture are three trademark education policies advanced by neo-liberalism. While they are supposed to increase efficiency, all three are likely to amplify the differences between social classes. First, privatization transfers education from a right or duty to an opportunity or commodity (Beder, 2009; Hill, 2006) increasing risk for all classes. Feeling exposed, upper and middle classes seek to maintain their privileged position by buying educational advantages in the private sector (Ball, 2003). Parents who are well off may also have more social capital and are thus better able to navigate the education system (Apple, 1999). This leaves the lower classes and the poor, which often lack the political clout to fight for equality, stuck absorbing the direct costs associated with education (Arnove, Franz, Mollis, & Torres, 2003).

Second, decentralization is "essentially the practice in which sub-national units are given responsibility for governing the education sector (finance and curriculum)" (Arnove et al., 2003, p. 327). It facilitates the neo-liberal aim of reducing the power and expenditure of the state. Bonal (2002) explains the rationale behind decentralizing education: "if public schools get the same level of autonomy as private schools and school competitiveness is boosted through quasi-market policies, the quality of education and the school cost effectiveness will improve substantially" (p. 10). Beder (2009), however, argues that the real goal behind decentralizing schemes is not local control and school autonomy, but to enable governments to abdicate responsibility for funding shortfalls.

Three types of decentralization affect the education sector: de-concentration, delegation, and devolution (Bray, 2003; Cueller-Marchelli, 2001). De-concentration occurs by transferring responsibilities to lower levels with only limited decision-making authority. Delegation is a horizontal move that shifts responsibilities from one government entity to another, and devolution is the complete reallocation of responsibility and authority to the lower level. Critics argue that by dispersing responsibility, the critical mass needed to push progressive and equalizing education reforms diminishes. For example, de-concentration, commonly seen in developing countries, reallocates the financial liability to the regional or local level. Lower class municipalities however typically lack the economic resources to fill the void left by the central government, leading to greater geographic disparities in education (Nickson, 2002).

Another policy component of neo-liberalism is the expansion of a competitive testing culture. Shifting attention from student needs to student performance reflects the promotion of market competition and the rush to secure limited resources in a capitalist system. In an attempt to maximize test scores and secure funding, schools are encouraged to transfer resources to those most capable, while diverting support from those most in need (Apple, 1999). Students who are unable to meet the given standard are tracked into opportunities more "appropriate" for their level. Hill (2006) suggests that such testing is used with the intent to produce laborers with just enough skills to fulfill their role in a capitalist society.

General finance reform has been used to support the three aforementioned neo-liberal policies. The basic logic of neo-liberal education finance was identified by Colclough (1996). First, user charges are installed for those attending school. This creates a need for scholarships to ensure equity. Second, student loans are introduced to ensure equity. Third, privatization of schooling opens up public capital for others to use. Lastly, the savings generated through privatization can be used to expand primary schooling. Unfortunately, the application of the corrective measures required to ensure equity is often unequal or omitted. Thus, neo-liberal policies such as privatization, decentralization, and deregulation often result in "intensified hierarchical differentiation between education institutions on the basis of social class" (Hill, 2006, p. 19). Additionally, these reforms aim to reduce the authority of the state, disengaging it from the education sector (Klees, 1999). By removing responsibility and accountability from the government, blame can be shifted the individual (Apple, 1999; Harvey, 2005; Lincove, 2009).

The victim is therefore culpable for the transgressions of a policy pressed upon them. Lower classes are especially vulnerable when social safety nets are removed and where there is a race to the bottom to cut wages and expenses (Hill et al., 2008). By aiming to convert education into a private rather than public good, neo-liberal policies transform the character of schooling to become "selective and differential rather than collective and equal" (Labaree, 1997, p. 51). Labaree (1997) argues that the long-term results of a private good emphasis on education include a devaluation of learning, the reinforcement of social stratification patterns, and education credential inflation.

### *Policy Impact on Equality*

Having examined four influential approaches to education policy, we now compare their presumed impacts on increasing or decreasing equality as shown in Table 2. Based on our analysis we expect the social class equalization approach to place the most emphasis on equality as it seeks to consciously narrow the education gap between the center (dominant classes) and periphery (subordinate classes). Education policies stemming from this perspective aim to increase social mobility so that a child born into a destitute family has a chance to move up the social ladder while a child born into a privileged family has a chance to move down. We expect the public goods approach to also emphasize a relatively high degree of education equality although not as much as an approach that aims explicitly to achieve equality between social classes. When education is treated as a public good,

***Table 2.*** Comparing Four Approaches to Education Policy.

| Policy Approach | Goal of Education | Emphasis on Equality |
|---|---|---|
| (1) Social Class Equalization | To reduce the gap between social classes | Highest |
| (2) Public Goods | To provide collective and individual benefits | 2nd Highest |
| (3) Human Capital | To increase economic productivity and growth | 2nd Lowest |
| (4) Neo-Liberalism | To be a private commodity | Lowest |

the state has an incentive to provide education to all because the social benefits that arise from a more educated population are believed to be worth the cost.

On the other hand, we expect the human capital approach to bring about less equality than the public goods approach because it only seeks to invest in education when there will be positive economic returns. The human capital approach is more likely to view education as a mix of public and private goods. It also does not see an intrinsic value in providing the same degree or quality of education to all in society, favoring investment in the most able students. Lastly, we expect the neo-liberal approach to bring about the lowest degree of equality because of its emphasis on education as a private commodity. Since private schooling increases the costs of education to families, privatization of schooling will make quality education unaffordable to many from the lower strata. As a result, over time there will be a wider gap between the well-educated core and less educated periphery in society.

Although some neo-liberal proponents may disagree with their position on this continuum, empirical studies of school privatization have mostly failed to substantiate the claim by supporters that new private schools would increase access, create competition that would increase performance, and open up resources to strengthen the remaining public schools. The positive results found regarding privatization have always been conditional. In their overall review of the marketplace on education, Levin and Belfeld (2003) found a modest increase in test scores; a one standard deviation rise in competition resulted in a 0.1 standard deviation rise in test scores. The improvement, however, was heterogeneous as some groups benefited while others did not. Overall, they concluded that the costs of maintaining a privatization program may outweigh the miniscule gains. Additional growth in testing scores were found to mask widening gaps between social classes (Ball & Youdell, 2007) and be temporal in nature, providing little lasting impact on student learning or the larger education system (Bing, 2008).

Schiefelbein and Schiefelbein (2002) in their study of the Chilean voucher system found an increase in the quantity of private education, a rise in the net primary school enrollment rate, and an increase in government resources allocated to education. However, this expansion was concentrated in urban areas, did not promote better education practice, and led to the dumping of poor students in public schools as private schools exhibited a selection bias. It was apparent that "the expected improvement in quality and functioning of the educational system derived from market choice, public choice, local bargaining, and a national testing system did not materialize" (p. 296).

Further studies done on the Chilean system found no evidence of increased test scores (Bettinger, 2006; Hsieh & Urquiloa, 2006) but significant increases in social stratification (Carnoy, 1998; Torche, 2005).

As in the case of Chile, two of the primary reasons privatization often fails to increase educational equality are public school flight and private school selection bias. Public school flight results in the departure of the most vocal advocates for education (Arnove et al., 2003) as well as the decline of public education quality (Carnoy, 1998; Roemer, 1992; Torche, 2005) and school facilities (Arnove et al., 2003). Some families simply lack the resources or capacity to take advantage of school choice opportunities (Lee, 1993; Levin & Belfeld, 2003; Patrinos, 1990). In the increasingly competitive atmosphere of education, private schools have also been shown to be selective in their student intake. Private schools may deny students or reject vouchers to maintain their privileged student body (Levin & Belfeld, 2003; Schiefelbein & Schiefelbein, 2002). The fight for access is based on the perceived notion that private schools provide better quality education. Upon controlling for student demographics, however, studies have repeatedly found no difference between the quality or value added of private schools and public schools (Carnoy, 1998; Levin & Belfeld, 2003; Schiefelbein & Schiefelbein, 2002; Wells, 1992).

Increased inequality due to privatization is not only an outcome found in developing countries. In the United States, voucher programs in Milwaukee (Witte, 1992) and Cleveland (Levin & Belfeld, 2003) had a neutral effect on test scores. Moore and Davenport (1990) in their analysis of school choice programs in New York, Chicago, Philadelphia, and Boston, find that these programs expanded social stratification between schools. Private schools in the United Kingdom and the United States have also been found to set prices high to create entrance barriers to low-income families (Hill et al., 2008). Overall, strong evidence points to privatization increasing economic and educational inequality while shifting the financial burden to the student consumer (Colclough, 1996; Mok, 1999). In summary, Torche (2005) finds that vouchers and privatization reform may not have created educational inequality but the practice has created an education sector "in which inequality was actualized and reproduced" (p. 335).

The related issue of whether an increased focus on testing and assessment will increase or decrease educational equality has largely been absent in past literature. The recent rise of a culture of testing is fueled by the belief that serious consequences are needed to spur real change in the education system (Braun & Kanjee, 2006). Paris and McEvoy (2000) define high stakes tests as "a variety of assessments that have control, content, and consequences imposed on students and teachers from forces external to the school" (p. 146). Assessments are commonly used by national authorities to select who receives funding, monitor the efficiency and academic progress of schools, and hold schools accountable (Braun & Kanjee, 2006). Unfortunately, these results can be misinterpreted, creating a "policy trap" where problems are created to benefit groups that stand to profit from pre-created solutions (Baker & LeTendre, 2005).

For low-income schools, the testing culture may be synonymous to a Trojan horse – presented with great popular support but riddled with dangers (Paris & McEvoy, 2000). Schools that serve the poor tend to score lower on standardized tests regardless of the instructional skill or strategy of their teachers. The low scores of these schools place them under intense scrutiny (Froese-Germain, 2001) and their diminished reputation makes the recruitment of high performing students difficult (Ball & Youdell, 2007). To ensure their livelihood many of these schools teach to the test (Froese-Germain, 2001; Glewwe, Ilias, & Kremer, 2003; Muruane & Cohen, 1986). This practice may further diminish education quality by eliminating curriculum areas deemed nonessential or not tested.

Additionally, high stakes testing has led to the increased tracking of low-income students, diminishing their opportunity to learn (Barr & Skrbis, 2008; Froese-Germain, 2001; Paris & McEvoy, 2000). Desperate to sustain themselves, some schools have even turned to dismissing students. This tactic is compounded by private school selection bias when privatization and testing culture are implemented simultaneously. Competition for funding has led schools to ensure that their population represents those that would perform well in relation to external measures (Ball & Youdell, 2007). There is also evidence that low achieving students are being dismissed on test day, placed in special education classrooms, refused admissions, or encouraged to drop out of school (Froese-Germain, 2001). These practices can widen disparities in school quality and limit the economic chances of low-income students.

## IDENTIFYING THE POLICY PARADIGM OF THE WORLD BANK EDUCATION STRATEGY 2020

Past assessments of the World Bank find its education policy has emphasized a neo-liberal or "human capital" approach to education. As discussed above, this is likely to bring about less equality than either a public-goods or social-class equalization approach to education. However, the Bank's new 2020 strategy as initially released in 2010 claims to represent a shift in World Bank policy toward a different education paradigm. To assess the degree of policy transformation we applied a combination of quantitative and qualitative content analysis to the Bank's strategy document.

Content analysis is a method that "aims at a classification of content in more precise, numerical terms than is provided by impressionistic 'more or less' judgments of 'either-or'" (Kaplan & Goldsen, 1949, p. 83). Commonly applied in the social sciences, this method has also been used to study the World Bank. For example, by comparing word frequencies in the World Bank's Global Road Safety Partnership (GRSP) with World Health Organization (WHO) safety guidelines, Roberts, Wentz, and Edwards (2006) discovered the GRSP did not incorporate many recommendations of the WHO. Building off their approach, we use quantitative content analysis (QCA) to consider whether the WBES 2020 overlaps or differs in emphasis with the four education policy approaches discussed above.

QCA generally assumes that words, concepts, and topics which appear more frequently indicate the degree to which significance is placed on them while words or concepts absent or infrequently used reflect issues of lesser emphasis (Starosta, 1984). Strengths of word count analyses include low interpretative burden in coding and high transparency, reproducibility, and reliability in terms of both inter-coder and intra-coder agreement, whereas coding of sentences and paragraphs is necessarily more subjective and open to interpretation (Cronbach, 1990; Hagelin, 1999; Hruschka et al., 2004; Weber, 1983, 1990).

In conducting our word count analyses, we compiled keyword lists from relevant literature on neo-liberal education policies (Hill, 2006; Levidow, 2002), human capital (Lanzi, 2007), public goods (Kohlrausch & Leuze, 2007), and social class equalization approaches to education (Hill et al., 2008). Recognizing that the four policy approaches are not mutually exclusive in all aspects, we selected separate keywords ("manifest content") for each policy approach reflecting their differing core emphases as a means of reflecting distinct underlying policy categories ("latent content") (Gray & Dentsen, 1998).

Following Rourke and Anderson (2004, p. 11) we made initial coding decisions based on the authors' judgements (in mutual consultation) prior to coding the November 2010 draft strategy. Since researchers should "ensure that a coding protocol neither leaves out behaviors that should be included, nor includes behaviors that should be left out" (p. 9), after our preliminary round of coding we made several revisions to our coding scheme to capture relevant keywords and synonyms previously left out (Weber, 1990). We then re-coded both the draft strategy and the April 2011 final strategy document. As a result, several candidate keywords were either discarded or not shown here because they did not appear in the document. For quantitative coding, we used the word search function for Adobe PDF files excluding endnotes, bibliographies, and annexes. We assessed frequency of word usage through keyword counts and total document word counts as calculated by Microsoft Word. To check for accuracy, the authors and a research assistant separately compiled word counts and the inter-coder reliability correlation came out to 0.99 (near perfect reliability).

Table 3 displays representative keywords for each of the four policy approaches as they appeared in the WBES 2020 policy document. These initial results support the argument that the World Bank is continuing to approach education from a neo-liberal and human capital perspective. Altogether the combined human capital and neo-liberal keywords outnumbered social class and public goods keywords by ratios of over 6 to 1 and 21 to 1 with discursive emphasis most heavily focused on the concepts of "private sector" and "market." Neo-liberal keywords appeared 65 times including "private sector" (29), "market" (29), "fee" (4), "decentralization" (2), and "competition" (1). There were also 44 appearances of human capital keywords including "(economic) growth" (24), "efficiency" (6), "productivity" (8), "economic development" (4), and "human capital" (2).

We found little support for the idea that the World Bank intends to shift toward a public goods or social class equalization approach. There were very few mentions of keywords related to public goods. The word "public sector" appeared only four times and "public good" once while there was no mention of "social return," "spillover," or "externality." There were 18 appearances of keywords possibly related to social class equalization. The words "class," "discrimination," and "Marx" did not appear but the word "equality" was mentioned more often in the finalized April 2011 document than in the draft November 2010 strategy, usually in the context of gender equality. "Human right," a term one might expect to find in a policy aiming to equalize educational opportunities, appeared only four times.

Our next analytical strategy was to compare content in the WBES 2020 to the World Bank's education strategy document issued in 1999. Table 4 compares the two documents for frequencies of keywords reflecting three neo-liberal policy prescriptions: privatization, decentralization, and testing culture. Keywords were selected from the vast literature on neo-liberal

***Table 3.*** Quantitative Content Analysis of WBES 2020.

| Education Policy Framework | Keywords | Nov 2010 Keyword Appearances | Apr 2011 Keyword Appearances |
|---|---|---|---|
| **I. Social class approach** | **Total (5 Keywords)** | **4** | **18** |
| | "Class" | 0 | 0 |
| | "Equality" | 3 | 14 |
| | "Discrimination" | 0 | 0 |
| | "Marx" | 0 | 0 |
| | "Human Right" | 1 | 4 |
| **II. Public goods approach** | **Total (5 Keywords)** | **4** | **5** |
| | "Public Good" | 0 | 1 |
| | "Public Sector" | 1 | 4 |
| | "Externality" | 0 | 0 |
| | "Spillover" | 0 | 0 |
| | "Social Return" | 3 | 0 |
| **III. Human capital approach** | **Total (5 Keywords)** | **32** | **44** |
| | "Human Capital" | 1 | 2 |
| | "Economic Development" | 4 | 4 |
| | "Productivity" | 4 | 8 |
| | "Efficiency" | 9 | 6 |
| | "(Economic) Growth" | 14 | 24 |
| **IV. Neo-liberal approach** | **Total (5 Keywords)** | **28** | **65** |
| | "Private Sector" | 9 | 29 |
| | "Decentralization" | 1 | 2 |
| | "Market" | 13 | 29 |
| | "Fee" | 4 | 4 |
| | "Competition" | 1 | 1 |

*Note*: Bold Represents to distinguish the 4 different policy approaches.

education policy[1] and comparisons were drawn between each neo-liberal policy category and the total neo-liberal rhetoric of the two documents.

As Table 5 shows, there is almost exactly the same degree of emphasis on the private sector in both 1999 and 2011. Keywords related to privatization comprised 0.24% of total words in both documents. The more recent document however talks more about "efficiency" and "fees" than the previous document, which featured terms like "private financing," "competition," and "student loans." Although neither document uses the word "privatization" explicitly, there is much discussion and promotion of the "private sector" in education and the "market" for education in both

***Table 4.*** Neo-Liberal Keywords in World Bank 1999, 2010, and 2011 Education Strategy Documents.

| | 1999 Word Count | 2010 Word Count | 2011 Word Count |
|---|---|---|---|
| *I. Privatization policies* | | | |
| Privatization | 0 | 0 | 0 |
| Private sector | 15 | 9 | 29 |
| Private financing | 4 | 0 | 0 |
| Voucher | 3 | 2 | 2 |
| Fee | 1 | 4 | 4 |
| School choice | 0 | 0 | 0 |
| Competition | 3 | 1 | 1 |
| Efficiency | 4 | 9 | 6 |
| Contracting out | 0 | 2 | 0 |
| Student loans | 3 | 0 | 0 |
| Market | 19 | 13 | 29 |
| Deregulation | 0 | 0 | 0 |
| *Total* | 52 | 40 | 71 |
| *Percent of total words (%)* | 0.24 | 0.23 | 0.24 |
| *II. Decentralization policies* | | | |
| Decentralization | 15 | 1 | 2 |
| Deconcentration | 0 | 0 | 0 |
| Delegation | 1 | 0 | 0 |
| Devolution | 1 | 0 | 0 |
| School-based management | 0 | 3 | 3 |
| *Total* | 17 | 4 | 5 |
| *Percent of total words (%)* | 0.08 | 0.02 | 0.02 |

documents. There is, however, a major shift in keywords related to decentralization. Whereas "decentralization" appeared 15 times in 1999, it appeared only twice in 2011. The related term "school based management" comes up in the new strategy three times whereas it did not appear in 1999.

A second major shift detectable through content analysis of keywords is the increased emphasis on testing culture in 2011 compared to 1999. In 2011, the words "test," "assessment," "accountability," and "results-based" appeared 94 times compared to only 20 times in 1999. As a whole, keywords related to testing culture made up 0.50% of total words in the 2011 policy strategy compared to 0.29% in 1999.

In trying to make sense of the quantitative content analysis, two initial features stand out. First, there is a high degree of continuity in emphasizing the private sector and the market in the delivery of schooling. Second, in

***Table 5.*** Testing Keywords in World Bank Education Strategy Documents.

| Testing Culture | 1999 Word Count | 2010 Word Count | 2011 Word Count |
|---|---|---|---|
| Test | 2 | 13 | 5 |
| PISA/PIRLS/TIMSS (International tests) | 1 | 8 | 25 |
| Assessment | 16 | 51 | 55 |
| Accountability | 2 | 15 | 32 |
| High stakes | 0 | 0 | 1 |
| Standard | 11 | 9 | 6 |
| Benchmark | 1 | 5 | 2 |
| Results-based | 0 | 11 | 2 |
| Monitor | 8 | 13 | 4 |
| Achievement | 22 | 7 | 20 |
| Merit pay | 0 | 0 | 0 |
| *Total* | 63 | 132 | 152 |
| *Percent of total words (%)* | 0.29 | 0.76 | 0.50 |

*Note*: PISA, Program for International Student Assessment; PIRLS, Progress in International Reading Literacy Study; and TIMSS, Trends in International Mathematics and Science Study.

2011 there is increasing emphasis on testing culture, assessment, and accountability with much discussion of comparative international tests. This new focus on testing and assessment may represent an emphasis on what Freire (2000/1970) has called the "banking concept of education" in which schooling revolves around students memorizing pre-set information for standardized tests. The question this raises is whether test-based education may be crowding out emphasis on well-rounded skills, personality development, and critical thinking that might come from a more problem-solving or dialogic approach to education.

In addition to measuring the *presence* (or *absence*) and *frequency* of keywords, we used qualitative content analysis as part of a multimethod triangulation to interpret the location (introduction, middle, and conclusion) and contexts (sentences, paragraphs, and sections) in which policy keywords appeared in the text. This enabled us to assess whether keywords were used in line with policy approach expectations. As George (1959) notes, "In order to make valid inference of intended meaning in each specific instance of communication, the investigator also takes into account the situational and behavioral contexts of the communications ... to determine which of the possible meanings of the words in question the speaker intends to convey in the instance at hand and the precise shading of his intended meaning" (p. 23).

Corroborating our earlier findings, the first sentence of the WBES 2020 executive summary, "Education is fundamental to development and growth" (p. i), reflects the Bank's view of education as primarily a means to an economic end rather than as an end in itself. Consistent with the human capital approach, the importance of education for economic growth is reiterated multiple times via "the development of a skilled, productive, and flexible labor force and the creation and application of ideas and technologies that contribute to economic growth" (p. 5). Emphasis on a "flexible" labor force is compatible with a neo-liberal orientation seeking an insecure and commodified workforce without guarantees to employment whereby employees (including teachers) are vulnerable to being laid off at any moment.

Unlike the public goods approach, but consistent with neo-liberalism there is repeated encouragement of private for-profit enterprises in the education sector. "The new Bank strategy redefines the term 'education system' to encompass all learning opportunities in a given society, whether within or outside of formal education institutions" (p. 16). Such nonstate entities include for-profit "private enterprises" which the Bank lists prior to "community organizations" and "faith-based organizations" rather than listing these entities in alphabetical order (p. 16). Not only has the Bank "set up a department focused on financing private education providers" (p. 11), but two of its four "key areas of education policy" (p. 25) are "involving the private sector in education" and "linking education systems to labor markets" (p. 25). In fact, the "rapid growth of private-sector provision of education services, sparked by the limited ability of many governments to meet growing demand for education" (p. 11) is seen by the Bank as a positive development.

In contrast to a social class equalization or public goods approach, but consistent with neoliberalism is support in the WBES 2020 for dispensing education of different quality to different strata of pupils. Aside from promoting private schooling there is de-emphasis on formal schooling in the new slogan "learning for all, beyond schooling" (p. vii) which ensures educational inequality by condoning a lesser degree of education for those who cannot afford to attend formal schooling. Instead of trying to bring all or even most children into formal public schooling, the Bank implicitly supports different levels/quality of education by explicitly endorsing nonformal education. This makes the Bank's claim that "growth, development, and poverty reduction depend on the knowledge and skills that people acquire, not the number of years that they sit in a classroom" (p. vii), come across as a pretext for not funding and not encouraging all students to spend the same number of years in school.

Also consistent with neoliberalism, the Bank places heavy emphasis on fostering a testing culture in education, particularly "assessments of student learning and achievement that cover the basic competencies of reading and numeracy, as well as other skills, including critical thinking, problem solving and team skills" (p. xii) While this proposal may be well intended, other types of education which aim to promote equity and equality or which encourage solidarity, egalitarianism, and cosmopolitanism in the minds of pupils (including democracy education, human rights education, moral education, and peace education) do not appear in the WBES.

The Bank also aims to "develop a culture of results monitoring and assessment" (p. 41) by assessing "the overall performance of education systems on a regular and systematic basis" (p. 23) through "more robust monitoring and evaluation (M&E)" (p. 33), but has chosen neither the equalization of education inputs, education outcomes, nor equality-encouraging curriculum as bases of assessment (p. 53). Under the WBES, those teachers teaching curricula related to human rights, peace, democracy, or social justice might even be assessed negatively if math and literacy become the sole or primary assessment criteria. The emphasis on testing culture by promoting participation in international tests like TIMSS and PISA may also lead to growing education inequalities. In Singapore, where testing culture takes its most extreme form, the tracking of students from elementary school guarantees not only educational inequality from an early age but also dramatic income inequality later on (Barr & Skrbis, 2008). This type of system leads to parents paying a large share of their income to private cram schools, which is precisely the aim of neo-liberalism, to turn education into a private commodity whereby those with more wealth have a market and marked advantage over those who do not (Barr & Skrbis, 2008; Harvey, 2005).

Ironically, in reading the WBES, one is struck by the importance of equality for educational performance. For example, the WBES reports that countries "with the narrowest gaps in learning achievement" are the most successful (p. viii). Yet, whereas the world's most successful education systems (based on international test scores) have free or almost free formal public education systems at least at the primary and lower secondary level, the Bank appears to be encouraging exactly the opposite: nonformal and private for-profit education. Instead of helping developing countries build up the necessary tax base to fund their own standardized quality public education systems the Bank appears to be encouraging not only private and nonformal education but also the accrual of debts incurred by borrowing from the Bank.

Though the Bank's own research has identified free schools, welfare payments to poor families, more schools in rural areas, and higher incomes in rural areas as the most important factors for bringing poor children into schools (p. xiv; p. 5), none of these policies are pillars of the WBES. Similarly, the Bank recognizes that "the period between birth and young adulthood is especially critical" (p. 12), especially between conception and age 5, but it does not prioritize this age group at all in its education strategy even though providing equal nutritional, health care, and developmental support to children prior to age 5 is essential for equal opportunities later in life. Even the claim that, "the learning for all strategy thus promotes the equity goals that underlie the education MDGs" (p. 12), is suspect as according to the WBES the Bank intends to finance MDG schools only "through 2015" (p. 33) even though such schools presumably need funding for a much longer period.

## CONCLUSION

Our content analysis highlights how the Bank plans to promote private sector education and a testing culture emphasizing assessment and accountability. In terms of policy orientation, its emphases reflect neo-liberalism and the human capital approach, and we expect neither of these strategies to significantly improve educational or economic equality in the absence of significant additional measures. In fact, the market-based solutions to education promoted by the World Bank may actually "serve to reproduce – not subvert – traditional hierarchies of class and race" (Apple, 1999, p. 8).

As Johnson and Howard (2008) point out, schools serve a function within the capitalist system to reproduce the existing class structure. Without the state serving to empower the lower classes by providing them equal educational opportunities, those groups with the power to reject a prescribed role in the economy are prone to separate themselves from the powerless, lower classes (Apple, 1978). This process reinforces class inequalities. With reduced state control and financing, the government's new role in the capitalist system, as endorsed and promoted by the World Bank, is to increasingly promote competition among private enterprises in the supply of education as a private commodity.

As discussed above, privatization, decentralization, and increased emphasis on testing culture are, however, likely to produce segregated schools attending to different social classes, thus resulting in unequal outcomes. As school choice increases, class disparity will rise (Hill et al., 2008) and poor performing schools will sink further as they absorb lower achieving students (Hill, 2006). Caught in a vicious cycle, the children of these students may have few opportunities for advancement and are likely to attend the same distressed schools, reproducing their subordinate class position across generations (Johnson & Howard, 2008; Reimers, 1999).

The alternative to this neo-liberal spiral of increasing segregation across social classes is for the state to provide free quality compulsory public education as a public good and as a means of equalizing the educational opportunities that children from different socio-economic classes have available to them (Weiner, 1991). This means not only providing public education and pre-primary health care and nutritional support to all strata of the population as a human right and entitlement of citizenship, but standardizing the quality of education and equalizing the financing of schools on a per pupil basis. This generally requires an increase in the state's tax revenue through increased tax enforcement and progressive taxation whereby those with greater wealth and inheritance pay a commensurate share in the provision of collective goods that can benefit all of society, especially the most disadvantaged. There is no reason why the Bank cannot and should not switch to supporting these policies for the provision and enforcement of compulsory public education in the developing world, as these are the very policies that most of the major industrialized country shareholders of the Bank apply in their own countries.

## NOTE

1. Asher (1994), Ball and Youdell (2007), Barksdale and Thomas (2000), Bray (2003), Cueller-Marchelli (2001), Hill (2006), Hunter (1995), Klees (1999), Mok (2000), Moses and Nanna (2007), Yin and Gordon (1994).

## REFERENCES

Apple, M. (1978). The new sociology of education: Analyzing cultural and economic reproduction. *Harvard Education Review*, *48*(4), 495–502.

Apple, M. (1999). Rhetorical reforms: Markets, standards and inequality. *Current Issues in Comparative Education*, *1*(2), 6–18.

Arnove, R., Franz, S., Mollis, M., & Torres, C. A. (2003). Education in Latin America: Dependency, underdevelopment, and inequality. In R. Arnove & C. A. Torres (Eds.), *Comparative education: The dialectic of the global and the local* (pp. 313–337). Lanham, MD: Rowman and Littlefield Publishers, Inc.

Asher, M. (1994). The role of the state in economic restructuring and development: The case of Singapore. In V. T. Anh (Ed.), *The role of the state in economic development: Experiences of the Asian countries*. Hanoi: Social Science.

Ayeni, O. (2003). *Relationship between training and employment of technical college graduates in Oyo State between 1998 and 2001*. Unpublished PhD thesis. University of Ibadan, Ibadan.

Babatunde, M., & Adefabi, R. (2005). Long run relationship between education and economic growth in Nigeria: Evidence from the Johansen's Cointegration Approach. Paper presented at the Regional Conference on Education in West Africa: Constrants and Opportunities, Dakar, Senegal.

Baker, D., & LeTendre, G. (2005). *National differences, global similarities: World culture and the future of schooling*. Stanford, CA: Stanford University Press.

Ball, S. (2003). The risks of social reproduction: The middle class and education markets. *London Review of Education*, *1*(3), 163–175.

Ball, S., & Youdell, D. (2007). *Hidden privatisation in public education*. Brussels: Education International.

Barksdale-Ladd, M., & Thomas, K. (2000). What's at stake in high stakes testing: Teachers and parents speak out. *Journal of Teacher Education*, *51*(5), 384–397.

Barr, M. D., & Skrbis, Z. (2008). *Constructing Singapore: Elitism, ethnicity and the nation-building project*. Copenhagen: Nordic Institute of Asian Studies.

Barro, R. (2002). Education as a determinant of economic growth. In E. Lazear (Ed.), *Education in the twenty-first century* (pp. 9–24). Stanford, CA: Hoover Institution Press.

Becker, G. (2002). The age of human capital. In E. Lazear (Ed.), *Education in the twenty-first century* (pp. 3–8). Stanford, CA: Hoover Institution Press.

Beder, S. (2009). *This little kiddy went to market: The corporate capture of childhood*. New York, NY: Pluto Press.

Bettinger, E. (2006). Evaluating educational interventions in developing countries. In J. Cohen, D. Bloom & M. Malin (Eds.), *Educating all children: A global agenda* (pp. 355–387). Cambridge, MA: MIT Press.

Bing, W. K. (2008). Education and inequality in the developing world. In D. Holsinger & W. J. Jacob (Eds.), *Inequality in education: Comparative and individual perspectives* (pp. 86–123). Hong Kong: The University of Hong Kong.

Bonal, X. (2001). Is the World Bank education policy adequate for fighting poverty? Some evidence from Latin America. *International Journal of Educational Development*, *24*, 649–666.

Bonal, X. (2002). Plus ca change ... The World Bank global education policy and the Post-Washington Consensus. *International Studies in Sociology of Education*, *12*(1), 3–21.

Braun, H., & Kanjee, A. (2006). Using assessment to improve education in developing countries. In J. Cohen, D. Bloom & M. Malin (Eds.), *Educating all children: A global agenda* (pp. 303–353). Cambridge, MA: MIT Press.

Bray, M. (2003). Control of education: Issues and tensions in centralization and decentralization. In R. Arnove & C. A. Torres (Eds.), *Comparative education: The dialectic of the global and the local* (pp. 204–228). Lanham, MD: Rowman and Littlefeld Publishers, Inc.

Buchmann, C., & Hannum, E. (2001). Education and stratification in developing countries: A review of theories and research. *Annual Review of Sociology*, *27*, 77–102.

Carnoy, M. (1998). National voucher plans in Chile and Sweden: Did privatization reforms make for better education? *Comparative Education Review*, *42*(3), 309–337.

Colclough, C. (1996). Education and the market: Which parts of the neoliberal solution are correct? *World Development*, *24*(4), 589–610.

Cooray, A. (2009). The role of education in economic growth. Paper presented at the 38th Australlian Conference of Economists, Adelaide, Australia.

Coraggio, J. (1994). Human capital: The World Bank's approach to education in Latin America. In J. Cavanagh, D. Wysham & M. Arruda (Eds.), *Beyond Bretton Woods. Alternatives to the global economic order* (pp. 166–171). London: Pluto Press.

Corrales, J. (2006). Political obstacles to expanding and improving schooling in developing countries. In J. Cohen, D. Bloom & M. Malin (Eds.), *Educating all children: A global agenda* (pp. 231–299). Cambridge, MA: MIT Press.

Cronbach, L. (1990). *Essentials of psychological testing* (5th ed.). New York, NY: Harper and Row.

Cueller-Marchelli, H. (2001). Decentralization and privatization of education in El Salvador: Assessing the experience. *International Journal of Educational Development*, *23*, 145–166.

Delgado-Ramos, G. C., & Saxe-Fernandez, J. (2005). The World Bank and the privatization of public education: A Mexican perspective. *Journal for Critical Education Policy Studies*, *3*(1). Retrieved from www.jceps.com/index.php?pageID=article&articleID=44. Accessed on November 15.

Denison, E. F. (1967). *Why growth rates differ: Postwar experiences in nine western countries*. Washington, DC: Brookings Institution.

Devarajan, S., Swaroop, V., & Zou, H. F. (1996). The composition of public expenditure and economic growth. *Journal of Monetary Economics*, *37*, 313–344.

Eginli, I. (2010, May 30–31). World Bank education policy: The impact of World Bank education projects (1997–2007) on Turkey. Paper presented at the World Bank's Annual Bank Conference on Development Economics (ABCDE), Stockholm, Sweden.

Fagerlind, A., & Saha, L. J. (1997). *Education and national developments*. New Dehli: Reed Educational and Professional Publishing.

Farrell, J. (2003). Equality in education: A half-century of comparative evidence seen from a new millennium. In R. Arnove & C. A. Torres (Eds.), *Comparative education: The dialectic of the global and the local* (pp. 146–175). Lanham, MD: Rowman and Littlefield Publishers, Inc.

Freire, P. (2000/1970). *Pedagogy of the oppressed* (30th Anniversary ed.). New York, NY: Continuum.

Froese-Germain, B. (2001). Standardized testing+high-stakes decisions=educational inequity. *Interchange*, *32*(2), 111–130.

Galtung, J. (1971). A structural theory of imperialism. *Journal of Peace Research*, *8*(2), 81–117.

Garba, P. K. (2002). Human capital formation: Utilization and development in Nigeria. Paper presented at the 2002 Annual Conference of the Nigeria Economic Society, Nigeria.

Gemmell, N. (1996). Evaluating the impacts of human capital stocks and accumulation on economic growth: Some new evidence. *Oxford Bulletin of Economics and Statistics*, *58*, 9–28.

George, A. L. (1959). Quantitative and qualitative approaches to content analysis. In I. Sola Pool (Ed.), *Trends in content analysis* (pp. 7–32). Urbana, IL: University of Illinois Press.

Glewwe, P., Ilias, N., & Kremer, M. (2003). *Teacher incentives.* NBER Working Paper Series 9671. Harvard University, Cambridge, MA.

Gonzales, M. (1999). The World Bank and African primary education: Policies, practices, and recommendations. *Africa Today*, *46*(1), 119–134.

Gray, J. H., & Dentsen, I. L. (1998). Integrating quantitative and qualitative analysis using latent and manifest variables. *Quality & Quantity*, *32*, 419–431.

Hagelin, E. (1999). Coding data from child health records: The relationship between interracter agreement and interpretive burden. *Journal of Pediatric Nursing*, *14*, 313–321.

Hannum, E., & Buchmann, C. (2006). Global education expansion and socio-economic development: An assessment of findings from the social sciences. In J. Cohen, D. Bloom & M. Malin (Eds.), *Educating all children: A global agenda* (pp. 495–534). Cambridge, MA: MIT Press.

Harvey, D. (2005). *A brief history of neoliberalism.* New York, NY: Oxford University Press.

Heyneman, S. P. (2003). The history and problems in the making of education policy at the World Bank 1960–2000. *International Journal of Educational Development*, *23*, 315–337.

Hill, D. (2006). Class, capital and education in this neoliberal and neoconservative period. *Information for Social Change*, *23*, 11–34.

Hill, D., Greaves, N., & Maisuria, A. (2008). Does capitalism inevitably increase inequality? In D. Holsinger & W. J. Jacob (Eds.), *Inequality in education: Comparative and individual perspectives*(pp. 59–85).

Hruschka, D. J., Schwartz, D., St. John, D. C., Picone-Decaro, E., Jenkins, R. A., & Carey, J. W. (2004). Reliability in coding open-ended data: Lessons learned from HIV behavioral research. *Field Methods*, *16*(3), 307–330.

Hsieh, C. T., & Urquiola, M. (2006). The effects of generalized school choice on achievement and stratification: Evidence from Chile's voucher program. *Journal of Public Economics*, *90*(8–9), 1477–1503.

Hume, D. (1961). *A treatise of human nature.* Garden City, NJ: Dolphin Books.

Hunter, R. (1995). Privatization of instruction in public education. *Education and Urban Society*, *27*(2), 168–194.

Ilon, L. (2002). Agent of global markets or agent of the poor? The World Bank's education sector strategy paper. *International Journal of Educational Development*, *22*, 475–482.

Johnson, E., & Howard, T. (2008). Issues of differences contributing to US education inequality. In D. Holsinger & W. J. Jacob (Eds.), *Inequality in Education: Comparative and Individual Perspectives* (pp. 444–460). CERC Studies in Comparative Education. The University of Hong Kong: Hong Kong.

Jolly, R. (2003). Human development and neo-liberalism: Paradigms compared. In S. Fukuda Parr & A. K. Shiva Kumar (Eds.), *Readings in human development* (pp. 82–92). New York, NY: Oxford University Press.

Kane, L. (2008). The World Bank, community development and education for social justice. *Community Development Journal*, *43*(2), 194–209.

Kaplan, A., & Goldsen, J. M. (1949). The reliability of content analysis categories. In H. D. Lasswell, N. Leites and Associates (Eds.), *Language of politics: Studies in quantitative semantics* (pp. 83–112). New York, NY: George W. Stewart.

Kaul, I., Grunberg, I., & Stern, M. (1999a). Introduction. In I. Kaul, I. Grunberg & M. Stern (Eds.), *Global public goods: International cooperation in the 21st century* (pp. XIX–XXXVIII). New York, NY: Oxford University Press.

Kaul, I., Grunberg, I., & Stern, M. (1999b). Defining global public goods. In I. Kaul, I. Grunberg & M. Stern (Eds.), *Global public goods: International cooperation in the 21st century* (pp. 2–19). New York, NY: Oxford University Press.

Klees, S. (1999). Privatization and neo-liberalism: Ideology and evidence in rhetorical reform. *Current Issues in Comparative Education*, *1*(2), 19–26.

Kohlrausch, B., & Leuze, K. (2007). Implications of marketization for the perception of education as public or private good. In K. Martens, A. Rusconi & K. Leuze (Eds.), *New arenas of education governance* (pp. 195–213). New York, NY: Palgrave Macmillan.

Krugman, P. (1994). The myth of Asian's miracle. *Foreign Affairs*, *73*, 67–78.

Labaree, D. (1997). Public goods, private goods: The American struggle over educational goals. *American Educational Research Journal*, *34*(1), 39–81.

Landau, D. (1986). Government and growth in less developed countries: An empirical study. *Economic Development and Cultural Change*, *35*, 35–75.

Lanzi, D. (2007). Capabilities, human capital and education. *Journal of Socio-Economics*, *36*, 424–435.

Lee, V. (1993). Education choice: The stratifying effects of selecting schools and courses. *Educational Policy*, *7*(2), 125–148.

Levidow, L. (2002). Marketizing higher education: Neoliberal strategies and counter-strategies. In K. Robbins & F. Webster (Eds.), *The virtual university? Knowledge, markets and management* (pp. 227–248). New York, NY: Oxford University Press.

Levin, H., & Belfeld, C. (2003). The marketplace in education. *Review of Research in Education*, *27*, 183–219.

Levine, R., & Renelt, D. (1992). A sensitivity analysis of cross-country growth regressions. *American Economic Review*, *82*, 942–963.

Lincove, J. (2009). Are markets good for girls? The World Bank and neoliberal education reforms in developing countries. *The Whitehead Journal of Diplomacy and International Relations*, x(1), 19–35.

Mankiw, G., Romer, D., & Weil, D. (1992). A contribution to the empirics of economic growth. *Quarterly Journal of Economics*, *107*, 407–437.

Mok, K. H. (1999). Education and the market place in Hong Kong and Mainland China. *Higher Education*, *37*, 133–158.

Mok, K. H. (2000). Marketizating higher education in post-Mao China. *International Journal of Educational Development*, *20*, 109–126.

Moore, D., & Davenport, S. (1990). School choice: The new, improved sorting machine. In W. Boyd & H. Walberg (Eds.), *Choice in education* (pp. 187–223). Berkeley, CA: McCutchan.

Moses, M. S., & Nanna, M. J. (2007). The testing culture and the persistence of high stakes testing reforms. *Education and Culture*, *23*(1), 55–72.

Muruane, R., & Cohen, D. (1986). Merit pay and the evaluation problem: Why most merit pay plans fail and few survive. *Harvard Educational Review*, *56*(1), 1–17.

Nickson, A. (2002). Education reform in Latin America: Decentralisation or restructuring. In C. Abel & C. Lewis (Eds.), *Exclusion and engagement: Social policy in Latin America* (pp. 266–284). London: Institute of Latin America Studies.

Olaniyan, D. A., & Okemakinde, T. (2008). Human capital theory: Implications for educational development. *European Journal of Scientific Research*, *24*(2), 157–162.
Patrinos, H. A. (1990). The privatization of higher education in Colombia: Effects on quality and equity. *Higher Education*, *20*, 161–173.
Paris, S., & McEvoy, A. (2000). Harmful and enduring effects of high-stakes testing. *Issues in Education*, *6*(1), 145–159.
Pritchett, L. (1996). *Where has all the education gone*? The World Bank Policy Research Working Paper 1581, Development Economics Research Group, The World Bank, Washington, DC.
Poot, J. (2000). A synthesis of empirical research on the impact of government on long-run growth. *Growth and Change*, *31*, 516–547.
Ranis, G., Stewart, F., & Ramirez, A. (2000). Economic growth and human development. *World Development*, *28*(2), 197–219.
Reimers, F. (1999). Educational opportunities for low-income families in Latin America. *Prospects*, *29*(4), 535–549.
Roberts, I., Wentz, R., & Edwards, P. (2006). Car manufacturers and global road safety: A word frequency analysis of road safety documents. *Injury Prevention*, *12*, 320–322.
Roemer, J. (1992). Providing equal educational opportunity: Public vs. voucher schools. *Social Philosophy and Policy*, *9*(1), 291–309.
Rourke, L., & Anderson, T. (2004). Validity in quantitative content analysis. *Educational Technology Research and Development*, *52*(1), 5–18.
Rouse, C. (2007). Consequences for the labor market. In C. Belfield & H. Levin (Eds.), *The price we pay: Economic and social consequences of inadequate education* (pp. 99–124). Washington, DC: Brookings Institution Press.
Schiefelbein, E., & Schiefelbein, P. (2002). Paradoxes of Chilean education reform, 1989–2000. In C. Abel & C. Lewis (Eds.), *Exclusion and engagement: Social policy in Latin America* (pp. 285–300). London: Institute of Latin America Studies.
Seidman, G. (1999). Is South Africa different? Sociological comparisons and theoretical contributions from the land of apartheid. *Annual Review of Sociology*, *25*, 419–440.
Sen, A. (2003). Human capital and human capability. In S. Fukada-Parr & A. K. Shiva Kumar (Eds.), *Readings in human development* (pp. 35–37). New York, NY: Oxford University Press.
Sorokin, P. (1927). *Social mobility*. New York: Harper and Row.
Starosta, W. J. (1984). Qualitative content analysis: A Burkean perspective. In W. B. Gudykunst & Y. Y. Kim (Eds.), *Methods for intercultural communication* (pp. 185–194). Beverly Hills, CA: Sage.
Stiglitz, J. (1999). Knowledge as a global public good. In I. Kaul, I. Grunberg & M. Stern (Eds.), *Global public goods: International cooperation in the 21st century* (pp. 308–325). New York, NY: Oxford University Press.
Strudwick, J., & Foster, P. J. (1991). Origins and destinations in Jamaica. *International Journal of Educational Development*, *11*, 149–159.
Torche, F. (2005). Privatization reform and inequality of educational opportunity: The case of Chile. *Sociology of Education*, *78*(4), 316–343.
Vawda, A. Y., Moock, P., Gittinger, J. P., & Patrinos, H. A. (2001). *Economic analysis of World Bank education projects and project outcomes*. The World Bank Policy Research Working Paper 2564, Development Economics Research Group, The World Bank, Washington, DC.

Weber, R. P. (1983). Measurement models for content analysis. *Quality and Quantity, 17*, 127–149.

Weber, R. P. (1990). *Basic content analysis* (2nd ed.). Newbury Park, CA: Sage.

Weiner, M. (1991). *The child and the state in India: Child labor and education policy in comparative perspective*. Princeton, NJ: Princeton University Press.

Wells, A. (1992). The sociology of choice: Why some win and others lose in the educational marketplace. Presented at Economic Policy Institute symposium, Choice: What Role in American Education?

Whitty, G. (1997). Creating quasi-markets in education. In M. W. Apple (Ed.), *Review of research in education* (Vol. 22). Washington, DC: American Educational Research Association.

Witte, J. (1992). The Milwaukee private-school parental choice program. Paper presented at Economic Policy Institute symposium, "Choice: What Role in American Education?" Washington, DC.

World Bank. (1999). *Education sector strategy*. Washington, DC: World Bank Press.

World Bank. (2010). *Education sector strategy 2020: Draft strategy*. Retrieved from www.worldbank.org/educationstrategy2020. Accessed on November 15.

World Bank. (2011). *Learning for all: Investing in people's knowledge and skills to promote development: World Bank Group Education Strategy 2020*. Washington, DC: World Bank Press.

Yin, Q. P., & Gordon, W. (1994). The marketization of China higher education: A critical assessment. *Comparative Education, 30*(3), 217–237.

Zhou, X., Tuma, N. B., & Moen, P. (1996). Stratification dynamics under state socialism: The case of urban China, 1949–1993. *Social Forces, 74*, 759–796.

# CONSTRUCTING AND MEASURING TEACHER EFFECTIVENESS IN GLOBAL EDUCATION REFORM

Rachael Gabriel and Richard Allington

## ABSTRACT

*The primacy of teacher effects on student achievement has been well documented from a variety of methodological approaches within the field of education research. Governments across the globe have or will address educational equity, especially the education of the poor, by designing programs to attract, train, develop, retain, and study more effective teachers. In their Concept Note, the World Bank also raises "fundamental questions" that balance upon an understanding of the development and measurement of teacher effectiveness. These include question 1: "What are the most important challenges in the next decade for building knowledge and skills for life and work in different country contexts?" and question 3: "What educational results should the Bank be accountable for in the next ten years, and how would we measure these achievements?" In this chapter, we build upon the extensive research that suggests teacher effectiveness ought to be the primary goal of educational reform efforts across the globe. We highlight the complexity of measuring effectiveness,*

**Education Strategy in the Developing World: Revising the World Bank's Education Policy**
**International Perspectives on Education and Society, Volume 16, 203–228**

**ISSN: 1479-3679/doi:10.1108/S1479-3679(2012)0000016014**

*especially across countries and varied contexts for education. We argue that the ways in which effectiveness is measured will have a direct impact on the potential of any reform policy to positively influence the overall effectiveness of a teaching force and the achievement of its students.*

The primacy of teacher effects on student achievement has been well documented from a variety of methodological approaches within the field of education research. Governments across the globe have or will address educational equity, especially the education of the poor, by designing programs to attract, train, develop, retain, and study more effective teachers (Teach For All, 2010; U.S. Department of Education, 2010). Within their Education Sector Strategy for 2020, The World Bank Group has highlighted the trend in developing countries that "gains in access have also turned attention to the challenge of improving the quality of education and accelerating learning" (p. 1). This chapter builds upon the growing body of research that suggests teacher effectiveness ought to be the primary goal of educational development and reform efforts across the globe. Though studies of educational effectiveness in general, or school effectiveness specifically, have yielded important information for policymakers about the structure and development of schools, we argue that teacher effectiveness can and must be considered as a factor on its own as study after study finds teacher effects are the largest (though by no means the only) factor in student achievement (Nye, Konstantopoulos, & Hedges, 2004; Sanders & Rivers, 1996; Stuhlman & Pianta, 2009). Teacher effects remain relatively constant even when a teacher is asked to change grades, schools, or curriculum (Handley & Kronley, 2006). Indeed studies of exemplary elementary school teachers find that such teachers remain effective even when methods, materials, and administration change (Allington & Johnston, 2002). Moreover, teacher effectiveness, unlike poverty, generational illiteracy, health care, etc., is in many ways the factor in education with which educators and educational administrators or policymakers have the greatest leverage. Thus we focus this chapter on classroom-level analysis of teacher effectiveness. Further we use findings and examples from a range of studies generated by the current and unprecedented fervor (Gabriel & Lester, 2010; U.S. Department of Education, 2010) surrounding the notion of teacher effectiveness policies in the United States in order to illustrate the main tenets, pitfalls, and considerations for teacher effectiveness policies worldwide.

Within this chapter, a review of research on teacher effectiveness and evaluation highlights the complexity of defining and measuring effectiveness, especially across varied contexts for education. Given the contingent and constructive nature of what counts as effective teaching, the ways in which effectiveness is measured will have a direct impact on the potential of any reform policy to positively influence the overall effectiveness of a teaching force and therefore the achievement of its students. We therefore suggest encouraging local adaptations of global policies for encouraging and measuring effective teaching.

## PERSPECTIVES AND THEORETICAL FRAMEWORK

The goal of the World Bank Education Sector Strategy is to "improve the quality of education and accelerate learning" (World Bank, 2011, p. 2) among children in developing countries. A growing body of research provides evidence that teacher effects on student achievement have a greater impact than any other contributing factor (Nye et al. (2004); Sanders & Rivers, 1996; Stuhlman & Pianta, 2009). An effective teacher can overcome the predicted influence of poverty, parental educational attainment, prior school experience, ethnicity, socioeconomic status (Sanders & Rivers, 1996), and even class size (Nye et al., 2004). Studies have also shown that teacher effects are both cumulative and residual. That is, "differences in student performance of 50 percentile points were observed after only three years" (Sanders & Rivers, 1996). Specifically, the lowest achieving students are the first to benefit by exposure to more effective teachers. Stuhlman and Pianta (2009) report that a teacher who earns a high rating for both emotional and academic support on their Classroom Assessment Scoring System (CLASS) can close gaps in the achievement of students from different socioeconomic backgrounds by the end of first grade. Unfortunately, in many cases, the lowest achieving students are the least likely to be assigned to an effective teacher, and few teachers in their large-scale, national study earned high ratings in both areas. Though the findings of this study can not necessarily be extrapolated outside the United States, the idea that students in greatest need of educational support are often served by the least prepared teacher candidates is not at all uncommon in developing countries or within struggling educational systems. Indeed, as the World Bank has noted, "learning levels that have been measured in many developing countries are alarmingly low especially among disadvantaged populations" (p. 3).

These three studies of teacher effect are often cited as a foundation for arguments about the primacy of teacher effects on students' opportunity to learn. As the World Bank (2010) has noted, educational institutions are not solely responsible for education, as learning does not begin or end in school classrooms. Though schools cannot and should not take responsibility for the influence of student health, housing, poverty, and family status (Ravitch, 2010), there are countless examples of effective teachers leading students to overcome such odds in terms of their academic achievement. We therefore write from the perspective that teacher effectiveness is a key lever in the improvement of educational opportunity for all students, especially those at socioeconomic risk. We caution, however, that there are no static or universal definitions for effective teaching. What counts as effective is in part determined by the tools selected to measure it, and in part by local values about the goals of education (Anderson, 1991). In the past decade, the World Bank has made great strides toward connecting their systems and policies to local contexts and local feedback by decentralizing 40 percent of staff and placing them in country offices. Research in teacher evaluation suggests that increases in communication between local, regional, and countrywide stakeholders will only improve the relevance and accuracy of an evaluation tool.

Darling-Hammond (1990) writes, "Whether intentionally or not, a teacher-evaluation system represents the incentive structure and mode of accountability implicitly adopted by an organization or profession. It communicates conceptions about teaching and expectations regarding performance priorities, norms for behavior, and the nature of the work itself" (p. 21). In other words, by outlining criteria for incentives and systems of accountability, an evaluation system provides implicit guidelines that both set and limit possibilities for what counts as good teaching. They thus construct a version of education that privileges certain kinds of teaching and resists others. As Noblit (2004) has written, "how we choose to represent reality is also an act of power and alters the interpretations of reality" (p. 185). In the case of teaching and learning, how we choose to represent teaching within definitions of effectiveness and evaluation criteria alters the ways in which teaching is interpreted and understood. The standards and criteria used to evaluate teachers are constructive of the ways in which teacher effectiveness is understood. We argue that local participation in the goal-setting portion of the policy-making process increases the possibility that local values are reflected in conceptions of effective teaching, and that local stakeholders appropriately and productively interpret the results of teacher evaluation.

## DEFINITIONS AND MEASURES OF TEACHER EFFECTIVENESS

A review of research on effective teaching demonstrates a large range of possible methods for the identification and measurement of effectiveness in teaching. Each method rests upon a different set of assumptions about the ways in which teaching and learning can be understood and the goals of education. Some researchers rely on the nominations of inside experts (e.g., school principals, administrators, or students) when identifying effective teachers to study (Allington & Johnston, 2002; Bohn, Roehrig, & Pressley, 2004; Pressley, Allington, Wharton-McDonald, Block, & Morrow, 2001; Pressley, Rankin, & Yokoi, 1996). This method assumes that effective teaching can be observed and that people will "know it when they see it" based on their own frame of reference and personal judgment. It works to construct a version of effectiveness in which those who work with or around teachers are best able to judge their effectiveness, thus privileging local knowledge and contextualized notions of the role of the teacher and purposes of schooling. Dennis (2009) and Haynes (2008) have suggested that notions of effectiveness within U.S. schools are heavily influenced by the philosophy of the school's leader (principal). That is, the person who supervises and evaluates teachers influences notions of what counts as effective by supporting or praising certain practices, and discouraging others. Poplin and Rivera (2009) caution, however, that teachers whose students earn very high test scores in otherwise low-performing schools are often not considered effective or well accepted within their schools because their practices do not conform to the school's norms. In cases where the school's norms have not been linked to desired student outcomes, it can be helpful for other, less localized measures of effectiveness to be taken into consideration when evaluating and supporting teacher effectiveness. Thus specific, local knowledge might be productively balanced by other sources of evidence or sets of criteria.

Researchers who have studied large and diverse samples of teachers across contexts can be a valuable resource for describing themes and patterns across examples of effective teaching but do not guarantee that these themes match local values and goals for education. Instead of relying on local stakeholder opinions, some researchers have developed their own sets of criteria for identifying effective teachers as a result of their search for trends and patterns in effective teaching (Haberman, 2005; Liesveld, Miller, & Robinson, 2005; Stuhlman & Pianta, 2009). This method positions researchers as experts on what counts as effectiveness based on a large frame of reference (comparisons of teachers across regions and over time), but little specific or local knowledge to the task of identifying effective teachers. As Anderson (1991) cautions, teachers' effectiveness is predicated on their ability to consistently reach the implicit and explicit goals set both by them and for them by others. It is therefore possible that a teacher is effective in terms of some, but not all of the metrics they are held accountable for. This method also assumes that there are universals of effective teachers that can be applied and made visible across settings. In this case, local values would need to be applied in order to weigh conflicting metrics. Researcher-developed scales or rubrics are most often the result of studying trends in observable characteristics of a large sample of teachers (Liesveld et al., 2005). Though some include personal characteristics, others focus on a teacher's use of "best practices" or certain approaches to teaching and learning (Haberman, 2005); styles of leadership (Liesveld et al., 2005); or kinds of interactions with students (Stuhlman & Pianta, 2009). This method represents a middle ground between relying on local appraisals of effectiveness based on the opinions of individuals and standardized measures of effectiveness based on student achievement data. Unfortunately, such tools are rarely validated by entities other than the developers and are rarely applied to populations of teachers across countries or contexts.

The very notion of collecting and disseminating a set of "best practices" flirts with a reductionist, positivist notion that there is one way or set of ways to teach well and begs the question: who decides? In practice, however, what is considered "best practice" is often too broad to be prescriptive of specific actions. Rather it is descriptive of patterns and themes that have been linked with desired outcomes across contexts for teaching. For examples of the collection and dissemination of broad best practices, see Danielson's *Framework for Teaching* (1996) and Steven Farr's *Teaching as Leadership* (Farr, Kopp, & Kamras, 2010). Both use evidence from a large body of classroom observations in a single country to describe teaching along a spectrum of beginning to advanced proficiency. Danielson's model describes best practice in terms of what teachers do, while Farr's model describes best practice in terms of what students do as a result of a teacher's actions. The mechanisms, assumptions, and uses of evaluation tools like these and others will be described in the following section.

A third group of teacher effectiveness studies have used higher-than-average or higher-than-expected student test scores to identify effective teachers (Mathematica Policy Research, 2009; Poplin & Rivera, 2009;

Reffitt & Pressley, 2007). This positions student achievement as the deciding factor in teacher effectiveness and allows anyone with access to student test scores to judge effectiveness, thus diminishing the need for proximity or specific, local knowledge for decision-making. At first glance, it seems that such methods would minimize subjectivity, yet, as will be described later in this chapter, even statistical measurements operate on sets of assumptions about the nature of teaching and learning that must be considered as closely as subjective appraisals. Though sometimes viewed as more objective or authoritative, statistical measures are not exempt from bias or error (Ewing, 2011).

In attempts to take advantage of the perspectives of local, global, and statistical effectiveness indicators, several researchers have combined approaches by comparing local nominations to statistical analyses of student achievement scores and their own observations (Allington & Johnston, 2002; Bohn et al., 2004; Teddlie, Creemers, Kyriakides, Muijs, & Yu, 2006). Such studies offer important insights into the ways in which data from each approach can interact to inform an effectiveness rating and the circumstances under which various indicators tend to converge. Empirical studies that explore the interactions of different approaches will be an important contribution to the thoughtful application of each in future research but are currently underrepresented. Currently, there is no clear "right" way to define or balance measurements of teacher effectiveness since what counts as evidence of good teaching varies across contexts and over time. If the goal of good teaching is an "excellent education," a construct that itself requires definition, then goals for education inform definitions of good teaching. Such goals are not just context, but also time specific. They are therefore difficult to generalize across communities, let alone countries, and hard to standardize over time. Since different people use education for different reasons (the acquisition of specific knowledge, general knowledge, cultural capital, socioeconomic mobility, etc.) what counts as "effective" varies along with varied perceived purposes and possibilities for education.

Existing research on teacher effectiveness falls somewhere along a spectrum from privileging local knowledge and values to statistical objectivity, with more recent studies attempting to balance the two. Whether researchers believe effectiveness is something that can be calculated, seen, sensed, or otherwise decided, as Rabinowitz and Travers (1953) have written, "The effective teacher does not exist pure and serene, available for scientific scrutiny ... the ultimate definition of the effective teacher does not involve discovery but decree" (p. 212). That is, teacher effectiveness is *decided*, not discovered by researchers. It must thus be collaboratively constructed, not uniformly mandated by a single body of policymakers.

In the following section, an overview of teacher evaluation practices is presented in order to illustrate the ways in which policymakers have decided to construct effectiveness based on the tools they select to measure it. This overview builds upon reviews of research conducted by Goe, Bell, and Little (2008), Goe (2007), and the multiperspective volume on teacher assessment edited by Kennedy (2010).

## RESEARCH ON TEACHER EVALUATION

Similar to research aimed at investigating teacher effectiveness, syntheses of research on teacher evaluation (Goe et al., 2008; Kennedy, 2010) find great variation in the tools and criteria used to evaluate teachers. In their recent synthesis of research related to teacher evaluation, Goe et al. (2008) suggest teacher evaluation can be approached from three different, but related angles: inputs, processes, or outputs. For example, studies of teacher quality most often compare teachers based on evidence of preparation (certification, licensure, and degrees held), demographic information, or personal characteristics (Campbell, Kyriakides, Muijs, & Robinson, 2004; Cooper & Alvarado, 2006). Quality is thus often operationally defined as being synonymous with *qualifications* that people carry with them (inputs) into the profession. This can be problematic when comparing developing countries with developed countries as teachers in developing countries are frequently underqualified but may very well be meeting both local and international goals for education in their contexts (Anderson, 1991). Processes, on the other hand, include teacher actions and interactions with students, colleagues, and the larger community. Processes are usually measured by observation, survey or nomination from those who are privy to the everyday work of the teacher – the *process* of teaching. The evaluation of processes is the most subjective of the three as the interactions between students and teachers are famously value laden and culturally contingent (Au, 1993; Gay, 2000; Ladson-Billings, 1994; Philips, 1983). The last angle, outputs, involves the study of a teacher's effect on whatever is viewed as the *desired outcome* of their work. In many cases, this angle casts student test scores as the outcome of effective teaching and thus identifies effectiveness in teaching by the level or differential (expected versus observed) of student scores. In almost all cases outputs implicitly refer to scores on local or international standardized tests, but may also include attainment measures such as graduate rates, and pass or acceptance rates on performance or career assessments. Such reliance on output measures assumes extremely high reliability and validity for individual assessments. Moreover, it limits the evidence of teacher effect to constrained set of content that can be assessed using multiple choice questions.

Recently, teacher quality or effectiveness comparisons have included multiple measures of quality such as observations, artifacts, interviews, student scores, and surveys (Teddlie et al., 2006). The relationships between such measures, and the weights and balances of multiple streams of evidence, are still under investigation (MET Project, 2010) even as policies are being made surrounding their use in decisions about teacher preparation, recruitment, development, promotion, and termination. Internationally, teams of researchers have worked to produce differentiated models of teacher effectiveness (Campbell et al., 2004) that investigate the possibility that teachers have profiles of effectiveness that make them more or less effective depending on the content they are teaching and characteristics of the students they are teaching. Teddlie et al. (2006) have similarly developed a system for teacher observation and feedback with an international, interdisciplinary team multiple sets of criteria for evaluating teachers across varied contexts. Their instrument, the International System for Teacher Observation and Feedback (ISTOF) was developed in order to create a tool with international validity, using theory and evidence from existing effectiveness literature. Their criteria are therefore very similar to many of the commercially available rubrics (Danielson, 1996; Farr et al., 2010) for evaluating teaching with components that address classroom environment, instructional planning, adaptive teaching, etc.

In the following section, we provide a synthesis of teacher evaluation research from various angles and discuss the underlying assumptions and implications of each. We follow with a section describing the need for transparency in assumptions, as well as flexibility and local engagement in the choices of tools used to measure and encourage teacher effectiveness.

## INPUTS

International comparisons of teacher quality most often compare qualifications for teaching, rather than evidence of teaching or the outcomes of teaching. Goe et al. (2008) define such qualifications as: "what a teacher brings to his or her position, generally measured as teacher background, beliefs, expectations, experience, pedagogical and content knowledge, certification and licensure, and educational attainment." Historically, the measures of teacher quality have changed along with definitions of the role of the teacher and purpose of education. More recently, other teacher characteristics besides academic ability have been taken into consideration including certifications, degrees held, and personal characteristics. Input measures of teacher quality rest on two assumptions about the nature of teaching and learning. This first is that there is a significant, measurable difference between candidates with different input profiles. The second underlying assumption is that there is a causal link between student achievement and measurable or observable inputs. Each will be examined in the following paragraphs as a range of input measures are explored and critiqued.

It is both conceptually and technically difficult to construct convincing causal links between teacher background, beliefs, or expectations. It is conceptually difficult because it requires the assumption that beliefs and expectations are relatively static constructs – that they remained the same across the year(s) teachers taught and are thus connected to the effectiveness of their teaching. As Richardson, Anders, Tidwell, and Lloyd (1991) have pointed out, teacher beliefs can change even within the space of a single study and may change frequently over time. It is technically difficult because of the inherent difficulty in measuring beliefs and expectations and because of the possibility of conflict or distance between teachers' reported beliefs and actions. In his review of research on the impact of teacher beliefs on their practice, Fang (1996) reported that there are two conflicting theses within this body of research: consistency and inconsistency of beliefs and practice. Many studies have demonstrated that teacher decision-making is influenced by a variety of factors besides their beliefs about or expectations for their students. School culture, professional expectations, sense of autonomy, availability of resources, experience and other factors can muddy any observable link between beliefs and actions. Some researchers have suggested that teacher background, especially sharing a similar background to their students, is linked with increased effectiveness. Though controversial because of its implications for cross- and multicultural teaching and learning, such research has been the basis of programs that recruit teachers from within targeted communities (e.g., minority teaching fellowships, North Carolina Teaching Fellows, Teach For America, and Teach for All) but has not to our knowledge been empirically investigated on a large scale. In conclusion, there is evidence that both background and beliefs are important for teacher effectiveness, but the extent and mechanism of this importance are unclear.

Studies of teacher experience are likewise inconclusive when it comes to the link between years in the classroom and student achievement. Just as the World Bank has decided to focus on "the knowledge and skills that people acquire, not the number of years that they sit in the classroom" (2011, p. 3), studies of teacher effectiveness suggest that years of experience or preparation are not the most important predictors of success. The SAS Institute Inc. (2011) suggests that teachers follow a general trend of improving their effectiveness over the first 10–12 years in the classroom, at which point it reaches a plateau. After 20–24 years this plateau begins a downward slope, but they warn this is most likely due to persistent low performers staying in the classroom while higher performing teachers move on to administrative or other roles. Recent research similarly suggests that teacher experience does matter but adds that not all experience has a positive effect (Ost, 2009). That is, teachers who are placed in the same grade and content area for the first five years of their careers improve up to 35% faster than teachers who never repeat grade or subject assignments. Thus content- and/or grade-level specific experience can have a meaningful impact, but years in the classroom alone are not an adequate predictor of effectiveness. Large-scale studies of teacher quality to date have almost exclusively measured teacher experience in years, without differentiating where those years were spent.

The United States is an example of a country that has complex requirements for entry into the teaching profession, while some countries have little to no requirements for entry (Anderson, 1991; Teddlie et al., 2006). Paradoxically, the dramatic rise of alternative, expedited teacher certification programs in the United States was facilitated, in part, by the lack of convincing evidence that any single amount or format of teacher preparation makes a measurable impact on teacher effectiveness as measured by student outcomes. For example, in their study of multiple of pathways into the teaching profession in New York City, Boyd et al. (2008) found that there are more similarities than differences between teacher preparation pathways including those that do not involve extensive coursework, testing, or certification before teachers enter the classroom. They further argued that programs varied greatly in the effectiveness of teachers they produced. Evaluations of teacher preparation programs in the states of Louisiana and Tennessee both reported that alternative programs were more effective than traditional programs that featured longer and more intensive preparation, and that there are large differences in the performance of candidates from the same program (Louisiana Board of Regents, 2008; Tennessee State Board of Education & Tennessee Higher

Education Commission, 2010). A federally funded comprehensive review of alternative and traditional education programs in the United States (Constantine et al., 2009) found that there is no significant difference in the performance of teachers from traditional and alternative programs, and that there is great variation in the preparation and performance of teachers within both. It is therefore difficult to argue that a holding a degree that implies a certain amount or type of preparation can be a measure of teacher quality. Similarly, even strong proponents of teacher licensure and certification agree that there is too much variation in the rigor and quality of standards for teachers across regions, even within one country, to claim that licensure or certification can be associated with greater teacher quality (Darling-Hammond, 1990).

In addition to evaluation tools that focus on inputs that would appear on a teacher's resume or personnel file, some evaluations rate teachers based on patterns in their personal characteristics and styles (Haberman, 2005; Liesveld et al., 2005). The difference in scope and content across scales is evidence of the lack of consensus for what matters in effective teaching. Where some scales focus on leadership qualities, others focus on certain beliefs about teaching and learning, or evidence of persistence, self-reliance, and critical thinking. Though it is difficult to argue that characteristics like persistence and critical thinking are not part of effective teaching, it is even more difficult to explain how their existence or their impact can be measured, analyzed, and distilled into an interview protocol that would be valid and reliable across cultures and contexts. Like all other input measures, screening tools and interviews rest upon the assumption that the potential for effective teaching is evident outside the context of a teacher's practice. They further assume that the characteristics that contribute to effective teaching are observable and measurable, though there have been few, if any, efforts to independently validate any of the commercially available screening tools, which are most often produced by for-profit organizations.

Some of the most discouraging evidence about the utility of policies aimed at *inputs* is that United States has pursued a set of policies aimed at improving the inputs of the teaching force for more than 50 years without measureable effect (Hanushek, 2002). Currently, U.S. federal policies required all teachers to become "highly qualified" and earn master's degrees and high scores on test of teacher knowledge (No Child Left Behind Act of 2001, 2008) before being allowed to teach, yet an achievement gap between rich and poor students persists. Similarly, individual cities (e.g., New York) in which the quality of applicants was raised significantly by a series of reform initiatives do not demonstrate any accompanying significant difference in student achievement (Boyd et al., 2008). Districts that use screening tools to identify promising candidates are not significantly different than districts that do not – though their hiring processes may be more efficient. Lastly, contrary to those who have argued for stricter standards for teachers, more levels of licensure, and greater requirements for certification (Akiba & LeTendre, 2009; Darling-Hammond, 1990), Hanushek (2002) explains, "teacher quality cannot be readily linked to teacher characteristics; therefore, new and more extensive certification and training standards are unlikely to be effective" (p. 11).

Darling-Hammond, a longtime advocate of increased rigor in teacher certification and licensure, explains that certification practices vary so widely across contexts that they cannot be interpreted as reliable measures of quality. In other words, there are often greater differences in the performance of certified teachers than between those who are certified and uncertified. The same holds true for varying levels of certification (Sanders, Ashton, & Wright, 2005). Teachers who opt to earn National Board Certification, the highest available level of certification for teachers in the United States, are not significantly different than the scores of those taught by teachers who have not opted to pursue that level of certification. Since such certification is optional, it could be that teachers who earn it are more effective than those who would not pass, but many teachers who are equally effective do not attempt to earn it. Alternatively, the criteria used to judge teachers for National Board Certification in the United States may not be linked to the elements of teaching that lead to higher student test scores. Taken together, the evidence against the provision of a nationalized set of prerequisites for entry into the profession seems not to be a strategic development investment in places where ongoing feedback on the process of teaching are available.

In this section, we have described the challenges and critiques associated with research policies that focus on the *inputs* a teacher brings with them to the profession. In the following section, we consider measures of effective teaching that consider the process of teaching, and those that consider the outcomes of teaching.

## PROCESSES

Classroom observations; artifacts of teacher plans, reflections, and student work; and the results of surveys or nominations are all tools researchers use to investigate the *process* of teaching. The underlying assumption of any observational method is that the factors that make teaching effective can be seen. This is somewhat tempered in the case of frameworks for teaching in which classroom observations are accompanied by examination of classroom artifacts (plans, activities, and materials) and evidence of the teachers' involvement in the school community (communication skills, leadership, professionalism, etc.). Research on effective teachers since the 1960s (Allington & Johnston, 2002; Bond & Dykstra, 1967; Knapp & associates (1995); MET Project, 2010) has cautioned that no single set of materials, strategies, or instructional philosophies are associated with more effective teaching. Rather, effective teachers use a range of materials and formats for instruction, often flexibly and interchangeably. Though effective teaching may look different across contexts, researchers have often attempted to find broad patterns and themes across observations of effective teachers in order to identify "best practices" and criteria for evaluation.

Goe et al. (2008) point out that compared to the large number of available observation instruments and frameworks for teaching within and outside of the United States, very few have been validated by anyone apart from the tool's developers. Though publishers of such tools rarely claim they have isolated the *only* set of criteria for effective teaching, most argue that the frameworks they provide are valid and reliable measures across contexts. The two most-researched examples of classroom observation instruments are good evidence of the differences in the structure and content of such tools. Charlotte Danielson's (1996) *Framework for Teaching* provides a set of components of instruction that evaluators can use to focus their observations on different aspects of teaching. The original set contains 22 components and 76 smaller elements for evaluators to consider. Since components are not weighted or averaged in order to calculate a final score, districts often select from the 22 components rather than using the whole framework. Danielson suggests, "The *Framework* may be used for many purposes, but its full value is realized as the foundation for professional conversations among practitioners as they seek to enhance their skill in the complex task of teaching" (Charlotte Danielson Group, 2011). Thus, the strength of such a tool may lie in its ability to foster professional conversations and opportunities for reflection on teaching rather than simply generating scores or ratings on a finite set of criteria.

Pianta, Paro, and Hamre (2008) developed and validated a classroom observation scale called the Classroom Assessment Scoring System (CLASS), which rates the teacher-student interactions and the classroom environment over a series of 30-minute observation cycles. They rate classrooms based on the degree to which they are considered socio-emotionally supportive and intellectually or academically supportive. They found that many teachers offer one kind of support, but not the other, while some offer both and some neither. They also report that teachers who offer both emotional and academic support in their interactions with students are highly effective at producing desired student outcomes regardless of the socioeconomic status of their students (Stuhlman & Pianta, 2009). This scale does not attempt to outline domains of teaching or describe indicators of effectiveness across different aspects of the teaching task. Rather, by focusing on teacher–student interactions, the tool reliably predicts student achievement and social adjustment. Unlike an observation rubric or framework for teaching, the results of the CLASS would not be used as a basis for professional conversations or discussions aimed at teacher professional development. They do, however, offer insight into the overall quality of educational experiences being offered within classrooms. It can therefore be used to formatively assess overall quality of a classroom setting and suggest areas for the improvement of a classroom experience in terms of emotional, academic, and environmental supports for learning.

The benefit of process measures is that they have the potential to inform immediate changes to instruction or action steps for future changes. Structures that increase the possibility of immediate feedback and suggestions for teachers are thus preferable to those that withhold or collect feedback for late or summative reporting. For example, some teacher evaluation systems require a single observation every one to five years followed at some distance by written feedback, while others require up to 10 observations a year with a face-to-face conference immediately following each observation. In the second case, the opportunity to discuss, adjust, and enhance instruction is increased 10-fold and stands to have a significant effect on the education of current students. In the former case, only one set of feedback is provided and it may not be viewed as relevant after time has elapsed or classes have changed. Since studies of effective teachers have identified professional conversations as an important factor in the development of effectiveness (Gabriel, Day, & Allington, 2010) evaluation systems that increase the possibility of such conversations increase the likelihood that effective teaching is fostered. Teachers who were nominated by their colleagues and confirmed by analysis of student test scores as exemplary teachers attribute their expertise, in part, to opportunities to talk with colleagues. As Lave and Wenger (1991) have suggested, teachers learn their craft by participating in communities of practice: that is, by collaborating with others in the field. Conversations about teaching are not only opportunities for feedback or reflection on practice but also forums for sharing new ideas, and offering emotional and material support. Conversations with colleagues are thus the foundation of embedded professional development efforts both informally and formally as in the case of systematized Professional Learning Communities (Dufour, 2004), Critical Friends Groups (Bambino, 2002), and other team initiatives. The assumption here is that these conversations lead to more, instead of less, effective practices. This depends, in part, on the validity of the observation tool, the knowledge of the evaluator, and their ability to communicate effectively with the teacher.

The major concern with process measures, as referenced at the beginning of this section, is that there is little consensus across available instruments about what evaluators should be looking for. Though guidelines for selecting an evaluation instrument have recently been published (The New Teacher Project, 2010) these criteria set standards for the structure, not the content of a helpful evaluation tool. Observer bias and the reliability and validity of any given instrument stand to confound the feedback and ratings provided based on classroom observations or the examination of other aspects of a teacher's practice. Though such measures stay closest to the practice of teaching (rather than examining preservice characteristics or the outcomes of instruction) they are also the hardest to validate. The classic trade-off between reliability and validity in evaluation is thus alive and well in the study and practice of identifying teacher effectiveness.

## OUTPUTS

Over the last 20 years, advances in statistical measurement including Hierarchical Linear Modeling, Structural Equation Modeling, and Value-Added Modeling (VAM) have paved the way for more sophisticated estimations of a teacher's effect on student achievement as measured by standardized test scores. Such modeling casts test scores as the desired outcome of an educational system and links evidence of student growth or achievement to individual teachers. Such *output* measures rest on three assumptions: (1) standardized tests are a reliable and valid measure of student growth and/or achievement; (2) teachers have a direct, one-way impact on student achievement in the content area they are responsible for; and (3) student growth and achievement should proceed at a relatively constant or predictable rate. Though a variety of factors complicate each assumption, teacher effect calculations offer a statistical answer to what was once an unavoidably subjective question.

Within this section, VAM will be used as an illustrative example of an output measure in order to discuss the assumptions and implications of the statistical modeling of teacher effectiveness in general. Though formulas vary across available models, VAM is most often used to isolate the effect of a teacher on student achievement from other possible influences. One of the largest challenges to measuring teacher effects has historically been the theoretical, but immeasurable, impact of students' individual differences. VAM circumvents these challenges by comparing individual students' performance to their own past performance, and not the performance of their peers. The influence of a student's background, prior educational experiences, and aptitude are thus held constant as each student's progress is tracked over time. In most cases, VAM provide a measure of expected versus actual performance on standardized tests based on a student's prior performance. For example, a student who scored in the 90th percentile in 5th and 6th grade would be expected to score in the 90th percentile in 7th grade. If they scored higher than their historical average score in 7th grade, their 7th grade teacher would be credit with "adding value" to the student's education. If instead they scored lower than their historical average, that is lower than would be expected, the teacher would be credited with adding negative value to the student's education. Students who maintain a constant level of performance earn their teachers a "zero" or neutral value-added score, which indicates that the student learned as much in the current year as they did in previous years – the expected and actual performance are equal.

Though VAM requires complex, sophisticated statistical modeling, it is conceptually relatively simple: Students scores are projected based on past performance and teachers are rated based on how closely their students match up to their projected scores. The statistical methods used to actualize this simple explanation come from the fields of economics and biochemistry. In fact one of the most commonly used model in the United States, the Education Value-Added Assessment System (EVAAS) system developed by Sanders at SAS Institute Inc., is based on a type of modeling that used to estimate the effects of radiation on livestock over time. It is designed to function with large sets of incomplete or "messy" data like that generated by student test scores. It is not, however, designed to reliably link the impact of teacher or classroom-level variables on student achievement to an individual teacher.

VAMs are becoming increasingly prevalent in U.S. state policies and increasingly linked directly to high-stakes decisions about teacher promotion, compensation, tenure, and dismissal. Even when the assumptions outlined above are accepted, however, researchers still question the reliability of such tools. For example, Papay (2011) reports that the same teacher would fall into drastically different pay scale categories depending on which reading test is used to measure their students' achievement. In order to demonstrate this he used the performance pay categories from Houston, TX, on data from teachers in Massachusetts where three different standardized reading tests are routinely given. As many as one-third of the teachers changed performance pay categories depending on which test was selected to calculate their value-added score though all three tests reported the achievement of the same students during the same school year. Papay suggests that differences in time of year as well as in standardized tests confound the reliability of VAM. Other large-scale investigations of error rates with VAM confirm his assertion that a large number of teachers are routinely misclassified. Schochet and Chiange (2010) report that there is a 35% error rate when using VAM that considers one year of data (rather than averaging three years at a time). If three years of data are taken into account the error rate is closer to 25%. Still, even with multiple years of data, such models may misclassify one in four teachers.

Despite the possibility of large error rates, limited reliability and a set of substantial assumptions about teaching and learning, the seeming objectivity of VAM and other statistical measurements make them a popular policy choice. They also provide data in a form that the general public can easily consume and understand. Though people may not agree on what effective teaching is or looks like, they can agree that one goal, if not the only goal, of effective teaching is that it should be measured in terms of student outcomes. Since these are the only evaluation instruments that explicitly link student outcomes to individual teachers, they are considered the best of many imperfect options for measuring effectiveness (Gabriel & Lester, 2010). As *The Los Angeles Times* has written, these models are not without flaws, but they are the best we have (*Los Angeles Times*, 2011). In the following section the inputs that make VAM possible will be described, as will the complexities of the set of assumptions that support it.

The assumption that standardized tests are a reliable and valid measure of student growth and/or achievement has raised several concerns for the quality of education offered in contexts with frequent high-stakes testing. Overreliance on student test scores can create a vicious cycle in which teachers teach with the narrow and explicit goal of raising student test scores instead of with the goal of differentiating instruction to match the needs, styles, and goals of individual students toward broad educational goals that include, but are not limited to, demonstrating proficiency on standardized assessments. Research has shown that this cycle has negative effects on two domains of student learning.

The first negative effect of high-stakes testing is a narrowing of the curriculum: Teachers have an incentive concentrate most on what will be tested, which is not always representative of the most important or relevant concepts within their purview. Rather tests are designed to focus on content and question types that are having the highest reliability and validity, regardless of their place in the curriculum. Resnick (2010) has pointed out that states often set minimum proficiency standards in an effort to raise student achievement. The risk of minimum proficiency standards and high-stakes standardized testing is becoming "caught in a basics trap," in which teachers have an incentive to focus on those skills that would lead to minimum proficiency, rather than to reach beyond them.

The second negative effect is nurturing a performance orientation rather than a task mastery orientation to learning. Task mastery orientations are associated with students who demonstrate long-term engagement, resilience, and achievement as well as intrinsic motivation to learn. They are invested in the development of mastery or expertise of a given task and will persist through challenges and over a long period of time. On the other hand, a performance orientation is associated with an approach to learning for the test's sake, short-term engagement, and anxiety around testing situations (Guthrie, 2001). An emphasis on testing as the reason and the measure of learning, rather than authentic outcomes (the ability to know or be able to do something) or intrinsic value of mastery can be both demotivating and anxiety producing. Motivation, along with other socioemotional factors, is tightly linked with increases in student learning and achievement (Guthrie & Humenick, 2004). Thus an emphasis on standardized tests scores as a measure of teacher effectiveness may put undue weight on the material and outcomes associated with a single standardized test, and establish one-time-performance, as the implicit goal of learning. Though international comparisons based on standardized test data are useful at a policy level, the countries with the highest scores on these (e.g., China and Finland) do not require annual testing as a measure of teacher or school effectiveness. Indeed some have attributed part of their relative success to their comparative lack of emphasis on standardized tests (Darling-Hammond, 2010). With this in mind one could say that any measure of teacher effectiveness that relies on frequent standardized testing is anathema to the mission of the World Bank to "unleash the potential of the human mind" (p. 1).

Similarly, VAM reduces the definition of value to a change in test score, a metric that is wholly unconnected with other possible goals of education including motivation to learn, socioemotional development, cultural knowledge, discipline-specific knowledge (in science, social studies, art, music, and athletics), citizen development, etc. Though these goals may be valued with or above content knowledge they cannot be measured using VAM. They are therefore positioned as an "other," qualitative measure, with questionable weight next to the oft-presumed objectivity of statistics. The maxim "what you test is what you get" serves as a warning against the use of VAM in isolation, as such tools pin the construct of effectiveness to a small, and possibly low value, set of testable constructs.

The second assumption of VAM is that learning should proceed at a constant and predictable rate. When projections of a student's expected level of performance are calculated, difference between expected and actual scores is attributed to the teacher. It is also possible, however, that students learn at different rates during different developmental stages, or that temporary outside factors influence their rate of achievement. For example, if a student missed several weeks of school due to illness, moved, or experienced trauma his or her academic performance may be significantly different than his or her performance in the previous year because of individual circumstances, even though more permanent individual differences such as race, class, and parental education are held constant. Theoretically, individual student circumstances would cancel out when calculations for an entire class are averaged together to come up with the teacher's overall effect score, but the assumption of linear, constant development is rarely addressed in the literature.

The third assumption of VAM is that a single teacher can be credited or held responsible for a student's achievement in a given subject. Since VAM is calculated using standardized test scores, reading and math are most often used. Teacher effect scores cannot be calculated for teachers who are assigned to subjects or grades that do not have a standardized test, or whose scope goes beyond the content of standardized tests. In some places, this has led to the mounting of massive efforts to design new tests for all subjects and grades. In other places, a schoolwide value-added score is distributed across teachers rather than to an individual teacher by subject-grade assignment (only 6th grade math teachers are linked with 6th grade math scores). Croninger and Valli (2009) have suggested that it is nearly impossible to attribute a single source for instruction in a given content area, especially in schools that place a high premium on student performance on standardized tests. In such schools math and reading are not only taught by teachers in different subjects (science, social studies, relate arts, etc.) but may also be taught by specialists, tutors, instructional aides, etc. throughout the school day. They describe the ways in which reading instruction permeates the temporal boundaries of time allocated to literacy learning as well as boundaries between adult teaching assignments. Though Croninger and Valli did not examine out-of-school reading instruction, it is also possible that some or all students receive tutoring, exposure, or extra support in academic areas after school. Thus the attribution of a student's test score to a single teacher is impractical. Yet, assigning a teacher effect score to a whole group of teachers cannot provide the specificity of information required to make strategic recommendations for individual improvement.

Despite methodological challenges, VAM brings statisticians closer than they have ever been to estimating teacher effects. The published consensus of education researchers is that VAM is an interesting and valuable tool, but not yet reliable or valid enough to be used in high-stakes decisions about a teacher's career or student's future (Baker et al., 2010). Policies that take up VAM as a measure of teacher effectiveness have the benefit of linking evaluation to student outcomes but must be transparent about the tenuous nature of that link. If VAMs are to be used effectively, their results must be interpreted with caution and appropriately tailored implications.

If evaluation is meant to help increase teacher effectiveness it must be used to continuously identify and act on areas for growth. For this reason it is important to note that process measures provide a unique opportunity to link evaluation to improvement throughout the school year. Input measures may be able to identify areas for improvement (someone might need to earn another degree or higher score) but are not specific enough to guide individualized support or add insight into the teaching process. Similarly, output measures may show a broad area where teachers need improvement (the teaching of math or reading; the teaching of a certain subgroup of students) but do not provide the level of detail needed to provide targeted professional development or to understand a specific aspect of the teaching process. Moreover, output measures provide information at the end of a teaching process – usually the end of a term or school year – at which point teachers often have little or no time to adjust their instruction before taking on a new group of students. In conclusion, conversation-driven evaluations of the process of teaching provide the most relevant and actionable information for the improvement of teaching, while measures of many outputs provide a counterpoint that describes the degree to which the local, subjective framing of effectiveness is having its desired effects on student outcomes. Process measures provide the most volume and highest quality information for countries seeking to continuously improve their collective understanding and execution of teaching, while output measures may assist policymakers in gauging relative success or urgency for reform. As the World Bank moves toward broad educational goals for 2020, goals that reach beyond traditional schooling, their mission requires broader measures of effectiveness that are not limited to constructs measurable on standardized tests. Likewise, a focus on the processes teaching and the development of systems that encourage conversation and collaboration among teachers will work to build both regional and global knowledge bases for effective teaching and educational reform.

## CONCLUSION

When tools for teacher evaluation are selected they become the authoritative source of "what counts" as good teaching and thus work to define and limit the kinds of teaching that are supported and allowed to occur. A review of research on teacher effectiveness and evaluation does not reveal any one formula or set of ideas for the definition or measurement of effectiveness. In order to evade the inevitable unintended consequences of blindly accepting a set of definitions or tools without first examining the assumptions that underlay their construction, policymakers must purposefully render transparent the assumptions of their polices so teachers, administrators, and the public can apply and interpret them as intended.

We suggest that policies aimed at increasing teacher effectiveness should be a top priority within global education development and reform efforts, yet we caution that effectiveness is not a single, unitary entity that can be easily measured. Rather it is contingent on context and local values about the purposes of education. Studies on teacher effects on student achievement demonstrate that a focus on teacher effectiveness, more than other school, system, or curricular factors, will be necessary in order to accelerate learning, especially in schools where students currently graduate without having developed basic literacy skills. In order to increase educational opportunities, the World Bank could provide leadership in the form of a vision for and focus on effective teaching that countries and local education agencies can adapt to their settings. This vision must include an emphasis on the utility of process measures as well as transparent guidance for capitalizing upon the specific strengths of varied tools for measuring effectiveness, while not falling prey to an oversimplified wholesale adoption of one type of measurement at the expense of another (process over outcome; outcome over process). This global vision may be used to check and balance local versions of effectiveness in order to ensure teacher effectiveness can be understood in both rigorous and relevant terms. Transparent and inclusive teacher effectiveness policies are of primary importance to any education reform effort and to the direction and measure of the World Bank's education strategy worldwide.

## REFERENCES

Akiba, M., & LeTendre, G. (2009). *Improving teacher quality: The U.S. teaching force in global context*. New York: Teachers College.

Allington, R., & Johnston, P. (2002). *Reading to learn: Lessons from exemplary 4th grade classrooms*. New York: Guilford Press.

Anderson, L. (1991). *Fundamentals of educational planning series: Increasing teacher effectiveness*. Paris: UNESCO: International Institute for Educational Planning.

Au, K. H. (1993). *Literacy instruction in multicultural settings*. New York: Harcourt Brace.

Baker, E., Barton, P., Darling-Hammond, L., Haertel, E., Ladd, H., Linn, R., ... Shephard, L. (2010). *Problems with the use of student test scores to evaluate teachers*. Washington, DC: Economic Policy Institute.

Bambino, D. (2002). Critical friends. *Redesigning Professional Development*, *59*(6), 25–27.

Bohn, C., Roehrig, A., & Pressley, M. (2004). The first day of school in the classroom of two more effective and four less effective primary grade teachers. *Elementary School Journal*, *104*, 269–287.

Bond, G., & Dykstra, R. (1967). The cooperative research program in first-grade reading instruction. *Reading Research Quarterly*, *2*, 5–142.

Boyd, D., Grossman, P., Hammerness, K., Lankford, R., Loeb, S., McDonald, M., ... Wycoff, J. (2008). Surveying the landscape of teacher education in New York City. *Educational Evaluation and Policy Analysis*, *30*(4), 319–343.

Campbell, J., Kyriakides, L., Muijs, D., & Robinson, W. (2004). *Assessing teacher effectiveness: Develping a differentiated model*. London: Routeledge.

Constantine, J., Player, D., Silva, T., Hallgren, K., Grider, M., & Deke, J. (2009). *An evaluation of teachers trained through different routes to certification*. Final Report (NCEE 2009-4043). Washington, DC: National Center for Education Evaluation and Regional Assistance, Institute of Education Sciences, U.S. Department of Education.

Cooper, J., & Alvarado, A. (2006). *Preparation, recruitment and retention of teachers*. Paris: International Institute for Educational Planning (UNESCO) and International Academy of Education (Belgium).

Croninger, R., & Valli, L. (2009). "Where is the action?" Challenges to studying the teaching of reading in elementary classrooms. *Educational Researcher*, *38*(2), 100–108.

Charlotte Danielson Group. (2011). *The framework for teaching*. Retrieved from http://charlottedanielson.com/theframeteach.htm. Accessed on January 9, 2011.

Danielson, C. (1996). *Enhancing professional practice: A framework for teaching*. Alexandria, VA: Association for Supervision and Curriculum Development.

Darling-Hammond, L. (1990). Teacher evaluation in transiton: Emerging roles and evolving methods. In J. Millman & L. Darling-Hammond (Eds.), *The new handbook of teacher evaluation: Assessing elementary and scecondary school teachers* (pp. 17–34). Newbury Park: Sage.

Darling-Hammond, L. (2010). *The flat world and education: How America's commitment to equity will determine our future*. New York: Teachers College Press.

Dennis, D. (2009). The haves and the have-nots: A comparison of classroom reading instruction in high and low SES schools. *Presentation to the annual meeting of the National Reading Conference*, Albuquerque, NM.

DuFour, R. (2004). What is a professional learning community? *Educational Leadership*, *61*(8), 6–11.

Ewing, D. (2011). Leading mathematician debunks "value-added." *The Washington Post*, April 5. Retrieved from http://www.washingtonpost.com/blogs/answer-sheet/post/leading-mathematician-debunks-value-added/2011/05/08/AFb999UG_blog.html

Fang, Z. (1996). A review of research on teacher beliefs and practices. *Educational Researcher*, *38*(1), 47–65.

Farr, S., Kopp, W., & Kamras, J. (2010). *Teaching as Leadership: The highly effective teacher's guide to closing the achievement gap*. San Francisco, CA: Jossey Bass.

Gabriel, R., Day, J., & Allington, R. (2010). What effective teachers taught us about learning to teach effectively? In I. Saleh & M. Khine (Eds.), *Teaching teachers: Approaches in improving quality of education*. Hauppague, NY: Nova Science Publishers.

Gabriel, R., & Lester, J. (2010). Public displays of teacher effectiveness. *Week*. Retrieved from http://www.edweek.org/ew/articles/2010/12/15/15gabriel.h30.html

Gay, G. (2000). *Culturally responsive teaching: Theory, research, & practice*. New York: Teachers College Press.

Goe, L. (2007). *The link between teacher quality and student outcomes: A research synthesis*. Washington, DC: National Comprehensive Center for Teacher Quality.

Goe, L., Bell, C., & Little, C. (2008). *Approaches to evaluating teacher effectiveness: A research synthesis*. Washington, DC: National Conprehensive Center for Teacher Quality.

Guthrie, J. (2001). Contexts for engagement and motivation in reading. *Reading Online*, *4*(8). Retrieved from http://www.readingonline.org/articles/art_index.asp?HREF=/articles/handbook/guthrie/index.html

Guthrie, J., & Humenick, N. (2004). Motivating students to read: Evidence for classroom practices that increase motivation and achievement. In P. McCardle & V. Chhabra (Eds.), *The voice of evidence in reading research* (pp. 329–354). Baltimore: Brookes.

Haberman, M. (2005). *Star teachers of children in poverty*. West Lafayette, IA: Kappa Delta Pi.

Handley, C., & Kronley, R. (2006). *Challenging myths: The Benwood initiative and education reform in Hamilton County*. Chattanooga, TN: Public Education Foundation/Benwood Foundation.

Hanushek, E. (2002). Teacher quality. In L. Izumi & W. Evers (Eds.), *Teacher quality* (pp. 1–12). Stanford, CA: Hoover Institution Press.

Haynes, K. (2008). Through the nominations of principals: Effective teachers of African American students share limitations of high-stakes testing. *Teaching and Teacher Education*, *24*, 2157–2167.

Kennedy, M. (2010). *Teacher assessment and the quest for teacher quality*. San Francisco: Jossey-Bass.

Knapp, M., & associates. (1995). *Teaching for meaning in high-poverty classrooms*. New York: Teachers College Press.

Ladson-Billings, G. (1994). *The dreamkeepers: Successful teachers for African-American children*. San Francisco, CA: Jossey-Bass.

Lave, J., & Wenger, E. (1991). *Situated learning: Legitimate peripheral participation*. New York: Cambridge University Press.

Liesveld, R., Miller, J., & Robinson, J. (2005). *Teach with your strengths how great teachers inspire their students*. Washington, DC: Gallup Corporation.

*Los Angeles Times*. (2011). *Los Angeles teacher ratings. FAQ & About*. Retrieved from http://projects.latimes.com/value-added/. Accessed on April 1, 2011.

Louisiana Board of Regents. (2008). *Regents study shows teacher certification matters*. Baton Rouge, LA: Board of Regents.

Measures of Effective Teaching Project. (2010). *MET Project. About the project*. Retrieved from http://www.metproject.org/project. Accessed on April 1, 2011.

Mathematica Policy Research. (2009). *Measuring school and teacher effectiveness in the EPIC charter school consortium-year 2*. Washington, DC: Mathematica Policy Research, Inc.

Nye, B., Konstantopoulos, S., & Hedges, L. (2004). How large are teacher effects? *Educational Evaluation and Policy analysis*, *26*(3), 237–254.

Noblit, G. (2004). Postcritical ethnography: An introduction. In G. Noblit, S. Flores & E. Murillo (Eds.), *Postcritical ethnography: Reinscribing critique* (pp. 1–54). Cresskill: Hampton Press.

No Child Left Behind Act of 2001, 20U.S.C. § 6319 (2008).

Ost, B. (2009). *How do teachers improve? The relative importance of specific and general human capital*. Cornell Mimeo.

Papay, J. (2011). Different tests, different answers: The stability of teacher value-added estimates across outcome measures. *American Educational Research Journal*, *48*(1), 163–193.

Pianta, R., Paro, K., & Hamre, B. (2008). *Classroom Assessment Scoring System (CLASS)*. Baltimore, MD: Brookes.

Philips, S. (1983). *The invisible culture: Communication in classroom and community on the Warm Springs Indian Reservation*. Prospect Heights, IL: Waveland.

Poplin, M., & Rivera, J. (2009). High-performing teachers in low-performing urban schools. *Presentation at the effective pathways to teaching conference*, Washington, DC.

Pressley, M., Allington, R., Wharton-McDonald, R., Block, C. C., & Morrow, L. (2001). *Learning to read: Lessons from exemplary first grade classrooms*. New York: Guilford Press.

Pressley, M., Rankin, J., & Yokoi, L. (1996). A survey of instructional practices of primary teachers nominated as effective in promoting literacy. *Elementary School Journal*, *96*, 363–384.

Rabinowitz, W., & Travers, R. (1953). Problems of defining and assessing teacher effectiveness. *Educational Theory*, *3*(3), 212–219.

Ravitch, D. (2010). *The death and life of the great american school system: How testing and choice are undermining education*. New York: Basic Books.

Reffitt, K., & Pressley, M. (2007). Effective literacy instruction in a rural school district: How do they do it? *Presentation to the annual conference of the American Educational Research Association (AERA)*, Chicago, IL.

Resnick, L. (2010). Nested learning systems for the thinking curriculum. *Educational Researcher*, *39*(3), 183.

Richardson, V., Anders, P., Tidwell, D., & Lloyd, C. (1991). The relationship between teachers' beliefs and practices in reading comprehension instruction. *American Journal of Educational Research*, *28*(3), 559–586.

Sanders, B., & Rivers, J. (1996). *Cumulative and residual effects of teachers on future student academic achievement*. Knoxville, TN: University of Tennessee Value Added Research and Assessment Center.

Sanders, W., Ashton, J., & Wright, S. (2005). *Comparison of the effects of NBPTS certified teachers with other teachers on the rate of student academic progress*. SAS. Arlington, TX: National Board for Professional Teaching Standards.

SAS Institute, Inc. (2011). *Teaching effectiveness and years of experience*. Cary, NC: SAS.

Schochet, P., & Chiange, H. (2010). *Error rates in measuring teacher and school performance based on student test score gains*. Washington, DC: Institute of Education Sciences.

Stuhlman, M., & Pianta, R. (2009). Profiles of educational quality in first grade. *Elementary School Journal*, *109*(4), 323–342.

Teach For All. (2010). *Teach for all: The global network for expanding educational opportunity*. Global challenge. Retrieved from http://www.teachforall.org/network_challenge.html. Accessed on April 1, 2011.

Teddlie, C., Creemers, B., Kyriakides, L., Muijs, D., & Yu, F. (2006). The international system for teacher observation and feedback: Evolution of an international study of teacher effectiveness constructs. *Educational Research and Evaluation*, *12*(6), 561–582.

Tennessee State Board of Education & Tennessee Higher Education Commission. (2010). *Report card on the effectiveness of teacher training programs*. Nashville, TN: State Board of Education & Tennessee Higher Education Commission.

The New Teacher Project. (2010). *Rating a teacher observation tool*. Brooklyn, NY: New Teacher Project.

U.S. Department of Education. (2010). *A blueprint for reform: The reauthorization of the Elementary and Secondary Education Act*. Washington, DC: U.S. Department of Education.

World Bank. (2010). *Concept note for the World Bank Education Strategy 2020*. Washington, DC: World Bank.

World Bank. (2011). *Learning for All: Investing in people's knowledge and skills to promote development*. World Bank Education Strategy Group. Washington, DC: World Bank.

# DELIBERATIVE EDUCATIONAL PLANNING: INCLUDING EDUCATORS' DELIBERATIONS IN EDUCATIONAL POLICY MAKING

Athena Vongalis-Macrow

## ABSTRACT

*The objective of this chapter is to argue a case for the need to include teachers and professional educators in the policy making and implementation processes of the World Bank's Education Sector Strategy 2020. By drawing on evidence from the Consultation Plan, the chapter investigates how communicative practices about teachers are embedded in the discourse of the plan and how these influence the rationalisation of the policy. In doing so, the chapter will examine the relationships between social actions, systems rationalisation and life world rationalisation. Much like commercial and entrepreneurial organisations focus on the voice of the customer (VOC), that is on satisfying the stakeholders and end users in their processes, in this chapter, the voice of the teacher (VOT) is highlighted. The skills and knowledge of key stakeholders need to be leveraged and engaged in order to ensure that the policy achieves its desired aims. In order to frame this argument, notions of Habermas' communicative action theory is used to show how policy engages in*

**Education Strategy in the Developing World: Revising the World Bank's Education Policy**
**International Perspectives on Education and Society, Volume 16, 229–247**

**ISSN: 1479-3679/doi:10.1108/S1479-3679(2012)0000016015**

*systems steering. Rather than understanding education strategy and reform as a process of engaging only government and policy makers, this chapter suggests that by engaging the practitioners and listening to the practical discourse around reform, teachers can be leaders of reforms rather than obfuscated agents.*

Initiating any conversation about the World Bank's education policy is to engage in a conversation ripe with contradictions, successes, failures and ongoing controversy. This chapter is an extension of such discourses as it considers and analyses the current World Bank policies addressing educational planning for the next decade. Reading through the ambitions and targets for education in the World Bank Education Sector Strategy 2020 (ESS2020) there is a great deal of continuity from previous strategies and plans. In a rapidly changing world, continuity of planning can be a signal for furthering the successful strategic planning of ongoing growth and development. However, the rapid social, economic and political changes over the past few years would suggest that policies that insist on a too close continuity with the past may meet problems. The objective of the paper is to argue a case for broader deliberations in educational strategising and planning, specifically for the greater inclusion of professional educators and education researchers in the policy making and implementation processes of the World Bank's ESS2020. The exclusion of educators' perspectives around education reform in World Bank education policies and planning has been an ongoing issue and one which irritates the integrity and successful implementation of policy.

## DEFINING POLICY

More inclusive deliberations, in policy making, begin with a common understanding of the purpose of policy. In the 1990s the World Bank defined policy as a process or a guide for the flow of money (World Bank, 2001). This definition varied widely from other academic definitions. For example, Easton's (1965) definition of policy as a 'an authoritative allocation of values' sustained the thesis that the battle ground for policy lay in the ideas contained within the text and discourse. For Prutny (1985) and others (Ball, 1994) the ideological content of policy, evident in the value-laden text, framed a pervasive narrative which positioned and legitimised the views and values of the policy makers and their representative interests. In contrast, World Bank definition of policy gave it a more strategic purpose in which policies allocated and mobilised capital and resources. While it could be argued the way policy seeks to guide the distribution of money is through a value-laden text, the discursive analyses unpacking hidden meanings of policy and how to read between the lines of policy text, is somewhat disarmed by the declaration that policy guides funding. That is not to say that World Bank policy is more transparent or less nebulous, the issue is that policy is more than a value-laden text, it is a strategic tool. A strategic tool seeks to represent a perspective or worldview, seeks legitimacy in its application and seeks to achieve a consensus around the strategy and implementation. Therefore, in order to examine policy as a strategic tool, a way to unpack strategy is through the framework of communicative action. Policy is communicative action because it outlines plans about what should be done (Flyvbjerg, 1998, p. 208).

Habermas' (1987, 1996) theory of communicative action (TCA) aims to clarify the rational processes of reaching understanding. These processes are dependent on 'consensus building discourse' (Flyvbjerg, 1998, p. 212) in which different actors negotiate their subjective ideas through deliberations and arrive at cooperative actions. The aim is for validity, or consensus without force. Such a process is required when implementing policy. In framing the understanding of policy as communicative action, the focus is on the process of consensus. It can be argued that policy, as a mechanism for guiding and coordinating actions, presents one side of the deliberations, that is the subjectivities of the policy-maker and their version of what should be done. However, framing our understanding of policy as a communicative action begins with the premise that the act of communicating policy and devising new strategies is based on the implied understanding that differences in what should be done will emerge. The issue is how to come to a mutual agreement about the way forward. Essentially, the effectiveness of policy is based on the shared understanding of the stakeholders in the outcomes around what should be done. In order to achieve the complex shared understanding that would be required to implement the Bank's global policy, Habermas emphasises widespread public participation in policy and planning as well as the need for sharing of information and public dialogue. As suggested by Bolton (2005), policy authority is not based on anything more than communicative rationality and the deliberations of reflective planners. By participating in the co-creation of policy, citizens' participation as well as the reflections of planners, allows those with an interest in the policy outcomes, to express their concerns and opinions in the creation of a common culture around policy making (Habermas, 1996, 1998). By referring to the work of Habermas, policy making is inclusive of the political interactions that co-create new institutions rather than reform and change of institutions being thought of as a planning process (Dryzek, 1995). It is difficult therefore to separate policy from politics.

## ONE-SIDED DELIBERATIONS AND EDUCATION POLICY

Reaching consensus through public dialogues and cooperative processes in the formulation and implementation of policy avoids the privileging of certain experts and bureaucrats raising issues of legitimacy and processes of democracy (Bolton, 2005). World Bank policy specifically about education reform and change has drawn criticism because of the way the Bank privileged its own powerful position in forcing change (Vongalis-Macrow, 2008). Omitted from influencing reforms and changes were the opinions and deliberations of other civil and social agents, who would be affected and impacted by policy. The often one-sided deliberations, associated with neoliberal reforms for example in South American countries in the 1990s, have raised issues of legitimisation, that is, that the World Bank was only concerned with implementing its strategies to maximise capital gain and create prosperity for a select few.

Reforming education has been a key goal in World Bank policy since the 1960s. Reforms to education were closely aligned to broader social and economic development goals such as improving health, improving prosperity and building capacity in the local population. The World Bank undertook significant education reforms in the late 1980s and during the 1990s in a range of countries spread across Africa, Asia and South America. The impetus for education reforms grew from the emergence of economic globalisation, which linked economies and financial interests at a greater speed and intensity. The vast improvements in ICTs, especially the popularisation of the internet meant that instantaneous communication, rapid movement of information and new forms of knowledge fuelled a new economic growth based on information, data, knowledge and technology.

Social and economic institutions deregulated, privatised, enterprised and downsised in order to function in flexible, competitive, adaptable and international ways. They no longer represented the localised interests but new ways were sort to combine the global economy with the local and national institutions. Education was not exempt from large-scale revision. Education systems were steered by notions of the global economy and how education could both enable knowledge economic growth and be transformed by knowledge economic growth. As Marginson (1999) noted, education became the subject and object of globalisation reform.

The World Bank pursued an active agenda in education reform identifying education as a spearhead in the alleviation of poverty and backwardness by helping to modernise developing nations so they could become key players in a global market. World Bank policies presented the future outlook as highly aspirational and within the reach of all nations. World Bank policy summed up the era as the 'flowering of globalisation' (Vongalis-Macrow, 2009, p. 72). However, while the policy extolled the virtue and possibility of globalisation and the fluidity of capital, the way the policy action plans were carried out raised serious concerns about the interests of the World Bank and whose interests most were served by policy.

For many developing nations, the World Bank policy meant large-scale restructuring of local education systems (Jones, 1992; Rhoten, 2000; Vongalis, 2009). The aim was to represent and link ideas about the global economy, knowledge making and the role of education. For example, table one outlines of policy foci evident in the education policy of three leading global players in the 1990s. While a fuller discussion of the OECD and UNESCO policies fall out of the scope of this chapter, a more detailed discussion is available elsewhere (Vongalis-Macrow, 2009). A number of researchers have critically examined how each global organisation directed and managed education reform during the globalisation era of the 1990s (Taylor, Rizvi, Lingard, & Henry, 1997; Willmott, 1999). The table shows that World Bank policy focussed more on education investment, management, budgetary decision-making, setting educational objectives and outcomes. The policy emphases reflect the monetary and financial underpinnings driving education reforms and provide a strategic roadmap illustrating the funding priorities.

The issue of legitimacy was raised in this era because the strategies around what should be done where not sufficiently deliberated among social and civil groups whose opinions and perspectives may have been very different. The policy process could be characterised as goal orientated, that is, to meet its objectives and assist the flow of capital rather than seeking consensus around how to build capacity in the interests of a range of different interpretations and expectations from globalisation. There was little opportunity to contest the validity claims in World Bank policy of the times. As a result, there was large-scale criticism of World Bank policies and to a large degree, it could be argued that these policies were not effective.

By the end of the 1990s, World Bank education specialists were admitting that the 1990s approach to education policy making was too simplistic (Zagha, 2005) and that contextual social and economic variations of each country, needed to play a greater role in determining a sustainable policy roadmap for growth and development. In other words, policy had to enter into a more mutually contractual agreement between policy makers and takers.

For example, consider the perspectives of teachers during this era represented in Fig. 1. Teachers, left to carry the implementation of reforms and create workable education systems were one group of education personnel consistently at odds with World Bank policy. For many educators in the 1990s, one of the key concerns around globalisation did not centre on how it enabled economic growth and financial flows, rather, about the meaning of education and knowledge. For educators grappling with globalisation, the epistemological foundations of education and knowledge had shifted and they wanted to examine how this shift necessitated foundational re-thinking about educational purpose, knowledge construction in relations to globalisation. However, these basic and fundamental educational concerns that represented the strategic interests and pursuits of educators were not prioritised in policy. Rather, education policy focussed on a balance sheet approach to reform, where issues around budgets,

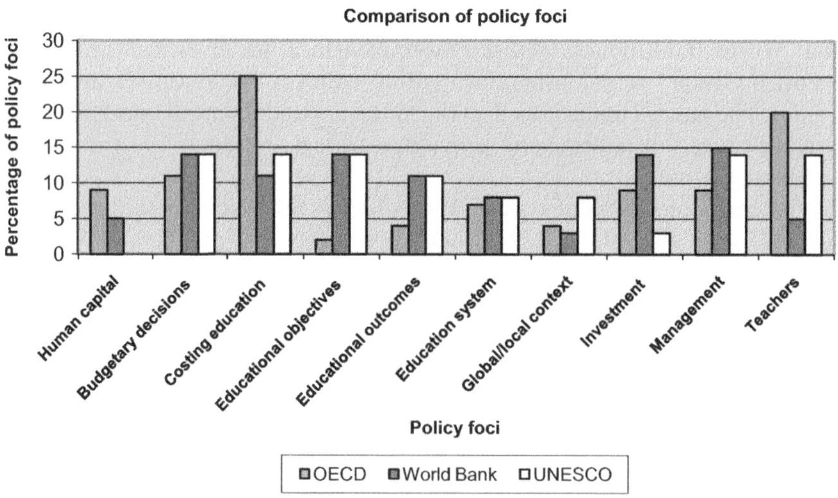


*Fig. 1.* Education Policy Foci of Supra Agencies in the 1990s.

education costing, education investment, human capital and management steered policy development.

As noted by Heyneman (2003), 'the Bank's tendency to become 'captured' by single methodologies beginning with manpower forecasting and later rate of return techniques. This tended to bias its views with respect to particular sub-sectors, educational functions and purposes'. For educators critical of the bank's singular methodologies, this era represented the most fervent infiltration of neoliberalism in the field of education.

Economic interests steered education systems in such a way as to transform knowledge and the processes of knowledge making in such a way that the constituents of knowledge making would dovetail with the new demands and potential growth in the knowledge economy. For many educators and educational researchers, the restrictive conditionality of World Bank loans fuelled further criticism about the Bank's interest in education. Heyneman (2003) points out that under these conditions, local actors are reduced to 'passive recipients'.

> Some argue that its loan covenants are too restrictive. Its policy reforms are based on narrow, neo-liberal assumptions about the role of the state. Local policy makers have become passive recipients of the Bank's agendas. To obtain loans, countries have agreed to raise education fees, which have exacerbated divisions between rich and poor. (p. 315)

As educational issues became increasingly reduced to how to improve and other technical matters, those involved in education, especially principals, teachers and educators, felt increasingly marginalised from the processes of reform and change. Carr and Kemmis (1986) cited in Lauglo (1996) argued that within technicist approaches to education reform, 'teaching and learning behaviours are elements in a system that can, in principle, be controlled as the means to a given end'. The pedagogic view was almost totally ignored in policy and consolidating the view that 'bankers' and 'pedagogues' tend to look at education through quite different professional lenses'.

The rationality of this line of thought translated into education policy and reforms. The impact of the rationality became evident in the way that education systems, around the world, were re-organised to reflect the views of knowledge-constitutive interests (Habermas, 1981). Country education strategies, lending and non-lending tasks are shaped by Country Assistance Strategies (CASs), budget constraints and dialogue among the Bank's country directors and sector teams. This instrumental rationality of these policy strategies reconfigured education as a system to be governed, controlled and managed by rules and measures stemming from economic management. Over time, these measures and the criteria assumed effective control over education systems. The goals, feedback control and interventions took on and implemented the ideological values of neoliberalism.

## WHAT SHOULD BE DONE: ESS2020

Framing of policy as a communicative act, that is, as a communication and strategic tool enables a comparative analysis between the policy directions of the 1990s and the current policy around education reform. ESS2020 presents a consensus building discourse which aims for validity, or consensus, without the implied coercion evident in previous policies. The emphasis is on a democratic consensus building, strengthening civil society and institutional development. Rather than policy focussing on the flow of capital, as had been flagged as the purpose of policy previously, this current strategy instead emphasises social and economic capacity building. The shift towards capacity building is a more socialised strategy and less of a blunt statement about the flow of capital. For this reason, there is continuity between previous strategies and ESS2020. For example, the language of investment continues to frame discourse of policy. Thus, invest early, invest smartly, and invest in learning for all is a catch-cry. However, there are key differences in the approach taken by the World Bank in this current education strategy. These differences will be analysed through the lens of communicative action.

## THE OBJECTIVE TRUTH ABOUT EDUCATION

For Habermas, truth is defined as an external objective in how we represent the world (Habermas, 2003). The truth represents the first feature of communicative action because it establishes how actors' 'idealising presuppositions' (Levine, 2006) that represent their objective world and what should be done. The external objective view of the world is captured in the Bank's policy imaginary. The policy imaginary of how the World Bank depicts the place and role of education in the world and in the future, sets the scene for initiating the deliberations around policy implementation and uptake. At the initial stages of proposing a new strategy for education, key questions prompting educational reform are, 'What will the world look like in ten years and how can the Bank best tailor its work in education to help countries achieve a prosperous and equitable future?' (World Bank,

2010a, p. 1). With these questions in mind, the World Bank began the process of soliciting views.

The web page announces,

> The World Bank has launched its Education Strategy for the next ten years. The strategy focuses on "learning for all" and investing early, investing smartly, and investing for all. Consultations with governments, development partners, students, teachers, researchers, civil society, and business representatives from more than 100 countries informed the strategy. (World Bank, 2011)

Focus on coordination of strategic actions suggests that ESS2020 is a communicative tool that presents a rationale for action and governance. The quality of communication, who is involved and represented and how changes will be managed and governed are therefore at the forefront of policy.

The consensus building around policy communication is captured initially in the concept note (World Bank, 2010a) which emerged from a range of consultations that sought to capture different the policy responses. Phase 2 of drafting the new strategy (World Bank, 2010a) highlights communicative action, aiming to building consensus in policy making. Communicative actions include, availability of different languages so there is no privileging of English, face to face consultations, blended consultations using Webinar and teleconferencing, online consultation, and feedback to stakeholders. Consultations included, sector and non-sector staff, internal stakeholders, representatives from client countries and global partners inclusive of NGOs, teachers' unions, youth groups and the private sector.

In addition to the consensus building around socialising the policy among different stakeholders, the discursive persuasiveness of the new strategy is that it draws education into the interconnected systems of quality necessary for a country's prosperity (World Bank, 2010a, p. 1). The new strategy links notions of quality, creativity, capability, with the health and education prospects of children. The connections are engaging, indicative of its 'whole-sector approach' to policy making for education. The policy communicates rich social connections for education and this further implicates the need for consensus building with a range of other actors in order to lead towards cooperative interpretation of education change. In other words, the reconceptualising of educational purpose in the light of imagining the future 10 years acts to connect education to broader social goals and to build a consensus around this imaginary future. The Concept Note (World Bank, 2010b), represents the first articulations and negotiations around the idealised truth about new education purpose and change and represents the key tenets of education reform.

A key shift in this imagined future is shifting education policy away from the framework of Education for All to the notion of Learning for All. The new education strategy stipulates that this shift is based on the lessons learnt from previous strategies as the Bank shaped the future directions of education development for the next decade. Underpinned by global educational goals such as the Millennium Development Goals, the onus is to continue to support nations to reach their targets of universal primary education and gender equality in schools. However, these goals continue to challenge educational planners and different nations. Despite the number of children attending school has fallen from 100 million more children to an estimated 72 million, this number still remains a challenge for policy. Policy states,

> However, progress towards Education for All has been uneven, with many areas of the world not on track to achieve the MDGs by 2015. In 2007, almost half of the world out of school children lived in sub Saharan Africa and a quarter of them lived in south Asia; estimates show that one third of out of school children live in areas affected by conflict. (World Bank, 2010d)

Despite shortcoming and uneven progress towards meeting the Millennium Goals, the demand for education increases and the demand for quality learning require new policy initiatives to ensure access and equity. These initiatives prioritise quality learning for all; skills and knowledge for growth and competitiveness, and education systems for results.

The focus on *Learning for All* compared with *Education for All* is that learning for all concentrates on systemic capacity building aimed at achieving set learning goals and objectives.

> The new education strategy differs from the past strategies in its focus on learning which may be attained partly by more investments in inputs such as more trained teachers or university professors, a better curriculum, and more learning materials, but which needs also institutional changes in the education system. (World Bank, 2010c)

The policy states that the mere act of attending school is not enough to ensure that learning is taking place. The Bank's briefing on education reform states, 'Yet access to and completion of schooling is insufficient if children are not learning what they need to learn' (World Bank, 2010c, p. 2). ESS2020 presents a more focussed understanding of education as not only schooling, rather education refers to the outcomes of schooling beyond attendance, that is, on learning. Compared to the previous strategies which aimed at actions plans to improve school attendance and thus meeting goals of access to school, this current strategy suggests that the individual learner, their learning experiences and how these are supported, managed and accounted for are the measures by which the effectiveness of educational systems can be monitored.

> The new strategy emphasizes the importance of getting governance arrangements, financing, incentives and accountability mechanisms, and management tools aligned with education goals. (World Bank, 2010c)

The key focus on learning and skills is referenced against a future imaginary based on technological progress, globalisation and national quotas for skilled workers to enable economies to grow and compete within a global economy.

> Literacy and numeracy are not the only skills that are needed in the labour market. The Bank helps countries provide education that creates a skilled and productive labour force, leading to economic productivity and competitiveness, knowledge generation, and increased earning potential. (World Bank, 2010d, p. 2)

The new strategy reinforces the connection between education, the provision of skilled labour, economic productivity and competitiveness, knowledge generation and earning capacity. The purpose of education is as an economic lever however, the shift evident in policy is on the meaning and purpose of education. Rather than education as a school-based system, the focus on learning for all reconceptualises educational outcomes that target individuals acquiring skills and knowledge that can fuel economic growth. The acquisition of these skills is not the confine of education/schools.

## ARGUMENTATION, NEGOTIATION AND ACTORS

In order to arrive at consensual strategies, Habermas' concept of rightness describes how the processes of argumentation and negotiation between actors is necessary to achieve consensus. Communicative action is dependent on cooperative action, and is arrived at through mutual deliberations of the stakeholders involved. ESS2020 has stressed the importance of wide consultation in policy deliberations. However, the key policy shift from Education for All to Learning for All is especially relevant for teachers and educators as it has a direct impact on the purpose and value of their work. The issue raised by this policy shift is whether there was sufficient consultation with educators in order to achieve the consensual shift announced in this policy.

The World Bank's 1999 Education Sector Strategy focussed on quality education for all, especially targeting poor children, girls and the necessity for early childhood education. The 2005 education strategy focussed on teacher recruitment, retention and training. The current strategy, based on learning for all, takes a more systemic view of teachers' work by coalescing teachers' practice and performance with broader systemic educational goals.

> The new strategy adds a systemic view of teacher reforms in which policy goals relate to setting clear expectations for teachers, ensuring that pay and benefits are competitive so as to attract the best into the teaching profession, prepare teachers through both pre-service training and classroom practice, monitoring the performance of teachers, as well as supporting and motivating them as needed. (World Bank, 2010c)

The necessity for better quality teaching underpins much of the policy shift towards quality education systems that focus on learning outcomes. Policy states,

> it will pay a high degree of attention to teacher issues given their key role in learning and the very large share of spending in education to pay for teachers'salaries. To improve the teaching force, policies must provide teachers the incentives for good performance besides establishing and enforcing proper qualifications (through pre- and in-service training and support services, in which most teacher-related investments are focused on. (World Bank, 2010c)

A criticism of World Bank policy in the past is the way that the actions of teachers were controlled and shaped in order to implement change (Vongalis-Macrow, 2008). Teachers were cast as potential obstacles to reforms and an element of 'political constraint' (World Bank, 2010a, p. 12) in the implementation of education reform. There is some continuation of this discourse in the current policy. Policy discussions identify the resistance of teachers and other civil servant in education agencies as factors which needed further 'input for concrete actions' (World Bank, 2010a, p. 11). This acknowledged need to prepare and strategise ways to deal with teachers suggests that some of the previously held assumptions about teachers and how they relate to policy making are still evident.

Teachers are not adversarial actors in the policy process, because as with policy makers, teachers are orientated towards creating a successful education system (Bolton, 2005). Therefore, in terms of consensus building, it can be surmised that while a number of other partnerships and collaborations are sought to affirm and implement policy, educators are still not part of the inner circle. Reviewing a World Bank blog on education, (http://blogs.worldbank.org/education/teacher-unions-friend-or-foe-to-reform) focuses mostly on the political actions of teachers through their unions and the negative impact of such actions. For example, the tendency to strike is an issue. Citing an example from Sao Paolo teachers,

> Sao Paula teachers went to strike over a proposal to make new recruits take tests before they start work to ensure they are qualified; last year they created a furore when the state government asked them to teach from standard textbooks. They proposed a plan to pay staff bonuses depending on their school' performance, but surprisingly went silent since 70% of the state teachers received a bonus. (http://blogs.worldbank.org/education/teacher-unions-friend-or-foe-to-reform. p. 1)

Such examples are supposed to illustrate the self-interest of teachers' unions and that this interest interferes with better education systems. However, when you analyse the motives for strike action it is usually a difference of opinion about how to achieve success. For teachers, a large part of achieving success means having an engaged and empowered teaching force that retains the value of teachers. Creating esteem and valuing the work of the profession is a critical factor in education systems that are high performing such as Finland, Singapore and Hong Kong (Simola, 2005). Therefore, rather than construing the tendency to strike as adversarial, strike action is an extension of teachers' argumentation about education reforms. The strike actions are also symptomatic of a communicative failure between actors interested in reforming education. When World Bank policy targets teachers for reforms, then good policy as communicative action, would affirm that reforms are dependent on cooperative actions derived through mutual deliberations of the stakeholders involved. Those critical to reforms are invested in how their work is 'overhauled'.

> The effectiveness of teacher policies (e.g., training, hiring, compensation, deployment, supervision) is critical to an education system's performance; this is one area that typically needs a major overhaul in order to motivate and support teachers. These reforms have to be consistent with a quality assurance framework. (World Bank, 2010d, p. 4)

Both teachers and policy makers are policy actors who are success orientated in wanting a more effective and supportive education system. The challenge is to better coalesce the concerns educators, working within the political reality of an education system, with the goals of education reform, as demanded by policy makers.

While there is recognition that teachers' unions are stakeholders in the consultation around education reform, they are still identified as potential disruptors of change. However, continuing to flag teachers as potential adversaries to reforming education in the reimagining of the educational future creates unnecessary division and tensions around reforms. Just as the World Bank policy adopted a more open and consultative approach to policy making, this openness should also extend to re envisaging teachers and their professional groups and associations as the co-creators of reform and not as adversaries. For educators, ESS2020 is not an effective communicative tool since their perspectives and inputs continue to be questioned and their interests politicised.

## BRINGING IN THE VOICES OF THE TRANSFORMATION AGENTS

Communicative actions require that the parties involved in the negotiations present their argumentation and negotiate their perspectives about achieving target goals. Habermas argues that the personal and subjective opinions and expressions, truthfulness, represents the invested interests of the actors (Habermas, 2003). While the new strategy creates an objective vision of what education should be and do, then socialises this vision through extensive consultations, the perspectives of educators, their truthfulness is under represented in policy.

The case of System Assessment and Benchmarking for Education Results (SABER) illustrates this point.

> is an initiative that helps countries systematically examine and strengthen the performance of their education systems to achieve learning for all. The World Bank is working with partners around the world to develop diagnostic tools that benchmark education policies according to evidence-based global standards and best practice. By leveraging global knowledge, SABER fills a gap in the availability of policy data, information and knowledge on what matters most to improve the quality of education. (World Bank, 2011)

This means representatives of the World Bank will create a teacher reform platform based on building evidence and developing a set of benchmarks and best practices in a range of measures designed to reform the profession. These measures include guidelines around teacher selection process, teacher management and incentives, best practices around pedagogy, curriculum and assessments, and professional development. The analytical work will cover all facets of teachers' work and professionalism. The World Bank presents its argumentation about what teachers should do essentially through its 'analytical work' (World Bank, 2003c). The analytical work involves the strategic planning of teachers' reforms through collection of data and diagnostics to build a knowledge base around what it means to be an effective teacher. This means representatives of the World Bank will create a teacher reform platform based on building evidence and developing a set of benchmarks and best practices in a range of measures designed to reform the profession. These measures include guidelines around teacher selection process, teacher management and incentives, best practices around pedagogy, curriculum and assessments and professional development. The analytical work will cover all facets of teachers' work and professionalism. In other words, the analytical work will reconfigure what it means to be a quality teacher within a quality education system.

While reconfiguring the work and practices of effective teachers and teaching may follow a quasi-scientific method of data collection and deriving best practices from evidence, teaching is a political activity. The previous World Bank strategies have neglected this reality to much criticism from educators, teachers and other educational interests. The current strategy acknowledges that the political context is a factor in the success or failure of reforms. This recognition is therefore included in the analytical work of teacher reforms and the knowledge base around teacher reforms in inclusive of the political economy of education and system reform (World Bank, 2010c). The political context in included in reform measures. Outlining key steps in reforming teachers, they include:

> (i) Build access to expertise on teacher quality and performance issues through a combination of expert database, staff training, and hiring. (ii) Train staff on topics including: i) effective practices for teacher selection, management and incentives; ii) effective pedagogical practices and professional development; iii) analysis of political economy of education reform. (iii) Pilot analysis of political economy of teacher reform during project preparation. (World Bank, 2010c)

The issue remains whether the many different perspectives or truthfulness of educators, representing their different and diverse education systems will be included and their concerns integrated into the knowledge base around effective quality teaching and teachers. How far will teachers' deliberations be sought and acknowledged within the guiding principles and benchmarks around good practice?

Habermas (1996, 1998) addresses the political implications of including deliberative processes as part of the development of deliberative politics. Within these processes the participation of actors, especially those with interests in developing a particular common political culture would be expressed. Including the concerns of education professionals in deliberations around reforming education, improving practice and reforming the profession is an example of democratic policy making through deliberative processes. Taking on board the concerns of the teachers, the political culture encasing policy actions is acknowledging an actual negotiation process in which invested groups all work towards relevant, legal and normative educational reforms that are instituted as part of a negotiated common political and educational culture.

The deliberative process is not without tensions and friction because the nature of the negotiations can involve argumentation and polarisation. However, the purpose of argumentation is to allow rational arguments to prevail and negotiate action plans. This is perhaps the most difficult element of policy planning because it does not focus on the action plans of only a privileged minority, but seeks ways to come to consensual decisions. As Mardi (2004) notes, the inclusion of those who are usually policy takers can make for more effective policy that works.

> Traditionally, only a privileged minority has had the chance to participate in the scientific process considering these decisions as objective. If we are analyzing the factors that understand dropouts, for example, we will need to take into account the adolescents' reasons for dropping out or continuing their studies. The scientific explanation about these factors cannot only be based in the subjectivity of the expert or the researcher that is considered objective; it should also be based in the intersubjectivity resulting from the dialogue among the parents and the researchers. (Mardi, 2004)

By consulting and inviting extensive input from a diverse range of educators representing the range of nations likely to be covered by World Bank policy, a more inclusive and sustainable process of reform can implemented.

Deliberative educational policy would seek to improve educational policy and governance, since it invites a range of voices to participate in the communicative actions, that is, in the construction of truth, rightness and truthfulness of policy. In doing so, the processes for improving the effectiveness and legitimacy of World Bank educational decision-making and planning would be enhanced, especially among educators.

While heightened emphases on broader consultation are evident in ESS2020, deliberations need to be more widely inclusive of educators in system steering policy action plans. For example, when examining the emerging themes advanced in ESS2020, teachers' actions and professional work intersects extensively in the successful outcomes. The emerging themes of a new strategy (World Bank, 2010c, p. 5) include: (a) focussing on learning and (b) using the comparative advantage of a global institution. Successful outcomes from both these emerging themes are highly dependent on the skills, knowledge and professional work of engaged and committed teachers. Teachers' work builds capacity and underpins the comparative advantage that education systems can leverage to help create a prosperous future. Educators understand the context and diversity of teaching and learning that are required to achieve the educational as well as the social aims of education. The trend for educators to take on leadership and governance of education also highlights the willingness of the profession to take on the responsibility of governance of schools and local systems. Educators are strategic actors in implementing action plans, it follows that their voice and input should be more evident in the deliberations of policy.

## DELIBERATIVE POLICY MAKING

Education policy making cannot afford to alienate those agents orientated towards success of the education systems and those agents whose professional identity is so embedded in the system. Global policy making can no longer assume a common and normative understanding of that policy from all participants. Rather than dealing with potential differences through exclusion of different perspectives and minimising the representations of those with conflicting views, continued efforts should be made to achieve a democratic consensus around reform. World Bank policy has been criticised for representing the interests of the privileged few and further open deliberations around policy and what should be done would help to change this perception. Policy making in a complex world needs to acknowledge and negotiate around differences and politics for the long term effectiveness of policy. Any deliberative conversation about education needs to account for the truthful perspectives of all those concerned, especially those who have an understanding of education as responsive and democratic. For this reason, the greater inclusion of educators in the consultation and in the implementation of policy is critical for its success. Deliberative educational planning ensures reforms are relevant and mutually inclusive.

> The form of communication is to ensure the full inclusion as well as the equal, uncoerced participation oriented toward reaching mutual understanding on the part of all those affected so that all relevant contributions to a given topic can be voiced and so that the best arguments can carry the day. (Habermas, 2003, p. 251)

Deliberative planning will also address ongoing criticism of World Bank policies (Heyneman, 2003) so it can continue to influence education access and quality across the world. Heyneman states,

> The World Bank has become the single largest source of development capital in the field of international education. These resources help expand educational opportunities for young women in South Asia and rebuild primary schools following civil conflict in

> Sub-Saharan Africa. They support textbooks, school meals, new curriculum, and teacher training in thousands, perhaps hundreds of thousands, of locations in over 100 countries in six regions. (Heyneman, 2003, p. 315)

By reviewing the way policy is communicated and how policy draws in other actors, the World Bank can continue to build a more accessible and open policy-making process. By considering policy as communicative action, better ways can be employed, throughout the policy-making process to build consensus which means involving those whose actions enable policy in the deliberations about policy. If key actors, such as educators, are left out of the process of argumentation and negotiation, some groups, with an interest in achieving the goals, will continue go outside the controlled process of consultation to ensure their views are heard.

## REFERENCES

Ball, S. (1994). *Education reform: A critical and post-structural approach.* Buckingham, UK: Open University Press.

Bolton, R. (2005, April). Habermas's theory of communicative action and the theory of social capital. Paper presented at meeting of Association of American Geographers, Denver, CO (previous version read at meeting of Western Regional Science Association, San Diego, CA, February 2005). Retrieved from http://web.williams.edu/Economics/papers/Habermas.pdf

Easton, D. (1965). *A framework for political analysis.* Englewood Cliffs, NJ: Prentice-Hall.

Dryzek, J. S. (1995). Critical theory as a research program. In S. K. White (Ed.), *The Cambridge companion to Habermas* (pp. 97–119). Cambridge: Cambridge University Press.

Flyvbjerg, B. (1998). Habermas and Foucault: Thinkers for civil society? *British Journal of Sociology*, *49*(2), 208–233.

Habermas, J. (1987). *The theory of communicative action.* Boston, MA: Beacon Press.

Habermas, J. (1996). *Between facts and norms.* MA: MIT Press.

Habermas, J. (1998). *The inclusion of the other.* In C. Cronin & P. De Greiff (Eds. & Trans.). Cambridge, MA: MIT Press.

Habermas, J. (2003). *Truth and justification.* Cambridge, MA: MIT Press.

Heyneman, S. P. (2003). The history and problems in the making of education policy at the World Bank 1960–2000. *International Journal of Educational Development*, *23*(3), 315–337.

Jones, P. W. (1992). *World Bank financing of education: Lending, learning, and development.* New York, NY: Routledge.

Lauglo, J. (1996). Banking on education and the uses of research. A critique of: World Bank priorities and strategies for education. *International Journal of Educational Development*, *16*(3), 221–233. World Bank's education sector review: Priorities and strategies for education.

Levine, S. (2006). Review of truth and justification by Jürgen Habermas Constellations *12*(3), 437–444.

Marginson, S. (1999). After globalization: Emerging politics of education. *Journal of Education Policy*, *14*(1), 19–31.

Prunty, J. (1985). Signposts for a critical educational policy analysis. *Australian Journal of Education*, *29*(2), 133–140.

Rhoten, D. (2000). Education decentralization in Argentina: A 'global-local conditions of possibility' approach to state, market, and society change. *Journal of Education Policy*, *15*(6), 593–619.

Simola, H. (2005). The Finnish Miracle of PISA: Historical and sociological remarks on teaching and teacher education. *Comparative Education*, *41*(4), 455–470.

Sorde Marti, T. (2004). Truth and justification. *Harvard Educational Review*, *74*, 209–308.

Taylor, S., Rizvi, F., Lingard, B., & Henry, M. (1997). *Educational policy and the politics of change*. London: Routledge.

Vongalis-Macrow, A. (2008). *Deployed to deliver*. Amsterdam: Sense Publishers.

Vongalis-Macrow, A. (2009). The simplicity of educational reforms: Defining globalization and reframing educational policies during the 1990s. *International Journal of Educational Policies*, *3*(2), 62–80.

Willmott, R. (1999). Structure and agency and the sociology of education: Rescuing analytical dualism. *British Journal of Sociology of Education*, *20*(11), 5–21.

World Bank. (2001). *Definition of policy*. Retrieved from www.ecdgroup.com/policy.htm#policy. Accessed on May.

World Bank. (2010a). *Concept note for World Bank education strategy, World Bank*. Retrieved from http://siteresources.worldbank.org/EDUCATION/Resources/ESSU/Concept_Note_ESS2020_Feb8.pdf. Accessed on 31 March 2011.

World Bank. (2010b). *World Bank Group's education sector strategy 2020 consultation plan, 2010 updated 17 June 2010*. Retrieved from http://siteresources.worldbank.org/EDUCATION/Resources/ESSU/ConsultationPlan_v2_English.pdf. Accessed on 31 March 2011.

World Bank. (2010c). *Learning for all: Investing in people's knowledge and skills to promote development World Bank Education Strategy 2020, World Bank*. Retrieved from http://siteresources.worldbank.org/EDUCATION/Resources/ESSU/Education_Sector_Strategy_draft_for_comment.pdf. Accessed on 31 March 2011.

World Bank. (2010d). *Education*. Retrieved from http://siteresources.worldbank.org/EDUCATION/Resources/ESSU/463292-1269917617150/6915424-1279137061297/WB_Education_Strategy_Executive_summary_For_Consultations_Phase_II.pdf. Accessed on 30 August 2010.

World Bank. (2011). *The World Bank Education web page*. Retrieved from http://web.worldbank.org/WBSITE/EXTERNAL/TOPICS/EXTEDUCATION/0,,menuPK:282391~pagePK:149018~piPK:149093~theSitePK:282386,00.html. Accessed on September 18, 2011.

Zagha, R. (2005, December 14). Economic growth in the 1990s: Learning from a Decade of Reform. A paper delivered in Melbourne, Melbourne, Australia.

# THE APPROACH OF THE WORLD BANK TO PARTICIPATION IN DEVELOPMENT AND EDUCATION GOVERNANCE: TRAJECTORIES, FRAMEWORKS, RESULTS

D. Brent Edwards Jr.

## ABSTRACT

*This chapter takes as its focus a series of issues related to participation and the World Bank. First, it traces from 1980 to the present the trajectory within the Bank of thinking related to participation in development generally. Second, it unpacks the framework within which that thinking has been crystallized – namely, the Framework for Service Provision (FSP) delineated in the 2004 World Development Report,* Making Services Work for Poor People. *Third, it shows how the work done by the Bank in the education sector has both paralleled and furthered the concepts embedded in the FSP. Focusing on the education sector is essential because it is the sector in which the Bank has perhaps been most active in theorizing and most successful in implementing its conception of participation. As the chapter shows, a particular approach to decentralization is central to the way the Bank advances that conception of*

**Education Strategy in the Developing World: Revising the World Bank's Education Policy**
**International Perspectives on Education and Society, Volume 16, 249–273**

**ISSN: 1479-3679/doi:10.1108/S1479-3679(2012)0000016016**

*participation and to the way that it supports the realization of participation in practice, both generally and with regard to education governance. Lastly, the chapter reviews and discusses the results of Bank-supported education decentralization projects in light of the theory elaborated to promote them.*

Given that the World Bank (hereafter, the Bank) has been a major proponent of participatory approaches to development, it is imperative to have a clear understanding of how the Bank conceives of participation, and how that conception has developed over time. This is particularly the case with regard to education, perhaps the sector in which the Bank has been most successful in adapting and promoting its conception of participation in development. At the same time, it is essential to have an understanding of what is known about the results of the Bank's participatory mechanisms in implementation. A firm grasp on each of these issues better enables one to critically engage with them and to consider whether alternative conceptions of participation should be pursued.

In this chapter, I address the above-identified tasks. First, I trace from 1980 to the present the development of the thinking within the Bank behind participation in the context of sector reform. Doing so shows how the thinking behind participation has evolved over time within a theory of market dynamics. More recently, this thinking was crystallized in the "framework for service provision" (FSP), as presented in the Bank's World Development Report (WDR) 2004, *Making Services Work for Poor People.*[1] The second task of the chapter is to present and unpack the theory of the FSP. This is essential because it is the overarching framework within which the Bank attempts to operationalize participation. Third, I show how the concepts behind the FSP have been developed, advanced, and applied over time in the Bank's education work. This section demonstrates that, in the education sector, participation occurs through a specific accountability-based conception of decentralization. Lastly, I synthesize and evaluate the results of Bank-supported, participation-related projects in education, which, as noted, fall under the label of decentralization.[2] In so doing, I provide a macro level picture of what is (and is not) known about the effects of such reforms. Given that the discussion contained in this chapter is the result of combing through a vast array of Bank literature, it is necessary in the next section to comment on the strategy adopted to guide the review of that literature.

## METHODS

Three pools of literature were examined in the research for this chapter. First, in order to trace the overall trajectory of the thinking behind participation in the Bank, I researched all those official publications from the 1970s to the present that represent the Bank's general approach to development. These include, for example, the annual WDRs – all of which were systematically reviewed for the concept of participation. Second, in order to see how the concept of participation has filtered into Bank thinking around education sector reforms, I reviewed not only all official education strategy documents but also other literature by the Bank and its staff related to education and participation, including working papers, evaluations, research publications, and theoretical discussions. The purpose here was not only to appraise the logic of participation in education governance but also to be attentive to the trends in thinking over time associated with how the Bank conceives of participation in the education sector. As well, education documents were assessed for the extent to which the embedded concepts mirror the way in which the Bank has more generally conceived of participation.

Third, discussing the effects of the Bank's participation-related projects in the education sector requires that one reviews reports on decentralization. However, because reviewing the dozens of individual decentralization evaluations and research studies that have been performed by the Bank is beyond the scope of this chapter, for my discussion of results, I rely on those Bank reports that specifically review in multiple countries the effects of decentralization projects that have been supported by the Bank. While we may miss some of the details that emerge in assessments of individual reforms, what the literature reviewed for this chapter helps bring to the fore is the bigger picture of what we know (and don't) about the functioning and effects of these projects. In that I include only those studies that review projects supported by the Bank, we can be sure that the reforms considered here have a common theory of action, thereby adding a dimension of conceptual clarity to the discussion of results. The common theory of action underlying the reforms discussed in this chapter is important to note because many other conceptions of participation (Edwards & Klees, forthcoming) and decentralization (Lauglo, 1995) exist in the literature on education governance.

The next section presents the findings on how the Bank's thinking in relation to participation in development has evolved since 1980, the first year in which the concepts that the Bank currently relates to participation began to appear.

## THE BANK'S APPROACH TO DEVELOPMENT AND THE TRAJECTORY OF PARTICIPATION

Although a particular conception of participation has taken center stage in the 2004 WDR, *Making Services Work for Poor People* (World Bank, 2003), as well as in the more recent Education Strategy 2020, *Learning for All*, the underlying, accountability-based perspective on participation and service provision has been evident in the Bank's thinking since 1980. When placed in the context of Bank literature spanning thirty plus years, one sees that the call for a rise in participation by communities and individuals has occurred along with a concomitant call to reduce state service provision and to decentralize the functions it previously coordinated centrally.

A raft of publications and documents demonstrate the Bank's shift in thinking toward strategies that reshape the state and invoke participation. The first was the *World Development Report 1980*, which indicated that the Bank now considered the organization and operation of central governments to be fundamental obstacles to progress (World Bank, 1980). This document pointed to both "inappropriate administrative structures" and an "undue emphasis on central control" as "institutional problems" impeding development (p. 76). At the same time, it also suggested that both (a) state – or provincial – level decentralization and (b) involving beneficiaries through their own organizations in service provision could lead to more effective service delivery (World Bank, 1980). These recommendations would mark the beginning of a general reorientation of Bank rhetoric, which had not previously taken the organization and operation of the state to be a central development problem.

Within a couple years, the profile of these ideas had been raised significantly, and they became the theme of the 1983 WDR, *Management in Development* (World Bank, 1983). Here, we continue to see the emphasis on participation as instrumental to the success of the Bank-favored reforms. Two statements are particularly insightful in this regard: The Bank first asserts that "some partnership with local communities in the design of programs is essential, if plans are to meet beneficiaries' needs and encourage contributions of money and labor" (p. 93); and, second, that "corruption can also be checked by community participation in the design, operation, and financing of programs, since this increases the accountability of field staff to local people" (p. 94). Increasing local participation was thus seen as a way to increase project effectiveness and to reduce the financial burden on national governments while simultaneously holding local implementers to account. The importance of these statements is that they laid the groundwork for the framework in which the Bank presently considers participation. That is, more than expressing that central governments are the problem, the 1983 WDR began to elaborate the rationale for why and how an increased role for communities and individuals is part of the solution.

The strategy of tapping community capacity and the logic of relying on local accountability were again declared in 1989, with the publication of *Sub-Saharan Africa: From Crisis to Sustainable Growth* (World Bank, 1989). This time, however, the declaration is more sweeping. As Barber Conable, then-President of the Bank, asserted in this document:

> A root cause of weak economic performance in the past has been *the failure of public institutions*. Private sector initiative and market mechanisms are important, but they must go hand-in-hand with *good governance* – a public service that is efficient, a judicial system that is reliable, and *an administration that is accountable to its public*. And a better balance is needed between the government and the governed. Thus the report sets out a range of proposals aimed at *empowering ordinary people*, and especially women, to *take greater responsibility for improving their lives ....*" (World Bank, 1989, p. xii, emphasis added)

Under the rubric of good governance, this excerpt connects all the dots for the participation template that emerged in the 1980s. It asserts the failure of public institutions, calls for public administration that is accountable to its public, and states that ordinary people should take responsibility for their own development. While this statement by Conable would conclude the evidence on participation from the 1980s, it would also set up the decade of the 1990s as a period in which the blueprint of good governance, decentralization, and participation would be advanced extensively in the Bank's development theory and practice. As the report itself states: "The watchwords for the future are delegation, community participation, and cost recovery" (World Bank, 1989, p. 7).

In the 1990s, we encounter numerous publications that reinforce the reorientation of the roles of both governments and individual citizens in development. Just as before, these publications emphasize a redefinition, reduction, and reallocation of the functions and organization of the state by promoting the overlapping notions of good governance, decentralization, and better management (Burki, Perry, & Dillinger, 1999; Litvack, Ahmad, & Bird, 1998; Peterson, 1994; World Bank, 1991, 1992, 1994, 1997). Moreover, as with the 1980s, the idea of participation was concomitantly elevated (World Bank, 1996, 1997).

To that end, in 1996, *The World Bank Participation Sourcebook* noticeably adopted a robust definition of participation in which "stakeholders influence and share control over development initiatives and the decisions and resources which affect them" (World Bank, 1996, p. xi). However, as the document makes clear, the "influence" and "control" aspects of this definition are equated with the ability to act as either a consumer or provider of services in market-based relationships. Specifically, according to the Bank, "as the capacity of poor people is strengthened and their voices begin to be heard, they become 'clients' who are capable of demanding and paying for goods and services … . these clients ultimately become the owners and managers of their assets and activities" (World Bank, 1996, p. 8). In this context, as the *Sourcebook* explains, participation boils down to accessing information, engaging in contracts, and owning and managing assets (World Bank, 1996).

Taken together, the numerous publications on good governance, decentralization, and participation indicate that the emphasis on the latter was not just about providing individuals with access to information or ensuring that a legal framework to uphold contracts existed, but rather also about promoting market-based service provision arrangements and then involving the population in them as clients and as do-it-yourself providers. The more it is possible to shift the responsibility for service provision to private citizens who take on ownership, management, and financing functions, the better (World Bank, 1996). Where this is not wholly possible, however, the push for good governance – through decentralization and better management practices – suggests that the provision of services should at least be brought closer to the end users, or clients. Said another way, direct government provision should be greatly reduced, and the operations relinquished should be sent to lower levels that, in theory, can be held more accountable by "partnering" with communities, where partnering means instituting policies that require citizens to construct, manage, and/or fund basic infrastructure, education, and healthcare projects (Burki et al., 1999; World Bank, 1997). The Bank's conception of participation and the framework in which it nests evolved to support the idea that, as opposed to central governments delivering basic services, individual citizens, communities, and local governments should participate in development by engaging in market-oriented relations based on choice, competition, self-financing, automanagement, and accountability.[3]

## THE FRAMEWORK FOR SERVICE PROVISION

A particular perspective on participation had been developing for twenty plus years before taking center stage in the 2004 WDR, *Making Services Work for Poor People* (World Bank, 2003).[4] Given the focus on the need for accountability in the preceding decades, it is not surprising that the resulting FSP has this concept at its core. Indeed, as presented in the 2004 WDR, this framework – reproduced here in Fig. 1 – has embedded in it both a "long route" and a "short route" to accountability. The long route to accountability between citizens and the state represents what "we would recognize as comprising both the aggregation of interests at a national level and the operation of formal democratic politics" (Mundy, 2008, p. 3). Per the Bank, however, this route is not desirable because official government channels engender "a large bureaucratic machine and strong interest groups whose lobbying could result in … inertia" (Di Gropello, 2006a, p. 1). The accountability relationships of democratic processes are presumed to break down, thus rendering government unresponsive and therefore an impediment to development.

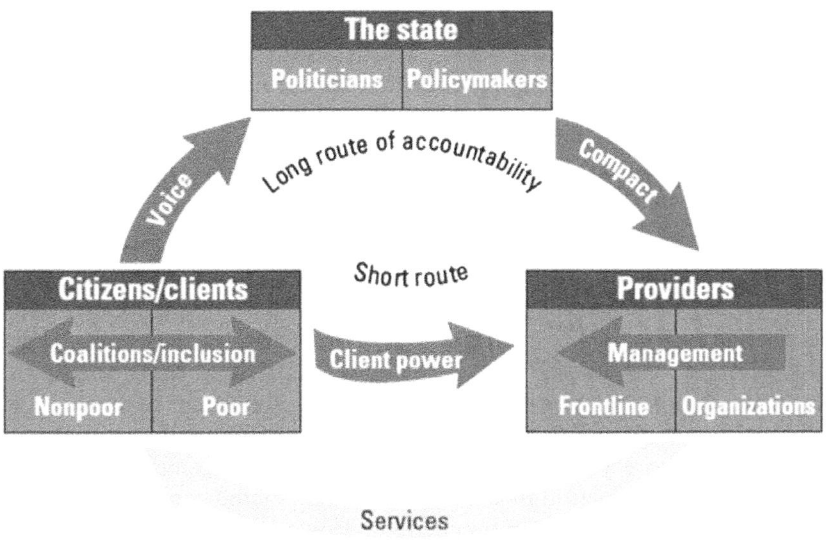


*Fig. 1.* Relationships of Power in the Service Provision Framework. *Source*: © World Bank (2003).

The solution, then, according to the logic of the framework, is to change the nature of the relationship between citizens and their services by largely removing the government from the equation. Citizens should be given the upper hand to become, or interact directly with, service providers. This is accomplished in short route relationships by localizing service providers so they can be held accountable for the quality of services delivered. As delineated by the Bank (2003), these local-level, short route relationships are (a) premised on a set of mechanistic interactions in which one set of actors (i.e., principals) enter into a relationship with other actors (i.e., agents) in order to (b) receive a service (such as education) in exchange for monetary compensation, and through which (c) the principals have the ability to enforce via recourse (normally some form of data-based correctional action) the delivery or the improvement of the service in question from the agent.

This definition is the heart of the way in which participation continues to be conceptualized by the Bank. The thought is that "citizens must reveal to providers their demand for services and [then] monitor the providers' provision of services" (World Bank, 2003, p. 51). Citizens are conceived as "conscientious consumers and vigilant observers" who will switch service providers when they are unsatisfied (Ackerman, 2005, p. 15). This form of participation is presented as the glue that holds (or should hold) together a variety of important relationships. Such relationships include those between consumers and providers, citizens and their elected officials, and government ministries and public servants. This is also true for communities and their schools in the provision of education, as the next section shows.

## PARTICIPATION AND EDUCATION GOVERNANCE

Bank thinking on participation and the reform of education governance has mirrored the trends within the Bank on the role of participation in development more generally. Shortly after the Bank began to encourage decentralization and the involvement of beneficiaries in their own service provision (as with the 1980 and 1983 WDRs), these ideas emerge as recommendations for how the education sector should be reformed (e.g., Psacharopoulos, Tan, & Jimenez, 1986). In the late 1980s and early 1990s, as calls became more vociferous from senior Bank management about "the failure of public institutions," the need for "good governance," the imperative of "an administration that is accountable to its public," and the desirability of "ordinary people ... tak[ing] greater responsibility for their lives" (World Bank, 1989, p. xii), we witness an increase in the attention given by the Bank to education decentralization. This increase in attention occurred with regard to theory (Winkler, 1989), research (Jimenez & Tan, 1987; Prawda, 1993), and practice (especially in Latin America; see, e.g., Di Gropello, 2006b; World Bank/IEG, 2006). Both the literature produced and loans supported during this time demonstrate that the participatory ideas at the center of the Bank's approach to development generally had been adopted and adapted within its work on education sector reform.

In the mid-to-late 1990s, the push in education reform for accountability-based participation in a context of decentralization, competition, and choice accelerated. This push was evinced by the fact that the 1995 *Priorities and Strategies for Education* (World Bank, 1995) dedicated two chapters to elaborating the thinking behind it, under the headings "household involvement" and "autonomous institutions." It stated, for example, that though "most households already contribute, directly or indirectly, to the costs of education, ... they could participate in school management and oversight, along with their wider communities, and they could be given the possibility of choosing among schools" (World Bank, 1995, p. 120). The 1999 *Education Sector Strategy* (World Bank, 1999) then went beyond discussion to make decentralization one of the Bank's official lending priorities in education sector reform. Just as it did in the Bank more generally (World Bank, 1996), this focus on governance and decentralization appeared in tandem with the definition of participation as equivalent to being a consumer. Indeed, one of the central operating principles guiding education reform in the 1999 *Education Sector Strategy* was a "focus on the client." This meant: "developing operations that respond to the local needs of clients and facilitate their participation as full partners ... The client owns its programs and sets the pace for change" (World Bank, 1999, p. 37). Thus, in both of these major 1990s' publications, the emphasis was on moving responsibility for education governance to the local level, where participation could occur through consumer engagement in market-based relations. If school control could be transferred to the community level and if the conditions for school choice could be created, then parents would participate in education as managers and consumers.

Surrounding these two high-profile publications were numerous other works by the Bank from the 1990s through the early 2000s that reinforced or reviewed the conception of participation in education reform. These included, for example, publications on the virtues and challenges related to community and/or household financing of decentralization (Bray, 1996a, 1996b; Patrinos & Ariasingam, 1997), the national politics that surround the decision to decentralize (Fiske, 1996), and the legal issues one must consider when implementing decentralization (Florestal & Cooper, 1997). By the end of the decade of the 1990s, as decentralization policies were increasingly implemented around the world, the Bank conducted reviews of them in Latin America (Winkler & Gershberg, 2000) and Africa (Winkler & Gershberg, 2003). Not only did ideas of decentralization appear in major publications, but the Bank also produced a series of publications that reviewed, buttressed, and encouraged these ideas.[5]

In practice, the Bank has attempted to pursue the vision it set out in its major 1990s' publications (see, e.g., Di Gropello, 2006b; Nielsen, 2007). That is, in operationalizing its conception of participation, the Bank has supported decentralization reforms in which (a) responsibility for individual schools is given to the community and (b) a council of volunteer parents is elected to manage each community's school. Ideally, students also have access to both a traditional school and a decentralized school so parents can choose which one their child will attend. As for the parents on the school council, the Bank encourages arrangements where they are responsible for hiring, firing, distributing payment to, and holding accountable the school's teacher(s). Financing for these schools should then come either in whole or in part from the central government. Commonly, decentralization reforms have been supported in which the government provides part of the costs associated with education provision, while the community, either officially or unofficially, contributes the rest – either in kind or in cash (Bray, 1996a, 1996b).

Thus, though the FSP was not crystallized until the 2004 WDR (World Bank, 2003), the thinking behind it was at the core of how the Bank understood and sought to realize education governance and, within that, participation. In terms of the FSP, through the arrangements described in the previous paragraph, parents engage in local-level relationships and become the principals (in the economic sense) who provide monetary compensation (supplied by either the government and/or the community) in exchange for services from teachers (i.e., agents). In that parents have the authority to manage, hire, and fire teachers, a set of accountability relationships has also been instituted, just as the FSP states is ideal.

While it is evident that the rationale of the FSP, per the WDR 2004, is reflected in the Bank's work in education decentralization, it should also be noted that, within that overarching framework, more extensive theoretical justifications for the decentralization of education governance have been elaborated by Bank education specialists. These justifications relate to social and technical efficiency, quality and effectiveness, the financial burden on central governments, service access, and equity (Behrman & King, 2001; Winkler, 1989; World Bank, 2003). First, to the extent that parents (a) can hire and fire teachers, (b) have increased information on or knowledge of the quality of their child's school, and (c) can choose among schools, then their preferences will, through these accountability mechanisms, be better met (social efficiency) (Winkler, 1989). Second, to the extent that parents are responsible for paying teachers and spending discretionary funds, they will seek to minimize costs (technical efficiency) (Winkler, 1989).[6] Third, the enhanced accountability relationships between parents and teachers give the latter an incentive to work harder and perform better, thereby raising quality and effectiveness. Fourth, to the extent that communities fund and volunteer to manage these services, it both reduces the financial burden on national governments[7] and results in increased supply of (i.e., access to) educational services. Fifth, it is suggested that to the extent that there is increased information available on the quality of service providers, equity will benefit because the poor (who otherwise normally experience greater difficulty in accessing such information) will be able to make better choices about which provider to choose, assuming parents have a choice of provider (Behrman & King, 2001). A later section of this chapter examines whether the results of Bank-supported decentralization reforms corroborate these theorized outcomes.

Though the conception of education management decentralization put forth by the Bank has remained rather stable over time, there have been three noticeable developments since the late 1990s. The first pertains to the increasing emphasis on student achievement as measured by standardized tests (Bruns, Filmer, & Patrinos, 2011; Lewis & Pettersson, 2009; World Bank, 2003, 2005; World Bank/IEG, 2006), which was formally endorsed by the Bank in its 1999 *Education Sector Strategy* (World Bank, 1999). The implication is that the success of participation through decentralization to raise education quality should be measured primarily in terms of test scores. Per the Bank literature, though the central government should reduces its responsibility for the management of education, it should still monitor the performance of those schools through standardized testing.

The second development relates to the language used to frame decentralization. Though the "ultimate form of decentralization" (World Bank/IEG, 2006, p. 44) is still based around a school council made up of community members who hire, fire, and monitor teachers, as well as spend a discretionary portion of the school budget, the term used to refer to education decentralization is now "school-based management" (Barrera-Osorio, Fasih, Patrinos, & Santibáñez, 2009; Bruns et al., 2011; World Bank,

2005, 2007, 2008).[8] Changing the terminology to school-based management reflects a more narrow conception of decentralization. To the extent that the community dimension is being written out of consideration by replacing the language of decentralization with the phrase school-based management, we see a further atomization of the relevant level for thinking about local participation in education governance. Such language implies that resources from neither the community, national, nor international levels are seen as relevant factors that may impact either local-level educational success or the ability of communities to participate in the provision of that education. Nevertheless, in that community members continue to fund and/or partake in the management of their schools in practice, participation continues to be at the heart of education decentralization.

A third shift has become evident with the recent publication of the Bank's Education Strategy 2020, *Learning for All* (World Bank, 2011). What this publication makes explicit is that the Bank now sees it as necessary to reform not only community-level provision of education per the FSP's accountability-based relationships but also entire national education systems and "all learning opportunities in a given society" along these same lines (World Bank, 2011, p. 29; see also Di Gropello, 2007). In putting forth this vision, the Bank has removed the language of participation and replaced it with the language of accountability exclusively. The concepts have not changed, however. We are simply witnessing the application sector-wide of the FSP, as first expressed in the 2004 WDR and as again reproduced in the *Learning for All* strategy document (in the latter, see pp. 29–31). It is a rephrasing, scaling up, and intensification of the same concepts. Whereas education governance reforms once invoked the language of participation, they now rely on a narrow yet more broadly applied conception of accountability. Any and all work done in the education sector, whether by the community or the central ministry of education, should follow the logic of mechanistic accountability.

These three shifts in thinking are concerning for multiple reasons. First, they conceive of a test-based accountability relationship between ministries of education and schools, which may foster adversarial and antagonistic dynamics that discourage rather than encourage local stakeholder participation (Edwards, 2010). Second, they isolate the school from its context and, in so doing de-emphasize the value of broad community participation. Third, at the system level, they place attention solely on accountability relationships and focus neither on increased financial inputs nor on support structures for students, teachers, communities, and the administrative levels within ministries of education charged with overseeing and facilitating decentralization reforms. Together, these changes in the way education reform and, within that, participation are conceptualized are unsettling because they have the potential to undermine collaboration and trust, as well as the administrative, technical, and financial support communities often need.

Before proceeding, it should be noted that participation is not something that the Bank only supports conceptually. It bears mentioning that the Bank funds in application what it conceives in theory. By 1999, after 15 years of encouraging it, the Bank commented how "virtually all the Bank's client countries are tackling education reform by involving decentralization" (World Bank, 1999, p. ix). In 2009, Barrera-Osorio et al. (2009) noted not only that a full 18 percent of all Bank project lending between 2000 and 2006 went to education decentralization, but also that the current portfolio includes countries in nearly every world region (Latin America; Eastern Europe; South, Central, and Eastern Asia; the Middle East and North Africa; and Sub-Saharan Africa). More recently, in 2010, in a Bank review of all lending to primary and secondary education since 2001, it was found that the percentage of projects incorporating school-level decentralization has continued to increase: While 48 percent of projects between 2001 and 2005 included support for school-level governance, this number jumped to 64 percent between 2006 and 2009 (World Bank/IEG, 2010, p. 28). Given that decentralization increasingly receives higher levels of funding, it is especially imperative that the results of Bank supported and funded projects be closely examined.

## RESULTS OF BANK-SUPPORTED PARTICIPATION REFORMS IN EDUCATION

The previous section made clear that the Bank understands participation in education governance within a framework of decentralization. Reviewing the dozens of individual studies on education decentralization that have been conducted by the Bank is beyond the scope of this chapter, however. Here, as noted earlier, I review only multicountry evaluations and reports produced by the Bank that assess or document the impacts of education decentralization projects that it has assisted in financing and supporting.[9] By relying on such multicountry evaluations and reports, we get a sense of the overall effects (or lack thereof) of Bank-supported, participation-related development activities in education – though we may miss some of the details that emerge in individual policy assessments and single-country case studies. An important benefit to including here only those studies that review projects actually supported by the Bank is that we can be sure that the results discussed here stem from the implementation of reforms with a common theory of action – that is, the theory of education decentralization detailed in the previous section.

Given the above criteria, the literature examined is Barrera-Osorio et al. (2009), Bruns et al. (2011), Nielsen (2007), and World Bank/IEG (2006).[10] Among these publications are two – Nielsen (2007) and World Bank/IEG (2006) – produced by the staff of the Independent Evaluation Group (IEG). Importantly, IEG reports directly to the Bank's president and executive directors, as opposed to department and research managers, who have been shown to discourage findings and/or publications that do not align with the Bank's official policy preferences (Broad, 2006). This allows the evaluators to be somewhat more frank in their assessments of Bank projects. In addition, given that their task is to evaluate Bank projects for an internal audience rather than to promote them for adoption (Verger, 2012), IEG reports assess more aspects of Bank projects, including equity and implementation issues, than do the Bank's other broad reviews.

The results discussed below have been identified and grouped by systematically reviewing the above-noted studies in light of the theory of education decentralization presented in the previous section. In addition to synthesizing the findings of these multicountry reports, I also reflect on the implications of the results they present and highlight those aspects of theory to which these studies do not speak. In what follows, I discuss results related to the intertwined concepts of quality, accountability, efficiency, finance, access, and equity. I also comment on the implementation issues raised in the analyzed eports.

Often, in the current reform climate, the first question to be asked of education reform is whether it improves quality, most commonly as measured by student test scores. Each of the four studies reviewed here speaks to this point. Nielsen (2007), a senior evaluation officer in the Bank's IEG, concludes, after reviewing Bank studies of education decentralization in 12 countries, that "in none of the cases ... is there any evidence that community empowerment has helped improve the quality of the teaching and learning in the classroom" (p. 90). Similarly, World Bank/IEG (2006), upon reviewing Bank lending to primary education between 1990 and 2005 asserts that, though "decentralization of educational management is supported by an increasing share of Bank primary education projects, ... the effects of this on educational access and quality, especially for the disadvantaged, have not been established" (p. 43). Barrera-Osorio et al. (2009), who examine dozens of studies on more than 20 countries, and Bruns et al. (2011), who analyze tens of evaluations on 11 different countries, both conclude that, on the whole, the evidence with regard to student test scores is mixed. They both point to the limitations of existing studies and call for additional, more rigorous studies, many of which are underway at the moment. With regard to currently available evidence, however, they both point to a handful of countries that have shown positive results, such as El Salvador, Kenya, Mexico, and Nicaragua. It should be noted, however, that, with regard to El Salvador, Mexico, and Nicaragua, these conclusions are based on studies whose methods, interpretations, and/or findings have been challenged (Edwards, 2011; Kaester & Gershberg, 2002; Reimers & Cárdenas, 2007). At best, the evidence on quality is mixed; at worst, Bank studies contain misleading findings. Either way, the multicountry reports reviewed here do not show the general link to increased quality that is supposed by the Bank's theory of education decentralization.

This finding could be the result of weak linkages in assumed relationships of accountability, a concept that depends on a number of factors. One factor is the supply of teachers in areas with decentralized education governance, for the chance of a teacher being fired is mitigated if there are no replacements. To that end, World Bank/IEG (2006) states that "in most countries, [there are] serious teacher shortages in marginalized areas" and that "modest financial incentives are not sufficient to convince urban, university-educated women to move to or teach in poor rural areas" (p. 44). In that decentralization programs often occur in rural and marginalized areas (Di Gropello, 2006b), one of the fundamental accountability mechanisms is frequently not operationalized.

A second factor in accountability relationships is information availability and the ability of school councils to make data-based decisions. Nielsen (2007), however, concludes that, at the community level, "parents lack information and do not know what to push" (p. 90).[11] This is not to say that communities are completely unaware of the condition or functioning of their school, nor that communities are unable to manage local schools, only that available information in many cases is minimal and that school councils may require more training and support in order to assess and improve a teacher's effectiveness (Nielsen, 2007).

A third factor at the heart of accountability is competition. Noticeably, however, none of the reports reviewed speak to this point – that is, whether decentralization programs increased competition among locally and centrally controlled schools. This may be because, rather than introducing new, locally controlled schools to compete with centrally controlled ones, decentralization programs instead facilitate the creation of schools where none existed previously and/or because these programs prompt the conversion of existing schools from central to community control.

A fourth factor that may limit the ability of communities to hold their schools accountable is elite capture. This is the idea that, in a given community, a relatively more well-off individual or family will dominate the decision-making body (e.g., the school council) and direct committed resources to the uses that they most prefer. An example could be hiring one's relative to teach in the community school, rather than hiring a potentially more qualified candidate. Though Bank documents sometimes refer to this local accountability threat, no evidence is provided one way or the other on its existence.[12] On the whole, the evidence suggests that the presumed accountability relationships – those market-based dynamics at the core of how decentralization is thought to operate – have not to this point materialized in practice as they are hypothesized in theory.

The same market dynamics that promote accountability are also those that, in large part, engender both social and technical efficiency. Given the absence of these dynamics (as evidenced by the above discussion of accountability), perhaps it should not be a surprise that there is silence in the reviewed documents on social efficiency. When mechanisms based on information availability, community technical capacity, teacher supply, and school choice are not functional, we have little reason to expect increases in the extent to which parents' preferences are met (i.e., social efficiency). But what about technical efficiency, or the extent to which school councils seek to minimize costs? Expenditures may be reduced under decentralization, but, to the extent that this occurs, it does so because communities use their time and resources to build, rehabilitate, and maintain schools (Nielsen, 2007; World Bank/IEG, 2006). Put differently, evidence suggests that overall monetary costs may be reduced because communities pay fees and provide time, labor, and materials in kind, and not because school councils seek out the most economical mix of inputs. That, in turn, could reflect the fact that school budgets are largely dedicated to teacher salaries and because school councils have few (if any) discretionary funds. Indeed, rather than allocating publicly provided school budgets in such a way as to minimize costs, parents often pay additional fees to cover basic school inputs (Bray, 1996a, 1996b).

The one form of efficiency to which evidence relates is internal efficiency, or the extent to which levels of repetition, failure, and dropouts are affected. Both Barrera-Osorio et al. (2009) and Bruns et al. (2011) assert that a number of studies they review show positive effects in this regard. However, while repetition, failure, and dropouts may co-occur with the implementation of decentralization programs, in the absence of a counterfactual, we do not know that community control causes these outcomes. These positive effects could result from the increased levels of access that decentralization often engenders by shifting responsibilities to communities. In order to correctly attribute reductions in repetition, failure, and dropouts, the effects of increases in schooling availability must be separated from the effects of increases in community control. With regard to the present review, however, what stands out is that, though the idea of efficiency, like accountability, is a primary argument for pursuing decentralization, the Bank's own multicountry reviews of its projects do not comment on any of the dimensions of efficiency posited in theory.

Unlike efficiency, equity is not a concept often drawn upon in relation to decentralization. Though, as noted in an earlier section, the article by Behrman and King (2001) suggests that greater information availability will, in theory, disproportionately benefit the poor, this line of thinking is rarely encountered in other Bank documents. Similarly, the actual impact on equity is scantly discussed in the Bank's multicountry reviews of decentralization. Perhaps this is due to the inherent potential, in practice, for inequity to increase when the responsibility for managing and financing (either in cash or in kind) education is shifted to heterogeneous communities. World Bank/IEG (2006), the only Bank review to comment on equity, notes this inherent possibility for decentralization to adversely affect equity and refers to the cases of Ghana and Peru:

> The impact study in Ghana revealed how decentralization in that country (involving a greater share of financing by districts and communities) has led to disparities in resource availability between poor and non-poor areas. Similarly, case study managers in Peru perceived vast inequalities in district capacity to effectively manage education under the country's proposed new decentralization laws (p. 43).

Interestingly, this report by the Bank's IEG actually cites Uruguay – "perhaps Latin America's most centralized country" (p. 43) – as an exemplar to follow in addressing inequitable educational outcomes. In sum, however, with regard to equity, the reports reviewed do not speak to the theorized benefits, likely because evidence does not exist or has not been collected on that on which equity improvements are hypothesized to be based – such as greater information availability and increased competition and choice among schools. Instead, the few assertions that are made regarding equity relate to the negative impacts that stem from differences across communities in their levels of financial resources and technical capacity.

A mix of other findings pertains to the benefits and shortcomings of the implementation and adoption of decentralization programs. First, with regard to the benefits, both Barrera-Osorio et al. (2009) and Bruns et al. (2011) note that decentralization "policies actually changed the dynamics of the school, either because parents got more involved or because teachers' actions changed" (Barrera-Osorio et al., 2009, p. 40). The studies on which this finding is based show, for example, that parents more often visit the school and that teachers more frequently visit students' homes (compared with schools not in decentralization programs). Importantly, this finding demonstrates that decentralization reforms can lead to more participation by parents in school affairs.

However, though these changes in dynamics around the school are beneficial, there are serious implementation and adoption shortcomings. On implementation, World Bank/IEG (2006) finds that decentralization models have been prematurely scaled up. That is, in some countries, the reforms were scaled up "before their models were fully developed. Consequently, there is much ambiguity over what level of government is responsible for different functions and how functions transferred to local governments will be financed" (p. 44). These findings speak to larger issues at the level of system capacity. They suggest that, in addition to worsening inequity at the community level, decentralization reforms, as implemented, often weaken the ability of governmental administrative structures to provide the support recently decentralized communities may require. While this may not be the case in all instances of decentralization, to the extent that it occurs, it reduces the likelihood that the theorized functioning and outcomes of decentralization will come to fruition.

The findings on adoption may shed light on why reforms are hastily scaled up. Nielsen (2007), the only one to comment on adoption, asserts: "In most locations it appears that the model has been adopted without the benefit of pilot testing or good evidence that the approach can influence school quality and learning outcomes in a given context" (pp. 90–91). One one hand, it is surprising that widespread adoption of these policies would occur without pilot testing or good evidence. On the other hand, as Nielsen (2007) points out, it is consistent with the fact that, when decentralization became an official priority for lending in 1999, it did so without "any evidence that decentralization made a difference in valued education outcomes" but with a clear "determination [by the Bank] to support countries in their movement towards more local decision-making" (p. 84). Just as the adoption of decentralization occurs at the country level without good evidence, so too did the adoption of decentralization within the Bank's education work occur this way. Thus, the finding by Nielsen (2007) that the Bank typically neither engages in pilot testing nor demonstrates positive impacts on school quality can be understood as a by-product of the fact that the Bank is primarily an ideological institution that encourages a market-based approach to development and, within that, supports a narrow, accountability-based conception of participation through decentralization.

## CONCLUSION

In this chapter I have attempted to explore the approach to participation of the World Bank. In the first section I investigated those official publications that present the Bank's overall development approach in order to trace both the emergence of participation and the trajectory of thinking behind it. As was shown, the idea of participation within the Bank emerged in tandem with a call for governments to decentralize the provision of public services. The literature also showed that, despite some robust language in the 1996 *Participation Sourcebook* (World Bank, 1996), the operationalization of participation in the official Bank discourse rests on the notion of citizens engaging in market-based relations through which they can either exercise their purchasing power as informed consumers, act as accountability levers for service providers, or directly assume the role of public service management and delivery themselves.

The second section focused on the FSP, the overarching framework within which the Bank understands participation. In crystallizing the thinking that had been developing for over two decades, the Bank emphasizes through this framework the notion of short route accountability. Short route accountability is thought to be the solution to the inherently problematic organization of central government ministries. As was shown, the idea behind short route accountability relationships is that, by localizing relationships between service providers and consumers, one is able to institute a set of narrow, mechanistic relationships in which principals (i.e., clients) receive services from agents (i.e., providers) and through which the former can incentivize the latter to improve their services, or else risk losing business to competitors.

It was shown in the third section that the thinking in the Bank's education work with regard to participation has both paralleled and extended the thinking within the Bank more generally. At the same time that the Bank's education sector has adopted and worked within the FSP's thinking, it has also developed additional theoretical justifications around the functioning and benefits of participation in governance reforms. Specifically, by shifting the responsibility for school management to the community level, by receiving at least a portion of the financing for education from parents, and by assuming that competition among schools would increase, documents published by the Bank and its staff posit that decentralization leads to increased social and technical efficiency, improved quality and effectiveness, enhanced access, a reduced financial burden on central governments, and a more equitable distribution of information about school performance (which in turn facilitates the operation of the school choice mechanism, especially among poor parents).

The fourth section showed, however, that these hypothesized outcomes are not always realized, or even addressed in evaluation. The reviewed documents showed that, at best, findings on quality improvement are mixed. These documents also revealed that research has not addressed efficiency, at least not as theorized. Attention was given neither to the fulfillment of parents' preferences (social efficiency) nor to the minimization of costs by parents on school councils (technical efficiency). To the extent that decentralization reduces finance costs, it does so because central governments' expenses are reduced by shifting a portion of the costs to communities (either in cash or in kind). Equity, like efficiency, also received very little attention in the multicountry reports reviewed. Only one IEG study touched on equity, and it acknowledged that Bank projects can increase "disparities in resource availability between poor and non-poor areas" (p. 43). In addition, the reviewed literature showed that we do not have cause to believe that the theorized accountability dynamics emerge and operate in practice, which are presumed to bring about the benefits of the Bank's conception of participation. That is, those accountability mechanisms based on excess teacher supply, information availability, community technical capacity, and competition among schools are often not operationalized. Moreover, as pointed out, the probability of realizing the posited benefits is further reduced by the fact that implementation is sometimes prematurely scaled up. Despite these issues, however, it is of note that the Bank not only continues to push its version of participation at the community level, but also that, as made clear in Education Strategy 2020, it also seeks to reform all relationships in national education systems per the FSP's short route version of accountability (World Bank, 2003, 2011).

Thus, in the present research, I explored the Bank's approach to development and education governance and showed how a particular conception of participation is at the heart of them. I also reviewed the results of education governance reforms which are based in this thinking and supported by the Bank. By fleshing out these issues, the hope is that I have not only brought some clarity to how the Bank approaches participation, but that I have also shown that, despite theory to the contrary, a narrow, accountability-based version of participation in the context of nonfunctional market dynamics is problematic, and that it may be more fruitful to explore alternative approaches to participation in development and education governance (Edwards & Klees, forthcoming).

## NOTES

1. This framework for participation is separate from the framework for participation within which borrower countries develop poverty reduction strategy papers (World Bank, 2000), which delineate a national government's overall approach to development.
2. For literature outside the Bank on participation, see, for example, Cornwall (2006), Cornwall and Brock (2005), Edwards and Klees (forthcoming), and Leal (2007).
3. This is known as a neoliberal approach to participation in development. See Edwards and Klees (forthcoming) for more on how this approach contrasts with liberal and progressive forms of participation in development and education governance.
4. Although the FSP is featured in both World Bank (2003) and World Bank (2011), I focus predominantly on its presentation in the former because it is more fully and formally elaborated there. That is not to say, however, that the FSP is any less integral to the latter's reform approach, for it certainly is, as I show later in this section.
5. The exception to this is Bray (1996a, 1996b), who, as a visiting scholar in 1996 in the Bank's Human Development Department, gave substantial emphasis to the negative effects on equity of relying on communities and households to finance decentralization.
6. Not all economists agree on definitions of efficiency. Levin (1976), for example, discusses an alternative definition of technical efficiency in which it refers not to minimizing costs but rather to the extent to which schools are organized to produce the maximum possible output.
7. Bank discussions of government service provision always either implicitly or explicitly assume constrained government budgets (e.g., Winkler, 1989). See Klees (2008) for issues surrounding the logic of an assumed budget cap.

8. In the United States, school-based management is the label under which decentralization has been discussed since the late 1980s (see, e.g., Malen, Ogawa, & Kranz, 1990).

9. These criteria eliminate studies produced by the Bank that look at decentralization reforms that it has not financed or supported (e.g., Bray, 1996b; Gunnarsson, Orazem, Sánchez, & Verdisco, 2008; Prawda, 1993; Winkler & Gershberg, 2000, 2003).

10. Di Gropello (2006b) and Umansky and Vegas (2007) are not included here because they are based on studies that have been called into question (Edwards, 2011; Kaester & Gershberg, 2002; Nielsen, 2007).

11. The use of information in decision-making is a systemwide issue. World Bank/IEG (2006) found, for example, that "where functioning [monitoring and evaluation] systems have been established, ... rarely have results been used in decision-making" (p. 47). This is exacerbated by the poor quality (i.e., inaccurate nature) of the data (World Bank/IEG, 2006).

12. Bardhan (2002) suggests that we should not always assume the phenomenon of elite capture because it depends on a large number of factors that should be investigated on a case-by-case basis.

# REFERENCES

Ackerman, J. (2005). *Social accountability in the public sector: A conceptual discussion*. Social Development Paper No. 82, World Bank, Washington, DC.

Bardhan, P. (2002). Decentralization of governance and development. *The Journal of Economic Perspectives*, *16*, 185–205.

Barrera-Osorio, F., Fasih, T., Patrinos, H., & Santibáñez, L. (2009). *Decentralized decision-making in schools: The theory and evidence on school-based management*. Washington, DC: The World Bank.

Behrman, J., & King, E. (2001). Household schooling behaviors and decentralization. *Economics of Education Review*, *20*, 321–341.

Bray, M. (1996a). *Decentralization of education: Community financing*. Washington, DC: World Bank.

Bray, M. (1996b). *Counting the full cost: Parental and community financing of education in East Asia*. Washington, DC: The World Bank in collaboration with UNICEF.

Broad, R. (2006). Research, knowledge, and the art of 'paradigm maintenance': The World Bank's development economics Vice-Presidency (DEC). *Review of International Political Economy*, *13*, 387–419.

Bruns, B., Filmer, D., & Patrinos, H. (2011). *Making schools work: New evidence on accountability reforms*. Washington, D.C: World Bank.

Burki, S., Perry, G., & Dillinger, W. (1999). *Beyond the center: Decentralizing the state*. Washington, DC: World Bank.

Cornwall, A. (2006). Historical perspectives on participation in development. *Commonwealth & Comparative Politics*, *44*, 49–65.

Cornwall, A., & Brock, K. (2005). What do buzzwords do for development policy? A critical look at "participation," "empowerment" and "poverty reduction". *Third World Quarterly*, *26*, 1043–1060.

Di Gropello, E. (Ed.). (2006a). *Meeting the challenges of secondary education in Latin America and East Asia: Improving efficiency and resource mobilization.* Washington, DC: World Bank.

Di Gropello, E. (2006b). *A comparative analysis of school-based management in Central America.* World Bank Working Paper No. 72, World Bank, Washington, DC.

Di Gropello, E. (2007). Education decentralisation and accountability relationships in Latin America and the Caribbean region. In T. Townsend (Ed.), *International handbook of school effectiveness and improvement.* Secaucus, NJ: Springer.

Edwards Jr., D. B. (2010). A comparison of local empowerment in education: Porto Alegre, Brazil and Chicago, USA. *Research in Comparative and International Education, 5,* 176–184.

Edwards Jr., D. B. (2011). *Appraising the evidence on decentralization in El Salvador.* Unpublished manuscript. College Park, MD: University of Maryland.

Edwards Jr., D. B., & Klees, S. (Forthcoming). Participation in development and education governance. In A. Verger, M. Novelli, & H. Kosar-Altinyelken (Eds.), *Global education policy and international development: New agendas, issues and programmes.* New York: Continuum.

Fiske, E. (1996). *Decentralization of education: Politics and consensus.* Washington, DC: World Bank.

Florestal, K., & Cooper, R. (1997). *Decentralization of education: Legal issues.* Washington, DC: World Bank.

Gunnarsson, V., Orazem, P., Sánchez, M., & Verdisco, A. (2008). *Does local school control raise student outcomes? Evidence on the roles of school autonomy and community participation.* Working Paper No. 09012, Department of Economics, Iowa State University, Ames, IA.

Jimenez, E., & Tan, J. (1987). Decentralised and private education: The case of Pakistan. *Comparative Education, 23,* 173–190.

Kaester, R., & Gershberg, A. (2002). *Lessons learned from Nicaragua's school autonomy reform: A review of research by the Nicaraguan reform evaluation team of the World Bank.* Paper written for the project "Empowering Parents While Making Them Pay: Autonomous Schools in Nicaragua." New York: New School University. Retrieved from http://www.newschool.edu/milano/cdrc/schoolreport/index.html

Klees, S. (2008). A quarter century of neoliberal thinking in education: Misleading analyses and failed policies. *Globalisation, Societies and Education, 6,* 311–348.

Lauglo, J. (1995). Forms of decentralization and their implications for education. *Comparative Education, 31,* 5–29.

Leal, P. A. (2007). Participation: The ascendancy of a buzzword in the neoliberal era. *Development and Practice, 17,* 539–548.

Levin, H. (1976). Concepts of economic efficiency and educational production. In J. Froomkin, D. Jamison & R. Radner (Eds.), *Education as an industry* (pp. 149–198). Washington, DC: NBER.

Lewis, M., & Pettersson, G. (2009). *Governance in education: Raising performance.* Washington, DC: World Bank.

Litvack, J., Ahmad, J., & Bird, R. (1998). *Rethinking decentralization in developing countries.* Sector Studies Series. Washington, DC: World Bank.

Malen, B., Ogawa, R., & Kranz, J. (1990). What do we know about school-based management? A case study of the literature – A call for research. In W. Clune & J. Witte (Eds.), *Choice and control in American education volume 2: The practice of choice, decentralization, and school restructuring* (pp. 289–342). New York: Falmer Press.

Mundy, K. (2008). *Civil society and its role in the achievement and governance of "Education for All."* Background paper prepared for the Education for All Global Monitoring Report 2009. UNESCO, Paris, France.

Nielsen, H. D. (2007). Empowering communities for improved educational outcomes: Some evaluation findings from the World Bank. *Prospects*, *37*, 81–93.

Patrinos, H., & Ariasingam, D. (1997). *Decentralization of education: Demand-side financing*. Washington, DC: World Bank.

Peterson, G. E. (1994). *Decentralization in Latin America: An overview of lessons and issues*. Washington, DC: World Bank, LATAD (May).

Prawda, J. (1993). Educational decentralization in Latin America: Lessons learned. *International Journal of Educational Development*, *13*, 253–264.

Psacharopoulos, G., Tan, J., & Jimenez, E. (1986). *The financing of education in developing countries: An exploration of policy options*. Washington, DC: The World Bank.

Reimers, F., & Cárdenas, S. (2007). Who benefits from school-based management in Mexico? *Prospects*, *37*, 37–56.

Umansky, I., & Vegas, E. (2007). Inside decentralization: How three Central American school-based management reforms affect student learning through teacher incentives. *The World Bank Research Observer*, *22*, 197–215.

Verger, A. (2012). Framing and selling global education policy: The promotion of public–private partnerships for education in low-income contexts. *Journal of Education Policy*, *27*, 109–130.

Winkler, D. (1989). *Decentralization in education: An economic perspective*. Population and Human Resources Department Paper. Washington, DC: World Bank.

Winkler, D., & Gershberg, A. (2000). Education decentralization in Latin America: The effects on the quality of schooling. LCSHD Paper Series No. 59. Washington, DC: World Bank.

Winkler, D., & Gershberg, A. (2003). *Education decentralization in Africa: A review of recent policy and practice*. Washington, DC: World Bank.

World Bank (1991). *Managing development: The governance dimension*. Discussion Paper, World Bank, Washington, DC.

World Bank. (1980). *World development report, 1980*. Washington, DC: World Bank.

World Bank. (1983). *World development report 1983: Management in development*. Washington, DC: World Bank.

World Bank. (1989). *Sub-Saharan Africa: From crisis to sustainable development*. Washington, DC: World Bank.

World Bank. (1992). *Governance and development*. Washington, DC: World Bank.

World Bank. (1994). *Governance: The World Bank experience*. Washington, DC: World Bank.

World Bank. (1995). *Priorities and strategies for education: A World Bank review*. Washington, DC: World Bank.

World Bank. (1996). *The World Bank participation sourcebook*. Washington, DC: World Bank.

World Bank. (1997). *World Development Report 1997: The state in a changing world*. Washington, DC: World Bank.

World Bank. (2000). *Poverty reduction strategies: A sourcebook*. Washington, DC: World Bank.

World Bank. (2003). *World Development Report 2004: Making services work for poor people*. Washington, DC: World Bank.

World Bank. (2005). *Education sector strategy update: Achieving education for all, broadening our perspective, maximizing our effectiveness*. Washington, DC: World Bank.

World Bank. (2007). *Guiding principles for implementing school-based management programs* (Retrieved from http://www.worldbank.org/education/economicsed). Washington, DC: World Bank.

World Bank. (2008). *What do we know about school-based management?* Washington, DC: World Bank.

World Bank. (2011). *Learning for all: Investing in people's knowledge and skills to promote development*. Washington, DC: World Bank.

World Bank, E. (1999). *Education sector strategy*. Washington, DC: World Bank.

World Bank/Independent Evaluation Group. (2006). *From schooling to access to learning outcomes: An unfinished agenda – an evaluation of World Bank support to primary education*. Washington, DC: World Bank.

World Bank/Independent Evaluation Group. (2010). *World Bank support to education since 2001: A portfolio note*. Washington, DC: World Bank.

# ICT, THE EDUCATION SECTOR, AND OPEN E-LEARNING: A UNIQUE OPPORTUNITY FOR THE DECADE AHEAD

Owen G. McGrath

## ABSTRACT

*As the World Bank approaches its fiftieth year of involvement in the education sector, its Sector Strategy for Education 2020 focuses on key challenges created in the past decade. With the successes in building up primary education systems, millions of matriculating students in many developing countries will now be seeking secondary and tertiary education. For most observers, this is a crisis: even if enough schools could magically be built in time, there would not be nearly enough trained teachers to staff them. For some observers, this is a crisis that can be coped with: information and communications technologies (ICT) have reached a stage where virtual schools and distance learning can be employed at scale to meet such challenges. Curiously, the Education Sector Strategy 2020 makes no mention of virtual schools or distance learning. In fact, it contains only a single, ambivalent reference to ICT for education. The curious silence belies the World Bank's vital leadership and active involvement over the years in identifying and funding model ICT uses in the education sector. However, this chapter is ultimately not*

**Education Strategy in the Developing World: Revising the World Bank's Education Policy**
**International Perspectives on Education and Society, Volume 16, 275–297**

**ISSN: 1479-3679/doi:10.1108/S1479-3679(2012)0000016017**

*about arguing over the extent to which ICT should be mentioned in the World Bank's Education Sector Strategy. Instead, the goal here is to draw attention to a specific opportunity that the World Bank has before it to shape and guide the many ICT-based virtual school projects that will be undertaken in the coming decade. The crucially important opportunity is one for which the World Bank is uniquely suited: to seed and grow an open e-learning movement based on open source, open educational resources, and open pedagogy for secondary and tertiary education in the developing world.*

## INTRODUCTION

As the World Bank formally began its activities in the education sector in 1962, more than half a dozen nations (e.g., Algeria, Burundi, Jamaica, Western Samoa, Rwanda, Trinidad and Tobago, and Uganda) gained independence from colonial rule. The year marked a peak in a post-war independence trend to which the World Bank's move into the sector was seen as an important response (Jones, 2007). It so happens that 1962 was also a landmark year in the formation of many key technologies that today we identify with the category of information and communications technology. J.C.R. Licklider published his initial musings about computer timesharing and systems that would allow simultaneous access to "vast quantities of information" (Licklider & Clark, 1962).[1] The year 1962 also saw the launch of the first commercially sponsored communication satellite,[2] the move to form the Institute of Electrical and Electronics Engineers (IEEE),[3] the release of what it believed to have been the world's first computer game,[4] and the initial field testing for the world's first solid-state mobile phone.[5] Nearly 50 years later as the World Bank releases the Sector Strategy for Education 2020, the remarkable growth of the networked information technologies and the ever-increasing penetration of low cost digital devices is on the minds of many in the field of information and communications technologies ICT for development. Yet the Sector Strategy's only mention of ICT for education is a passing reference to the need for more research into ICT's appropriate role in schools. For the ICT enthusiast, the Sector Strategy is a surprising disappointment. How is the lack of an ICT strategy to be interpreted? Perhaps in becoming so pervasive, the many enabling roles for ICT no longer need to be made explicit in education policy documents (Moonen, 2008). Or, perhaps ICT is falling out of favor due to the litigation that seems to surround it nowadays. Year 2010 saw mobile phone manufacturers bringing an unprecedented number of patent litigation suits before the International Trade Commission (Dowell, 2010). The venerable IEEE's newest working group established in 2010 is not about cutting-edge technology but about dealing with the nettlesome issues of digital rights management and digital property ownership.[6] And as the highly controversial Anti-Counterfeiting Trade Agreement (ACTA) reached the revised final agreement stage, it was met throughout 2010 with petitions and protests from many quarters, especially for its predicted detrimental effects on developing nations (Geist, 2010). Given all these legal wranglings, maybe it is just as well that ICT gets so little mention in the Sector Strategy. After all, the developing world has enough challenges, and lawyers are even scarcer than teachers.

More seriously, the challenges for secondary and tertiary education outlined in the Sector Strategy are insurmountable if we leave ICT out of the picture. Fifty to sixty years into independence, many developing nations are finally seeing significant enrollment success within primary level schooling, thanks in large part to learning-for-all initiatives of the past decade. Now, however, there simply is not enough time nor are there enough resources available to build up brick-and-mortar secondary and tertiary schools to meet the surging demand. One of the few sources of hope is that this crisis occurs at a remarkable moment in the evolution of ICT for the education sector. A convergence of enabling technologies (e.g., Internet, mobile phones, tablet computing devices, cloud computing, and satellite-based internet access) has opened up transcendent possibilities for using networked computing and communications technologies to extend teaching and learning opportunities in unprecedented ways. In particular, the coming decade of ICT for development will likely be remembered as the era of virtual schools. Accredited secondary and tertiary school systems delivering instruction fully online will become commonplace. The main argument of this chapter, however, is not that the World Bank should quickly scramble to identity and champion best models for virtual school instruction or management. Instead, the World Bank has before it an historic opportunity to influence fundamentally how such virtual schools will be designed, built, and deployed. This is a role for which the World Bank is uniquely suited: to form, fund, and nurture for the developing world virtual school era a global Open E-Learning Movement for open source, open educational resources, and open pedagogy. To make its case, this chapter looks to the existing open movement in global tertiary education while considering key aspects of how the far-flung organizations behind that movement formed, governed, and positioned themselves successfully to produce and distribute educational software and content on a global scale (Iiyoshi & Kumar, 2008). Among the important insights from the open movement that have implications for strategizing the use of ICT for the developing world are: (1) the trans-regional open movement achieved economy of scale in ways both compelling and surprising; (2) the resulting open software systems and open content have proven to be highly adaptable to local needs while accommodating of varied spectrum of teaching and learning approaches; (3) the trans-regional organizations that grew up around the processes and practices of open education production offer compelling examples of the kinds of capacity building and knowledge exchange communities that the World Bank seeks to create through many of the new operating principles stated in the Sector Strategy.

As we will see in the next section, such a role would well befit the World Bank, given its long-standing leadership in researching and undertaking ICT and distance education initiatives. As the second section will show, a powerful technology convergence is at hand, one that holds out the promise of virtual schools as a means of extending education to many who would otherwise not have it. Third section points to the need for considering how such virtual schools will be built, and makes the case for the benefits of collaborative open production processes found in the open movement. Fourth section suggest that guiding examples for the World Bank's appropriate role in the coming virtual school era can be found in the story of the nonprofit foundations behind the open movement. Fifth section looks briefly at a corollary set of policy issues around the World Bank's role as Knowledge Bank: virtual schooling's far-reaching implications on research and management methodologies, particularly in the areas of educational analytics and educational data mining.

## LOOKING FOR ICT IN THE SECTOR STRATEGY

In order to interpret well the way ICT is presented in the Sector Strategy for Education 2020, it helps first to look back at predecessor documents. The 1999 10-year Education Sector Strategy gave ICT a place of prominence. It held up ICT as a top priority for improving teaching and learning through innovative delivery via distance education, open learning, and the use of new technologies (World Bank, 1999). In particular, the World Bank showed a strong interest during that period in the ways ICT might help overcome education access barriers such as those around gender equality

(Hawkins, 2002). As early as 2006, however, one can begin to detect a de-emphasis on ICT. The midterm report for the sector strategy showed a surprising drop in the overall number of references to ICT and only a few brief references to distance education as a priority, despite having more than 20 projects then underway at the time with some form of distance education component (World Bank, 2006). In January 2010, looking toward the consultation process and drafting of the next sector strategy, the World Bank issued the Concept Note, which offered some telling insight into how little importance ICT would have this time around (World Bank, 2010a). For the first time there was no mention at all of distance education, while the scant references to ICT were mostly around background issues (e.g., knowledge economy jobs and policy coherence). The single reference to ICT in education in the Concept Note's main body would turn out to be more than a preview of things to come. In outlining how the knowledge economy requires a new sector vision for the coming decade, the Concept Note ends the globalization bullet item with a wait-and-see view of school-based ICT:

> As a result, education systems face increased challenges to equip post-basic education graduates with knowledge and skills relevant to a rapidly changing context, which is made more difficult in the cases where the enrollment growth of the past decades came at the expense of quality. More systematic information is needed about whether and how school-based ICT can enhance learning and raise school completion rates. (World Bank, 2010a, p. 2)

A similar sentence then became the only significant mention of ICT for education in the final version of the Sector Strategy for Education 2020. Here again there is no mention of distance learning; the few references to ICT are mostly around background issues (e.g., knowledge economy jobs and school accountability). The lone sentence about ICT for schooling appears at the end of a paragraph about cross-cutting issues that can addressed across country groups, trailing a list of preventative health measures such as deworming and hand washing:

> Confronting health conditions that affect learning is also important across country groupings; mechanisms for achieving this goal include more effective collaboration between health and education sectors and the adoption of proven school-based health and nutrition programs, such as deworming, school feeding, and hand washing (Bundy & O'Connell, 2010). Another example of a cross-cutting issue that may help accelerate learning is ICT investments in education, although much better monitoring and evaluation is needed to assess their impact and cost effectiveness. (World Bank, 2011, p. 71)

Formerly a strategic priority, ICT for schooling has now been relegated to the background, its use and value apparently unproven.

Whatever may be the reasons for the doubts and disaffection, it is worth noting how contrary they are to the World Bank's long-standing commitment to exploring and advocating innovative ICT use for education in general and for ICT-based distance education in particular. Until now, in fact, nearly every major World Bank education sector policy or strategy document since 1970 has emphasized the use of educational technology to improve instruction in one way or another (Verspoor, 1991). For more than 30 years, the World Bank has funded technology-based teaching and learning projects carried out across geographical and temporal distance. Early World Bank funded educational projects for television and radio involved a notable range of experiments with various instructional arrangements, different education levels, and a wide span of regions. Even from the hard-nosed perspective of cost analysis, those early distance education efforts revealed promisingly that whatever significant financial barriers existed were confined mainly to the costs around media production (Hawkridge, 1988). Far from being intractable, of course, media production and delivery are two domains where digital age ICT progress has continually and dramatically reduced costs over the years. In recent decades, the World Bank has placed new emphasis on educational lending not just for physical infrastructure (i.e., building schools) but also on the so-called"soft" inputs such as the production of learning and instructional materials (Boissiere, 2004). Indeed, since the mid-1990s, the 'soft' input prioritization seems to have fit well with the cross-sector positioning of the World Bank as it began providing even greater thought leadership for ICT with, for instance, the founding of InfoDev. In this same period, the World Bank also successfully initiated Africa Virtual University, a large-scale distance education project, which today serves tens of thousands of users throughout the African continent via both internet and satellite technology (World Bank, 1998).

So it is not unreasonable to read the Sector Strategy and wonder what happened. Why is ICT now played down so much? Nevertheless, speculating about the answer to such questions is beyond the scope of this chapter. ICT and distance learning will undoubtedly occupy some strategic and tactical positions in many of the World Bank's education sector endeavors in the coming decade, whether articulated or not. The rapid response needed to address the secondary and tertiary education crisis in the developing world will necessarily elicit ICT solutions. Virtual Schooling will be the most significant of them, and as a category it contains many forms and models worth trying. Left alone, these virtual school efforts will have one set of characteristics. Guided by World Bank policy, they could have quite another. What this chapter seeks to show is what some of those desirable characteristics (e.g., open, coordinated, trans-regional, collaborative, scalable, re-useable, and locally adaptable) are and how the World Bank can play that guiding role.

### *Lessons Learned: How Not to Do ICT in the Education Sector*

Before considering the World Bank's future role, it is worth briefly reviewing two of the long-standing critiques that have confronted ICT in education efforts of multilateral agencies like the World Bank in particular. As mentioned, the World Bank's ICT and distance learning efforts have a long and extensive history. They have garnered much attention and at times some criticism. In general, there have been two kinds of criticism offered up. The oldest, the return-on-investment critique, questions the purported value of ICT in education projects. This line of critique relates to a valid and important skepticism of ICT in education in general. ICT in education, it is argued, is typically oversold and underused (Cuban, 2001; Kenny, 2006). This sort of analysis scrutinizes the claimed functional values of ICT deployments in education projects to see if they are really adequate enough to justify the opportunity costs (Grace & Kenny, 2003). Would the money spent on technology be better spent elsewhere (e.g., on hiring teachers, buying books, etc.)? In the case of the World Bank, this line of critique has extra gravity, as it relates to an internal tradition of asking fundamental questions about the economic viability and effectiveness of lending for development in the education sector, a tradition still evident in the Sector Strategy. One of the World Bank's many noted areas of expertise in ICT for education over the past 30 years has been in developing methodologies for accurately measuring costs involved in distance education projects (Hülsmann, 2008). In practice, most return-on-investment analyses have tended to be retrospective. Therein lays one weakness of these critiques when applied to ICT. Retrospective analyses of technologies that have usually already been surpassed do not always generalize into the present or future. The valid complaints about what was oversold and underused in the microcomputer era, for example, should not be used as a sole and lasting indictment of everything that might come along since (Pal, Patra, Nedevschi, & Pawar, 2009).

The second line of criticism, the policy implementation critique, accepts the rationale for using ICT in education sector projects while focusing more on appraising the implementation details and actual effects. The pragmatic argument here is that getting the high level rationale correct is not sufficient. Project design and implementation must take into account salient aspects of the local context. These critiques accept the overall aims of those policies, but point to necessary adjustments and mediations, usually from the perspective of client countries. How to allow for local capacity development, local ownership, and local control are examples of crucial implementation issues (Mackintosh, 2005). This line of critique relates to a broader analysis of ICT and development that seeks to show how even subtly different policy approaches can result in dramatically different outcomes along a continuum of success and failure, based on how much choice and autonomy policies give individual client countries (Howkins & Valantin, 1997). Sensitivity to these implementation issues remains a stated concern of the World Bank as well. How to make policies more flexible and adaptable to individual nation's situations, how to balance state and private sector involvement, how to give nongovernmental organizations a role, and how to make goals more practical and realizable are themes repeated throughout the Sector Strategy.

As we will see, the open movement approach to ICT advocated in this chapter holds up quite well in the face of both the traditional return-on-investment critique and the policy implementation critique. The compelling arguments that many others have already made about the the cost–benefits of open source and open content will be noted further on, while the chapter's primary focus is mainly on the policy implementation benefits. For the coming virtual school era, open source and open content processes can enable new ways of balancing the many local and global issues that will undoubtedly confront any large-scale implementation of virtual schools in the developing world.

## VIRTUAL SCHOOLS: THE DECADE AHEAD FOR ICT IN THE EDUCATION SECTOR

The past criticisms of ICT projects for education in developing countries have obviously not been confined to the efforts of the World Bank. However, to overlook the unique role and reach of the World Bank in the education sector would be a mistake. While other agencies might only pursue modest pilot projects that showcase innovation, the World Bank's traditional interest has always been at a higher level, i.e., national education systems (Jones, 2006, p. 135). Where other agencies might only pursue and promote a portfolio of showcase projects, the World Bank can pursue major solutions that scale. The special interest in scale and systems is as evident as ever in the Sector Strategy. While most multilateral development agencies face the same challenges ahead, the World Bank as a global institution stands apart in being able to seek solutions on a global scale.

As pointed out in the Sector Strategy, the demands for secondary and tertiary education will be enormous. The traditional response, i.e., more bricks and mortar schools, cannot possibly happen with either the breadth or rapidity required to meet the demand. The ICT response, i.e., virtual schools, can. Some call them virtual schools, others call them cyber-schools or mega-schools. By any name, ICT-based virtual school offer a compelling way forward for rapidly expanding educational opportunities in the developing world, as a diverse and growing group of educational leaders and analysts agree (Daniel, 2010; Moe & Chubb, 2009). Whole books could be written in describing the many key enabling technologies that are allowing for virtual schools: the Internet, mobile phones, tablet computing devices, cloud computing, satellite-based internet, etc. Whole books have been written about the wide range of possible teaching and learning modes, methods, and models these virtual schools might use. Innovative ideas already abound for possible organizational structures, methods of delivery, modes of institutional alignment, and assessment models for best implementing ICT-based online schools and ICT-based teacher training for secondary and tertiary education in developing countries (Bramble & Panda, 2008). Across many of these varied proposals is also a shared sense that the sophistication and reach of low cost ICT creates an historic opportunity to make significant progress in overcoming some of the most vexing developing world education obstacles: disadvantages due to gender, place of residence, disability, and ethno-linguistic affiliation.

In terms of software and content for virtual schools, most commentators also agree that e-learning applications have been shown to succeed in small online learning projects focused on specific curriculum areas: mathematics, literacy, science, and language arts. Of course, online schooling involves more than individual elements of a curriculum. The software applications and content tailored to a particular aspect of the curriculum cannot simply be tossed together to form virtual schools. The aspects of enrollment management, record keeping, counseling, assessment, and progress monitoring are typical of what are generally expected as underpinnings in systems that can serve as the basis for online schooling. But how then to build and scale up these systems? Here, most observers do not yet have answers. Based on failures in previous ICT in education eras, most observers would agree on what will *not* work: unilateral approaches involving software systems wholly designed and built in the developed world. The one-size-fits-all mistake resonates with the previously mentioned policy implementation critique.

For Richard Heeks, such mistakes have doomed not just previous efforts in the education sector, but many ICT for development efforts overall. To avoid the mistakes of the past, argues Heeks, a new process approach for employing ICT for development (ICT4D) must include:

- Participation of beneficiaries in the design and/or construction of the ICT4D project.
- Flexibility and improvisation in the implementation of the ICT4D project.
- Learning in order to improve implementation of the ICT4D project (embracing both learning from past experience and iterative learning-by-doing during the project).
- Utilising and building local capacities including those of local institutions.
- Competent leadership of the ICT4D project that is able to promote the other four elements. (Heeks, 2009, p. 17)

Although he does not say how all this local participation and flexibility are to be achieved, Heeks does correctly pinpoint a key relation where many of these factors would come into play at the earliest stage of any ICT project design: the tensions between top-down and bottom-up requirements (p. 18). Some new set of processes is needed, Heeks asserts, for balancing local needs against the top-down constraints. What Heeks has put his finger on here, a process by which system functionality and local feature needs could somehow be balanced, happens to be a key distinguishing aspect of the open source development processes commonly seen in the open movement, as we will see in the next section.

## WHY THE OPEN MOVEMENT HAS SUCCEEDED IN TERTIARY EDUCATION

An understandable tendency in the discussion about the coming era of virtual schools is a focus on hardware, i.e., the low cost end-user devices such as laptop computers or mobile phones. These physical commodities are where innovation and dramatic costs reductions occur most tangibly. Usually missing from discussions of virtual schools, however, is any sustained consideration of the underlying software systems, especially around their design, production, and extension over time. To take software systems for granted as simply unitary "solutions" that will somehow get produced and appear as needed is to overlook many crucial issues: the flexibility of the software architecture, how the parts are built, who builds and extends them, their ownership, customizability, ongoing development, etc. For the virtual school era, overlooking these software design and production issues is an invitation to repeat many of the past ICT for development failures. Some leading advocates of virtual school do sense that open production processes are important. Though they mainly wonder about its implications for the business models of for-profit e-learning companies, Moe and Chub acknowledge the growing trend towards using open educational resources (Moe & Chubb, 2009, p. 71). Sir John Daniels goes a step further, noting not just cost–benefits but also some important collaborative processes of an open production approach (Daniels, 2010, p. 74).

There are, of course, many parallel and related "open" initiatives in tertiary education: open data, open access journals, open networking, and even open textbooks. The open movement of interest in this chapter has mainly to do with open software and open content development by and for tertiary education. Over the past 10 years, this open movement has not simply been about the "free-ness" but also about the opening up of collaboration among colleges and universities in ongoing development of software and content used for research, teaching, and administration . The next section examines some key open processes that have allowed these institutions successfully to build, extend, and adapt a specific class of large-scale, e-learning systems.

## *Scale and Balance: The Requirements Processes in Tertiary Education Open Source Projects*

The main story of the open movement in tertiary education over the past 10 years has been one of the collaboration, iterative production, sharing, re-use, and community. Three major areas addressed by the movement have been open source software, open content, and open pedagogy (Iiyoshi & Kumar, 2008). The open content effort is perhaps best known, drawing considerable interest in recent years from UNESCO. The modes of production and use of open content relate closely but are not identical to the modes of production and use of open source software (Vukovic & Martin, 2009). Especially relevant to the building of virtual schools in the coming decade is the open source software aspect of the open movement. These projects extend the general open source software model in new ways as open source software gets built by and for tertiary education institutions (McGrath, 2008). For more than a decade, academic institutions have become increasingly involved in collaborative efforts to develop open source alternatives to commercial software (e.g., portals, repositories, e-portfolios, and learning management systems). Typically, tertiary education open source projects such as Dspace, Fedora, and Moodle evolved with varied organizational forms while having in common some form of governance structures based upon membership at an institution level, allowing colleges and universities to coordinate distributed software development together.

A particularly important set of open source projects came to be produced by open movement organizations that used the so-called community source model (Wheeler, 2010). Consortia such as the Sakai Project, the Open Source Portfolio Initiative, and Kuali each consist of scores of institutions around the world designing, developing, and using a shared base of software. For example, Sakai Project member institutions all around the world build upon a shared base of software code for online collaboration environment that can be used by individuals, groups, and courses for managing a wide range of academic activities. From an institutional standpoint, the benefit of distributed development in the Sakai Project derives from shifting financial commitments away from commercial software vendor licenses. The Sakai code base can be downloaded by anyone anywhere for free. The concomitant costs of allocating developers to the project are viewed by participating institutions as a better use of their money. By contributing staff to a particular aspect of the project, institutions also gain influence in determining the project's direction and priorities. While the Sakai end-user sees a harmonious arrangement of tools that interoperate and share a common interface style, the ongoing development of Sakai software environment is very much a distributed and heterogeneous affair. In particular, responsibility for development of the framework and of the individual tools is spread across a dozens of institutions around the world.

In community open source consortia like the Sakai Project, a formal governance structure is put in place at the start. This formal founding and membership model stand in contrast to many smaller open source projects, where governance only emerges later if at all (O'Mahony & Ferraro, 2007). Indeed, the tertiary education open projects are more like cathedrals than bazaars, to use Eric Raymond's famous metaphor (Raymond, 1999). And unlike many projects in the general open source world, community source programming gets carried out predominantly by paid staff who work for the member institutions and who are managed within fairly traditional organizational structures. Levels of organizational participation by member institutions in these projects are also diverse and varied. The most heavily involved institutions might typically commit software programmers, project managers, instructional designers, user interface designers, etc. for significant periods to work on the overall project. Other institutions might contribute similar but smaller teams to focused work such as creating or extending a specific tool (e.g., SCORM player), translating for language localization, or improving the accessibility of the user interface. Smaller institutions may only be able to contribute technical writers to help produce documentation or event planners to help organize conferences and online meetings. At the very least, however, all institutions in the project face the work required in adapting and the system for use locally. This work includes branding,[7] integrating with other local systems, and selecting the particular tools and applications to present to local users.

This nexus between the consortium and individual member institutions is where we can see how the open movement processes successfully solve what Heeks sees as the most gravely important problem facing ICT: the balancing of local and community requirements. In order to decide whether and how to implement new tools features for the software system, the open movement consortia have developed processes that allow their member institutions to express their needs and to coordinate their development efforts to meet those needs effectively. Were it not a member of the consortium, an individual institution would just confine its efforts to meeting its own local needs. However, as a member of the consortium, the institution needs to address needs of the broader community as well, get input in the design process, and ultimately balance local and community needs if the two diverge. As the consortium grows, the requirements gathering process becomes more challenging, particularly in determining and reconciling the needs of very different teaching and learning practices in the wider community. Not surprisingly, the requirement process in these settings is characterized by flexibility and iteration. Traditional software requirements methodology involves careful elicitation of user needs, formal requirements specifications, and usually some sort of contractual obligation. The somewhat unconventional requirements process found in the community source projects tends to lack both the sequencing aspect and the formal obligation. Instead, a more iterative, community discourse approach tends to be common (Scacchi, 2009). For these distributed, open movement consortia, the requirements process becomes one of the key practices out of which community emerges. Collecting requirements, feature requests, and suggestions together in online meetings, shared online collaborative spaces, and occasional face-to-face conferences requires a great deal of communication for finding commonalities, negotiating priorities, and preview design solutions. The processes involved can result in open debate and fair negotiation of near and long-term development plans, thereby giving community representatives and decision makers a handle on what they can expect as they implement the software system at their local institutions. Ultimately, the communication channels formed across institutions also then get used for many broader forms of sharing across the community such as knowledge sharing around teaching and learning over time (Mackie, 2008).

## A ROLE FOR THE WORLD BANK

If the main story of the open movement is one of the collaboration, the back story is one of the nonprofit foundations (Stacey, 2010). All three major areas of the open movement – open source, open content, and open pedagogy – had important guidance and ongoing support respectively from the William and Flora Hewlett Foundation, the Andrew W. Mellon Foundation, and the Carnegie Foundation for the Advancement of Teaching (Iiyoshi & Kumar, 2008). The point of the previous section was to give some sense of the process benefits of the way the community source projects balance local and community requirements. As mentioned, the establishment of these sorts of governance and participation processes within projects such as Kuali, OSP e-Portfolio, and Sakai was far from accidental. The Mellon Foundation in particular worked very actively to form the consortia for these projects in ways that would create sustainable organizations. Even once the projects were well underway, a good deal of effort from the Mellon Foundation went into refining their organizational processes and business models that would allow them to coordinate their far-flung distributed software development better (Mackie, 2008). As mentioned, these community source organizations differ in fundamental ways from other open source efforts. The community source model would likely never have succeeded without the Mellon Foundation's organizational initiatives and ongoing involvement.

Certainly, there the many ways in which future virtual school projects in the developing world will hear about and benefit from the experiences of open movement successes like the Sakai Project. Individually, some regional projects may even self-organize and successfully enact similar processes in developing and maintaining online environments for virtual schools in their region. As mentioned, however, the ultimate prize that ICT observers are eyeing for the developing world in the decade ahead is always scale (Trucano, 2005). Scaling up is key. The open movement achieved scale. A handful of North American tertiary education institutions made up the original Sakai Project consortia, but seven years later the Sakai community is comprised of hundreds of institutions in more than 35 countries.[8] The variety of institution types and their uses of the Sakai software further attests to the success of the community source model for developing scalable and flexible frameworks that can meet both the general needs of the global organization and the local needs of the many and diverse individual institutions. This successful scaling up points us back again to consider the very special role played by the Mellon Foundation in setting up communities like the Sakai Project. In the open content area, a similarly pivotal role was played by the Hewlett Foundation.

It would be simplistic, however, to say that for the coming decade of virtual schools what the developing world education sector needs is simply a world foundation. The operational, technical, and financial assistance required are far beyond the capabilities and means of even the largest foundations imaginable. In their work with open source and open content, the Mellon and Hewlett foundations could instantiate projects with seed grants, while leveraging the deep resources and existing infrastructure of some of the world's largest and wealthiest educational institutions. Though economy of scale would be an equally important goal for any education sector virtual school consortia, no amount of seed grants alone would even begin to allow such an effort to scale up. In the developing world, the corresponding institutional players (e.g., ministries of education, nongovernmental organizations, economic development boards, and private companies) will vary widely in their resource readiness and infrastructure capacity for such endeavors. Flexible and varied forms of lending would be needed. The kinds of cross regional exchanges required for organizing global consortia are not easily brokered. Accomplishing all this would require more than a super foundation. In short, for the coming decade of virtual schools what the education sector needs is not a world foundation but a world bank.

### *Policy Coherence: Open Source as Process vs. Open Source as Product*

Putting aside the future need for collaborative production processes for virtual school software systems, there are still other compelling reasons why the World Bank should support open source strategically in the education sector. Focusing for a moment on open source as product (e.g., the Linux operating system and Open Office desktop suite), one can rightly say that the vast majority of users of open source products never participate directly in the ongoing software development process. Clearly, open source software as product stands on its own merits simply in terms of cost (Assar, El Amrani, & Watson, 2010; Papin-Ramcharan & Soodeen, 2007; Unwin, 2009). Observers have been advocating open source products strategies for the developing world from a variety of angles: seeing open source as a way to move forward on issues of copyright and intellectual property protection (Dravis, 2003; Dudley-Sponaugle, Hong, & Wang, 2007), as a sort of bulwark against potentially creeping reach of private ICT monopolies (Leye, 2007), as an opportunity for developing local capacity (Dravis, 2003; van Reijswoud & Mulo, 2006), and as a way to stimulate local innovation (Spence & Smith, 2010; Weber, 2004). Open source products have also been proposed to and by the World Bank as necessary and important elements of a larger open ICT ecosystem strategy across all sectors (Open ePolicy Group, 2005).

To reiterate, open source as process is about much more than free software. When viewed as products, open source software may rightly be relegated to lower level operational components of educational policies. When viewed as processes, however, open source software development of the kind that will be needed in the era of virtual schools should not. In the case of scalable e-learning systems like Sakai, open source as a process entails a far-reaching enterprise – a set of processes for the ongoing production, refinement, and extension of the software over many years. It also entails a far-reaching community – a globally networked, self-governing, trans-national organization. Tactics and policies at many levels of an education sector strategy can certainly benefit from an understanding of the formation, processes, and experiences of the open movement during the past decade. As can be seen in the Sector Strategy, the World Bank itself already has set out to approach the sector challenges by strengthening education systems not just at the country level but also at a global level. Advocating open source processes would be one very important way in which the World Bank could realize those global goals.

### *Further Implications: The World Bank as Knowledge Bank in the Era of Virtual Schools*

With or without the World Bank's involvement, many ICT-based attempts at creating virtual schools will spring up in the coming decade as developing nations try to address secondary and tertiary schooling demands. Within the context of these virtual schools projects, a corollary set of strategy and policy considerations arises. With teaching and learning activities increasingly moving online, important research and policy questions surface as to how users are to be studied, how their usage patterns should be captured, how that usage data will get analyzed, by whom and for what purposes. It would be difficult to overstate the importance that usage analytics and data mining already have as constitutive components of today's web-based e-commerce models and social computing paradigms. Tremendous amounts of money and research are being directed toward the science and practice of probing deeply into the mountains of activity data users leave behind in visiting web sites. Better known and ever more controversial is the increasing use of data mining for surveillance and profiling. Debates about the pros and cons of these kinds of tracking and monitoring technologies are just beginning in the developed world.

In recent years, the newer sub-fields called learning analytics and educational data mining have formed (Bach, 2010; Romero & Ventura, 2010). As related fields, learning analytics and educational data mining represent burgeoning research and policy areas where the World Bank's traditional thought leadership and policy expertise will be much needed in the virtual school era. Applying tracking and data mining techniques in online teaching and learning contexts, learning analytics and educational data mining encompass their own unique range of research questions and policy issues. A fair generalization can be made that much of the inquiry and practical wisdom developed so far center on applying computational techniques to large data sets about students. Learning analytics efforts in tertiary education settings have served as the basis for discovering categories and characteristics in student enrollment patterns. In the context online learning environments, data mining projects have examined similarities across thousands of online sessions to reveal useful characteristic aspects of students' interaction with e-learning content as well (McGrath, 2009).

The World Bank's tradition role as a thought leader in educational research has always stemmed in part from its methodological expertise in collecting, managing, and analyzing, large data sets (Jones, 2006). The Sector Strategy makes it clear that the World Bank will continue that tradition, as it intends to build high-quality knowledge bases for educational reform. The World Bank as "Knowledge Bank" will continue in its unique capacity as a leading contributor to educational research and policy. As it continues to develop its own in-house analytical expertise, the World Bank will likely find the need to immerse itself in the new knowledge domains of learning analytics and educational data mining. It will also find itself needing to identify and recommend policy around best practices, privacy, and data stewardship for both domains. It probably already has the need to do so now. Even the World Bank's networked-based projects of the previous decade revealed impossibility of evaluating ICT projects if measures were not in place to capture and gauge system usage carefully (Ballantyne, 2003; Tolani-Brown, McCormac, & Zimmermann, 2009; Trucano, 2005). Of course, many more issues and opportunities will come to light in the context of virtual school implementations. Suffice to say, if it were also to take the leadership role in creating a development sector Open e-Learning Movement for the virtual school era, the World Bank would be in a position to ensure that educational data mining technology development and implementation are guided systematically by enlightened policies and understanding of best practices.

## CONCLUSION

In putting together a 10 year educational sector strategy for the developing world, topics like software and content production processes might initially seem out of place. As the Sector Strategy makes clear, however, the developing world desperately needs more school and teachers. In the face of these challenges, many observers outside the World Bank cast an eye toward ICT. Will this finally be the time when ICT's promise can be realized in the education sector? Some skepticism of ICT is always warranted, but as a general stance, it is not enough. If the issue here were simply about the appropriate application of ICT within existing schools in the developing world, then a wait-and-see approach might be excusable. Instead, what is at stake in the developing world, as the Sector Strategy points out, is whether millions of children will obtain any form of schooling at all. Here the case for trying something with ICT quickly starts to look less like an option and more like an imperative. Even the biggest skeptics would have to agree that the underlying technologies are reaching a stage of global penetration and level of sophistication where virtual online schools and mobile learning will happen in the developing world in some form or other.

How those virtual schools can and should be built to meet the challenges is really the issue at hand. It should also be a matter of vigorous and creative debate. An understandable tendency among virtual school advocates so far has been an excited focus on the low costs and the wide reach of the hardware (e.g., of the thousands of satellites, millions of laptop computers, and billions of mobile phones). The costs and reach of the hardware is rightly an important focal point when considering ICT for the developing world, and the World Bank has usually led the way in performing such analyses. As this chapter has attempted to show, for the virtual school era, a focus on hardware's cost and reach will not be enough. The production of the software and content must not be left unexamined nor taken for granted. For the kinds of large-scale software frameworks that will be needed for virtual schools, it will be crucial to focus on how these systems can be built collaboratively and globally in order to meet a wide range of local needs while still achieving sustainable economy of scale. Drawing upon the successful experiences in tertiary education open movement of the past decade, the World Bank could take a leadership role in instantiating and guiding the kind of open, long-term, trans-institutional, trans-national, shared development needed for building the right kind of virtual school infrastructure.

This chapter has not been about wishing the World Bank had included more references to ICT in the Sector Strategy for 2020. Nor is this chapter about advocating ICT as panacea for all the challenges of the sector. The argument instead is that major ICT-based virtual school projects will be undertaken one way or another in the decade ahead. As it approaches its fiftieth year of involvement in the education sector, the World Bank occupies a unique position as the acknowledged global leader with deep expertise and tremendous capacity to plan, undertake, and guide educational endeavors at national and global scale. The World Bank is uniquely suited for the pivotal role of seeding and cultivating a global Open e-Learning Movement for secondary and tertiary education in the developing world for the virtual school era ahead. For any other organization, this historic opportunity to create and guide such a movement would be seen as a challenge too daunting. Only the World Bank has the combination of global stature, wisdom, experience, and resources required. For the World Bank alone, this historic opportunity to create and guide an education sector Open e-Learning Movement can be seen as a call to duty.

## NOTES

1. Licklider's writings together with the first published papers on packet switching mark 1962 as the year of conception for what would eventually become the Internet (Leiner et al., 1997). Interestingly, a third of the 1962 Licklider and Clark paper is a marvelous speculation on what computer-based learning for schoolchildren would someday look like.

2. Telstar 1 carried the first public, live, trans-oceanic television signal as well as the first telephone and fax relays through space. Telstar 1 project involved a multinational effort between several companies, governments, and agencies.

3. Particularly relevant to this chapter are the enabling aspects of the work done by the IEEE Standards Association (IEEE-SA). Also pertinent are the deliberation processes and mode of operations of the IEEE-SA as a global organization.

4. Created by MIT staff, SpaceWar!'s source code was made freely available on magnetic tape. Before long, the game was compiled and available around the world on most of the computers capable of running it.

5. Field testing for the Swedish Berglund Mobile Telephone System (MTB) began in Stockholm and Gothenburg. The project was one of many collaborations between Televerket, Sweden's public communications utility, and the Ericsson company (Karlsson & Calm, 2009).

6. IEEE working group, P1817, the Standard for Consumer-Ownable Digital Personal Property.

7. Even the act of naming and creating a visual brand for a local implementation of a system can have great significance attached. For an intriguing look at open source used as a way of preserving a sense of local identity, see Saloma-Akpedonu's study of "glocalization" (2006).

8. The Mellon Foundation brought together four research universities (Michigan, Indiana, Stanford, and MIT) as the original partner schools. Seven years later, the hundreds of Sakai member institutions represent a full range of tertiary institutions classifications as well as government and military training institutions, research societies and organizations, educational societies and organizations, and fully or predominantly online institutions.

# REFERENCES

Assar, S., El Amrani, R., & Watson, R. (2010). ICT and education: A critical role in human and social development. *Information Technology for Development*, *16*(3), 151–158.

Bach, C. (2010). Learning analytics: Targeting instruction, curricula and student support. In *Proceedings EISTA 2010 June 29 – July 2, 2010*. Orlando, FL: International Institute of Informatics and Systemics.

Ballantyne, P. (2003). *Evaluation of Swedish support to SchoolNet Namibia*. Swedish International Development Agency (SIDA). Department for Infrastructure and Economic Cooperation. Retrieved from http://www.schoolnetafrica.org/fileadmin/resources/schoolnetnamibia.pdf. Accessed on February 5, 2011.

Boissiere, M. (2004). *Determinants of primary education outcomes in developing countries. Background paper for evaluation of the World Bank's support to primary education*. Washington, DC: World Bank.

Bramble, W., & Panda, S. (2008). In *Economics of distance and online learning*. London: Routledge.

Cuban, L. (2001). *Oversold and underused: Computers in the classroom*. Cambridge, MA: Harvard University Press.

Daniel, J. S. (2010). *Mega-Schools, technology and teachers: Achieving education for all*. London: Routledge.

Dowell, A. (2010, December 27). The rise of Apps, iPad and Android. *Wall Street Journal* (New York). Retrieved from http://online.wsj.com/article/SB10001424052748704774604576035611315663944.html. Accessed on January 8, 2011.

Dravis, P. (2003). *Open source software: Perspectives for development. InfoDev.* Washington, DC: World Bank.

Dudley-Sponaugle, A., Hong, S., & Wang, Y. (2007). The social and economical impact of OSS in developing countries. In K. St. Amant & B. Still (Eds.), *Handbook of research on open source software: Technological, economic and social perspectives* (pp. 102–114). Hershey, PA: Information Science Reference.

Geist, M. (2010). The trouble with the anti-counterfeiting trade agreement (ACTA). *SAIS Review*, *30*(2), 137–147.

Grace, J., & Kenny, C. (2003). A short review of information and communications technologies and basic education in LDCs. *International Journal of Educational Development*, *23*(2003), 627–636.

Hawkins, R. (2002). Ten lessons for ICT and education in the developing world. In G. Kirkman, P. K. Cornelius, J. D. Sachs & K. Schwab (Eds.), *The global information technology report 2001–2002: Readiness for the networked world.* Oxford: Oxford University Press.

Hawkridge, D. G. (1988). Distance education and the World Bank. *British Journal of Educational Technology*, *19*(2), 84–95.

Heeks, R. (2009). *The ICT4D 2.0 manifesto: Where next for ICTS and international development.* Development Informatics Working Paper Series, Paper No. 42. Development Informatics Group, Institute for Development Policy and Management. Retrieved from http://www.sed.manchester.ac.uk/idpm/research/publications/wp/di/documents/di_wp42.pdf. Accessed on January 8, 2011.

Howkins, J., & Valantin, R. (1997). *Development and the information age: Four global scenarios for the future of information and communication technology*. Ottawa: IDRC Books.

Hülsmann, T. (2008). From Baobab to Bonsai: Revisiting methodological issues in the costs and economics of distance education and distributed e-learning. In W. Bramble & S. Panda (Eds.), *Economics of distance and online learning*. London: Routledge.

Iiyoshi, T., & Kumar, M. S. V. (Eds.). (2008). *Opening up education: The collective advancement of education through open technology, open content, and open knowledge.* Cambridge, MA: MIT Press.

Jones, P. W. (2006). *Education, poverty and the World Bank.* Rotterdam: Sense Publishers.

Jones, P. W. (2007). *World Bank financing of education: Lending, learning, and development* (2nd ed.). London: Routledge.

Karlsson, S. O., & Calm, A. (2009). *To change the world: A tale of Lars Magnus Ericsson and his successors.* Stockholm: Sellin & Partner.

Kenny, C. (2006). *Overselling the Web? Development and the internet.* Boulder, CO: Lynne Rienner.

Leiner, B., Cerf, V., Clark, D., Kahn, R., Kleinrock, L., Lynch, D., Postel, J., Roberts, L., & Wolff, S. (1997). A brief history of the internet. *Communications of the ACM 40*(2). New York, NY: ACM Press.

Leye, V. (2007). UNESCO, ICT corporations and the passion of ICT for development: Modernization resurrected. *Media, Culture & Society*, *29*(6), 972–993.

Licklider, J., & Clark, W. (1962, May 1–3). On-line man-computer communication. In *Proceedings of the Spring Joint Computer Conference, San Francisco, CA*. New York, NY: ACM Press.

Mackie, J. C. (2008). Open source in open education: Promises and challenges. In T. Iiyoshi & M. S. V. Kumar (Eds.), *Opening up education: The collective advancement of education through open technology, open content, and open knowledge*. Cambridge, MA: MIT Press.

Mackintosh, W. (2005). Can you lead from behind? Critical reflections on the rhetoric of e-learning, open distance learning, and ICTs for development in Sub-Saharan Africa (SSA). In A. Carr-Chellman (Ed.), *Global perspectives on e-learning: Rhetoric and reality*. Thousand Oaks, CA: Sage.

McGrath, O. (2008). Open educational technology: Tempered aspirations. In T. Iiyoshi & M. S. V. Kumar (Eds.), *Opening up education: The collective advancement of education through open technology, open content, and open knowledge*. Cambridge, MA: MIT Press.

McGrath, O. (2009). Mining user activity data in higher education open systems: Trends, challenges, and possibilities. In T. Kidd (Ed.), *Handbook of research on technology project management, planning and operations* (pp. 508–521). Hershey, PA: Information Science Reference.

Moe, T., & Chubb, J. (2009). *Liberating learning: Technology, politics, and the future of American education*. San Francisco, CA: Jossey-Bass.

Moonen, J. (2008). Policy from a global perspective. In En J. Vooght & G. Knezek (Eds.), *International handbook of information technology in primary and secondary education* (pp. 1171–1178). New York, NY: Springer.

O'Mahony, S., & Ferraro, F. (2007). The emergence of governance in an open source community. *Academy of Management Journal*, *50*(5), 1079–1106.

Open ePolicy Group. (2005). *Roadmap for open ICT ecosystems*. Berkman Center for Internet and Society. Retrieved from http://cyber.law.harvard.edu/epolicy/. Accessed on January 12, 2011.

Pal, J., Patra, R., Nedevschi, S., & Pawar, U. (2009). The case of the occasionally cheap computer: Low-cost devices and classrooms in the developing world. *Information Technology and International Development*, *5*(1), 49–64.

Papin-Ramcharan, J., & Soodeen, F. (2007). Open source software: A developing country view. In K. St. Amant & B. Still (Eds.), *Handbook of research on open source software: Technological, economic and social perspectives* (pp. 93–101). Hershey, PA: Information Science Reference.

Raymond, E. (1999). *The cathedral and the bazaar: Musings on linux and open source from an accidental revolutionary*. Sebastapol, CA: O'Reilly and Associates.

Romero, C., & Ventura, S. (2010). Educational data mining: A review of the state-of-the-art. *IEEE Transaction on Systems, Man, and Cybernetics, Part C: Applications and Reviews*, *40*(6), 601–618.

Saloma-Akpedonu, C. (2006). How to solve the 'Hotmail Problem': Global-local interfaces and Filipino technopreneurs. In A. P. D'Costa (Ed.), *The new economy in development: ICT challenges and opportunities*. New York, NY: Palgrave Macmillan.

Scacchi, W. (2009). Understanding requirements for open source software. In K. Lyytinen, P. Loucopoulos, J. Mylopoulos & W. Robinson (Eds.), *Design requirements engineering: A ten-year perspective*. Heidelberg: Springer.

Spence, R., & Smith, M. L. (2010). ICT, development, and poverty reduction: Five emerging stories. *Information Technologies and International Development*, *6*(2010), 11–17.

Stacey, P. (2010). Foundation funded OER vs. tax payer funded OER: A tale of two mandates In *Proceedings of Open ED 2010*. Barcelona: UOC. Retrieved from http://www.icde.org/filestore/Resources/Handbooks/ProceedingsOpenEd2010.pdf. Accessed on January 5, 2011.

Tolani-Brown, N., McCormac, M., & Zimmermann, R. (2009). An analysis of the research and impact of ICT in education in developing country contexts. *Journal of Education for International Development*, *4*(2), 1–12.

Trucano, M. (2005). *Knowledge maps: ICT in education. InfoDev*. Washington, DC: World Bank.

Unwin, T. (Ed.). (2009). *ICT4D: Information and communication technology for development*. Cambridge: Cambridge University Press.

van Reijswoud, V., & Mulo, E. (2006). Applying Open source software in a development context: Expectations and experiences. A case study of a university in Uganda. *e-Learning*, *3*(2006), 361–372.

Verspoor, A. M. (1991). Twenty years of World Bank support for basic education: Presentation and evaluation. *Prospects*, *21*(3), 313–329.

Vukovic, B., & Martin, C. (2009). Free and open source software (FOSS) and OER: An introductory note. In S. D'Antoni & C. Savage (Eds.), *Open educational resources: Conversations in cyberspace*. Paris: UNESCO Publishing.

Weber, S. (2004). *The success of open source*. Cambridge, MA: Harvard University Press.

Wheeler, B. (2010). Open source 2010: Reflections on 2007. *EDUCAUSE Review*, *42*(1), 48–67.

World Bank. (1998). *Knowledge for Africa: The African virtual university*. World Development Report 1998/1999 Background Papers. Washington, DC: World Bank.

World Bank. (1999). *Education sector strategy paper*. Washington, DC: World Bank.

World Bank. (2006). *Education sector strategy update*. Washington, DC: World Bank.

World Bank. (2010a). *Concept note for the World Bank Education sector strategy 2020*. Washington, DC: World Bank. Retrieved from http://siteresources.worldbank.org/EDUCATION/Resources/ESSU/Concept_Note_ESS2020_Feb8.pdf. Accessed on January 5, 2011.

World Bank. (2011). *Education sector strategy 2020*. Washington, DC: World Bank. Retrieved from http://siteresources.worldbank.org/EDUCATION/Resources/ESSU/Education_Strategy_4_12_2011.pdf. Accessed on September 4.

# PART IV
# REGIONAL EVALUATIONS

# WHAT DOESN'T THE EDUCATION SECTOR STRATEGY SAY? HOW THE FAST TRACK INITIATIVE AND MULTISECTOR OPERATIONS ARE CHANGING THE LANDSCAPE OF WORLD BANK EDUCATION FINANCING

Sarah Beardmore and John Middleton

## ABSTRACT

*Historically, the World Bank has been the largest external financier of education in the world, committing a peak amount of just over $5 billion in Fiscal Year (FY) 2010 through both its Education Sector projects and multisector projects managed by other sectors (World Bank, 2010b). The World Bank also hosts the Education for All-Fast Track Initiative (EFA FTI). Launched in 2002, EFA FTI is a partnership of governments, civil society organizations, and multilateral agencies such as United Nations Educational, Scientific and Cultural Organization (UNESCO) and the World Bank, which provides grant funding and technical assistance to*

**Education Strategy in the Developing World: Revising the World Bank's Education Policy**
**International Perspectives on Education and Society, Volume 16, 301–335**

**ISSN: 1479-3679/doi:10.1108/S1479-3679(2012)0000016018**

*implement the basic education components of national education strategies. By providing significant funding for education in low-income countries (LICs) through its own International Development Association (IDA) and by managing the majority of EFA FTI grant funding, the World Bank has a major impact on the direction of education development around the world.*

*In 2011 the Bank released a new Education Sector Strategy,* Learning for All, *which sets out the World Bank Education Sector's approach to education development over the coming decade. The analysis in this chapter examines the role of the EFA FTI and the growth of World Bank education operations managed outside the World Bank Education Sector, as well as their influence on Bank education lending objectives in sub-Saharan Africa. We examine trends in World Bank and EFA FTI basic education financing in sub-Saharan African countries that have joined the EFA FTI partnership to compare these two sources of financing for primary education and analyze the extent to which the World Bank is substituting its primary education lending with grants from the EFA FTI. We also assess the results frameworks of 10 multisector operations managed by noneducation sectors (Economic Management and Poverty Reduction; Urban Development; Rural Sector; Population, Health, and Nutrition; and Social Protection) to ascertain the extent to which they include education objectives and indicators. The chapter focuses its research around two questions:*

1. *Is there evidence that financing from the EFA FTI is substituting World Bank financing for education in sub-Saharan Africa?*
2. *Are World Bank multisector operations well designed to achieve education objectives in sub-Saharan Africa?*

*The research finds that the EFA FTI has almost certainly impacted the demand for IDA financing for basic education development. The comparison of IDA and EFA FTI primary education financing shows country-level substitution is occurring in a number of sub-Saharan African countries, with at least 13 out of 18 EFA FTI grant recipients in sub-Saharan Africa receiving a declining share of IDA financing for primary education since joining the EFA FTI.*

*Second, multisector operations now account for one-third of Bank education lending and have increased to comprise half of all new education commitments in sub-Saharan Africa. The research finds that multisector operations with education components are not as effective or accountable for education outcomes as those managed by the Education Sector, unless they are explicitly linked to national education plans. Given the disconnect between Education Sector managed education lending, and financing for education managed by other Bank sectors, it is unclear how the latter will be guided by the Bank's Education Sector Strategy, which will only apply to half of all Bank education lending for sub-Saharan Africa. Currently, there is no guarantee that both EFA FTI funding and noneducation sector managed lending will be measured against World Bank education strategy standards, and yet the Education Sector Strategy 2020 does little to address these challenges.*

## INTRODUCTION

### *EFA Goals*

In 2000, governments from around the world agreed to achieve six goals in education by 2015. The Education for All (EFA) goals include early childhood development, primary education, basic skills for youth and adults, literacy, gender equality, and quality education (UNESCO, 2000). As such, donor agencies have made variable efforts to scale up education financing targeted toward the achievement of these goals (ONE, 2011). The EFA goals were further narrowed within the international framework of the Millennium Development Goals (MDGs) which included two education objectives: to achieve universal primary completion and gender parity in primary education.

Additional financial, technical, and human resources are needed to continue the unprecedented expansion of education systems around the world so that they are able to provide high-quality education for all children. UNESCO estimates that the global financing gap to achieve universal basic education is $16 billion; with almost half of the world's out-of-school children and some of the world's highest rates of poverty, sub-Saharan Africa faces chronic resource constraints, which hinder many countries' ability to achieve EFA (UNESCO, 2010). The United Nations has estimated that the region will achieve universal primary enrollment in 100 years if progress continues at the current rate (UNICEF, 2008). In fact, UNESCO's Education for All Global Monitoring Report states that "Sub-Saharan Africa accounts for about 66% of the global financing gap, or US$10.6 billion" (UNESCO, 2010, p. 130).

### *Education for All-Fast Track Initiative*

To this end, in 2002 agencies such as the World Bank and UNESCO, civil society organizations, and donor governments including the United Kingdom and Canada established the EFA FTI Partnership to accelerate progress toward the MDGs (EFA FTI, 2004). EFA FTI sets out a global compact to coordinate the development, implementation, and resourcing of quality national education plans by bringing together donor agencies and governments around a common platform for educational development. The EFA FTI provides technical support and financing for the development and implementation of education sector plans, while creating a framework for donor cooperation in the sector.

As host of the EFA FTI Catalytic fund and Secretariat, and primary supervising agency for the delivery of the EFA FTI funding, the World Bank has played a central leadership role in establishing the EFA FTI partnership and defining its mandate and policies (Mokoro, 2010). Particularly important is Bank administration of the multidonor EFA FTI Catalytic Fund three-year grants to LICs (GDP below $1,335) to support the scaling up of national education strategies. Donors contribute to the EFA FTI's Catalytic fund, while coordinating and aligning their bilateral flows of aid around nationally developed education plans. The multidonor Catalytic Fund was intended to be a last resort source of financing for countries; however, it has become the funder of first resort in practice, having provided financial support to 37 countries (EFA FTI, 2011). By June 2010, the Catalytic Fund had allocated a total of $1.85 billion to 36 countries (World Bank IEG, 2011a).[1] With many countries now either joining the EFA FTI or applying for a second round of three-year grants the EFA FTI's trust fund has become a significant source of funding for EFA FTI countries.

### *World Bank Lending*

The World Bank provides loans to LICs through its IDA and to middle-income countries (MICs) and poorer countries deemed more credit-worthy through the International Bank for Reconstruction and Development (IBRD) (World Bank International Development Association Resource Mobilization Department (CFPIR), 2010a). The Bank provides considerable leadership and often has a powerful influence on development strategies. Country directors and Bank management interact with ministries of finance, developing Country

Assistance Strategies (CASs) (the Bank's three-year business plan for a given country), medium-term expenditure frameworks that cost out a countries public sector spending, and allocate funding for the various sector operations designed by World Bank technical experts (Woods, 2006).

New World Bank commitments to education totaled \$23 billion between 2001 and 2010 (World Bank (IEG), 2011a). In FY2010, the World Bank reported record levels of financing across all programs due to increased demand for assistance during the global economic crises, which lead to a doubling of commitments from its IBRD and IDA[2] lending arms (the Bank's executive directors approved lending of \$44.2 billion for IBRD and \$14.5 billion for IDA). While the percent of education lending as a portion of all Bank lending has been stable at 7–8%, overall absolute amounts of lending for education reached an all-time high of \$5.04 billion in loans in FY2010 (World Bank, 2010a).

## *The Education Sector Strategy*

Guiding the Bank's education policy and objectives for the next decade, the Bank's Education Sector Strategy sets the focus on learning (World Bank, 2011a). The Strategy emphasizes improving education systems at country level and generating a global knowledge base on education systems. In line with this approach, the Bank intends to focus its financial and technical support on "system reforms that promote learning," with a view that the "new education strategy is built on the premise that people learn throughout life, not simply during the years that they spend in formal schooling" (World Bank, 2011a, p. 25). The World Bank Independent Evaluation Group (IEG) raises two red flags in its Education Sector Portfolio Review regarding this shift in focus for the Education Sector: first, a systems approach will require a more complex project design, which tend to have weaker success rates, and second, the focus on *Learning for All* may lead to insufficient attention to access, and therefore to the poor (World Bank IEG, 2011b).

To ensure that it responds to these risks adequately, the Bank has allocated an additional \$750 million in IDA resources through 2015 to help achieve the education MDGs (World Bank, 2011c). The programming of this funding, which represents a 40% increase in primary education lending from IDA, and its interaction with external financing flows in EFA FTI countries over the next three years will depend in large part on how the Bank's Education Sector frames its strategic approach to achieving the intended impact of its education funding. It is also strengthening monitoring, evaluation and accountability, and its framework for system assessment and benchmarking to strengthen management oversight, identify areas for improvement, and better address systemic reform issues (World Bank, 2011c). While the strategy does provide some indication of potential solutions to mitigate the risks to both its corporate priorities in basic education and to its portfolio performance, the strategy fails to mention two very significant trends that may actually undermine the ability of the Bank to effectively address the issues raised by the IEG.

### *Aid Substitution*

The Bank manages two funding flows for basic education: IDA concessional loans, credits and grants, as well as grants from the EFA FTI's Catalytic Fund grants. With increasing flows of finance from the EFA FTI's Catalytic Fund, especially to sub-Saharan Africa, it is possible that this funding is substituting for traditional IDA loans for basic education. This substitution effect is also referred to as aid fungibility (Swaroop, Jha, & Rajkumar, 2000). Aid can be fully or partially fungible depending on the amount of aid used to supplement domestic resources. There has been evidence of fungibility in global health, though the causes and implications have been debated (Ooms et al., 2010). A study published in the *Lancet* in 2010 found that for every dollar of development assistance for health, government health expenditures from domestic resources drop by $0.43 to $1.14 (Lu et al., 2010). While studies have focused on substitution of domestic social sector resources, for example, by aid to global health or by lottery funding in the United States, there is evidence in the education sector that unlike in health, domestic education expenditures in sub-Saharan Africa have not decreased in tandem with increasing aid to the sector. In fact, a recent report by UNESCO indicated that over the past 10 years real expenditure on education has increased 6% annually (UNESCO-UIS, 2011), when education aid overall experienced significant increases. However, it is still possible that different sources of education aid are fungible, and this report addresses the prevalence of IDA substitution by the EFA FTI, the primary education focused multidonor trust fund managed by the World Bank. The research finds that the EFA FTI has almost certainly impacted the demand for IDA financing for basic education development. The comparison of IDA and EFA FTI primary education financing shows country-level substitution is occurring in a number of sub-Saharan African countries, with at least 13 out of 18 EFA FTI Catalytic Fund recipients in sub-Saharan

Africa receiving a declining share of IDA financing for primary education since joining the EFA FTI.

### *Multisector Operations*

The second issue that is not addressed in the new Education Sector Strategy, but that poses a risk to its implementation, is the effectiveness of multisector operations. In public statements regarding total lending for education, the Bank also includes investments managed by noneducation sectors that typically implement a multisector approach to deliver development finance. These operations have some portion of the loan coded as contributing to education even though they are managed by sectors such as Poverty Reduction; Social Protection; Health, Nutrition and Population; Public Sector Management; Rural Sector; Urban Development; Private Sector Development; Transport; Economic Policy; and others (World Bank IEG, 2011b). These operations typically have broader goals geared toward community development (rural and urban), job creation, youth empowerment, or other goals that transcend a specific sector. Education is folded into projects whose overall objectives are broader, for example, school building as a component of village resettlement, as a piece of broader governance reform, or through general budget support. Because overall lending in these operations is often not focused specifically on education outcomes, strong accountability for education objectives, especially on quality, is critical to ensuring a positive impact of these kinds of investments in the education sector.

Research on the effectiveness of multisector partnerships in health, for example, in Population Health Improvement, finds that the effect of such collaborations on health outcomes is seldom studied, partly due to the difficulty of such a study and the complexity of multisector project designs. The research states that though indeed multisector partnerships benefit communities through shared resources and intersectoral collaboration, more research on outcomes is needed so that such partnerships are based on evidence rather than conventional wisdom, as they are now (Woulfe, Oliver, Zahner, & Siemering, 2010). While in theory multisector programs allow multiple entry points for a given development objective, the specific needs or aims of a single sector may not benefit from such an approach.

The World Bank is considered a multisector organization, and the Bank claims to have a comparative advantage in this area, "leveraging its deep sectoral expertise on issues from water and urban development to education and health, and creating synergies across those areas" (Holland & Evans, 2010). This is especially relevant in terms of education, which is often included as a component in multisector operations to strengthen social protection, early childhood development, urban and rural development, for example. However, the results framework of any given operation in a multisector approach may or may not contain explicit indicators to measure the project's impact on a given education outcome, as it is instrumental but subsidiary to outcomes that focus on broader objectives such as, for example, job creation in a community. These complex projects, containing multiple sectoral interventions, have not typically reflected priorities in the education sector and therefore are not clearly tied to education-focused strategies by the Bank or by governments.

It should be noted, however, that a growing portion of lending managed outside the Education Sector is attributed to the increasing use of budget support (through the Bank's "Poverty Reduction Credits" or "Development Policy Loans") to channel education lending. Budget support has considerable advantages such as reducing transaction costs, increasing predictability of aid flows, strengthening national financial management systems, and supporting recurrent education costs (World Bank IEG, 2010). The Bank's Poverty Reduction Strategy Credits (PRSCs) often include indicative targets related to basic education – either as a percent of total education budgets, share of government budget, or education access and are therefore a useful mechanism to promote education policy dialogue with ministries of finance (Mundy, 2010). Multisector operations with education components are therefore not inherently disadvantageous to achieving education objectives; however, the significant level of funding channeled through both budget support and project aid outside of the Education Sector Board merits closer attention.

Indeed, the inclusion of education in World Bank multisector operations has been found by the IEG to comprise expenditures primarily for education inputs and outputs in a results chain designed to achieve other outcomes. Between FY2001 and FY2010, almost 1 out of 5 projects with over 20% of funding dedicated to education and 1 in 10 projects with 30% or more of the total loan dedicated to education did not contain education anywhere in the results chain (World Bank IEG, 2011b). Given the challenge of properly designing complex multisector operations, the proliferation the multisector operations in sub-Saharan Africa and the relatively weak inclusion of education outcomes in multisector project design, this chapter looks more closely at the nature of multisector operations managed outside the Bank's Education Sector. The research finds that multisector operations with education components are not as effective or accountable for education outcomes as those managed by the education sector, unless they are explicitly linked to national education plans. Given the disconnect between Education Sector managed education lending, and financing for education managed by other Bank sectors, it is unclear how the latter will be guided by the Bank's Education Sector Strategy, which will only apply to half of all Bank education lending for sub-Saharan Africa. Currently, there is no guarantee that both EFA FTI funding and noneducation sector managed lending will be measured against World Bank education strategy standards, and yet the Education Sector Strategy 2020 does little to address these challenges. What doesn't the Education Sector Strategy say?

## METHODOLOGY

This chapter has relied on World Bank and EFA FTI documents and data, as well as World Bank analytic work, IEG reports, and literature from international education research. In order to assess possible substitution of Bank financing by EFA FTI, the authors assessed all education financing from the World Bank for 18 EFA FTI partner countries in sub-Saharan Africa between FY2000 and FY2010. Data on World Bank financial commitments to education were accessed from the World Bank projects and operations database and the 2010 Education Sector Retrospective project data from FY1990 to FY2010. Information on Catalytic Fund grant allocations from the EFA FTI from 2003 to 2009 was obtained from the EFA FTI 2009 Annual Report.[3]

In order to assess the relationship of IDA financing and Catalytic Fund grants, all new commitments for primary education from the Bank (including Education Sector and Multisector operations such as PRSCs) were calculated for each country that had joined the EFA FTI and received grants from the Catalytic Fund by end 2009. The totals were then averaged over three-year periods and juxtaposed with Catalytic Fund grant commitments to reveal trends over the past 10 years.

To calculate the trend over time of the share of IDA and IBRD education lending managed outside the Education Sector, annual loan commitments from FY1990 to FY2010 of "Education Sector" lending totals and "Multisector Operations with Education Components" lending totals were calculated for all regions, and for just sub-Saharan Africa to show the proportion of finance managed by each sector over a 20-year period. Three-year averages were used in order to smooth out year-on-year fluctuations in lending amounts.

Finally, 10 CAS Progress reports for sub-Saharan African EFA FTI members were available and reviewed for reference to the EFA FTI to assess whether proposed financing explicitly references EFA FTI grant funding.

To assess the quality of operations managed by noneducation sectors in the Bank, the authors reviewed 10 multisector education operations in sub-Saharan Africa managed by the following Bank operations management units: Economic Management and Poverty Reduction; Urban Development; Rural Sector; Population, Health and Nutrition; and Social Protection.[4] The projects were all completed after FY2000, have an Implementation Completion Report (ICR), and education comprised 5% or more of total project loan. Half of the operations used budget support instruments (DPOs), while the other half were delivered through project investment loans (SILS). The analysis has relied on performance reviews in ICRs, which are prepared by Bank staff for all projects once they are closed.[5] Project goals and objectives were taken from the Project Appraisal Document (PAD), which is typically approved before project launch by the Bank's Board.

## RESULTS/DISCUSSION

An examination of World Bank PADs, (ICRs, CASs, and operation financing commitments from the World Bank Projects and Operations database revealed the following:

1. ***The World Bank is reducing its financing for basic education in sub-Saharan Africa, with 13 out of 18 EFA-EFA FTI Catalytic Fund Recipients in sub-Saharan Africa receiving a declining share of IDA for primary education between 2003 and 2010.***

The additionality of the EFA FTI's grant facility is a key element of global efforts after the Dakar Summit in 2000 to achieve Education for All and has contributed significant financing to 37 LICs (EFA FTI, 2011). Currently, donor governments provide financial resources to the World Bank's IDA and to the EFA FTI Catalytic Fund, but these two pools of funds are independent of each other despite being managed by the Bank's Education Sector. In addition to managing its own IDA lending portfolio, the Bank does play an important role in the EFA FTI partnership. Since the inception of the EFA FTI, the World Bank has hosted the EFA FTI Secretariat, serving as Trustee and Supervising Entity for the Catalytic Fund and the Education Program Development Fund (Mokoro, 2010).

Because the Bank implements the majority of Catalytic Fund financing (all but four grants to date), there has been confusion at country level over whether this funding, programmed through World Bank–type operations, is financed by IDA or the EFA FTI Catalytic Fund.

In its portfolio review of Bank education lending between FY2000 and FY2010, the World Bank IEG concurred that despite "levels of IDA support for primary education [being] on a par with levels from before the EFA FTI ... [t]his does not preclude the possibility of substitution of IDA primary education funding for EFA FTI funding in individual countries" (World Bank IEG, 2011b, p. 18). Indeed, this research that analyzes World Bank education financing in comparison with EFA FTI financing in 18 sub-Saharan African countries revealed substantial substitution (see Appendix A for Country Charts). As of 2010, there is evidence that the Bank is using EFA FTI to fund primary education in at least 13 of 18 sub-Saharan African EFA FTI countries, while reducing its primary education investments from IDA.

Although a thorough analysis of the displacement of World Bank financing would require a broader calculation of all aid flows to all sectors, the incentive structure for governments to request either IDA or Catalytic Fund financing for their basic education programs typically favors Catalytic Fund grants. It is likely Ministries of Finance prefer to allocate IDA to other purposes (given that their total IDA allocation is capped under the IDA Resource Allocation Index), selecting Catalytic Fund grants as another source of external education financing at their disposal. And the Bank's strong position, not only as the trustee of EFA FTI trust funds but also in EFA FTI processes at the country level, is likely to encourage Bank managers, including country directors who negotiate with finance ministries, to see EFA FTI as strategic financing for the education sector – and to allocate IDA to other objectives (RESULTS Educational Fund, 2010).

In addition to our simple quantitative comparison, we undertook a cursory review of 10 current CAS Progress reports (for sub-Saharan African EFA FTI member countries) to see if there was any evidence for preferential selection of EFA FTI funding for basic education. Seven CAS reports explicitly referred to EFA FTI's Catalytic Fund grants as the primary source of financing for basic education, either allowing the Bank to withdraw its own financing from the sector altogether or shift its focus to vocational and other post-primary education sectors (see Appendix B for a list of reviewed CASs). The following examples show that at least in some countries, the World Bank's own business strategy recognizes Catalytic Fund grants as the primary source of funds for basic education.

For example in Mali, the CAS Progress report states that World Bank financing is likely to focus on expanding higher education and vocational skills development, while EFA FTI continues to finance basic education:

> The Bank is expanding its support to higher education and skills development with the aim to build a solid foundation for growth and to create new opportunities for youth to access the labor market. The FY12 Higher Education Project aimed at improving the sector's relevance, management and efficiency will be complemented by an EFA-EFA FTI Grant Development Policy Support (currently under preparation) which focuses on policy and institutional reforms and the preparation of a Youth Skills Development operation (delivery in FY13) aimed at improving productivity, leadership, and competitiveness.

Similarly in Cameroon, EFA FTI is seen as a source of funding for basic education, while the Bank's analytic focus will shift to post-basic education and provide direction to the future focus of World Bank operations in the sector:

> As the supervising entity for the Education For All-Fast Track Initiative (EFA-EFA FTI) Catalytic Fund, the World Bank will provide additional trust fund support during the CAS period to help finance the implementation of the government's Education Sector Strategy. The grant will specifically finance the remuneration of contract teachers, whose salaries will eventually be integrated into the national budget. New analytic work will be undertaken during the CAS period to examine the linkages between education and economic growth. This will require a holistic review that examines all the different parts of post-basic education (secondary, higher and Technical and Vocational Education Training). The results of this sector work will help orient the subsequent focus of further interventions in the sector, which will most likely focus on one facet of the post-basic education.

In Sierra Leone the CAS indicates confusion between the Catalytic Fund and IDA, with no indication that the Bank will propose IDA for education sector financing needs in future:

> [African Development Bank] and IDA both provide ongoing support for education. AfDB is assisting through its ongoing Education III Project, of Support to Basic Education and Rehabilitation of Basic and Non-formal Education and Vocational Training, while IDA is assisting through the new multi-donor trust funded Education for All Fast Track Initiative (EFA-EFA FTI) and the recent Rehabilitation of Basic Education Project (closed in December 2009).

The logic of the Bank's shifting focus to post-primary education is certainly debatable; however, it does raise questions about the intention of EFA FTI to accelerate progress toward universal basic education by providing additional financing. In many countries Catalytic Fund grants are now the largest single source of external financing for basic education even where the Bank has a history of funding the sector. However, the EFA FTI's annual budget of roughly $200 million to $300 million a year pales in comparison to the $2 to $5 billion that the Bank may invest in education development annually.[6] The risk this poses is that Catalytic Fund recipients that are heavily dependent on funding from the EFA FTI have taken on related liabilities (including salaries for additional teachers) and face the prospect of weakened financial and technical basic education aid once the grant runs out, without a predictable source of external aid from the Bank or other bilateral aid agencies to replace it. The Bank has typically provided not only financing for basic education but also technical assistance to the sector, and more importantly, influence on policy dialogues with ministries of finance.

Furthermore, the displacement of IDA from the Bank poses several risks to the institution and its mandate. The first is the risk posed to the Bank's mandate to achieve the MDGs, and specifically to commit $750 million in additional financing for primary education (World Bank, 2011b). One of many reasons that donor governments provide funding to the IDA is in support of basic education in the world's poorest countries, yet with decreasing investments in primary education during the largest IDA replenishment ever, the Bank may be forced to report record lows in its primary education investments come IDA 17.[7]

The second risk posed is the following: Where the Bank is no longer investing in basic education, the technical assistance and policy advice normally provided are likewise withdrawn, leaving the Bank out of sector dialogues at the country level. The EFA FTI funding, while it does not count against the limited IDA allocation ceiling, is not integrated into portfolio management scenarios which trigger added staff capacity with greater amounts of lending, nor into Bank accountability mechanisms to ensure project performance is effectively tied to Bank (and/or EFA FTI) management structures. While the World Bank may still play a visible role in negotiating the implementation of EFA FTI grants, its accountability chain does not sufficiently ensure that staff capacity is increased to manage the additional burden of the EFA FTI grants, nor held to Bank performance standards and/or EFA FTI policy objectives when implementing EFA FTI grants (Mokoro, 2010; RESULTS Educational Fund, 2010). In short, there is a policy incoherence linked to the Bank's management of trust funds that substitute for and are governed by different bodies than IDA financing.

Finally there is a third risk: The Bank's role in implementing EFA FTI grants poses specific challenges to effective governance, with management of EFA FTI resources overseen by both the Bank's Board of Governors and the EFA FTI's independent Board of Directors and Financial Advisory Committee. With dual accountability, goals, processes, and agendas, the dominant role played by the Bank in the EFA FTI partnership creates a significant tension. This tension is further compounded by the different approaches taken by EFA FTI and IDA, where, on the one hand, the EFA FTI delivers sectoral funding, while, on the other, IDA claims to respond to demand for financing across multiple sectors. In part, the lack of financial investment by the Bank in primary education in EFA FTI countries is a symptom of the policy incoherence mentioned above.

The Bank's growing role in multidonor trust fund management has posed many new challenges to the Bank's governance and strategic directions, especially given the scale of trust funds currently managed by the Bank.[8] While the IEG has found that trust funds "may add value by compensating for the limited availability of grant funds and the absence of earmarking mechanisms in World Bank and other multilateral development banks (MDBs), although an alternative might be to eliminate these gaps through changes to multilateral financing arrangements" (World Bank IEG, 2011a). How the Bank manages its relationship with the EFA FTI's multidonor education trust fund will fundamentally shape the multilateral education aid architecture and influence the successful scale-up of domestic and external financing for basic education. If the Bank aims to support the achievement of the MDGs, deliver additional financing for primary education, and maintain its role in basic education in sub-Saharan Africa, it must directly address its relationship with the EFA FTI. The Education Sector Strategy has failed to do so adequately.

Given that the EFA FTI has effectively functioned to increase the availability of grant funding for basic education and has therefore influenced the use of Bank concessional financing for basic education, the Education Sector Strategy needs to explicitly address this fundamental change in the availability of Bank-administered financing for basic education. Although the Education Sector Strategy 2020 did not address how the Education Sector will respond to the shifting demand for and use of Bank lending for education, the Education Sector must now work with Bank Senior Management to explicitly address the potential dynamics of both IDA and EFA FTI funding in IDA countries. The Bank should assess the conditions under which it has successfully contributed additional funding alongside the Catalytic Fund, and the case of Ethiopia (which successfully secured new financing from both sources in FY2009), or Mozambique (which secured $71 million in education funding in FY2010) may hold valuable lessons for how to best structure a complete package of external financing for education.

Current discussions involve solutions such as decreasing EFA FTI grants so that they do not cover the full financing gap (and therefore maintain the need for additional IDA financing to fully fund education sector plans), creating a window of financing that can be automatically triggered without the full project appraisal process (referred to as a horizontal Adjustment Policy Loan), and reducing their role in supervising EFA FTI funds (which other EFA FTI partner donor agencies can take over, if they so choose). However, none of the proposed solutions will address the structural weaknesses that have led to a perfectly rational incentive by countries to use their IDA allocations for other sector investments. By creating explicit cofinancing arrangements with the EFA FTI and adjusting the terms of its financing for human development, the Bank can incentivize sufficient uptake in EFA FTI countries of its lending for basic education to mitigate "crowding out" and ensure that the Bank's financing is not skewed to higher education despite persistent financing gaps for basic education in sub-Saharan Africa.

The World Bank, with a considerably larger and more predictable pool of IDA financing, should be positioned to match or contribute directly to the EFA FTI's grant facility so that it has a catalytic effect that increases overall levels of aid to education. This is particularly important given the recent record-breaking IDA16 envelope and the current EFA FTI replenishment for 2011 to 2014 – both of which would benefit from an explicit cofinancing arrangement between the EFA FTI and the World Bank that would better align these two important external sources of education sector financing, and mitigate the risks now posed to the Bank's stated corporate priority to support basic education.

2. ***Multisector operations now account for one-third of Bank education lending and have increased to over half of all new education commitments in sub-Saharan Africa. They are more likely to contribute to education objectives if linked explicitly to national education plans, however investments operations (rather than policy operations) rarely, if ever, do so.***

### *Noneducation Sector Board Lending*

The Bank invested between 25%and 46% of its lending annually for education through multisector operations managed by other sectors – totaling roughly $7.5 billion in education investments between FY2000 and FY2010 (World Bank IEG, 2011b). Multisector operations are delivered through both budget support operations (DPOs) and sector investment operations (IOs), which have education as one of multiple-sector investments included in a single operation. In recent years (between FY2006 and FY2010), noneducation sector managed lending from IDA and IBRD amounted to over 45 percent of total education lending, at an average of $907 million annually (World Bank, 2010c).

Multisector operations nearly tripled in the last decade as the Bank has shifted toward greater reliance on large multisector operations to channel the delivery of its finance (see Fig. 1). Therefore the increases in World Bank lending for education in recent years is attributed in large part to increasing amounts of funding for education in these lending operations that are designed and managed outside of the Education Sector Board. Roughly half of projects with a substantial education component have an education objective, while the rest frame education as an input for other objectives (World Bank IEG, 2011b).

Financing education through noneducation sectors raises issues of performance and accountability in the long-term process of developing national education system capacity in the region. There is some strong evidence that these operations tend to lack sufficient oversight or measurement of education outcomes, including the impact of this financing on national education strategies and objectives (Mundy, 2010; World Bank IEG, 2011b; Frederikson, 2008). For example, Education Sector staff participates

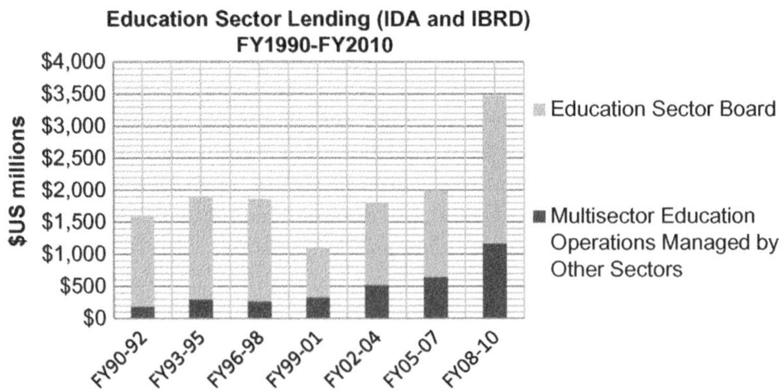


*Fig. 1.* ESB and Non-ESB Education Lending FY1990 to FY2010. *Source*: Data from the World Bank Education Sector Retrospective 2010.

in only half of the multisector operations with substantial investments in education (World Bank IEG, 2011b). Further compounding this issue is the fact that allocation of technical staff for any sector within the Bank is based on the size of the sector's loans portfolio, increasing the risk that channeling increasing amounts of education lending through multisector operations will bring about a decline in skilled education specialists, further reducing the quality of the Bank's education lending (Frederikson, 2008).

### *Noneducation Sector Lending in Sub-Saharan Africa*

Multisector operations managed by noneducation sectors in sub-Saharan Africa have increased especially rapidly, currently amounting to almost half of all education financing in sub-Saharan Africa. This financing is designed and managed outside of the education policy framework of the World Bank, with arguably less education expertise. The *African Education Sector Portfolio Review* commissioned by the Bank's Human Development Network states that multisector operations are less likely to be held accountable to education sector objectives than those managed by the Education Sector Board (Mundy, 2010). Given the growing amount of education financing channeled through multisector operations in sub-Saharan Africa and the ambiguous authority of the Education Sector Strategy 2020 over this channel of funding, a review of the performance of such operations was seen to be essential to an analysis of Bank education financing. This report therefore seeks to explore an initial sample of operations in sub-Saharan Africa, the region with the slowest progress toward universal basic education, in order to review the design objectives of such operations (Fig. 2).

While multisector operations have increased to account for between 25 and 45% of Bank education lending over the past decade, they now account for over half of all new education commitments in sub-Saharan Africa. These projects are less likely to be linked to national education strategies, to support education objectives and to monitor education indicators (Mundy, 2010). This chapter reviews a cursory analysis of 10 operations in sub-Saharan Africa. Five of these operations were sector investment operations and five were development policy operations.

A review of the ICRs and PADs revealed that no multisector IOs and only three of five multisector DPOs were designed to be aligned with national basic education strategies or to be accountable for contributions to education strategy objectives. None of the multisector IOs were linked to national education plans, contained education objectives or monitored

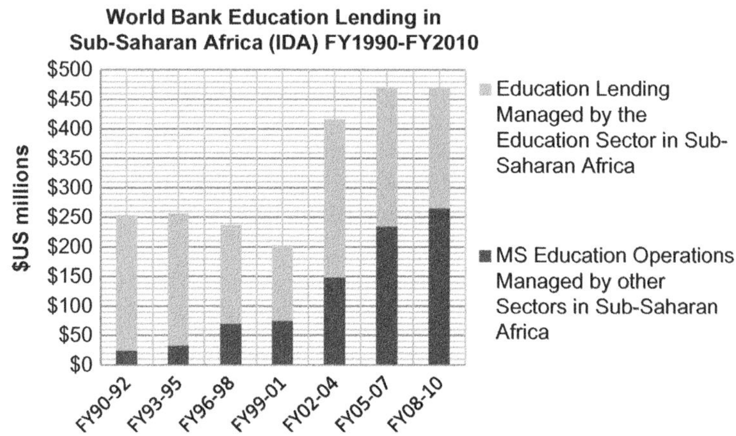


*Fig. 2.* ESB and Non-ESB Lending in Sub-Saharan Africa FY1990 to FY2010. *Source*: Data from the World Bank Education Sector Retrospective 2010.

education indicators. However, multisector DPOS that had access and quality indicators, were monitored on these objectives and were linked to national education plans performed well and were accountable for intended results. When education was financed through budget support, operations were more likely, but not necessarily, to be linked to national education plans, and be accountable for education objectives (see Appendix C for a list of operations reviewed and methodology.).

*Project Design and Monitoring of Multisector Investment Operations*

Although the multisector IOs reviewed were rated satisfactory in their achievement of the performance objectives set out in the results framework, these objectives were not related to education outputs or outcomes in education. The five multisector IOs reviewed did not refer to the national education plans and did not contain education objectives or indicators as part of the project design. Rather, multisector IOs invested in education as an input to achieving other objectives such as job creation or social protection. Because the multisector IOs aimed at other sector objectives, such as drought relief or community development, their contribution to the country's educational development strategy seems to be marginal. In general, the reporting on the education component in these projects was poor; some ICRs for multisector IOs did not report on education expenditures at all.

The main goal of these IOs in Madagascar, Tanzania, and Burundi was to support productive employment of community members in various aspects of infrastructure creation or rehabilitation, including classrooms – so education inputs were instrumental to the goal of job creation. While these projects typically involve community construction of classrooms and are a more cost-effective way of expanding education infrastructure, there is no clear indication of the links these construction projects have to national education strategies (Mundy, 2010).

None of the operations reviewed measured education outcomes such as student completion of primary school, repetition, learning outcomes, transition to secondary school, etc. However, they did contribute to education infrastructure objectives. Nearly 6,000 classrooms were built or rehabilitated in Madagascar, with a reported 98% utilization rate. Similar outcomes were achieved in Tanzania: 2,586 classrooms, 468 teacher offices, 335 teacher houses, 951 school toilets, and other education infrastructure. In Burundi, 230 classrooms were constructed but the ICR also states that education funding was not disbursed – the true impact of this investment on education inputs is therefore unclear. Similarly, the Mauritania project managed by Urban Development was aimed at improving access of the poor to urban infrastructure by building the capacity of municipal governments to contract with private firms for services. Contracts were signed and money spent for 42 education subprojects. However, no data on type and location of infrastructure are provided in the ICR, nor are data available on student utilization of the facilities. In all cases, the educational inputs and outputs, such as classrooms and school supplies, were not monitored for their outcomes so their impact on education objectives was not possible to determine.

Some of the multisector IOs had implicit education access objectives, but in four operations these objectives must be inferred from classroom construction objectives (i.e., from educational inputs purchased). None of these four multisector IOs monitored or reported on enrollments or completion. Where education objectives in school access were included, even implicitly, their contribution to and integration with education system development objectives were not explicitly measured. Only one of the five projects reviewed focused on education content or quality: The Burundi Multisector HIV and Orphans Project, which was managed by the Population, Health and Nutrition Sector, aimed at increasing the access of orphans and vulnerable children (OVC) to HIV education in schools and nonformal evening classes. However, the project inputs and outputs were reported within the framework of the National HIV program without reference to national EFA objectives.

None of the multisector investment operations were linked to national education strategies, monitored, or reported on student learning achievement. Given that the Education Sector Strategy has chosen to focus on "Learning for All" and on education system strengthening, it is significant that multisector IOs managed outside the Education Sector Board are not currently designed to focus on outcomes related to learning and none refer to the education system (Fig. 3).

### *Project Design and Monitoring of Multisector DPOs*

Three of the five DPOs had objectives for education access and quality and achieved their objectives. These were the Poverty Reduction Support Credits (PRSCs) in Burkina Faso and Uganda, and the Niger Public Expenditure Adjustment Credit. All three monitored and reported on enrollments, and two monitored completion rates as well (see Fig. 4). In each case the Bank supported three separate PRSCs over successive years. These operations explicitly supported government objectives in education access and quality. In Burkina Faso enrollments increased from 37% to 52% in the most disadvantaged districts and primary completion rates increased from 31% to 36%. Important to achieving these outcomes was a 22% increase in per

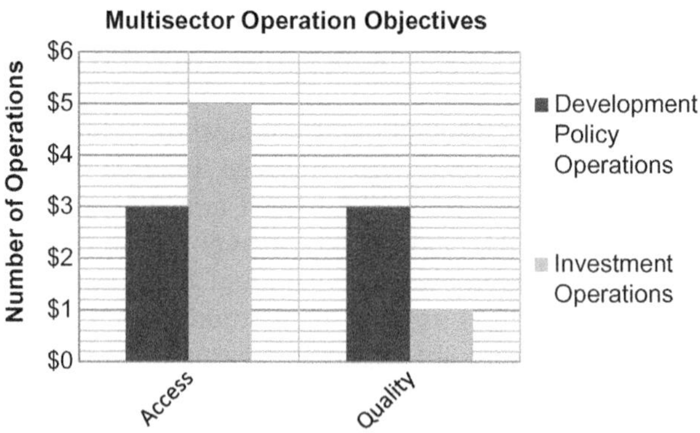


*Fig. 3.* Multisector Operations' Education Objectives. *Source*: Data taken from the World Bank Projects and Operations and Documents Database (based on analysis of Implementation Completion Reports and Project Appraisal documents) for 10 multisector operations.

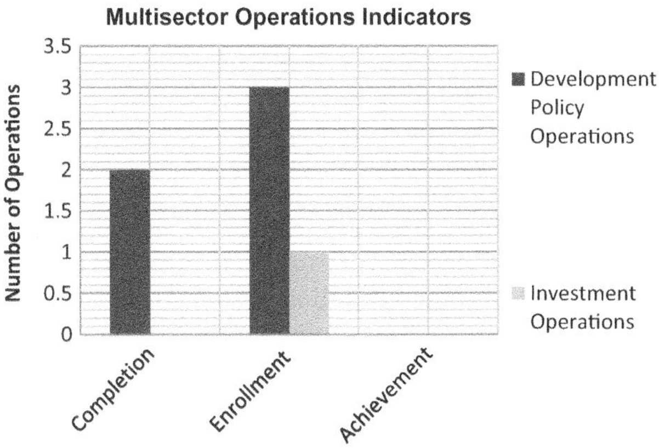


*Fig. 4.* Multisector Operations' Education Indicators. *Source*: Data taken from the World Bank Projects and Operations and Documents Database (Project Appraisal Documents and Implementation Completion Reports) for 10 multisector operations.

capita primary education expenditures. Over the three consecutive one-year PRSC operations years in Uganda, the gross enrollment in primary schools rose to 126% while gender balance was maintained; the cohort survival rate (students entering the final year of primary school) increased from 36% to 57%; and the pupil: textbook ratio was reduced to 2:1 (exceeding the target of 3:1).

The third successful DPO in the sample was Public Expenditure Adjustment Credit in Niger, which also measured and achieved positive education outcomes. Managed by the Poverty Reduction and Economic Management Sector, the operation was aimed at increasing public expenditures across the sectors.[9] In primary education, the project supported extending decentralized recruitment of contract teachers, strengthening teacher training, and piloting the involvement of local communities in the delivery of schooling. Budget expenditures for primary education increased from 70% to 90%. To the extent that they had favorable impact on education financing, the PRSCs in Burkina Faso and Uganda and the Niger Public Expenditure Credit are likely to have helped create a supportive environment for the Education IOs in those three countries to invest in learning achievement.

In contrast to the DPOs in Burkina Faso, Uganda, and Niger, DPOs for Emergency Drought Relief in Malawi and Zambia managed by the Rural Sector focused only on education inputs – school feeding programs

(Malawi) and education supplies (both projects). The ICR for Malawi reported that school feeding reached 325,000 pupils; neither ICR reported on the nature, value, or distribution of school supplies.

Overall, the findings strongly suggest that project design matters both to education performance and to accountability. Strong links with national educational development plans along with clear statements of outcome objectives, appropriate indicators, and collection and reporting of performance data were essential elements of project effectiveness. The PRSCs were consistently linked to national education strategies and objectives. These findings confirm the IEG's analysis of the Bank's PRSCs, which found that there was greater use of measurable indicators, drawn from country's own strategy, and more output-based conditions – as opposed to the input-based conditionality under sector investments operations (World Bank IEG, 2010). While the relative merits of multisector operations may be debated, clearly within the Bank's operational design the PRSCs seem to create a supportive and enabling environment for education development.

Seven operations did not incorporate basic elements of good design, including sufficiently linking outputs to education outcomes: two multisector drought relief DPOs, and all five of the multisector investment operations. These operations therefore may have diverted substantial education financing from more targeted and accountable investments in education. Sixty-eight million dollars of IDA financing was committed to the seven multisector DPOs and IOs that were not linked to national education development. The design pattern of the multisector IOs was especially weak; none of the projects had objectives or indicators that that were aligned with or linked to national education plans. From the ICR data, it is impossible to determine whether or not these education investments were seen by the country, or by the Bank, as part of national basic education strategies. If omission of information can be a partial indicator, they were not. Unless multisector IOs are better linked to education objectives, education sector expertise, and national education plans their contribution to the aims of the Bank's education strategy will be weak.

Despite the variable quality of multisector operational design in support of education objectives, it is clear that the Bank's Education Sector Strategy – which aims to support education system strengthening to achieve "Learning for All" – will face significant challenges if it is to be applied to the operations managed by other sectors. Based on a small sample of projects in sub-Saharan Africa that were managed by other sectors, there is no guarantee that the noneducation sector managed lending for education will align with its Education Sector Strategy. On the contrary, unless the Bank proactively implements more coherent oversight and accountability of operational designs that include education, a growing portion of Bank "education" lending will be irrelevant to the Bank's education strategy.

## RECOMMENDATIONS

The Bank can and should take concerted action to ensure that it continues to provide important financing for basic education in sub-Saharan Africa and elsewhere, both as a core part of its mandate and as a sound investment to reduce poverty and inequity. In order to target financing for countries off-track to achieving EFA and mitigate competition between the Bank and the EFA-EFA FTI grant funding, the Bank should implement match funding from IDA on grant terms, pooled at country level and delivered through a single channel. This can most easily be accomplished by directly transferring $750 million from IDA to the EFA FTI trust fund to ensure that its financing is allocated to basic education. In addition, the World Bank should exempt social sector spending for the achievement of the MDGs (including funding for education) from the allocation limits imposed by the IDA Resource Allocation framework, maximizing the use of grant funding from IDA and decreasing the debt burden of education financing to ensure sufficient incentive for countries to request IDA for education. Finally, the World Bank should direct all country directors, especially in sub-Saharan Africa, to program IDA for basic education development, and ensure that dialogues with ministries of finance include and prioritize basic education investments in order to fill financing gaps in the sector.

To improve the impact of multisector operations on education outcomes, including those set out in the Education Sector Strategy 2020, the Bank's IEG should undertake a comprehensive evaluation of all financing for education managed by other sectors to measure the strength of education indicators and outcomes, and reform current design processes to ensure coherence with the current Education Sector Strategy and national education plans. The Bank should also ensure that Ministries of Education and education sector specialists are engaged in prior review, planning, and implementation of proposed operations and multisector components. All multisector operations should involve sufficient education specialists in the design, monitoring, and evaluation of education components, link education investments to national education strategies. Finally, as an oversight provision, the World Bank should publically report on its contribution to education objectives in countries that are off-track to achieve the MDGs, and ensure that all projects coded as providing finance for education, especially multisector investment operations, are aligned with national education strategies through objectives, indicators, and institutional linkages with broader education development strategies and plans, or not be counted as part of the Bank's financing for education.

The World Bank stands at a crossroads in terms of its role in basic education development. Over the next decade, its Education Sector Strategy may well apply to financing managed by the Education Sector. However, it will certainly not apply to funding from the EFA FTI, nor is there reason to believe that other Bank sectors will understand and implement the Strategy in their education investments in multisector operations. The Bank's ability to promote progress toward the achievement of basic education outcomes is therefore fundamentally at odds with the policy incoherence presented by the Bank's management of the EFA FTI funding, and its implementation of growing sums of lending through noneducation sectors. Without buy-in from Bank senior management and country directors on the priority of basic education in their IDA allocations, nor strong oversight of education components in other operations, the Bank will continue to underperform in its contribution to the Education for All goals in sub-Saharan Africa. What the Education Sector Strategy doesn't say is that its relevance is limited by a failure to ensure institutional accountability for its aims.

## NOTES

1. It should be noted that the EFA FTI is undergoing a significant reform process that provides a unique window of opportunity for the donor community to address its financial arrangements and technical capacity in order to improve the Education for All aid architecture and the Bank's role within that.

2. Of the roughly $1.5 billion in annual average lending that is managed by the Education Sector Board, over half is allocated from the World Bank's concessional lending arm, the International Development Association, designated specifically to support those countries with a per capita GDP of under $1,335. This lending is critical to the World Bank's overall claim to "work for a world free of poverty" and is foundational for the other sector development objectives for which the World Bank also provides lending. It is therefore this pool of funds, intended for the poorest countries in the world, that provides the most resources for those nations furthest from reaching the Education for All goals.

3. The quality of the World Bank's lending – much less its impact – cannot be assessed because both World Bank and country evaluation processes are weak, inconsistently applied, and unevenly reported. However, the quantity, allocation, and modality of IDA for education can provide a numeric picture of the Bank's role in education development. Thus the analysis for questions concerning the

quantitative spread of education allocations assumes that more lending, better targeted at the poorest countries, is a positive contribution to education development initiatives that aim to achieve the Education for All goals. The methodology for question d relies on the Bank's own self-assessments of projects to determine their effectiveness according to their own standards.

4. These sector terms were used when projects were developed are do not necessarily correspond to the current sector structure of the Bank.

5. ICRs then rate the performance of projects against the objectives set by Bank staff in their own project design. Despite some weaknesses, ICRs are the single most comprehensive form of publicly available project evaluation from the Bank.

6. Further analyses need to be undertaken to ascertain whether bilateral aid has also declined in response to the availability of Catalytic Fund grants, and, importantly, whether countries are increasing their domestic education budgets in proportion to the external resources provided for education through budget or sector support.

7. The recent IDA replenishment secured a record $49 billion in financing for development in low-income countries.

8. Between FY2002 and FY2010, the World Bank administered $57.5 billion in trust funding (IEG, 2010).

9. Budgets are allocations; expenditures are how much money is actually spent in a financial year from a given budget. Inability to spend education budgets in a timely manner has long been a constraint on development.

10. The indicators selected have been endorsed by the UNESCO, the Education for All-Fast Track Initiative and the World Bank.

## REFERENCES

Education for All-Fast Track Initiative. (2004). *EFA Framework: Accelerating progress towards quality universal primary education*. Retrieved from http://www.educationfasttrack.org/media/library/FrameworkNOV04.pdf

Education for All-Fast Track Initiative. (2011). *Support we offer: Catalytic fund*. Retrieved from http://www.educationfasttrack.org/financing/catalytic-fund

Frederikson, B. (2008). *The evolving allocative efficiency of education aid: A reflection on changes in aid priorities to enhance aid effectiveness*. Washington, DC: World Bank Group.

Holland, P., & Evans, D. (2010). *Early childhood development operations in LCR: Jamaica, Mexico, and Brazil in focus* (Retrieved from http://siteresources.worldbank.org/INTLAC/Resources/257803-1269390034020/En_Breve_152_Web.pdf). Washington, DC: World Bank Group.

Lu, C., Schneider, M., Gubbins, P., Leach-Kemon, K., Jamison, D., & Murray, C. (2010). Public financing of health in developing countries: a cross-national systematic analysis. *The Lancet*. Retrieved from http://www.thelancet.com/journals/lancet/article/PIIS0140-6736%2810%2960233-4/fulltext

Mokoro. (2010). *Midterm evaluation of Education for All Fast Track Initiative*. Retrieved from http://mokoro.co.uk/content/EFAFTI

Mundy, K. (2010). *Africa education sector portfolio review*. Toronto: Ontario Institute for Studies in Education, University of Toronto.

Ooms, G., Decoster, K., Miti, K., Rens, S., Leemput, L., Vermeiren, P., & Van Damme, W. (2010). Crowding out: Are relations between international health aid and government health funding too complex to be captured in averaged only? *Lancet, 375*(9723), 1375–1387.

ONE, The DATA report 2011. Retrieved from http://one.org/data/en/media/

RESULTS Educational Fund. (2010). *World Bank education financing: Less or more for the poor in IDA 16?* Washington, DC: RESULTS Educational Fund.

Swaroop, V., Jha, S., & Rajkumar, A. (2000). Fiscal effects of foreign aid in a federal system of governance: The case of India. *Journal of Public Economics, 77,* 307–330.

UNESCO. (2000). *The Dakar Framework for Action.* Paris: UNESCO.

UNESCO. (2010). *Education for All global monitoring report: Reaching the marginalized.* Paris: UNESCO.

UNESCO-UIS. (2011). *Financing education in Sub-Saharan Africa: Meeting the challenges of expansion, equity and quality.* Paris: UNESCO-UIS.

UNICEF. (2008). *The state of the world's children, 2008: Child survival.* New York: UNICEF.

Woods, N. (2006). *The globalizers: The IMF, the World Bank, and their borrowers.* Syracuse, NY: Cornell University.

Woulfe, J., Oliver, T., Zahner, S., & Siemering, K. (2010). *Multisector partnerships in population health improvement.* Centers for Disease Control, Preventing Chronic Disease Dialogue. Retrieved from http://blogs.cdc.gov/pcd/2010/10/15/multisector-partnerships-in-population-health-improvement/

World Bank. (2010a). *Education Year in Review 2010: Focusing on what works in education [CD-ROM].* Washington, DC: World Bank Group.

World Bank. (2010b). *The World Bank Annual Report 2010: Year in Review.* Washington, DC: World Bank Group.

World Bank. (2010c). *IDA16 Financing Framework.* Washington, DC: World Bank Group.

World Bank. (2011a). *Education Sector Strategy 2020* (Retrieved from www.worldbank.org/educationstrategy2020). Washington, DC: World Bank Group.

World Bank. (2011b). *Press briefing: Education for All Fast Track Initiative.* Retrieved from http://go.worldbank.org/56G27PY2C0

World Bank. (2011c). *Millennium development goals.* Retrieved from http://www.worldbank.org/mdgs/

World Bank Independent Evaluation Group. (2010). *Poverty reduction support credits: An evaluation of World Bank support.* Washington, DC: World Bank Group.

World Bank Independent Evaluation Group. (2011a). *An evaluation of the World Bank's Trust Fund Portfolio.* Washington, DC: World Bank.

World Bank Independent Evaluation Group. (2011b). *A Porfolio Note: World Bank Support to Education since 2001.* Washington, DC: World Bank.

World Bank International Development Association Resource Mobilization Department (CFPIR). (2010a). *IDA's Non-concessional Borrowing Policy: Progress Update.* Washington, DC: International Development Association, World Bank Group.

# APPENDIX A: WORLD BANK AND EFA FTI FUNDING COUNTRY CHARTS

The following charts represent funding for primary education from the World Bank (IDA) and from the EFA FTI (Catalytic Fund grants) between 1990 and 2010 in 18 sub-Saharan African countries. Data was taken from the World Bank Projects and Operations Database and from the EFA FTI 2010 Annual Report. IDA funding for primary education was calculated using 100 percent of funding coded for primary education and 50 percent of funding coded for general education. Financing for primary education from the EFA FTI includes 100 percent of Catalytic Fund grants.

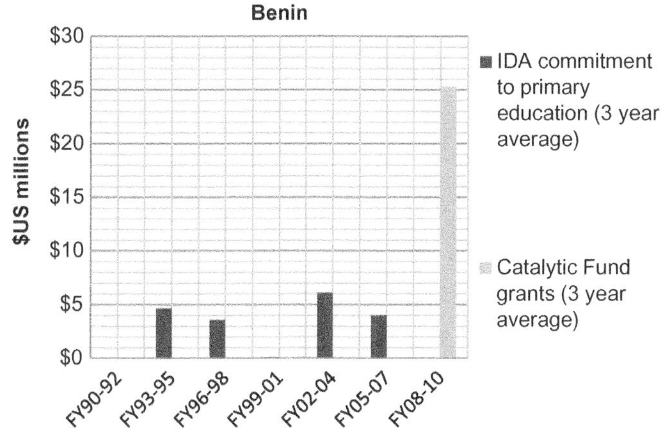


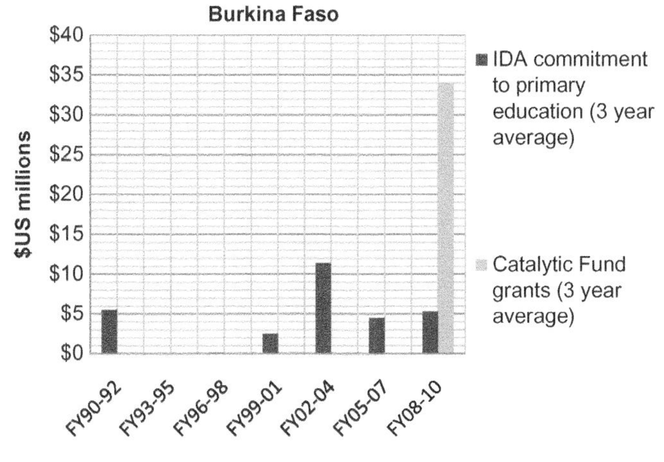

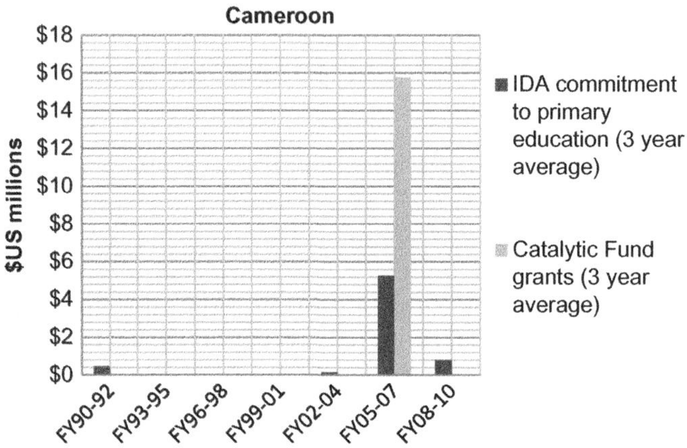
Cameroon
$18
$16
$14
$12
$10
$8
$6
$4
$2
$0
$US millions
FY90-92
FY93-95
FY96-98
FY99-01
FY02-04
FY05-07
FY08-10
IDA commitment to primary education (3 year average)
Catalytic Fund grants (3 year average)

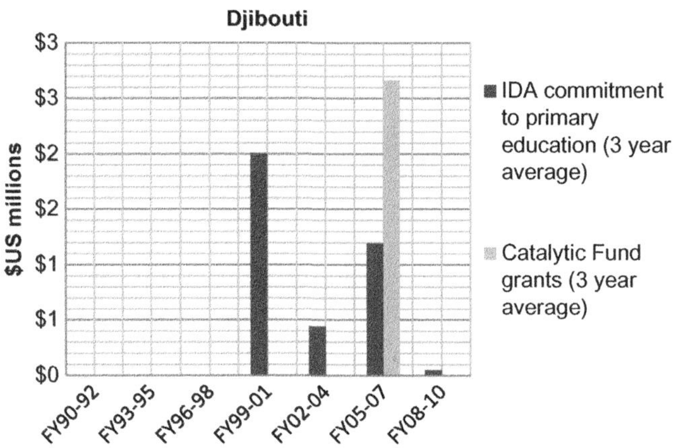
Djibouti
$3
$3
$2
$2
$1
$1
$0
$US millions
FY90-92
FY93-95
FY96-98
FY99-01
FY02-04
FY05-07
FY08-10
IDA commitment to primary education (3 year average)
Catalytic Fund grants (3 year average)

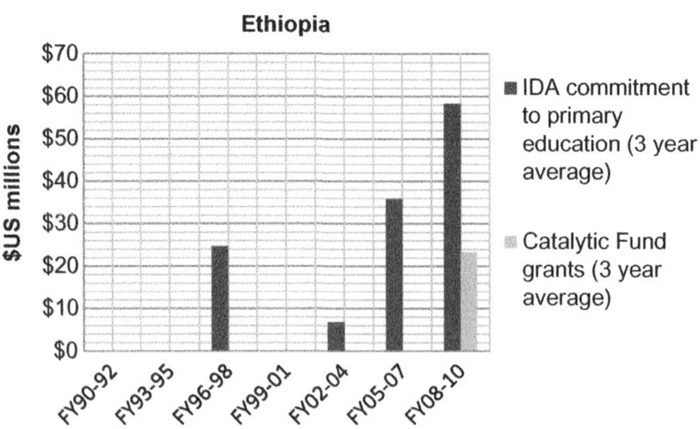
Ethiopia
$70
$60
$50
$40
$30
$20
$10
$0
$US millions
FY90-92
FY93-95
FY96-98
FY99-01
FY02-04
FY05-07
FY08-10
IDA commitment to primary education (3 year average)
Catalytic Fund grants (3 year average)

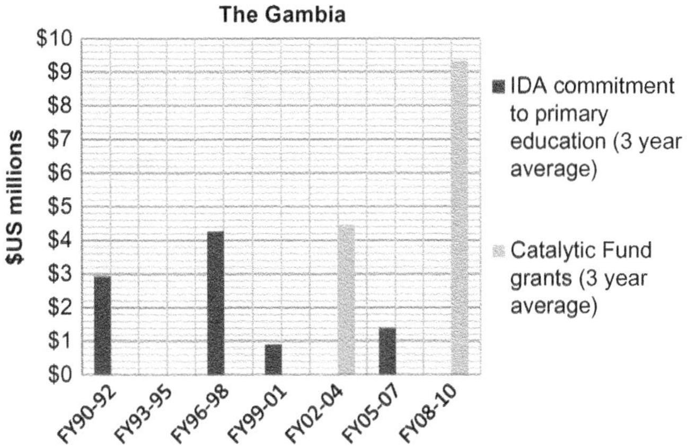
The Gambia
$10
$9
$8
$7
$6
$5
$4
$3
$2
$1
$0
$US millions
FY90-92
FY93-95
FY96-98
FY99-01
FY02-04
FY05-07
FY08-10
IDA commitment to primary education (3 year average)
Catalytic Fund grants (3 year average)

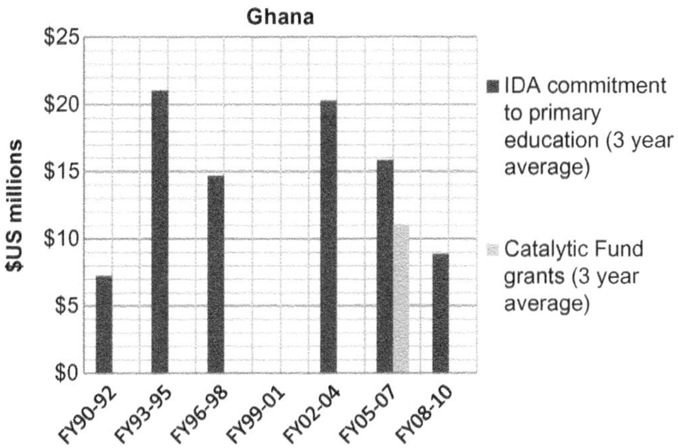
Ghana
$25
$20
$15
$10
$5
$0
$US millions
FY90-92
FY93-95
FY96-98
FY99-01
FY02-04
FY05-07
FY08-10
IDA commitment to primary education (3 year average)
Catalytic Fund grants (3 year average)

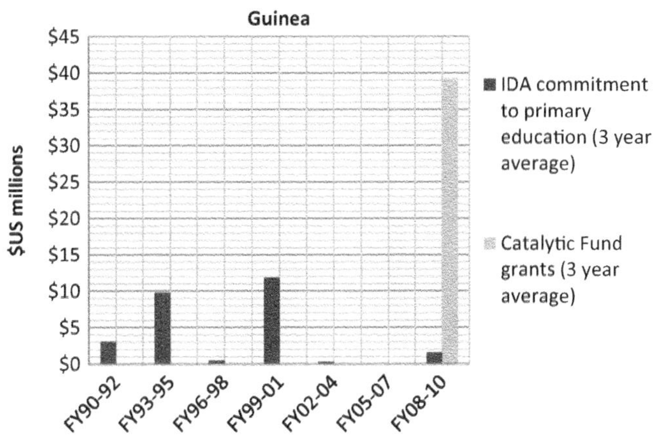
Guinea
$45
$40
$35
$30
$25
$20
$15
$10
$5
$0
$US millions
FY90-92
FY93-95
FY96-98
FY99-01
FY02-04
FY05-07
FY08-10
IDA commitment to primary education (3 year average)
Catalytic Fund grants (3 year average)

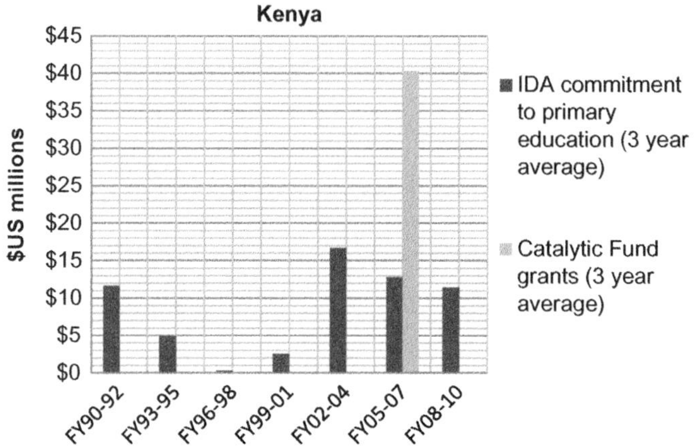
Kenya
$US millions
$45
$40
$35
$30
$25
$20
$15
$10
$5
$0
FY90-92
FY93-95
FY96-98
FY99-01
FY02-04
FY05-07
FY08-10
IDA commitment to primary education (3 year average)
Catalytic Fund grants (3 year average)

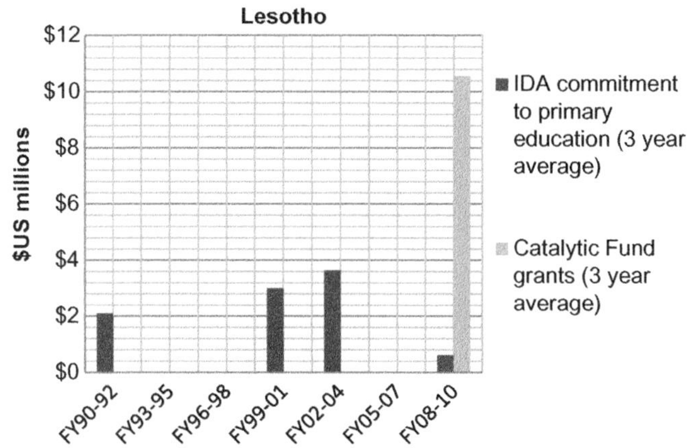
Lesotho
$US millions
$12
$10
$8
$6
$4
$2
$0
FY90-92
FY93-95
FY96-98
FY99-01
FY02-04
FY05-07
FY08-10
IDA commitment to primary education (3 year average)
Catalytic Fund grants (3 year average)

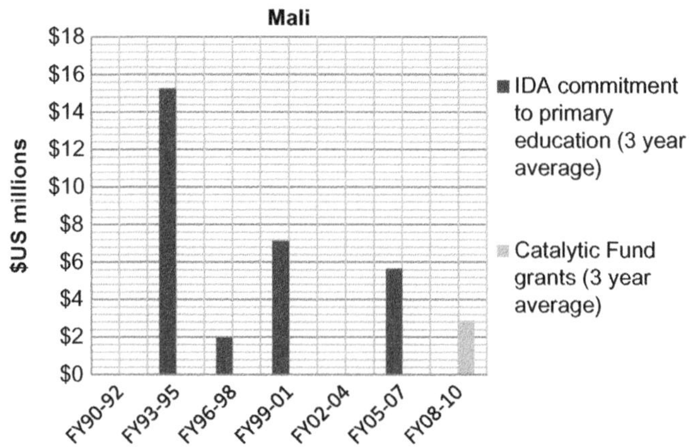
Mali
$US millions
$18
$16
$14
$12
$10
$8
$6
$4
$2
$0
FY90-92
FY93-95
FY96-98
FY99-01
FY02-04
FY05-07
FY08-10
IDA commitment to primary education (3 year average)
Catalytic Fund grants (3 year average)

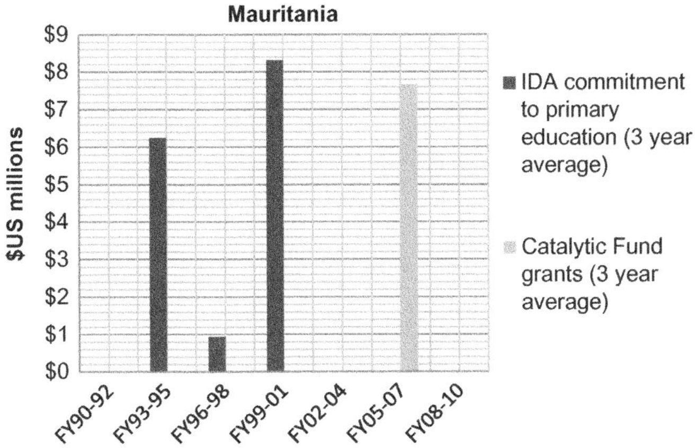
Mauritania
$US millions
$9
$8
$7
$6
$5
$4
$3
$2
$1
$0
FY90-92
FY93-95
FY96-98
FY99-01
FY02-04
FY05-07
FY08-10
IDA commitment to primary education (3 year average)
Catalytic Fund grants (3 year average)

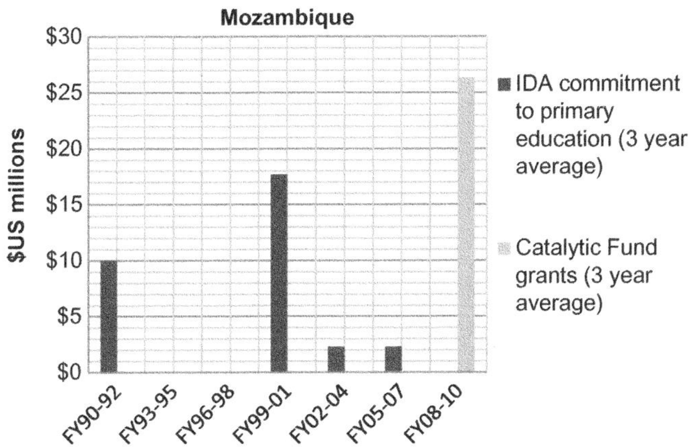
Mozambique
$US millions
$30
$25
$20
$15
$10
$5
$0
FY90-92
FY93-95
FY96-98
FY99-01
FY02-04
FY05-07
FY08-10
IDA commitment to primary education (3 year average)
Catalytic Fund grants (3 year average)

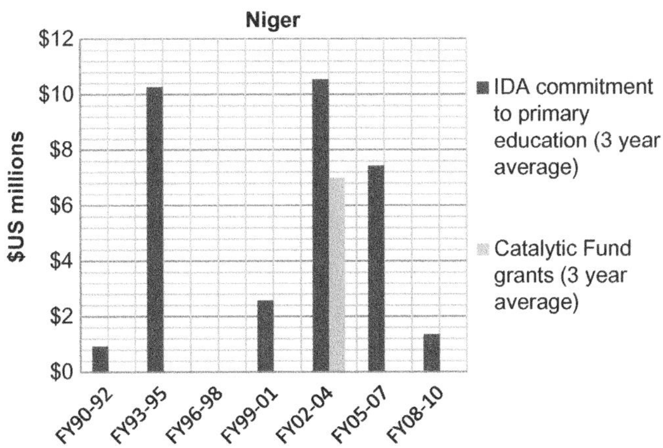
Niger
$US millions
$12
$10
$8
$6
$4
$2
$0
FY90-92
FY93-95
FY96-98
FY99-01
FY02-04
FY05-07
FY08-10
IDA commitment to primary education (3 year average)
Catalytic Fund grants (3 year average)

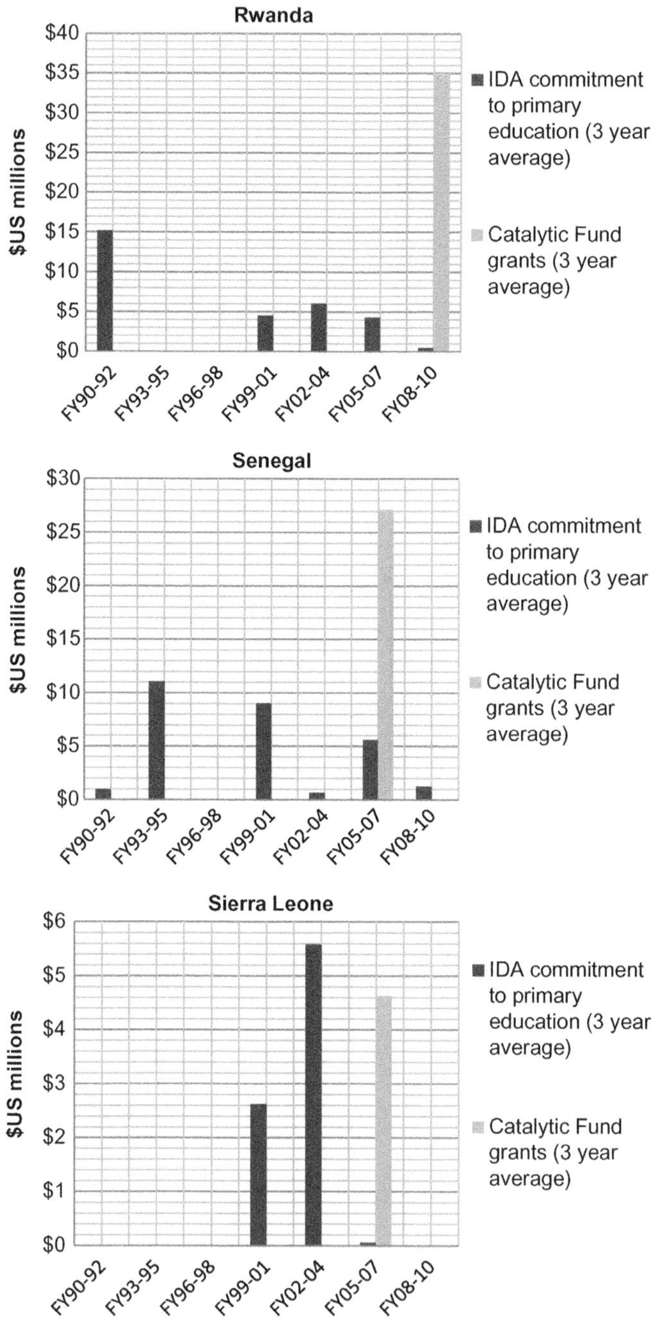
Rwanda
$US millions
$40
$35
$30
$25
$20
$15
$10
$5
$0
FY90-92
FY93-95
FY96-98
FY99-01
FY02-04
FY05-07
FY08-10
IDA commitment to primary education (3 year average)
Catalytic Fund grants (3 year average)
Senegal
$US millions
$30
$25
$20
$15
$10
$5
$0
FY90-92
FY93-95
FY96-98
FY99-01
FY02-04
FY05-07
FY08-10
IDA commitment to primary education (3 year average)
Catalytic Fund grants (3 year average)
Sierra Leone
$US millions
$6
$5
$4
$3
$2
$1
$0
FY90-92
FY93-95
FY96-98
FY99-01
FY02-04
FY05-07
FY08-10
IDA commitment to primary education (3 year average)
Catalytic Fund grants (3 year average)

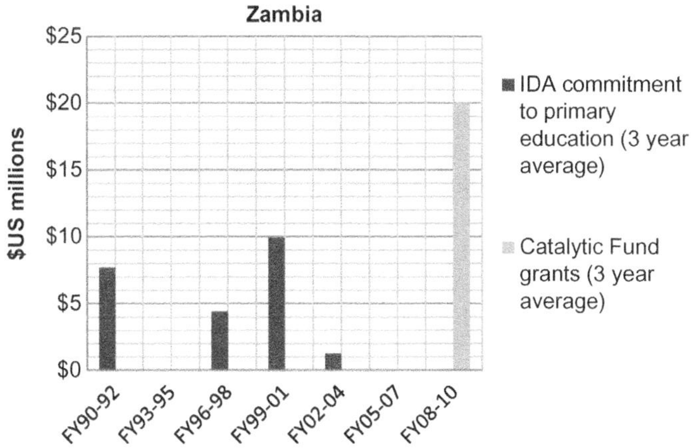


## APPENDIX B: LIST OF COUNTRY ASSISTANCE STRATEGIES

The following documents were retrieved from the World Bank Documents Online Database for all sub-Saharan African EFA FTI partner countries for the years 2008–2011.

| Country | Report | Year |
|---|---|---|
| Burkina Faso | Country Assistance Strategy for Burkina Faso, for the Period FY2010–2012 | 2010 |
| Ethiopia | Country Assistance Strategy Progress Report for the Federal Democratic Republic of Ethiopia | 2010 |
| Kenya | Country Partnership Strategy for the Republic of Kenya for the Period FY2010–2013 | 2010 |
| Lesotho | Country Assistance Strategy for the Kingdom of Lesotho | 2010 |
| Mali | Country Assistance Strategy Progress Report for the Republic of Mali for the Period of FY2008–2011 | 2011 |
| Niger | Country Assistance Strategy for the Republic of Niger for the period of FY08–2011 | 2008 |

| Country | Report | Year |
|---|---|---|
| Rwanda | Country Assistance Strategy Report for The Republic of Rwanda | 2011 |
| Senegal | Country Assistance Strategy Report for the Republic of Senegal | 2009 |
| Sierra Leone | Joint Assistance Strategy for the Republic of Sierra Leone | 2010 |
| Zambia | Country Assistance Strategy for the Republic of Benin FY2009–2012 | 2009 |

# APPENDIX C: SUB-SAHARAN BASIC EDUCATION PROJECTS SELECTED FOR REVIEW

| | Sector Investment Operations (Year Completion Report Issued – IDA commitment amount for education) | Development Policy Operations |
|---|---|---|
| Multisectoral (ECMOS) | Burundi Public Works (2001 – $8.4 million) | Burkina Faso Poverty Reduction Strategy Credit (PRSC) 4, 5, and 6 (2007 – $27.0 million) |
| | Burundi Multisector HIV and Orphans (2002 – $7.2 million) | Malawi Emergency Drought Relief (2003 – $7.5 million) |
| | Madagascar Community Development Fund (2001 – $16.5 million) | Niger Public Expenditure Adjustment Credit (2009) – $15.0 million) |
| | Tanzania Social Action Fund (2001 – $18.0 million) | Uganda PRSC 1,2, 3 (2002– $60.0 million) |
| | Mauritania Urban Infrastructure and Pilot Decentralization (2002 – $2.8 million) | Zambia Emergency Drought Recovery (2003 – $8.4 million) |

The qualitative analysis used project documents to compare the project design and performance of EDSIOs and ECMOS. To identify differences in design and monitoring across the categories of operations, six simple binary indicators were used: three focused on links to national basic education plans and strategies and three on the monitoring of generally accepted education outcome indicators.[10] This part of the comparative analysis was based on the hypothesis that there would be no design differences among the categories of projects (EDSIOs, multisector SIOs, and multisector DPOs).

1. Is there evidence in the ICR that the project is linked to the country's national education plan?
2. Is there evidence that the Ministry of Education (or equivalent) was consulted in the preparation of the ICR?
3. Does the ICR mention "Education for All" or "EFA"?
4. Does the ICR report on the EFA indicator of primary education completion?
5. Does the ICR report on the EFA indicator of student enrollment?
6. Does the ICR report on student learning achievement?

# TAMING THE YOUTH BULGE IN AFRICA: RETHINKING THE WORLD BANK'S POLICY ON TECHNICAL AND VOCATIONAL EDUCATION FOR DISADVANTAGED YOUTH IN THE KNOWLEDGE ECONOMY

Chijioke J. Evoh

## ABSTRACT

*This study presents an innovative approach to Information and communication technology (ICT) skill training and employment generation for out-of-school and disadvantaged youths in Africa. With technical and policy assistance from the World Bank, ICTs can be used to revitalize technical and vocational training to meet skill and employment needs of disadvantaged youths in the region. The deplorable conditions of out-of-school youth and the state of secondary education in Africa underscore the urgency to engage disadvantaged youth in productive economic activities. An ICT-enhanced technical and vocational training program in*

**Education Strategy in the Developing World: Revising the World Bank's Education Policy**
**International Perspectives on Education and Society, Volume 16, 337–369**

**ISSN: 1479-3679/doi:10.1108/S1479-3679(2012)0000016019**

*Africa provides both private and social gains: it provides economic prospects for disadvantaged youth and; it adds to the development of the knowledge economy in Africa. The NairoBits Digital Design School in Kenya is presented as a model of a vocational and training school that uses ICTs to improve skill formation among disadvantaged youths in informal settlements in urban Africa. Meeting the objectives of an ICT-based training and employment generation program for underprivileged youth in Africa require strong regulatory frameworks and contributions from the World Bank. The involvement of the bank, particularly through private sector grants for ICT skill train in Africa will help to revitalize technical and vocational education and training in the region. Above all, the collaboration of government agencies, private businesses, other international development agencies and civil society groups in ICT skill training will help to meaningfully engage African youths in the development of their communities in the emerging knowledge economy.*

## INTRODUCTION

The purpose of this study is to identify and propose some promising ways in which ICTs can be employed to meet skills and employment needs of youths, particularly, out-of-school and slum youths in Africa that have the creativity and zeal but without the means for self-employment. The focus of this study is on ICTs-based skill development for youths in sub-Saharan Africa (SSA). In recent years, changes in communication technologies have influenced skilled occupations as well as the cognitive and theoretical knowledge required for productivity. Unlike other regions of the world, vocational and technical education and training have played a little role in education and development strategies in countries in Africa. This explains why the investments in TVET in the region by governments and development agencies such as the World Bank have not yielded the expected results. This chapter addresses the need for restructuring and reorientation of vocational education and workforce development for disadvantaged youth in SSA by leveraging modern information and communication technologies (ICTs) in the process. Vast majority of the World Bank's support for ICT in education is predominantly focused on the provision of computers and internet connectivity to schools. The bank has paid little attention to using ICT tools to meet the demand for ICT skill training and entrepreneurship for the knowledge economy, particularly among special need youth in poor communities.

The above underscores the need for a comprehensive strategy for the education and training of youth in Africa with the 21st-century skills. In a time of high rate of unemployment among youth, particularly those in Africa, there is a strong demand on technical and vocational skill training to impart, retool and enhance job-related skills. To meet the labor market demands of the present knowledge economy, TVET in Africa needs to be enhanced with the potential of modern ICTs. According to the Commission on Growth and Development (2008), modern ICTs and digital tools are transforming every aspect of human endeavor including but not limited to how people live and communicate, how enterprises do business, what jobs are available, and what skills are in greater or lower demand. How digital tools can be used to enhance and retool technical and vocational education and training and build job-relevant skills among disadvantaged youth in Africa is the focus of this chapter. Besides, the study examines what these new communication technologies offer out-of-school and slum youths in Africa by creating new and innovative careers and skills in the global knowledge economy.

Many scholars have analyzed the role of modern ICTs in all levels of educational development in Africa. Some of the benefits of integrating ICTs in education in Africa, which include expanded access, greater equity, and the improvement in the quality and relevance of education management, have also been examined by many scholars (Evoh, 2010; Farrell & Isaacs, 2007; Naidoo, 2004). In addition to using ICTs to improve education quality, quantity, and relevance, new technologies can also be used to develop new and highly demanded vocational skills in African economies. Particular skills and vocations that are ICT-biased have proven essential in the development of the emerging workforce in the knowledge economy. This study focuses on how ICTS can be used to develop new and essential ICTs-based TVET for out-of-school youth in the knowledge economy in Africa. However, the practical knowledge of the prospects and challenges facing ICT-based skill training and employment generation ventures for out-of-school youths remain largely unavailable, and at best fragmented to policy makers, donors and prospective social entrepreneurs. This study is an attempt to bridge this gap by using the case of NairoBits, a youth and ICT-based vocational training organization in Kenya, as a "knowledge map" of what works and what is needed for a sustainable scale-up of multimedia technical training for out-of-school youths in African in the present knowledge economy.

Premised on the theoretical and conceptual frameworks of human capital and Positive Youth Development, this chapter puts forward the following arguments. First, it argues that developing the latent talents of disadvantaged African youth will entail innovative application of ICTs for skill training and employment generation. It argues for the introduction of technical and visual design skills supported by digital and multimedia technologies in vocational training programs in the region. Equipped with 21st-century skills, out-of-school and slum youth in Africa can contribute to economic and civic development. Second, this study argues that making TVET relevant in Africa will require more than the efforts of policy makers in different African countries: given its central role in development practice in the region, the World Bank will be required to exert policy influence in the retooling and integration of ICTs in TVET practice in Africa.

This study is guided by the following primary questions. First, besides its use for curriculum delivery, how can ICTs be used to revitalize vocational education and skill training in SSA? Second, to what extent can ICT-enhanced vocational training create employment opportunities for disadvantaged youth in a less formal setting? Three, to what extent can ICT-based vocational training help African countries to meet the Millennium Development Goals (MDGs) as well as the World Bank's education policy goals in Africa? Fourth, what strategic partnership models will enable the World Bank to accomplish the goals of ICT-based vocational training in Africa?

## OVERVIEW OF RESEARCH METHODOLOGY

Data for the study was gathered through qualitative research method, and theory-driven case study approach was adopted (Yin, 2004). Due to the nature of ICT-based TVET, multiple strategies were used to gather data. This includes a review of extant literature, which provided a rich source of information. In addition, data collection was carried out through online research, e-mail communication and telephone interview with managers and staff of the NairoBits organization and digital vocational training school in Kenya. A field study was conducted in June 2011 during which nonparticipant observation and semi-structured interviews were conducted with staff, current and past students of the institution in Nairobi, Kenya. Five knowledgeable individuals were interviewed. A personal observation session of classroom activities was also part of the field research. Besides, desk research was used to gather additional information from sources such as the printed media, institutional websites and blogs. Documents analyzed include official reports and policy documents from institutions such as the World

Bank, International Labor Organization (ILO) and the African Union. The use of multiple sources of data and review of documents provided multiple methods to validate and crosscheck the findings of the study.

The study alternated between data collection and data analysis. Data was analyzed by themes and keywords. This involves the use of descriptions of widely held views and perception of the use of ICTs in skill training for youths as expressed by informants. The primary goal of analysis is to use the data collected on the case studies to answer the research questions that drive the study.

The use of qualitative methodology in this study was essential for deriving rich descriptions within as natural a setting as possible (Merriam, 1998). These sources are used to understand the wider perspectives of how the World Bank can implement ICT-based vocational education system in Africa. The study is conscious of the fact that the NairoBits Digital Design School is a private/nonprofit institution and has not been rigorously evaluated. This is a major limitation of the study. However, this study draws the attention of the World Bank and other donor agencies to the human capital development needs of youth in informal settlements and poor communities in Africa. This gap in training can be bridged through the involvement of private nonprofit institutions such as the NairoBits School as partners. This is an area that has attracted little or no policy considerations among policy makers in the region.

## THEORETICAL FRAMEWORK

This study is informed by the human capital theory (Evoh, 2007; Olaniya & Okemakinde, 2008; Schultz, 1963) and the conceptual framework of Positive Youth Development (PYD) (EQUIP3/Youth Trust, 2005; Pittman, Irby, Tolman, Yohalem, & Ferber, 2005). The theory of human capital is based on the assumption that individuals and the society at large derive economic gains by investing in people. Such investment is instrumental in the improvement of production capacity of the people. The framework argues that investments aimed at exploiting the utmost potential of people should target areas such as education, health, and nutritional improvement (Evoh, 2007; Schultz, 1963).

Human capital theoretical framework centers on the development and improvement of human potential through education, training, and healthcare investments for private and social benefits (Becker, 1964). The investment in the development of human capital of the youth through vocational and technical training is vital for the sustainable development of any community both in developed and developing countries. As in many developing countries, secondary education in Africa, which includes technical and vocational training (TVT), is faced with many challenges among which are, budgetary constraints, low quality and limited access. The magnitude of these challenges has made it difficult for governments to unilaterally, meet the educational needs of the people. However, secondary schooling and technical and vocational education are positively associated with high value-added production capacity for the economy (i.e., human capital creation). Technical and vocational education is a way through which, human capital is developed. It contributes to the improvement of peoples' lives and reduction of poverty. As illustrated in Fig. 1 by the World Bank, education develops human capital through multiple pathways, among which are:

(1) helping people to become more productive and earn more;
(2) improving health and nutrition;
(3) enriching lives directly; and
(4) promoting social development through strengthening social cohesion and giving more people better opportunities (World Bank, 1999, p. 5).

By following the above step, the concept of Positive Youth Development framework helps to promote long-term investment in the development of the human capital of youths. It involves the engagement of youth in the development of a long-term and sustainable plan, and the support necessary

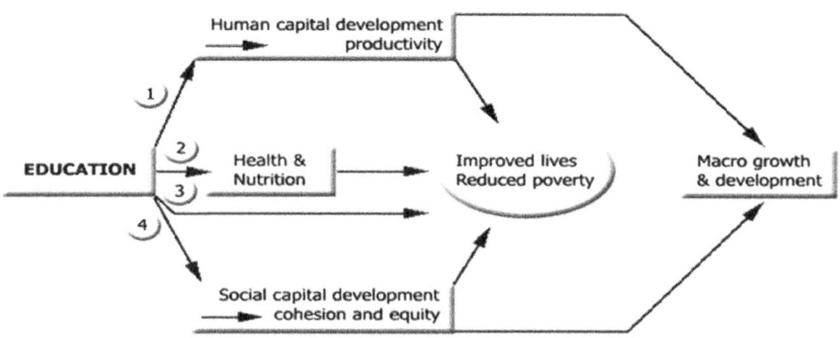


*Fig. 1.* The Importance of Youth Education and Training. *Source*: The World Bank (1999).

for the implementation of such a plan of action. Positive youth development aims at preparing the youth to earn a livelihood,[1] provide for their family and contribute to the development of their community (EQUIP3/Youth Trust, 2005).

Therefore, in this age of the "youth bulge" (World Bank, 2006), it is a necessity to invest in young people who are critical actors in the development process. Failure to train millions of unskilled and low-skilled out-of-school youth in Africa will amount to higher social and economic cost to the society in the feature. One way to accomplish this goal is to revitalize TVET in Africa partly by integrating the potential of modern communication technologies. This approach to skill acquisition and employment generation for marginalized youth in the region will boost efforts to realize the core objectives of the Millennium Development Goals (MDGs).

As used in this study, ICT-based workforce means labor and employment demands that require the application of modern information and communication technologies, especially, computer peripherals. ICT-based workforce encompasses production processes and services (i.e., employment demands) that are computer based. This has implications for the workplace organization and changing labor demand. Given that ICT-based workforce tends to require lower levels of traditional skills and greater abstract and synthetic reasoning skills (Mansell & Wehn, 1998; Yigitcanlar & Baum, 2009), employment and employability have changed tremendously. As argued by Yigitcanlar and Baum, such changes have occurred in two major ways by:

(1) expanding final demand or shifting its composition from tangible goods to intangible, information and knowledge intensive services and
(2) changing the composition of intermediate demand both in services and manufacturing toward information and knowledge based inputs and processes (Yigitcanlar & Baum, 2009, p. 44).

Therefore, a knowledgeable ICT workforce is needed to implement, maintain, and manage the knowledge economy. Hence, ICT-based workforce development describes a relatively wide range of activities such as training, policies and programs used to create, sustain and retain the workforce that can support the emerging knowledge economy. The developments of such skills are primarily based on the application of modern ICT tools.

## YOUTH BULGE IN AFRICA: A DEMOGRAPHIC ASSET OR LIABILITY?

The concepts of "youth," "adolescent," or "young people," which are used interchangeably in this study, refer to a broad range of people who fall in the age range of 12–24 years (World Bank, 2006). SSA is one of the most youthful regions of the world. The International Conference on Population and Development (ICPD, 2009) estimates that the youth and children aged 25 and below constitute about 70 percent of the population in some African countries like Kenya, Tanzania, Zimbabwe, and Zambia. The study further maintains that children and young people below age 15 constitute over 40 percent of the total population in Africa (*ibid.*), and children under 14 make up 43 percent of Kenya's population (Bremner et al., 2010). In the face of this "youth bulge" (World Bank, 2006), it is essential to invest in young people who are critical actors in the development process. Failure to train millions of unskilled and low-skilled disadvantaged youths in Africa will amount to higher social and economic cost to the society in the feature. As aforementioned, SSA has one of the largest populations of young people in the world. In global terms, the World Development Report 2007 (World Bank, 2006) estimates that out of 1.5 billion people between the age group of 12–24 years, 1.3 billion of them are in the developing regions of the world.

For the most part, the education system in Africa has failed to address the livelihood needs of African youths. In essence, the human capital of African youths, particularly, their knowledge and skills are not being developed. This makes it difficult for African youths to have a healthy and educated family and engage meaningfully in economic development and civic life in their respective communities. Out-of-school youths are young adults, which are neither in formal schools, training and vocational apprenticeship programs nor in the labor force. These youths have an uncertain future. This particular group of youth needs assistance in upgrading their skills. This group cannot be categorized as discouraged workers because they have never been employed in the labor market in the past (Guarcello et al., 2005). In 2005, the total population of young people in Africa aged 15–24 was 157 million, and the population of this age group is projected to reach 200 million in 2015 (World Youth Report, 2008). As illustrated in Table 1, a broader definition of "youth" to include people between 15 and 34 years of age will bring additional 100 million people to this young population in Africa. For this reason, Africa is seen as the most "youthful" continent in the world. Given that the age structure of a country's population has major

***Table 1.*** Size and Share of the Youth Population in Sub-Saharan Africa, 1980–2015.

| Year | Population by Age | | | Youth Aged 15–24 Years as Percentage of Total Population | Youth Aged 15–34 Years as Percentage of Total Population |
|---|---|---|---|---|---|
| | Youth aged 15–24 years[a] | Youth aged 15–34 years[a] | Total population | | |
| 1980 | 73,457 | 124,274 | 388,063 | 18.9 | 32.0 |
| 1985 | 85,260 | 144,690 | 449,349 | 19.0 | 32.2 |
| 1990 | 99,418 | 168,292 | 519,391 | 19.1 | 32.4 |
| 1995 | 116,356 | 212,674 | 596,402 | 19.5 | 35.7 |
| 2000 | 136,099 | 228,043 | 679,873 | 20.0 | 33.5 |
| 2005 | 156,899 | 263,753 | 769,348 | 20.4 | 34.3 |
| 2010 | 177,255 | 302,591 | 866,948 | 20.4 | 34.9 |
| 2015 | 197,878 | 343,410 | 971,522 | 20.4 | 34.9 |

*Source*: The Department of Economic and Social Affairs of the United Nations (2007).
[a]The table includes figures based on the United Nations definition of youth (aged 15–24 years) and that used by the African Union (15–34 years).

implications for development, this can be both a positive or negative force when viewed within the context development potential. Some scholars have observed that countries with a large youth population stand to benefit economically due to the increased productivity associated with young people (Birdsall, Kelley, & Sinding, 2001; Bloom, Canning, & Sevilla, 2003; Curtain, 2003). Robert Okello (2005, p. 2) reinforced this idea is when he argued that:

> A youthful population offers many economic advantages-in terms of a dynamic aggregate supply of labor, with all its implications for macroeconomic management, opportunities for mass production and hence development-enhancing economies of scale in production, and a buffer for social security and pension systems.

However, it needs to be said that such demographic dividend can only be realized with an educated and skilled youth population. With increasing youth population, countries in Africa face the daunting task of expanding learning opportunities to tap into the potential of this fast-growing demography, particularly out-of-school youths. If supported and encouraged, the young African population can represent a positive socioeconomic force as productive workers and citizens. As the International Labor Office estimates, "halving the rate of youth unemployment in sub-Saharan Africa could add up to 19 percent to the GDP of the region" (ILO, 2004; United Nations Office for West Africa, 2006, p. 2).

The present condition of out-of-school youth in Africa raises significant concerns about their role in the development process. The out-of-school adolescent populations in Africa have a high level of illiteracy, and the least skills required for productive participation in the economy and social and political activities. For these reasons, teenagers experience more than three times the unemployment of workers aged 20 and over (Bade & Parkin, 2006).

What characterizes out-of-school youth in Africa is a combination of common environments, lack of employable skills, shared experiences of neglect and alienation by the government and the ruling elite. Arguably, unskilled and uneducated young people are more likely to engage in criminal activities and social misconduct. As Richard Curtain (2003) observes, there is a correlation between the possibilities of civil conflict a given society with the size of its youth bulge in the population. This is truer when the youth in such society lack education and employment opportunities. In fact, a jobless youth is not only a vulnerable person, but a liability to the society. According to a World Bank study by Richard Curtain (2003) "the average country that experienced civil conflict during the period 1965 to 1999 had only 45 percent of its young males in secondary education" (p. 5). In essence, out-of-school youths are prime targets for recruitment for civil wars and disorder. This trend has been illustrated in many African countries. For instance, the political changes and upheavals in North African and the Middle Eastern countries are masterminded by unemployed and disgruntled youth. These crises are dress rehearsals of potential youth crisis in Africa.

The vulnerability of young people in the hands of African warlords and political elite was equally demonstrated in former war-torn countries of Liberia and Sierra-Leone. As observed by some scholars (Abdullah, 1999; Chigunta, 2002), young people who are involved in armed conflicts and insurgent activities across Africa cannot read or write and none of them are from the middle class or elite families. Rather, these are marginalized and estranged youths who are economically unskilled and socially disconnected from the mainstream as they struggle to survive in the "underground" economy.

The International Labor Office (2004) estimates that 27 percent of youths in Africa are neither in school nor at work. According to the World Youth Report 2007 (The Department of Economic and Social Affairs of the United Nations, 2007), and the 2008 Global Employment Trends for Youth (ILO, 2008), the level of unemployed among African youth increased by about 34 percent between 1995 and 2005 (see Fig. 2). In countries with the largest population in Africa such as Nigeria (149 million people) and Ethiopia (85 million people), the unemployment rate among young people is estimated at 70 percent (*The Economist*, 2008). This is not surprising in view of the estimated number of young people that are added to the labor force in Africa every year. For instance, Johanson and Adams (2004) estimate that about 500,000, 700,000, and 250,000 young people are annually added to the labor force in Kenya, Tanzania, and Zimbabwe, respectively. It is estimated that African countries are faced with the task of finding gainful employment for about 7–10 million new entrants to the labor force each year (African Union, 2007). As the fastest growing labor force in the world (*The Economist*, 2008), youth in Africa desperately needs to channel their potential into productive economic activities.

Several factors have contributed to increasing rate of unemployment among disadvantaged and out-of-school youth in Africa. African population grows at a rapid rate of between 2.7 and 3.00 percent per annum (Okojie, 2003). This trend leads to unprecedented growth in the labor force. Consequently, the demand for jobs among youth in the labor force outweighs the supply of jobs (Chigunta, 2002; Okojie, 2003). Another factor driving unemployment among youth in the region is the increasing rate of rural–urban migrations. The continuous influx of young people from rural areas in different African countries to the cities and urban centers in search of better life adds to the frustration of unemployment among disadvantaged youth. Besides, the geographical mobility of youth in Africa adds to the

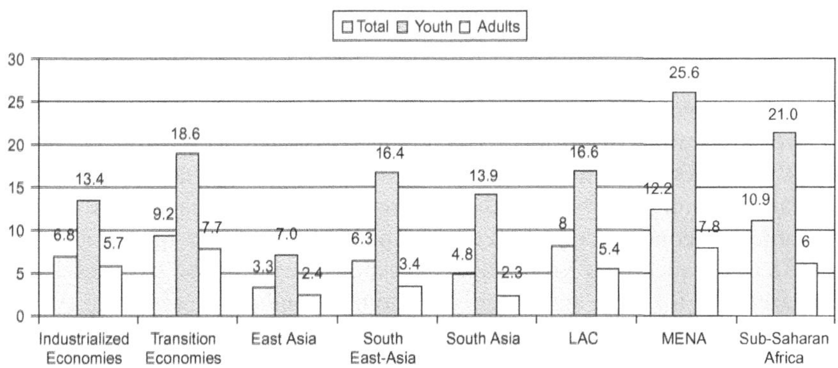


*Fig. 2.* Regional Unemployment Rates, Total, Youth, and Adults, 2003. *Source*: Guarcello et al. (2005, p. 3).

urbanization rate of African cities, which is among the highest in the world (Okojie, 2003; Palen, 2008). As explained in the following section, the traditional secondary education system in Africa (including the technical and vocational aspects of it) has created a pool of graduate with little or no employable skills in the job market. As summed up by Okojie, the major causes of unemployment among youth in Africa are:

- rapid population growth;
- small private sectors;
- rapid rural-urban migration; and
- inappropriate school curricula and poor quality education that is largely irrelevant to the needs of the labor market in most African countries (Okojie, 2003, p. 5).

## TVET AND POST-PRIMARY EDUCATION IN AFRICA

As part of the public education system, the fundamental goal of TVET in Africa is to enable the youth acquire practical knowledge and skills thereby developing the human capital among youths. At the personal level, this effort in human capital development creates opportunities for employment, and at the public level, it brings economic development for communities. The practice of TVET in Africa varies from one country to another. At the same time, technical and vocational education is delivered at different levels of educational institution. Such institutions include, technical and vocational schools, which are also called "Trade Centers" (both public and private) in some countries, polytechnics, enterprises, and apprenticeship training centers (African Union, 2007). To understand the imperative of integrating ICTs in vocational training in Africa, it is crucial to first grasp how vocational education, which is part of the secondary education system in most countries in Africa, is faring. According to the United Nations Educational, Scientific and Cultural Organization (UNESCO, 2006; World Bank, 2008), secondary education belongs to the zone that lies between basic education and higher education. Secondary education enables pupils between the ages of 11 or 12 and 18 to broaden their knowledge and experiences from the basic level and prepare them for work or higher education. Secondary education in Africa can be either academic, vocational or a combination of the two.

Vocational and technical education has been described as that part of phase of secondary education that "seeks to help students acquire specific manipulative skills required to function adequately in a dynamic society"

(Gayus, 2003, p. 11). As the UNESCO International Standard Classification of Education (1997 cited in African Union, 2007, p. 19) puts it, the aim of vocational and technical education is to "acquire the practical skills, know-how and understanding necessary for employment in a particular occupation, trade or group of occupations or trades." In more specific terms, the National Policy on Education in Nigeria defines technical and vocational education as "education, which is designed to prepare individuals to acquire skills, basic and scientific knowledge and attitude required as craftsmen and technicians at a sub-professional level" (Mohammed & Nafada, 2003, p. 47).

## THE NATURE OF TECHNICAL AND VOCATIONAL TRAINING IN AFRICA

Most TVET programs in SSA countries are school-based and some countries have maintained policies and practices established during the colonial era (African Union, 2007). As Bello et al. (2007) report, the provision of vocational education starts at the Junior Secondary level in Nigeria, which is the equivalent of the Middle School. In countries like Burkina Faso and Kenya, students switch to technical and vocational track after primary school. Other countries such as Ghana, Mali, and Swaziland commence technical and vocational education at the beginning of senior secondary school (African Union, 2007). Although the course content has elements of introductory technology, the focus is different. The technology content is comprised of "some theoretical knowledge and practical skills in electricity and electronics, woodwork, metal work, and building trades" (Bello et al., 2007, p. 57). These are subjects that make up the "old technology generation," which formed the backbone of the old economy.

Despite its potential for employment generation and economic growth, vocational education and training in SSA have been characterized by institutional deterioration, lack of funding and innovation and supply driven. As Braimah and King (n.d.) argue, the skill training and development industry in Ghana and other African countries are ill-prepared and ill-equipped to absorb the number of youths who are unable to continue with the formal education system. In many countries, vocational education exists only in the name. This trend is supported by a recent World Bank study, which argues that "Where they [TVET] exists, these schools offer under-financed, low-quality programs catering to small numbers of mostly poor students" (Verspoor, 2008, p. 194). Thus, it is hardly surprising that many young people and their families see vocational education as a "road to nowhere" in their quest for economic improvement.

Besides, in most countries in Africa, courses offered in vocational education and training programs were designed to carter for the needs of the "old economy." For instance, the National Education Policy in Nigeria recognizes a range of vocational and technical courses for Nigerian schools. These courses include: plumbing, electrical installation, brick-laying and concreting, painting, carpentry, joinery and furniture making. Others are, printing, sign-writing, metal fabrication, motor vehicle mechanics, electronics, radio, and television servicing (Gayus, 2003, p. 11). Suffice it to say that these disciplines are still relevant in the present economic structure. In some extreme cases, some African countries are beginning to experience shortage of basic vocational and technical skills such as carpentry and plumbing. The paucity of such skills in African economies is partly due to the increasing lack of interest of the youths in such technical and vocational professions that are classified as "dead-end job." Other factors include the apparent lack of adequate government support for TVET in the region. In many countries, these disciplines are integrated in the traditional secondary school education structure. As Verspoor (2008) observes, curriculum structures and examination systems in secondary schools in SSA countries reflect education styles of their former colonial masters such as France and the United Kingdom in the 1970s and 1980s. Thus, students are required to take the technical subjects alongside other subjects in the school curriculum. The implication of this integrated and formalistic approach to TVET in SSA is confusion and chaos. The system has made it difficult for students who need immediate technical and vocational skills to separate their area of interest from the academic-oriented secondary education structure designed for and dominated by the elite. Under such circumstances, many TVET students are forced to drop out of the school system. These students have the impression that academic secondary school environment, under which technical and vocational training exists is not designed for their interest. In addition to the course contents and apparent lack of funding, TVET programs in SSA countries lack incentives that can attract and retain students in the program. Above all, many course contents in many TVET programs do not match the labor market demands of the knowledge economy. This mismatch between labor supply and demand stresses the need to reorganize technical and vocational training programs in SSA.

On the other hand, efforts have been made by private businesses and non-for-profit groups to provide ICT-based skill training services for disadvantaged in different African countries. Unfortunately, such private initiatives in skill training and workforce development among youth have fallen short of their objective due to some problems. Prominent among these problems are: lack of quality assurance measures; lack of recognition by the appropriate government authority; and high tuition cost associated with such programs (Braimah & King, n.d.). The implication is that private ICT-based skill training initiatives are faced with challenges that are similar to those facing governments TVET, particularly, high dropout rate among participating youth.

Besides restructuring TVET programs in SSA, there is the need for a concomitant update and reform in the course contents. Such update will include technical and vocational courses involving modern information technologies. This will be in line with the demands of African economies in the digital age where such technologies as computers, mobiles phones and the Internet have become integral parts of the economic system. The reform of TVET program contents should be linked to employment generation priorities for the interest of out-of-school youth in SSA, particularly in the ICT sector. Central to this process is the organization of TVET programs as independent institutions, thereby separating them from the academic secondary school system. This view is reinforced by the African Union when it comments that:

> technical and vocational education for employment is unlikely to be effective when delivered concurrently with general education in junior secondary schools. This is because employment-oriented training requires inputs in human (qualified instructors) and material resources that are not available or too expensive to provide in all junior secondary schools or even in a cluster of secondary schools. (2007, p. 21)

Thus, the process of separating vocational schools from mainstream secondary schools will allow the various courses in the TVET program to receive sufficient attention in terms of funding and administration. Second, such a separation will allow the TVET programs to recognize and integrate the demands of the labor market into vocational and technical training of students. This form of reorganization will eventually remove some obstacles faced by underprivileged and vulnerable youth in the acquisition of practical skills, and create incentives for economic growth and poverty reduction in SSA.

## ICT SKILL AND THE REVITALIZATION OF TVET IN AFRICA

Vocational development and engagement among Africa youths are a crucial part of positive youth development (Pittman et al., 2005). This entails the acquisition of functional and organizational skills necessary for employment, especially in today's labor force. Thus, the prospect of youth employment and integration into the mainstream development process in the present digital economy depends largely on the resolve of governmental and nongovernmental groups to harness the potential of information technologies in a collaborative fashion. Skilled workers and technicians in the ICT industry enhance the quality and efficiency of production and maintenance in the local and global knowledge economy. The economic potential of informational and communication technologies (ICTs) informed the recommendation of the panel of eminent persons, a body appointed by the U.N. Secretary general, to focus on the application of modern technologies for job creation for young people (Braimah & King, n.d.). This strategy entails exploiting opportunities created by the boom cycle of new small and medium scale business ventures that use ICTs as tools.

The optimism in the prospects of the ICT industry in SSA is derived from the impact of modern information technologies in poverty alleviation and economic growth (Williams, 2008). The increasing rate at which countries in the region have adopted modern technologies such as mobile telephone and Internet connectivity points to the growth potential of the industry in the region. The increased capacity of international internet connectivity in SSA countries has experienced astronomical growth in recent years. For example, Telegeography (2008, cited in Williams, 2008, p. 4) reports that "between 2004 and 2007, the international internet bandwidth connected to Sub-Saharan Africa grew at 96 percent per year, compared with a global average annual growth rate of 51 percent per year." The effect is that today, countries in SSA are experiencing increased use of ICT services. For instance, $23 billion was invested in the ICT sector in the region between 1996 and 2006 (Williams, 2008). Despite the constraints of high cost, poor network quality and limited availability, the continuous growth of mobile telephone, internet subscriptions and other ICT services in SSA illustrates the potential of modern ICT industry in the region. In the same vein, this trend points to potential employment opportunities in these economies, if the necessary skills are available. These emerging businesses represent new and broad economic opportunities in the digital economy.

These economic and technical artifacts can be used to create and foster what the World Development Report (World Bank, 2006) called the "Second Chances" for the youth. Such second chances for young people, argues the report, will allow them to recover from deprivations and misfortunes of the past (*ibid.*, p. 45). In the information age, the deployment of ICTs in vocational training and interventions for out-of-school youth promises to bring significant economic and social returns to the society.

More importantly, a strategic investment in youth through the deployment of information technologies in vocational training provides an opportunity for a "catch up" in human capital development. This is more important when viewed against the opportunity cost in time lost by many young people in Africa in social vices such as youth pregnancy, insurgency and prostitution to mention a few. As observed by Knowles and Behrman (2006), the private and social rate of returns to different investments in youth depends on the context of such investments.

The rate of returns to interventions such as the deployment of information and communication technologies for vocational training for youth can be understood given the level of technology adoption in social and economic activities in African countries. The application of modern communication technologies such as computers, the Internet and mobile phones have reached a critical mass in the region because these technologies have become part of everyday life in both rural and urban Africa. ICTs can be used in TVET both as subject of study and a tool that can be used to study other subjects and for content delivery. This study underscores the need to use ICTs as a method of content delivery in mainstream secondary schools in Africa. However, the aim of this study is to encourage the incorporation of ICT knowledge and skills as part of the TVET program for out-of-school youth in Africa. Therefore, modern communication technologies are part and parcel of the aggregate socio-cultural and economic tools essential for expanding education and vocational training options but also artifacts for promoting community economic development.

This new learning environment for TVET will provide students with the basic processes and skills that underpin information storage, retrieval and processing in the modern knowledge economy. ICTs offer new opportunities for the youth to enter the labor market by lowering barriers of entry and degree of formality in employment relationship. ICT also "eliminates geographic boundaries and provides flexibility in the value chain thereby enabling the youth to compete for high-level jobs due to specific skill advantage in technology" (La Cava, Rossotto, & Paradi-Guilford, 2011, p. 2). La Cava et al. (2011) observe that as a high-growth industry, ICT companies absorb a high share of youth, especially in the mobile phone sector. The increasing adoption of mobile technology across Africa has made this argument even stronger. According to them, fewer formal jobs are generated for youth by IT-enabled services, particularly in Information technology Enterprises (ITES) and Business Process Outsourcing (BPO), due to increasing demand from European countries that suffer from shrinking and aging workforce (*ibid.*). This makes ICT an area of specialization in TVET programs across Africa. It is expected that after completing ICT-based training program, young people will acquire ICT skills that are in demand in their local economies. New ICT-based skills (such as those identified in Fig. 3) can be put to work either by self-employment initiatives or existing private and public employers and ventures. This will be an additional source of employment generation for low-middle income opportunities in the overall economy. Some technical and ICT-driven and entrepreneurial activities for out-of-school youth, which can be added to TVET programs, are:

- Internet-café management and operations
- Mobile Tele-centers
- Video technology
- Web design
- Computer and Phone technicians
- Local Area Network (LAN) technicians
- Digital photography and video studio work
- Wireless Internet technicians
- Computer graphic design
- Software configuration and installation
- Computer literacy training
- Computer hardware assembly
- E-commerce activities

The above enterprises (further illustrated in Fig. 3) are parts of the new frontier in the digital economy. If properly designed and managed, these enterprises have the prospects of generating employment opportunities for the youth in disadvantaged communities across Africa.

It is expected that the call for the application of ICTs for skill training and employment generation for less privileged youth in shanty towns and slums across Africa will attract some criticisms. Many critics have questioned the wisdom behind the provision of ICTs for the poor in Africa, rather than providing them with nutritional foods, healthcare, good roads, and basic education resources (e.g., employing more teachers and constructing more school classroom buildings) (Fife & Hosman, 2007). This criticism is the essence of what Fife and Hosman (2007, p. 3) called the "bread vs. broadband" debate. Although the above argument is salient, however, many scholars (Fife & Hosman, 2007; Wilhelm, 2003) observe that investment in ICTs for the poor in the developing countries promises long-term economic benefits in the overall social and economic development of these regions. Among such core benefits are; improved cognition among learners, improvement in local small business

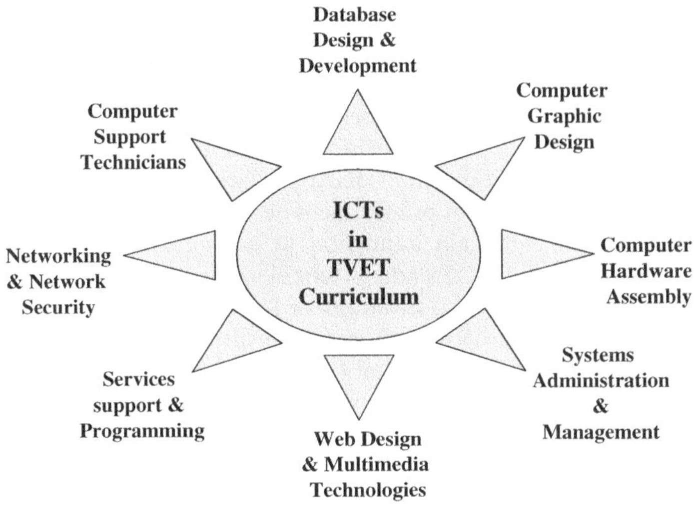


*Fig. 3.* Potential of ICTs in TVET Curriculum. *Source*: Figure created by C. J. Evoh.

entrepreneurship, tele-education and tele-health capabilities. Therefore, we have to reject the notion that resource investment in ICTs for out-of-school youth would be of greater value if invested in other areas. It needs to be emphasized that ICTs are tools; they are not ends to themselves in terms of youth training. Following the increase in demand for new skills in the new knowledge economy, ICTs have become means to reach economic ends. This is because technology, according to Theodore Lewis (1999), is a manifestation of human creativity channeled towards problem solving. Such innovative application of modern ICTs in skill development among disadvantaged youth has been the driving force behind the NairoBits Digital Design School. While much remains to be known about the integration of ICTs in education, the NairoBits School has emerged as an appropriate model and good practice in ICT skill formation by the private sector.

## ICT-BASED VOCATIONAL TRAINING – THE NAIROBITS DIGITAL SCHOOL MODEL

This section presents the profile of NairoBits Digital School as a model of social enterprise that uses ICT in an innovative way to develop the human capital among disadvantaged youth in the urban community. Generally, these institutions fall under the Ministry of Youth Affairs (Hooker, 2008; Nyerere, 2009). These institutions are responsible for training youths in vocational and technical skills, particularly primary and secondary school graduates who could not pursue further academic training at the secondary or university levels. Within the education landscape in Kenya, about 600,000 pupils graduate from primary schools and only 55 percent of these graduates (i.e., 350,000) gain admission to secondary schools (Nyerere, 2009). At the end of the secondary school cycle in Kenya only 20,000 graduates proceed to higher institutions of learning (*ibid.*). The remaining 330,000 who could not proceed to a tertiary institution of learning, coupled with the 250,000 pupils who could not go beyond primary schools, pursue vocational education and training in various public and private institutions across Kenya. The NairoBits Digital Schoolbelongs to the nongovernment/nonprofit TVET sector in Kenya. Within the Directorate of Youth Training in Kenya, there are over 750 public Youth Polytechnics, out of which, 350 receive government assistance (*ibid.*). The inadequacy of public Youth Polytechnics and other government institutions to meet the increasing demand for TVET underscores the need for private and nonprofit TIVET institutions like the NairoBits Digital School in Nairobi, Kenya.

NairoBits, a youth and ICT-based vocational training organization, stands out as a model considering the conceptual and organizational imperatives integrating ICTs, not just in skill development among youth, but more importantly, in revitalizing TVET curriculum in Africa. The organization has made significant contributions to sectoral development and employment generation for disadvantaged and vulnerable youth in slums in Nairobi through the application of modern information and communication technologies. The activities of NairoBits are focused on youths who lack basic job skills in poor communities. In essence, this group of youth has few opportunities to gain employment in the traditional job market. Social enterprise institutions like NairoBits play strategic roles of tackling economic and social concerns and challenges that "neither public agencies nor for-profit enterprises can address effectively" (Carlo, Giulia, & Rocío, 2008, p. 5). Both from its economic and social perspectives, entrepreneurs create value in the society. Within the context of economics, production can imply the production of tangible good or services. As Dee (1998) argues, the function of entrepreneurs is to revolutionize production processes.

The NairoBits Digital Design School was established in 1999 by Emer Beamer and Hester Ezra as a web design school for disadvantaged young people in Nairobi, Kenya (NairoBits, 2011). The school is registered as a

Trust to work in the field of vocational education, training and development of ICT and Multimedia skills. The school aims to ensure socioeconomic inclusion of marginalized of the youth, aged between 17 and 21 years, who come from the informal settlements within Nairobi. These are the famous slums like Kibera, Mathare, Mukuru, Juakali slums, and Korokocho slum (Ikiara, 2011). These youths are faced with many social and economic challenges such us drug abuse, early pregnancies, lack of skills and education opportunities, lack of information, and lack of basic healthcare among others. The mission of the school is "To promote positive change in the lifestyles of less privileged African youth by equipping them with multimedia skills and promoting cross-cultural exchange" (NairoBits, 2011). The realization of this goal was succinctly described by one graduate of the program when she said that the NairoBits:

> created the environment that did not discriminate anyone, despite the fact that we came from environment which was not that conducive e.g., where I came from is Kibera one of the largest slums in the world and it was not easy as sometimes one lacks basic needs but you have to put a smiling face and forget what is happening at home and take the happiness face the Nairobits environment created for us. (Fatuma, 2011)

In addition, the establishment of the school was to meet the exponential demand for new digital skills and competences for employment in the emerging knowledge economy. ICT is currently the major driver of growth in the Kenyan economy. Hence, as the World Bank puts it, the Kenyan economy is experiencing a triple technology transformation (i.e., mobile phones, mobile money, and internet). According to the World Bank, the ICT sector in Kenya grew by 23 percent annually from 1999 to 2009, thus outperforming every other sector (World Bank, 2010). By contrast, the agricultural sector, which is the largest in the economy, shrank by an annual average of nearly 2 percent per annum (*ibid.*).

The seed fund for the project was secured from different sources, including the Prince Claus fund, the Dutch Embassy, and many others. However, the practical training of young people in digital technology began, in earnest, in January 2000 with 20 students. As explained by the General Manager of NairoBits Digital School, another rationale behind the establishment of the school is that:

> There had been numerous vocational training centers offering traditional courses such as carpentry and masonry but none offering ICT and multimedia skills to the youth from the informal settlement ... it pays to be different and to deviate from the norm, though it is normally difficult in the beginning. It is the right thing to do given the global trends. (Ikiara, 2011)

Students are admitted from Community-based Organizations (CBOs) that are partners with NairoBits. Students attend the vocational courses free of charge. However, students are required to pay a commitment fee to the CBO centers that brought them into the program. The commitment fee varies from one center to another depending on the overhead costs incurred and the utility bills in such centers. However, on average, the commitment fee is about 800 Ksh (about US$8.49) per student or 10 weeks in course one. As a donor funded organization, the NairoBits School has a group of promising donors who fund their programs such as IYF, Samsung, KNH, TDH, EU, and Turing foundation Terre Des Hommes (Ikiara, 2011).

As a private school, NairoBits was first in a unique field of ICT-based vocational and technical training for the slum youth, and there was no source for institutional reference. Thus, the school fumbled through challenges and successes in its own unique way. Two months after the commencement if training, the students did not only have self-designed websites, but also mastered the use of software applications such as Adobe PhotoShop, Macromedia Dreamweaver, Microsoft Word, GIF Builder and Netscape. At its inception, the institution encountered a number of challenges, most of which have been resolved. For example, due to the uniqueness of the courses offered in the school, the NairoBits Digital School had serious problems acquiring accreditation from the local education institutions in Kenya. These authorities insist that the courses in the school be tailored along the traditional system of TVET.

The vocational and technical training curriculum of the school is structured in four levels of training, namely: course one, two, three, and media lab (see Table 2). In all, the school enrolls the total of 770 each year in different technical and vocational training courses.

What factors have contributed to the success of ICT-based vocational training programs at NairoBits School? One factor is the involvements of the private sector in the design and delivery of the school's educational curricula. The institution partners with major web design and technology companies in Nairobi. This partnership has two major advantages. First, these companies are involved in designing training curriculum for the school based on labor market demands. Second, they also provide internship and full employment opportunities for students and graduates of the institution. As one graduate of the school puts it, "Nairobits played a pivotal role in securing my employment, they basically arranged everything, and I just went for my internship, and I had to work my way through from that" (Onyango, 2011).

***Table 2.*** Vocational and Technical Curriculum at NairoBits.

| Course | Vocational Training | Duration | Annual Enrollment |
|---|---|---|---|
| Course one | • Introduction to computers<br>• ICT<br>• Entrepreneurship life-skills | 10 weeks | 550 |
| Course two and three | • Web environment<br>• Introduction to web design | 6 weeks | 120 |
| Medialab | • Advanced web design and development<br>• Project management | 6 weeks | 100 |

NairoBits graduates are employed in the ICT-based industries, particularly in the design and development industries in Kenya. To a large extent, the course contents, training and graduates of the school are demand-driven. This is crucial given that Kenya has been rated as a pioneer in the use of phone and phone technologies in Africa and the world. Thus, to meet the employment demand in the economy, the school works closely with the market players in the ICT industry in Kenya. As partners, these companies monitor NairoBits students during the training period and upon graduation absorb them either as interns or as employees. The training methodology is also in line with ICT industry specifications for the production of digital skills demanded by the industry. The school has 99.9 percent success rate in internship and job placements for its graduates. The success of the NairoBits School in placing its students after graduation is mainly due to its ongoing partnership with private companies in the economy. Over the years, the NairoBits School has established a working relationship with many private organizations and industry in Kenya. These entities contribute to the curricula offered at the school and also offer students internship opportunities. Thus, right from the onset, students are vocationally and technically trained to meet industries' workforce demand and specification.

By training youth from informal settlements on entrepreneurial and digital skills, the NairoBits Digital School is contributing to the productivity growth in ICT-using sectors in the Kenyan economy. Given that the knowledge develops in an evolutionary fashion, it is expected that rapid technological progress in ICT producing sectors and the greater use of ICT by firms would help raise multifactor productivity (MFP)[2] growth in the

Kenyan economy. ICT areas of skill development focus on multimedia, web design, database design and management, and creation of digital contents among others. These are emerging sectors in the Kenyan economy that demand agile, skilled and ICT-based workforces. In addition, the alumni of the school give back to the community by helping to train other youths and by leading self-help groups in the use of ICT in business and life and employability skills.

As an innovative approach to skill formation, barriers exist to the operations of the NairoBits School. First, the school finds it challenging to cope with the technological advancement. It is quite expensive for the school to keep updating its courses and to retrain trainers. Paradoxically, the innovative nature of vocational and technical training offered in the schools also makes difficult it to fit very well in the formal education sector. Unfortunately, this has hindered the accreditation of the courses offered by the school. Besides, as a capital-intensive undertaking, both personnel and technical resources are replaced or upgrade.

Against this background, the NairoBits School is engaged in the development of human capital of hundreds of slum youths in Kenya. These are youths who have been excluded from the mainstream education system in the country due to poor family background. However, in line with the basic principles of positive youth development (EQUIP3/Youth Trust, 2005; Pittman et al., 2005) and through ICT-based vocational and skill training programs, the NairoBits School prepares and supports this slum youth and young adults to become confident, effective members of the new workforce in the knowledge economy in Kenya. Through an outcome-based ICT training, the institution builds the foundational, vocational and ICT skills essential for success in future educational pursuit, the workplace and the community at large.

## THE WORLD BANK AND ICT-BASED VOCATIONAL TRAINING IN AFRICA

Over the years, the World has used education to promote equity and reinforce positive youth development across Africa. According to the World Bank (2011), the overarching goal of its 10-year education strategy (i.e., Education Sector Strategy, 2020) is not just schooling, but "Learning for All." As the Bank explains, the new strategy is built on the premise that "growth, development, and poverty reduction depend on the knowledge and skills that people acquire, not the number of years that they sit in a classroom" (World Bank, 2011, p. 2). The strategy advocates for "alternative ("second-chance" or "catch-up") learning opportunities that take into account the reasons why they [disadvantaged youths] are not in school" (*ibid.*, p. 26). The strategy further argues that the challenge to governments and other education providers is to,

> give these young people appropriate opportunities to consolidate their basic knowledge and competencies, and then equip them with technical or vocational skills that promote employment and entrepreneurship. (*ibid.*)

Furthermore, the Bank's new education strategy redefines the concept "education system" to include "all parties who participate in the provision, financing, regulation, and use of learning services" (*ibid.*, p. 29). This includes both private providers and nonstate organizations. Such an expanded redefinition underscores the fact that governments alone, particularly those in the developing countries, cannot meet the educational demands of the day.

Therefore, as a nonstate and private vocational education provider, the activities and programs of the NairoBits Digital School align with the World Banks new education strategy and principles, which is focused on "Learning for all" to "support innovative strategies for serving underserved populations ..." (*ibid.*, p. 28). Setting up and maintaining ICT-based modeled along the NairoBits Digital School model in Africa will require the investment of substantial financial and technical resources. This calls for a collaborative partnership of public and private entities such as private businesses, national and provincial departments/ministries of education and community-based organizations. Above all, an effective and sustainable integration of ICTs in technical and vocational education and training in Africa requires the involvement of the World Bank and other international development agencies.

Historically, the World Bank has financed TVET in Africa more than any other development agency. Such concessional aid for skill training comes in the form of grants and low-interest loans (Adams, Middleton, & Ziderman, 1992). However, continuous funding from the World Bank will go a long way to ensure the sustainability of ICT-based skill training and employment generation programs for disadvantaged adolescents in Africa. The World Bank can make its impact to be felt in ICT-based TVET in three ways.

First, the bank can strengthen the capacity of national departments/ministries of education to achieve ICT skill formation through vocational and technical education. The Bank can do this by making financial contributions in the form of seed funds to countries that are committed to establishing innovative technical and vocational schools that are focused on digital and ICT skills training and development. Early funding for ICT skill training in technical and vocational schools can be offered to both public and private institutions that have the capacity to deliver skill training and those that show preference for disadvantaged youths. The involvement of the private sector in ICT skill training will help to reduce pressure on public finance and delivery of digital skill training in Africa. ICT in education initiatives have a high cost of operation and the initial funds for the deployment of ICT hardware and software as part of TVET programs are not available in African countries. Hence, funding from the bank will enable ICT-skill training schools to keep with the pace of technological innovations. Assistance to the private sector in Africa for ICT skills, vocational training and employment can be facilitated through the World Bank Group's International Finance Corporation (IFC), which has began to invest in private education projects in Africa (World Bank, 2011). This strategy will require the IFC to refocus attention from providing funding primarily private universities to funding for capital-intensive vocational training institutions in Africa. Increased funding for ICT-based TVET in Africa will augment the bank's funding for vocational training, which has been on a decline since 2000 (World Bank, 2010).

Second, the World Bank can contribute to ICT-based TVET in Africa by providing strategic policy advises aimed at keeping African governments in check during the process of implementing ICT-based skill training and employment generation programs. Crucial to this role is the effectiveness of national policy on TVET program in Africa. The bank can encourage governments in SSA to elicit the support of the private sector in ICT skill formation by reducing barriers to entry into the emerging ICT skill training market. This can be done by allowing private institutions to be innovative in the design of their curriculum and ICT skill programs, which will be accredited by the appropriate government agencies.

Finally, the Bank can contribute to ICT-based TVET for disadvantaged youths in Africa in the next 10 years by monitoring the delivery of ICT skill training and vocational programs after their establishment. This can be done in conjunction with monitoring and evaluation agencies at the national level. In framing its new education strategy in SSA, the World Bank needs to leverage its technical expertise to assist African countries to incorporate ICTs in vocational education and training for out-of-school and disadvantaged youth. This policy approach on the part of the Bank will help to restructure and realign vocational training in Africa along the demands of the present digital economy. The policy will help to reinforce positive youth development through the Bank's strategic thrust, which is to help countries integrate education into national economic strategies and develop inclusive education systems in response to changing economic demands (World Bank, 2010).

## ELEMENTS FOR A SUCCESSFUL ICT-BASED SKILL TRAINING AND EMPLOYMENT IN AFRICA

As the world move towards global information order (Castells, 2000), advancements in ICTs can be used to promote positive youth development through ICT-based TVET. The innovative integration of ICTs TVET curriculum and employment generation in SSA needs to be implemented in phases. This is because the integration of technologies into education and skill training is a complex and multifaceted process. A phased implementation process will enable the managers of the program to learn from early mistakes. Pilot projects test-run development ideas by merging both the planning and implementation stages of project development. Batchelor and Norrish (n.d., p. 11) reports that "ICT pilot projects need to be assessed in terms of their contribution to core development priorities, and to be assessed as to whether they can be taken to scale." Thus, the ICT-based skill training and employment generation can be piloted. This will enable such schemes to make provisions for the adjustments of the program by providing constructive feedback.

Quantitative and qualitative data from the pilot project to project managers may be used to refine or adjust the project. Such data can also be used to determine the viability and sustainability of ICT skill training projects. Based on the adjustments made on the pilot programs, and the lessons learned, individual countries will be in a better position to scale up the programs. It is crucial that every ICT-based skill training and employment generation program in each country have basic components even before the pilot phase. Among these are: World Bank commitment; government agency/department of education and skill training for accreditation of courses; a project champion,[3] which may be an individual or agency; a plan of action; buy-in from the community and ICT industry; and institutional structure of the project. Like most ICT-related projects, the proposed project is multi-pronged in nature (see Fig. 4). To ensure its success, all the facets of the project need to be understood, engaged and monitored.

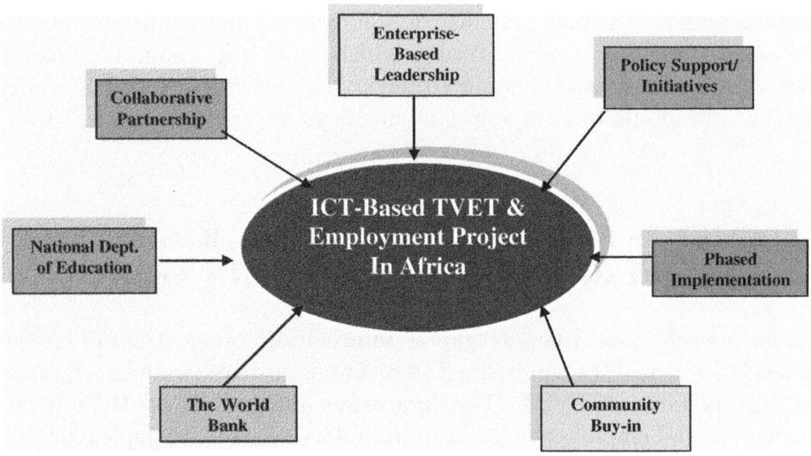


*Fig. 4.* Facets of ICT-Based TVET in Africa. *Source*: Figure created by C. J. Evoh.

## CONCLUSIONS

Investment in ICT skill training and strategies for youths promotes income generation opportunities activities, especially in many service industries in Africa. The NairoBits Digital School promotes positive youth development and the development of human capital among youths. The institution achieves this goal by engaging in the development of enterprise capabilities, increasing experience and raising awareness about ICT applications and employment opportunities for the youths. ICT-based TVET is not a panacea to youth unemployment in Africa. However, the development of ICT skill is an important strategy to exploit the potential of youth, enhance productivity, stimulate economic competitiveness and raise disadvantaged communities out of poverty in the region. To accomplish the goal of reforming TVET and to meet the increasing demand for ICT skills in Africa, it is imperative to recognize that learning opportunities go beyond those offered by the public sector and also beyond traditional formal programs (World Bank, 2010). As rightly observed by the World Bank (*ibid.*, p. 15) "the past education strategies have been very much about the Bank's role in supporting formal schools that are funded and/or operated by the government." In framing its new education strategy in SSA, the World Bank needs to leverage its technical expertise to assist African countries to incorporate ICTs in vocational education and training for out-of-school and disadvantaged youth. This policy approach on the part of the Bank will help to restructure and realign vocational training in Africa along the demands of the present digital economy.

Lack of productive skills and unemployment are direct causes of poverty among African youth. To take away out-of-school youth from the streets and slums in African towns and cities, and engage them in meaningful and productive economic activities is, no doubt, a huge development challenge for African governments and policy makers. The potential of out-of-school youth in Africa can be exploited for private and social gains by instituting ICT-based technical and vocational programs. The integration of ICTs in skill training for youth will excel for two main reasons: first, the prospects and rapid adoption of modern communication technologies for social and economic needs in Africa; and second, the extraordinary interest in ICT-based skills and employment among youths in the region. The proposed programs would be inward-looking and deliver innovative skill training and employment generation activities for the well being of youth in poor communities in Africa. The objective of transforming disadvantaged youth in Africa by creating employment opportunities cannot be accomplished through old institutional arrangements of technical and vocational training. This objective can be realized through a critical reevaluation and revitalization of existing technical and vocational training programs in countries across the region. The complex and capital-intensive nature of the ICT sector underscores the need for the involvement of the World Bank as well as other collaborative partners. However, it remains the responsibility of African governments to create the enabling environment to attract and encourage effective participation of other stakeholders.

## NOTES

1. EQUIP3/Youth Trust defined a livelihood as "occupation, work or other means by which one earns an income to provide necessities, growth and abundance for the individual and the family" (EQUIP3/Youth Trust, 2005, p. 5).
2. MFP measures the changes in output per unit of combined inputs. It reflects the joint efforts of many inputs in the production process (Bureau of Labor Statistics, U.S.A http://www.bls.gov/mfp/).
3. A champion is a strong, influential person or agency, with passion, focus, and energy to pursue the objectives of a given policy or project. A champion has a promotional and influencing role in the life of a project.

# REFERENCES


Adams, A. V., Middleton, J., & Ziderman, A. (1992). The World Bank's policy paper on vocational and technical education and training. *Prospects*, *XXII*(2), 127–140.

African Union. (2007). *Strategy to revitalize technical and vocational education and training (TVET) in Africa*. Retrieved from http://www.africa-union.org/root/AU/Conferences/2007/May/HRST/29-31/TVET_Strategy_english.doc. Accessed on October 16, 2008.

Bade, R., & Parkin, M. (2006). *Foundations of economics*. New York, NY: Pearson & Addison Wesley.

Batchelor, S., & Norrish, P. (n.d). *Framework for the assessment of ICT pilot projects Beyond Monitoring and Evaluation to Applied Research*. Washington, DC: InfoDev.

Becker, G. S. (1964). *Human capital*. New York, NY: Columbia University Press.

Bello, M. I., et al. (2007). A survey of vocational training needs of 15–25 years old out-of-school youths in Bauchi Metropolis. *Journal of Career and Technical Education*, *23*(1), 55–71. http://scholar.lib.vt.edu/ejournals/JCTE/v23n1/pdf/bello.pdf

Birdsall, N., Kelley, A., & Sinding, S. (Eds.). (2001). Population matters: Demographic change, economic growth, and population in the developing world. Oxford: Oxford University Press.

Bloom, D., Canning, D., & Sevilla, J. (2003). *The debate over the effects of population change on economic growth: A new perspective on the economic consequences of population change*. Rand Corporation.

Braimah, I., & King, R. S. (2006). Reducing the vulnerability of the youth in terms of employment in Ghana through the ICT sector. *International Journal of Education and Development using Information and Communication Technology (IJEDICT)*, *2*(3), 23–32.

Bremner, J., Frost, A., Haub, C., Mather, M., Ringheim, K., & Zuehlke, E. (2010). World Population Highlights. *Population Bulletin 65*(2). Retrieved from http://www.prb.org/pdf10/65.2highlights.pdf. Accessed on January 16, 2011.

Carlo, B., Giulia, G., & Rocio, N. (Eds.). (2008). *Social enterprise: A new model for poverty reduction and employment generation*. Bratislava: United Nations Development Program (UNDP). Retrieved from http://europeandcis.undp.org/poverty/show/2F171313-F203-1EE9-B687694A1F8C9AEC. Accessed on October 15, 2011.

Castells, M. (2000). *End of the millennium: The information age economy, society and culture* (Vol. 3). Oxford: Blackwell.

Chigunta, F. (2002, September). The socio-economic situation of youth in Africa: Problems, prospects and options. Paper presented at the Youth Employment Summit, Alexandria, Egypt. Retrieved from http://www.yesweb.org/gkr/res/bg.africa.reg.doc. Accessed on December 26, 2010.

Commission on Growth and Development. (2008). *The growth report: Strategies for sustained growth and inclusive development* (Retrieved from http://cgd.s3.amazonaws.com/GrowthReportComplete.pdf. Accessed on October 2, 2010). Washington, DC: The World Bank.

Curtain, R. (2003, June 21–24th). Promoting youth income generation opportunities through information and communication technologies (ICT): Best practices in Asia and the Pacific – A 2003 update. Paper prepared for Youth and ICT for Development: International Conference of the Information Society Malaysia, Equatorial Hotel, Melaka. Retrieved from http://www.curtainconsulting.net.au/download_controlled/Youth%20&%20Development/CurtainJune2003.pdf. Accessed on October 20, 2011.

Dee, G. J. (1998). The meaning of "social entrepreneurship." Retrieved from http://www.fuqua.duke.edu/centers/case/documents/dees_SE.pdf. Accessed on July 2, 2011.

EQUIP3/Youth Trust. (2005). Youth Livelihood Toolkit: Preparing Out-of-School for Livelihood. USAID.

Evoh, C. J. (2007). ICTs, secondary education, and the knowledge economy: Exploring the roles of the private sector in post-apartheid South Africa. *Journal of Education for International Development*, *1*(3), 1–25.

Evoh, C. J. (2010). The adoption and sustainability of technology-enhanced education in higher institutions of learning in Africa. In S. D'Agustino (Ed.), *Adaptation, resistance and access to instructional technologies: Assessing future trends in education*. New York, NY: Information Science Reference.

Farrell, G., & Isaacs, S. (2007). *Survey of ICT and education in Africa: A summary report, based on 53 country surveys* (Retrieved from http://www.infodev.org/en/Publication.353.html. Accessed on January 22, 2011). Washington, DC: World Bank.

Fatuma, R. (2011). Interview conducted on June 4.

Fife, E., & Hosman, L. (2007). Public private partnerships and the prospects for sustainable ICT projects in the developing world. *Journal of Business Systems, Government and Ethics*, *2*(3), 53–66 (Special Issue).

Gayus, B. (2003). Vocational and technical education for sustainable economic development. In D. Lawani (Ed.), *Reshaping education in Nigeria: A book of readings*. Potiskum: Federal College of Education (Technical).

Guarcello, L., Manacorda, M., Rosati, F., Fares, J., Lyon, S., & Valdivia, C. (2005, November). *School to work transition in Sub-Saharan Africa: An overview*. Working paper series. Understanding Children's Work (UCW) Project. ILO, UNICEF and the World Bank.

Hooker, M. (2008). *Models and best practices in teacher professional development*. Retrieved from http://www.gesci.org/old/files/docman/Teacher_Professional_Development_Models.pdf. Accessed on September 5, 2011.

Ikiara, A. (2011). General Manger, NairoBits Digital Design School. Nairobi, Kenya.

International Conference on Population and Development. (2009). *ICPD and the MDGs: Working as one* (Retrieved from http://www.uneca.org/acgs/icpd + 15/docs/Executive%20summary%20ICPD%20report.pdf. Accessed on November 2, 2010). Addis Ababa: United Nations Economic Commission for Africa, United Nations Population Fund and the African Union Commission.

International Labor Office (ILO). (2004). *Global employment trends for youth* (Retrieved from http://www.ilo.org/public/english/employment/strat/download/getyen.pdf. Accessed on October 28, 2010). Geneva: International Labor Organization.

International Labor Office (ILO). (2008). *Global employment trends for youth October 2008*. Geneva: International Labor Office.

Johanson, R. K., & Adams, A. V. (2004). *Skills development in Sub-Saharan Africa*. Washington, DC: The World Bank.

Knowles, J. C., & Behrman, J. R. (2006). Assessing the economic returns to investing in youth in developing countries. In C. B. Lloyd, et al. (Eds.), *The changing transitions to adulthood in developing countries: Selected studies*. Washington, DC: The National Academies Press.

La Cava, G., Rossotto, C. M., & Paradi-Guilford, C. (2011, February). Information and communication technologies (ICT) for youth in MENA: Policies to promote employment opportunities. *Arab World Brief*. No. 1. Retrieved from http://www.aicto.org/fileadmin/user_upload/Youth.pdf. Accessed on March 2.

Lewis, T. (1999). Research in technology education-some areas of need. *The Journal of Technology Education 10*(2). Retrieved from http://scholar.lib.vt.edu/ejournals/JTE/v10n2/lewis.html. Accessed on December 24, 2010.

Mansell, R. E., & Wehn, M. U. (1998). *Knowledge societies: Information technology for sustainable development*. Oxford: Oxford University Press.

Merriam, S. B. (1998). *Qualitative research and case study applications in education*. San Francisco, CA: Jossey-Bass Publishers.

Mohammed, M., & Nafada, A. U. (2003). Issues and challenges in technical and vocational education in Nigeria. In D. Lawani (Ed.), *Reshaping education in Nigeria: A book of readings*. Potiskum: Federal College of Education (Technical).

Naidoo, V. (2004). ICT in education policy – Reflecting on key issues. A paper presented at a Pan-African workshop on ICTs in African Schools at Gaborone, Botswana, 28 April 2003.

NairoBits Digital Design School. (2011). *History and start up*. Retrieved from http://www.nairobits.com. Accessed on January 25.

Nyerere, J. (2009). Technical and vocational education and training sector. The Dutch Schokland TVET programme. Retrieved from http://schoklandtvet.pbworks.com. Accessed on August 23, 2011.

Okello, R. (2005, March 4). Statement issued at the 7th Ethiopian youth forum youth and unemployment. Africa Hall, UNECA. Retrieved from http://www.unicef.org/ethiopia/ET_media_S_7_EYF05_Okello.pdf. Accessed on November 9, 2008.

Okojie, C. E. E. (2003, January 15–16). Employment creation for youth in Africa: The gender dimension. Paper presented at the Expert Group Meeting on Jobs for Youth: National Strategies for Employment Promotion. Geneva, Switzerland. Retrieved from http://www.un.org/esa/socdev/social/papers/youth_okojie.pdf. Accessed on December 23, 2010.

Olaniya, D. A., & Okemakinde, T. (2008). Human capital theory: Implications for educational development. *European Journal of Scientific Research*, *24*(2), 157–162.

Onyango, D. (2011). Interview conducted on June 4.

Palen, J. O. (2008). *The urban world*. Boulder, CO: Paradigm Publishers.

Pittman, K.J., Irby, M., Tolman, J., Yohalem, N., & Ferber, T. (2003). Preventing problems, promoting development, encouraging engagement. Retrieved from http://www.forumfyi.org/node/105. Accessed on August 23, 2011.

Schultz, W. T. (1963). *The economic value of education*. New York, NY: Columbia University Press.

The Department of Economic and Social Affairs, United Nations. (2007). World Youth Report 2007: Young people's transition to adulthood: Progress and challenges. New York, NY: United Nations.

*The Economist*. (2008). Opportunity knocks. *The Economist*, October 11–17.

UNESCO Institute for Statistics. (2006). *Teachers and educational quality: Monitoring global needs for 2015*. Montreal: UNESCO.

United Nations Office for West Africa. (2006). *Youth unemployment and regional insecurity in West Africa*. UNOWA Issue Papers. Dakar, Senegal.

Verspoor, A. (2008). *At the crossroads: Choices for secondary education in Sub-Saharan Africa*. Washington, DC: The World Bank.

Wilhelm, A. (2003). Connections between in-school and out-of-school ICT programs for youth. In: *Organization for economic cooperation and development (OECD) ICT and learning: Supporting out-of-school youth and adult*. OECD: Paris.

Williams, M. (2008). Broadband for Africa Policy for Promoting the Development of Backbone Networks. InfoDev/World Bank. Retrieved from http://www.infodev.org/en/Publication.526.html. Accessed on November 28, 2010.

World Banks. (1999). *Education sector strategy*. Washington, DC: The World Bank.

World Banks. (2006). *World development report: Development and the next generation*. Washington, DC: The World Bank.

World Bank, X. (2008). *Transitions in secondary education in Sub-Saharan Africa: Equity and efficiency issues*. Washington, DC: The World Bank.

World Banks. (2010). *Kenya at the tipping point? With a special focus on the ICT revolution and mobile money*. Nairobi: The World Bank.

World Banks. (2011). *Learning for all: Investing in people's knowledge and skills to promote development*. Washington, DC: The World Bank.

Yigitcanlar, T., & Baum, S. (2009). Providing youth with skills, training and employment opportunities through ICT Initiatives. In *Public-Private Partnerships and ICTs*. ICTs. Hyderabad, India: ICFAI University Press.

Yin, R. K. (2004). *Case study research: Design and methods* (3rd ed.). Thousand Oaks, CA: Sage Publications.

# FRAMING THE WORLD BANK EDUCATION STRATEGY 2020 TO THE INDIAN CONTEXT: ALIGNMENTS, CHALLENGES, AND OPPORTUNITIES

Supriya Baily

## ABSTRACT

*This chapter is a theoretical exploration of the relevance, challenges, and points of consideration to be taken into account as India prepares for the next stage of educational development. By providing context for the current challenges faced by India and aligning the framework of ESS2020 with government goals, this chapter seeks to inform the debate on ESS2020, especially in light of the significant gap in secondary education in India. Though the case itself focuses on India, in part due to its size, relative importance in the global economy and the relatively open nature of its government and media, there is much that would be relevant to other countries that have succeeded in addressing the first stages of educational development and that are poised to tackle the next steps. This chapter utilizes media reports, government documents, and in-country research to highlight how ES 2020 applies, falls short, or altogether misses the Indian context.*

**Education Strategy in the Developing World: Revising the World Bank's Education Policy**
**International Perspectives on Education and Society, Volume 16, 371–393**

**ISSN: 1479-3679/doi:10.1108/S1479-3679(2012)0000016020**

# INTRODUCTION

The emergence of the World Bank's Education Strategy 2020 (ESS2020) comes at a pivotal moment in time. It is situated during a worldwide financial crisis with widespread imbalances between the rich and the poor and records numbers of young people seeking opportunities for a better future. These crises require education to be the strongest hope for people to "live healthier, happier, and more productive lives" (World Bank, 2010a, p. 1). The World Bank's vested interests in education as it pertains to employment, economics, and globalization might be seen incongruent from education as a human right that promotes security, peace, and agency, but it is increasingly clear that notions of economics, employment, and happiness are linked especially for those people who do not have the luxury to question the philosophical merits of one over the other. While there is a demand for education to promote both individual and national economic success, the need for health and happiness is also equally important to consider.

In light of these vital yet often conflicting goals, this chapter seeks to present the alignments, challenges, and opportunities the new World Bank strategy faces in relation to one country case. In the concept note on its new educational strategy, the World Bank asks "What are the most important challenges in the next decade for building knowledge and skills for life and work in different country contexts?" (World Bank, 2010a, p. 5).[1] This is the primary question addressed in this chapter as it relates to the context of India.

The importance of India as a global partner and emerging powerhouse is rising. India shows evidence of a vibrant economy, a strong democracy, a pluralistic society, and an influential candidate for leadership in the region. India has been considered a useful case study in part due to "the democratic character of its struggle against colonial role and the sustenance of democratic governance afterward, in the face of bewildering internal and external difficulties" (Kumar, 2004, p. 11). The gains India has made over the past two decades are significant, yet there are major gaps in certain areas of education. For instance, the gains include a significant policy focus on addressing the "expanding the supply of education and increasing participation" (Hill & Chalaux, 2011, p. 5). Gaps include concurrent high levels of unemployment among educated young people (Sarkar, 2007) stemming from a mismatch between educational qualifications and employment opportunities. This chapter utilizes the case of India to explore how Education Strategy 2020 or "Learning for All" (World Bank, 2011) might be met, adapted, and deemed useful in this environment.

As the conversation around ESS2020 ratchets up, theoretical exploration of points of consideration to be taken into account as India prepares for the next stage of educational development are justified. By providing context for the current challenges faced by India and aligning the framework of ESS2020 with government goals, this chapter is a systematic study of policy documents from India and the World Bank, research publications on current trends and conditions of education in India, data presented in the Seventh All India School Education Survey, media reports pertaining to the concerns of the public on education as well as data collected in conversations with Indian principals on their views of the state of education to highlight how ESS2020 applies, falls short, or altogether misses the Indian context.

## BACKGROUND AND CONTEXT

The development of broad mandates at the international level requires national-level relevance and local-level acceptance if the policies are to make sense at the time of implementation. Articulation of these policies depends on the context and population of each country and this chapter seeks to focus on how India might receive ESS2020, especially as India seeks to move away from a former identity emphasized by need, poverty, and "third-world" status.

While this chapter does not seek to deconstruct the methodology of the World Bank process to design and develop ESS2020, I accept that the World Bank did commence on an "unprecedented level of global consultations, with stakeholders representing 90 countries" (World Bank, n.d., p. 1) emerging with an ambitious plan to expand, enrich, and capacitate the scope of education worldwide. The scope of ESS2020 appeared to be dictated by the needs of multiple countries at various stages of development. While primary education expansion has been the focus of most educational strategies in developing countries up until this decade (World Bank, 2010a), the rising challenges faced by countries require the development of more equitable policies if more people's lives are indeed expected to be "happier." Complexities emerging from the inequities of distribution of wealth, power, and opportunity continue to privilege certain groups over others. The importance of education as a tool for transformation for individuals and the communities and countries they reside in is rarely debated. Yet if countries are to provide an improved standard of living, education policies have to move beyond the relative success we have seen in many parts of the world in terms of access to primary education. Relying on numbers as an indicator of success, by World Bank accounts, enrollment rates in primary education are at the highest at nearly 80 percent while completion rates hover at 60 percent (World Bank, 2010b). Though the universal numbers are high, the challenges for countries at differing stages of development vary. It goes without saying that the challenges faced by education in Serbia will be very different from the challenges faced by a country like South Africa. In an effort to make ESS2020 relevant to the multiple countries at varying stages of development, the World Bank attempted to craft conversations around the needs of different groupings based on each country's income levels. Using a process of discussion between representatives of countries of similar economic status, visual "word clouds" were developed that highlighted areas of similar interest and levels of urgency. In the analysis in this chapter, the world clouds provided the first data set where, India, as a lower-middle-income country (World Bank, 2010a), identified with needs that intersected between those of the low-income and middle-income countries. These "word clouds" offered a pictorial representation of the most important issues for consideration in each income grouping. Looking for intersections between the two groupings in the order of importance, the data highlighted common needs including issues of quality, training, learning, and systems (World Bank, 2010b). Using those specific issues, further investigation of policy papers, media reports, interview notes, and research reports resulted in another layer of data that addressed the contextual factors underlying these issues. Finally, the two layers of data, namely, the themes from ESS2020 data and the findings and attitudes from the research media and in-country policy reports, were placed in the framework of alignments (synergy between World Bank goals and local level buy-in), challenges (discrepancies between World Bank goals and local-level attitudes and research) and finally opportunities (issues that offer some judicious openings for action).

## SITUATING EDUCATION IN THE CURRENT CONTEXT OF INDIA

India's recent success has allowed a feeling of general "optimism about (India's) social and economic development" (Kingdon, 2007, p. 168). The immediate postindependence needs required a specific focus on increasing the metrics of school-related indices. As the population continues to grow, passing the one billion mark, it is imperative to shift the spotlight from numerical accomplishments to those that measure broader educational goals, including those that are self-defined such as happiness and well-being.

The focus on primary or basic education has been the centerpiece of most educational programs and practices. In introducing ESS2020, the World Bank offers that its mission has been to "ensure ... basic education of adequate quality, and further opportunities to learn advanced skills throughout life" (World Bank, 2010a, p. 1). This mission has been well aligned with most developing countries including India. However, India is currently at a crossroads. With a largely agrarian workforce, a shortage of jobs for educated youth (Sarkar, 2007) and where the national average number of teachers in a school is 2.47 (Pandey, 2006), policy mandates including the newly enacted Right to Free Education Act have divided responsibilities for education between the central and state governments (Ministry of Human Resource Development, 2008), leading to a system that is both national in scope and local in implementation.

India's recent history highlights active partnerships with the World Bank and allows for some inferences to be made regarding its upcoming alliance with the World Bank with ESS2020. In 1994, India undertook an ambitious educational program called the District Primary Education Program (DPEP) in partnership with the World Bank, the United Nations Children's Fund (UNICEF), and the governments of the United Kingdom and the Netherlands. The key populations addressed by the DPEP were children between the ages of 6 and 14 with a target to provide at least five years of quality primary education in 149 districts covering 14 states (World Bank, 1997). To universalize primary education across the country, the program sought to increase enrollment, maintain attendance, and raise achievement in primary education with a special emphasis on improving access to those who have historically been denied such educational advantages, namely, girls, the disabled, and those in scheduled castes and tribes.

Over the course of the eight years the DPEP was in effect, the trajectory of enrollment and development and opening of new schools shows positive growth in meeting the goals of the DPEP. Utilizing the enrollment numbers provided in the CABE Report (2007), I have presented the data in the following figures to highlight the changes over time. Fig. 1 shows the growth in enrollment overall over the eight-year span of time showing increases at all levels but highlights the significant drop from the lower primary levels to the upper levels of primary and secondary education. Fig. 2 shows the steady growth of all educational institutions but again highlights the considerable separation between the numbers of lower primary schools and the subsequent drop at the upper levels.

Though the trajectory of the numbers has shown positive growth and development, critiques of the DPEP include "too much emphasis on the

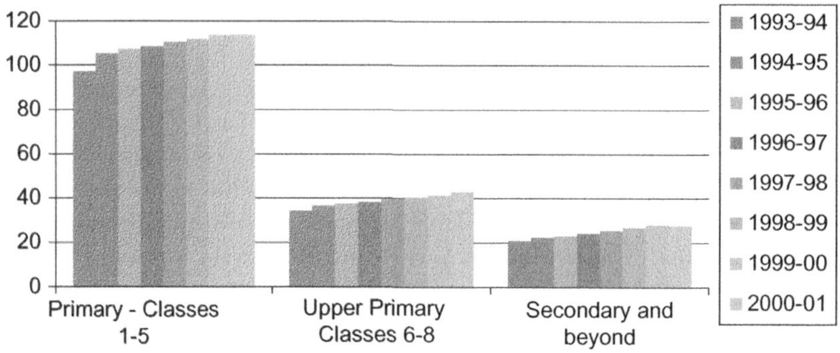


*Fig. 1.* Enrollment Growth Over the Course of the DPEP Across All Levels of Education.

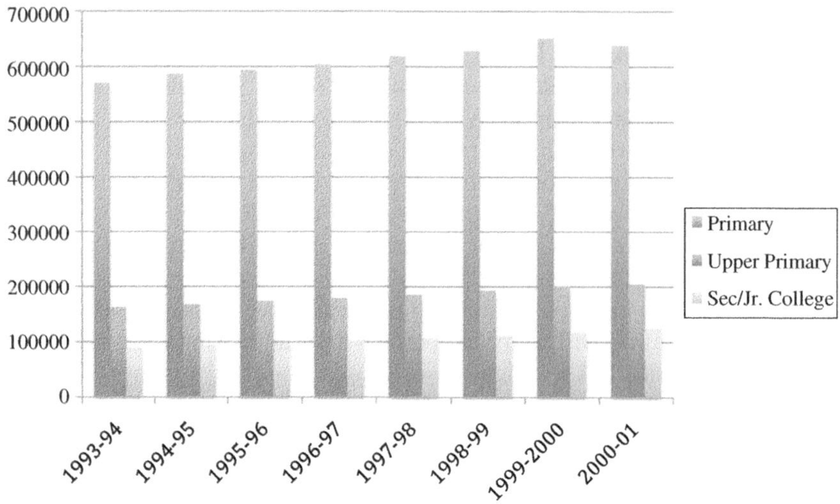


*Fig. 2.* Educational Institutions – Eight Year Growth.

technical aspects of the project … lack of focus on content orientation, lack of commitment on the part of teachers, uninspiring classroom environment, (and) improper evaluation" (Prabhu, 2003). Additionally, results were dissimilar in the various districts where the program was being implemented (Pandey, 2000) that might be expected, but it behooves researchers to better understand why that might have been the case. Finally, there are broader critiques and counter-critiques of the DPEP as a tool to promote Western hegemony and questions related to India's dependence on foreign investment to promote education are also found (Joshi, 2001; Kumar, Priyam, & Saxena, 2001). Finally, quality or the lack of measures to address it has also been a consideration (Kumar, 2004).

As the DPEP came to a close, India is seeing a fresh set of challenges as it pertains to issues of geography, socioeconomics, class, gender, caste, and religion. The rapidly expanding youth population is a major concern for India. As a "young country," India has a population of nearly 770 million under the age of 35 (over half the population), and the average age currently lies at 25. In comparison, the average age of the population in China is 34, while in the United States, Europe, and Japan, the average ages range between 40 and 45 (Aggarwal, 2010).

Another significant challenge India facing today is the continued marginalization of certain groups of people. The tribal groups (or *Adivasis* as preferred by members of the groups) have had limited if negligible changes to their economic status over the past 20 years (Das, Hall, Kapoor, & Nikitin, 2011). Women's status may have improved as well over time, but girls still face forms of discrimination in education including a preference for supporting boys in families and hesitations on the part of families to send girls to coeducational schools or for longer distances at the later stages of their education careers (Wu, Goldschmidt, Boscardim, & Azam, 2007).

Finally, there have been calls for greater focus on the quality of education in India instead of quantity (Kingdon, 1996). Issues of quality around the rural–urban divide, the need to recognize alternate forms of education, and better connections between work and school are critical to consider if education is to be useful and effective especially for those students in the middle years or of secondary school age. Training and learning are interwoven and this chapter further explores those linkages, both in scholarship and in context of ESS2020 and India. Finally, the idea of integrated systems, a multisectoral approach, and greater participation of stakeholders in the reform and design of education are examples of what systemic change might be important to consider in light of the ESS2020 strategy.

## FRAMING ESS2020 AND EDUCATION IN INDIA – A PLACE FOR DISCUSSION

Either shrewd observation or welcome serendipity has placed the timing of the ESS2020 to align with India's own debate and dialogue about what is to be its own next steps for education. As mentioned at the onset of this chapter, the four key areas stakeholders identified were quality, training, learning, and systems. Each of these four key components offers multiple constraints and depends on certain critical factors if they are to impact Indian education.

Because of the relative influence the World Bank has on education policy in India, evidenced by a long relationship between the two, it is important to understand how these four terms are defined in the context of ESS2020 rather than in terms of the national context. These definitions will inform the subsequent sections of this chapter to understand how the terms are deconstructed from the perspective of the World Bank as it is framed in the context of education in India.

- *Quality* – Quality is far the most nebulous of terms to define, but in the *Summary of Consultation Inputs* (World Bank, 2010b), discussions in the low- and middle-income countries focused on quality measures that included regulatory frameworks, relevance of bridging school and work lives, as well as addressing the differences between urban and rural education. Additional quality inputs focused on teacher accreditation and quality assurances for tertiary education (World Bank, 2010b). Additionally, ESS2020 addresses quality as not only those "visible inputs to education … but also the competence of teachers … (and) the relevance of what is being taught" (World Bank, 2010b, p. 10).
- *Learning* – Learning is considered to be the "acquisition of knowledge and skills (that) happen over a person's lifetime" but is especially critical between birth and the mid-20s as the learning that occurs in this timeframe provides a "foundation for more learning throughout life, including the ability of the adult workforce to re-skill" (World Bank, n.d., p. 2).
- *Training* – Training allows countries to better reach those who have been out of school for too long, provides options for vulnerable youth, and promotes lifelong learning. Through ESS2020, the World Bank is attempting to "explicitly (recognize) that learning opportunities go beyond those offered by … traditional formal programs" (World Bank, 2010c, p. 15).
- *Systems* – System has referred historically to the "schools, universities, and training programs that provide educational services" (World Bank, 2010c, p. 13), but the meaning has grown to encompass a far larger range of people, places, services, and entities that might include formal and nonformal programs while also incorporating the use of agency and voice to "drive the way the system works" (World Bank, 2010c, p. 13).

These four areas do not stand independently of each other. Though they are separated for the purposes of this analysis, there can be viewed as interlinked as interpreted in Fig. 3.

It is important to see that systematic change is directly linked to student learning (beyond the evidence of testing literacy and numeracy skills, but looking at learning that is about the whole development of the individual), training (those opportunities that afford training for employment in formal, informal, and nonformal venues), as well as quality (which is critical to support the underlying factors of inequity and marginalization in education).

Though there are clearly many more areas of critical need for those involved in education to address, these four foci represent the most urgent needs of countries in the groupings as articulated by those in the discussions at the World Bank consultations. They are also key elements of India's National Curricular Framework (NCF), which embarked on a similar process six years ago to establish new guidelines related to what counts as knowledge in India. In the NCF, the construction of knowledge (learning and training), quality, and systematic reforms is highlighted (NCERT, 2005). What might also be common between the two is the supposedly the deliberative and collaborative effort that took into consideration of multiple stakeholders and "experts." With the NCF, critiques have emerged that politics and a haphazard focus occurred during the process (Sadgopal, 2005) and this may yet be seen in the World Bank efforts. Yet, as long as influential institutions and governments are leading such efforts, exploring the ramifications within the context of the country becomes a logical next step. As such, these four areas will be addressed in the context of India in terms of alignments, challenges, and opportunities over three dimensions that have come to be seen as vulnerable areas for educational development in the post-DPEP period as determined by the analysis of policy documents that include the report prepared by the Central Advisory Board of

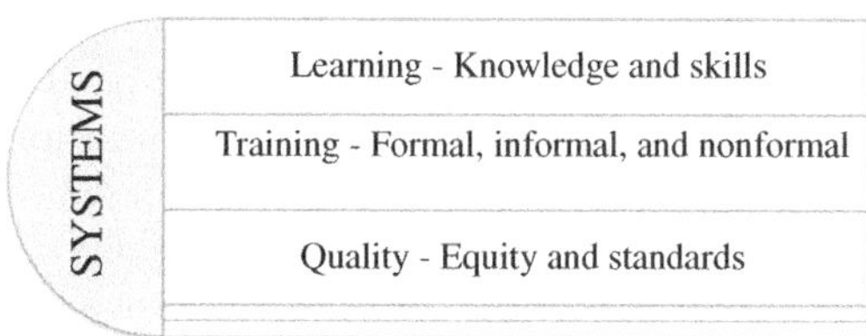


*Fig. 3.* Linking Critical Elements of ESS2020.

Education (CABE) in response to the universalization of secondary education in India, the Seventh All India School Education Survey as well as other related articles and publications. These three areas include calls for a number of improved opportunities for the supporting the youth population (alignment), strengthened systems of education especially in the postprimary years (challenge), and, finally, curriculum that is synchronized with the need for good jobs and fulfilling work (opportunity).

## ALIGNMENTS – THE ROLE OF EDUCATION FOR YOUTH

The growing youth population highlights an urgent need for a robust strategy on how countries plan to address the future of their young people. Early on, the World Bank cites statistics that draw attention to employment problems young people face including frequent layoffs, difficulty in finding employment, and a shortage of skills that are marketable in the 21st century (World Bank, 2010c). Education Strategy 2020 calls for the right to learn from birth to the mid-20s, which is highly relevant in the Indian context where over 35 percent of the population is under the age of 15 (Lall, 2005). Unfortunately, the capacity to keep learning until one is in their late teenage years or even into one's twenties requires financial security and the ability for families to sacrifice a potential earning member of the family if they are to continue their education. Though there are increased levels of unemployment among educated youth (Sarkar, 2007), the informal sector has seen growth and this is often seen as a critical area for both "economic growth and poverty eradication" (Singh, 2000, p. 600). Unfortunately, in many cases formal schooling has had little compatibility with the skills needed in leading to a disconnect between education for youth and the skills needed for work.

Additionally, training opportunities provided outside of the formal school system face problems in both the rural and urban environments. In urban environments, nonformal or technical education is considered less prestigious than formal education (Baily, 2007). In a postcolonial upwardly mobile society, there is a prestige attached to certifications, degrees, and diplomas that are considered the hallmarks of increased social status that are not available to those who participate in skills based, technical, vocational, or nonformal education (Fershtman, Murphy, & Weiss, 1996; Jarmul, 1987). Additionally, income, education, and occupation are clear indicators of socioeconomic status (Bradley & Corwyn, 2002). In a competitive system like what is found in India, education can determine occupation and subsequently income thereby becoming "more critical for the 'value' placed on education to be equitable for those with either extensive or limited means" (Baily, 2009, p. 91). In rural areas, training programs tend to be far from the villages where young people live, offer outdated curricula and training materials, and can be gender-specific limiting options for women as well as other marginalized groups. In terms of quality, for those students who do try to access nonformal or vocation training, there have been too many graduates "who are not needed by the industry and are not equipped with the basic technical know-how of their trade" (Aggarwal, 2010, n.p.), thereby adding to a growing unemployment problem as well.

Training for young people has to be timely, allow for 21st century skill development such as critical thinking and collaboration (Trilling & Fadel, 2009) and make strong connections between school, education, and jobs. This has been well recognized in ESS2020 where the World Bank cites the aim to respond to the "specific needs, capacities, and demands" of different countries (World Bank, n.d., p. 4). As India balances between its status as a low- and middle-income country, it is directly affected by the policy where the World Bank states that for low-income countries it will "expand learning opportunities for children and youth under fifteen" while also focusing on middle-income countries needs where there is a "growing demand for flexible skill acquisition programs" (World Bank, n.d., p. 4).

Expecting young people to learn while not thinking of adequate provisions for family support will be a strong hindrance to this goal of ESS2020. The focus on systems will continue to be a challenge as it pertains to the role of education for young people in India. The problem of affordability remains crucial and is often overlooked outside of the urban environments, which appear on the surface level, to be thriving with all manner of public and private opportunities to enroll in courses to gain employment. For young people to have a stake in the future, it is important to allow systems of higher education (which have been very successful at maintaining the structure of a postcolonial middle-class bastion of economic and political hegemony) to evolve into something more innovative. Asking institutions to blend knowledge and education with jobs-based know-how, public accreditation of institutions and improved connections between the fields of general and vocational education are some suggestions (Aggarwal, 2010, n.p.) that might help improve learning.

With the establishment of ESS2020, it really is learning that is at the heart of the effort. Learning that promotes "healthier, happier, and more productive lives" depends on quality, training, and systems, but with young people in middle-income countries this becomes more urgent where "stakeholders are particularly concerned about learning and relevance of education and equity of access to learning opportunities" (World Bank, 2010b, p. 2). For young people, it is the equity of access that continues to prevent stronger strides in leveling the playing field. For instance, India has a preponderance of upper- and middle-class students using private resources to protect their academic and educational interests through the use of private tutoring in a high-stake testing environment. Moving onward and upward requires extraordinarily high "marks" (grades) to get from one class level to the next. Additionally, to gain admission to one of the well-respected and highly sought after science or engineering tracks, demands almost no level of forgiveness in publicly administered tests. Some students hire tutors for years to supplement their school education to prepare for these tests. Others have resources that are able to buy them into the college of their choice.

In terms of the private tutoring, there have been limited if not negligible conversations related to its impact on the vast numbers of students who are unable to benefit from the higher education system due to poor schools, inadequate teachers, and limited and marginal resources. The benefit of private tutoring is unarguable, and Bray (1998) cites studies where 80 percent of Sri Lankan students at the advanced level received tutoring, while in Korea private tutoring "consumed 37.4 percent of out-of-school expenditures" and private tutoring is especially common in those years when students take public examinations (Bray, 1998, p. 639). This complication prevents the equitable access of learning and will continue to divide those youth who have access to resources and those who do not which will be one area that ESS2020 must take into greater account as it moves forward in India.

## CHALLENGES – SUPPORTING EDUCATION IN THE POSTPRIMARY YEARS

If working to provide young people more educational opportunities is one of the most direct alignments between ESS2020 and the current state of education in India, most challenging might be the advancement of secondary education. ESS2020 calls for improvements in secondary school education, which has also been a hot button issue in India over the last few years. As noted earlier, the DPEP was considered to be the most ambitious primary education program in the world (Alexander, 2000), and the demand for secondary schooling is growing especially as more students complete primary school. With almost universal rates of success in terms of enrollment, of 88.5 percent with a survival rate to the last primary grade of between 73 and 95 percent (UNICEF, 2009), secondary schools have to do some catching up.

The last national survey documented 90,741 recognized secondary schools, of which 70 percent were rural schools and 30 percent were located in urban areas (Sharma & Singh, 2007). In spite of these challenges, the demand for secondary education is rapidly rising. Improving access to secondary education has been defined as one of the main goals of the Department of School and Literacy (Ministry of Human Resource Development, 2008). Researchers have shown that secondary education is a relatively "lucrative level of education" (Kingdon, 2007, p. 172), where the returns on investment to individuals with secondary education is higher than any other forms of education. Yet, participation in secondary education remains relatively low at 47 percent.

These issues mirror the World Bank's concerns for both low- and middle-income countries. For low-income countries, the success of primary education has led to a "rising percentage of students (who) continue on to secondary education" and middle-income countries face challenges due to "classroom and teacher shortages and/or low demand for schooling" (World Bank, 2010a, p. 6). The problem for India is that any education strategy will have to deal with these parallel issues at the same time, dividing both limited resources and attention. An additional point under consideration in terms of secondary education is that access might be more easily addressed in the development and implementation of schools, but the disparity in quality will be much more difficult to address (World Bank, 2010a).

The scope of secondary education is quite vast and arises through the multifaceted nature of the players who are involved with developing educational goals in India. As evidenced by the DPEP, there are international, national, and local players who are actively involved in planning and implementing national goals for secondary education, yet there is limited understanding of how the public and private schools operate, the role of secondary educational institutions that focus on skills-based knowledge (vocational technical institutions), and the complications of moving from a system that has been compulsory until age 12 to one that expands to higher grade levels. Poor infrastructure and lack of core common examinations hinder broad understandings of quality of education. This is especially troubling when pass rates vary greatly, and the input of central and state roles in administering examinations vary from state to state (Kingdon, 2007).

The Government of India has designated that the constitutionally mandated eight years of education is no longer adequate for a country like India and therefore the CABE was tasked with exploring the universalization of secondary education in India. This board is the "highest advisory body relating to policy making in education in India" (CABE, 2007, p. 10) and allows a forum for the concurrent responsibilities of education at the central and state levels while evaluating and envisioning policies and programs for future implementation. The committee recommended four main areas of focus for the expansion of secondary education in India:

1. Universal access – Interweaving physical, social, cultural, and economic challenges to access with the creation of a "new cultural ambience and a child friendly curriculum" (CABE, 2007, p. 15);
2. Equality and social justice – Empowering children to understand, act, and deconstruct injustice;
3. Relevance and development – Recognizing the full potential of students and linking development of the individual with society focusing on citizenship, critical thought, skills and technology; and
4. Structural and curricular considerations – Reducing the gap between the "world of work" and the "world of knowledge."

The social justice component is an important undertaking for India where the divisions between the haves and the have-nots are strong, and continue to create inequities in education. These inequities come to light especially in the areas of training and learning, which follows a similar pattern when we look at the challenge of meeting the secondary school needs in India as it relates to ESS2020.

Obstacles to secondary education include a number of criticisms that span both issues of curricula and stakeholders. In terms of curricula, middle-income countries complained the content was often dull, "obsolete, irreverent, (and) boring" (World Bank, 2010b, p. 22). This is especially true in rural areas where a "poor learning environment ... combined with drab curriculum and lackluster teaching" (Rao, Cheng, & Narain, 2003, p. 164) increases student dropout rates and reduces effective learning for those who remain in schools.

Pedagogy is often "characterized by lectures where students are passive listeners" and students lack "higher order thinking and cognition and creativity" (CABE, 2007, p. 26). Such open critiques are refreshing, as India has often preferred not to publically highlight any shortcomings for fear of humiliation. However, to revamp curricula will be a mammoth task. Besides huge systemic, administrative, and financial hurdles to cross, social hurdles might be the most troublesome to address. Those who have been able to historically benefit from the status quo will not appreciate opening limited opportunities to far more competition that students are already facing.

This leads to another curricular issue in the form of hidden and oppressive curricula that exist in India as they do elsewhere. Nambissan (1996) documents cases where textbooks and curricula discount or ignore the contributions of low-caste or other marginalized groups in India. The "nature of social relations ... that influence the daily routine of teaching, learning and peer interaction" make for this hidden curricula to continue to hinder the success of "socially disadvantaged communities" where there is a "distinct message of social inferiority" (p. 1018). India is facing a complex future where there is both economic growth and political respect. Yet, socially, the links between groups/castes/religions are becoming more tenuous. The lack of open and socially just curriculum will limit the opportunities for social and cultural pluralism as defined both by the CABE and ESS2020.

The role of stakeholders can be an area of concern as it relates to secondary education in India. There is a large public/private divide in terms of schools in India. This is not uncommon in middle-income countries where upper and upper-middle-class families send their children to private schools and therefore remain unengaged in the "public education debate" (World Bank, 2010b, p. 21). As long as the perception and performance of private schools remains more respected, public secondary schools will continue to divide students on the basis of class, caste and income.

Teacher recruitment and retention for secondary schools has been one area that has grown rapidly. Over the course of the last 50 years, there has been a growth of nearly 50,000 new teachers at the secondary and higher secondary levels (Mehta, 2003). Though the numbers have grown, the teacher–student ratio has also grown, highlighting increased enrollment at the secondary level. Moving from a pupil–teacher ratio of 21:1 in 1950–1951 to 32:1 in 1999–2000 (Mehta, 2003), the larger ratio might mean quality as well as learning suffers. There are new efforts to prepare teachers for secondary education classrooms like courses being developed at the newly instituted Azim Premji University that addresses the gaps in current teacher training structures (Azim Premji Foundation, n.d). In these gaps, it might also be important to consider augmenting teacher preparation to address social justice and equity issues. Though the goals of the NCF address the need for better teacher training (NCERT, 2005), criticisms of the framework illustrate a continued problem that hinders the active participation of teachers in breaking down social inequities. Reports say it is "wrong to assume – as the NCF does – that teachers will be far removed from their own socio-political context, where biases and discrimination against people, based on their backgrounds" will not impact their classroom practice (Anaparra, 2005). These partnerships between private and public entities can also help advance the goals of secondary education, but it also presents multiple layers through which ESS2020 must operate if it is to be a viable and successful strategy in India.

Finally, there is a clear recognition of the urgency surrounding the need for secondary education in India, which may not always translate as quickly to larger projects emerging from often-complicated international partnerships. In the report on the universalization of secondary education, the report uses strong language to call for the improvement in secondary education. The "skyrocketing demand may completely destabilize the schools education system leading to significant frustration to the growing aspirations of the people" (CABE, 2007, p. 31) is how the report addresses the demand for secondary education. There is equal worry that any lack of movement on the part of the government to take charge of this will affect the economic and social structure of the country.

## OPPORTUNITIES – CURRICULUM THAT MOVES FROM THE SCHOOLHOUSE TO THE WORKPLACE

Of the three areas that have been highlighted in this chapter, the curriculum that moves from school to work might be the least developed as it relates to India. Yet ESS2020 does focus on this and it might be one of the key areas of opportunity that intersect between the two other foci discussed earlier: the role of youth and the improvement in secondary education. The question becomes how does one discern between education for work as purely an economic strategy (which one would expect from a bank) or an empowerment strategy that allows both the country and the individual to navigate a path to a productive and happy life? This is a balancing act and addressing one should not necessarily preclude or ignore the other.

In framing ESS2020, stakeholders discussed the gap between school-based learning and its relevance to the world of work. The changing nature of the Indian economy and curriculum that emerged in a postindependence, postcolonial mindset also needs to be taken into account. For students, especially for those between the ages of 10–15, "education has to be convenient, accessible, relevant, and goal oriented" (Baily, 2009, p. 93). There are challenges in both urban and rural environments where in rural areas distance to schools and the fees spent on uniforms and textbooks make education less appealing. In urban areas, the value of education is often not questioned, but the limited access to lucrative higher education opportunities makes for a more driven and competitive environment (Baily, 2009).

Bridging the world of school with that of work requires a number of inputs to improve the quality, scope, and reach of education. Inputs encompass both the visible and the invisible, where the visible inputs include infrastructure and supplies, while invisible inputs include training for effective teachers, relevant curricula, and linkages between public and private entities. In a country with multiple recognized languages and state curriculum that varies from location to location, collaborative efforts will be required to improve systems of delivery and accountability. These inputs and mechanisms help to transition students as they move out of school, where the kind of work they do "depends on the knowledge and productive skills they bring to the labor marker" (World Bank, 2010a, p. 6).

Learning and training that relate to how students use their school knowledge in their working lives have also been affected by factors of administrative and structural failure. There is a high level of cheating that pervades the system and discounts whether students are learning the material or are merely getting passing grades to make it through the high-stake examinations. The movement away from rote learning, memorization, and dependence on textbooks was a central facet of the NCF (NCERT, 2005), but the focus on high-level testing and assessments results in high pressure to keep to these outdated methods. Kingdon (2007) documents that when rigorous anticheating measures were implemented, pass rates fell from 57 percent to 14.7 percent in one state (where the passing grade was only 33 percent). When nearly 85 percent of the students are not even able to achieve one-third of the points needed to pass the exams, the concern has to center on issues more relevant to teaching, content, examination structure, and other administrative and pedagogical challenges rather than the student's inability to study (which also needs to be considered, but not at the detriment of the other factors responsible for student achievement). Such failures require policy steps to address the connection between knowledge and application and the discrepancy between regions and states does little to mitigate this shortcoming.

As mentioned earlier, there is a strong stigma attached to vocational and technical education in India, but there is a strong demand and need for skills that are developed through these tracks. Unfortunately, most countries promote the academic track for middle and upper- middle-class students and vocational and technical tracks to those who are from lower income levels. This form of tracking does little to remove stigmas, but also reduces opportunities for those who might not continue with school the way that it is currently structured. Diversifying secondary school curriculum (Grubb, 1985) might be one way to handle the stigma while also opening up technical and vocational skills to a broader swathe of student populations, including those who are more privileged.

ESS2020 highlights a multisectoral approach for systems to address as the most effective method to promote smoother transitions for students between school and work (World Bank, 2010b). Beyond working with economic partners, taking a multisectoral approach should consider health, nutrition, and political partnerships to engage in efforts to move between the two worlds. Such broad partnerships would be more helpful to take into considerations the diverse populations who are to be served by any changes in curricula and structures of education. For instance, this might reduce the misalignment of opportunities for rural and urban students. Facilitating a curriculum that meets the needs of a country with an economy that is both agrarian and knowledge based will be a gargantuan task, one that will especially need to take into account issues of equity and justice as well.

## CONCLUDING THOUGHTS

It is not just access and enrollment that are the hallmarks of education in India. The social inequities that hinder the equitable distribution of learning for all are a part and parcel of educational challenges in every country. In India, focusing on youth rather than students in the early or primary years, building a case for secondary education, and making curriculum work for those in higher grades are interlinked. Together they start to work to address the disparities in education that are slowly diminishing at the early years will not be eliminated until the structures of education in the later years continue those efforts. The rural/urban divide continues to ensure that education is a two-tier system that promotes the hegemony of the haves against the have-nots. Caste and religious discrimination also continue to maintain a hold of education. Overall, if the World Bank strategy is to allocate resources and maintain an overarching vision toward education over the next decade, maintaining a focus on the intersections of some of these issues may help ground the debate as it pertains to India.

The success of ESS2020 will depend on a number of factors. First, the exponential growth and the changes that are occurring at the speed of light will demand thoughtful yet rapid reactions. Changes that take too long or go through a lengthy and arduous bureaucratic process will quickly become the target of public criticism and will reduce any level of trust people might have in the future as a result of the policy. Considering that the NCF faced criticism including that if such "large scale change is … change (that) requires finances, structural co-ordination and bureaucratic efficiency, none of which is readily forthcoming" (Thapar, 2005, n.p.), a larger international effort may take on more financing, coordination, and bureaucratic efficiency that might not exist at any level, internationally or nationally. Media and the local governments are speaking about education in a state of crisis (Mahajan-Bansal & Prasad, 2010), and a dysfunctional or cumbersome bureaucracy will be a significant hurdle for any success that ESS2020 and its planners would intend for India.

There also needs to be some parallel efforts focused beyond 2020 and the role higher education will play in the future. Mahajan-Bansal and Prasad (2010) cite that India will need to "send 22 million people to college in 2014, an increase of 8 million from the 14 million that it currently sends" (n.p.). This is a tremendous undertaking and with significant connections to the themes presented earlier in this chapter, educational needs beyond what is outlined in ESS2020 as it relates to India must also be considered.

The Central Advisory Board on Education (CABE) is also calling for considerable investments in education. The financial resources that were expected to be allocated were never realized. For over four decades, the government has asked for at least 6 percent investment of the Gross Domestic Product in education. This has stagnated between 3 and 4 percent and has resulted in the "under investment in … access, enrollment, classrooms, teachers and other infrastructure facilities" (CABE, 2007. p. 38). The success of ESS2020 and the future of Indian education will depend on continued and stable financial support.

The continued marginalization of certain groups remains a challenge to India's development. Though policies have been set in place to right historic wrongs, India is still beset by the sizeable "persistence of social, religious, and gender bias" in the educational system which "given … returns to education rise with levels of education … any caste, gender and religious gaps in education will translate into further gaps in labor market earnings" (Rawal & Kingdon, 2010, p. 4). The need to maintain a focus on equity in education will have to remain an integral part of ESS2020 if India is to truly evolve in terms of its social, political, and economic future as a result of forward-focused education policies.

Finally, there are critical issues questions that must continue to be addressed across the board as they relate to the complexities of education in India. For instance, India has been characterized as having limited numbers of jobs available in the formal sector with the large-scale expansions occurring in the informal, service, or entrepreneurial sectors (Singh, 2000). What role do new technologies play in the educational arena that offer greater economic rewards and increased appeal for employers? Also, what are the factors that lead to low levels of secondary school participation? Given the fact that there are such high levels of progress in enrolling primary school students, what keeps the "pipeline" from creating the same level of demand at the secondary school levels? Lastly, what impact does teacher shortages and absenteeism play on the level of quality that is expected both from the NCF and the World Bank Strategy?

Continuing to explore these answers and debating the merits and drawbacks of multiple modes of education for the diverse population that needs to be served by education is critical to address in other studies if in fact educational development will meet the needs of all. The development and universal acceptance of Education for All and the Millennium Development Goals by most countries in general and India more specifically has meant that there has been a strong rhetoric that supports education as a goal for the country. Yet, there has been little understanding at the grassroots level of how those goals translate toward implementation. The development of ESS2020 might be yet another rhetorical treatise toward education, but history shows that multilateral vision tied directly to plans for implementation alongside the resources to make those changes usually bodes well for education. The situation in India, though it offers many challenges to an ambitious education policy that is outlined in ESS2020, is ripe for new directions and refreshed energy. The alignments, challenges, and opportunities in India are operating in a complex and ever-shifting structure. Yet, there is much that is offered in terms of the hope for education to create a happier, healthier, and more productive life for her citizens.

## NOTE

1. Various documents that emerged during the consultation process are referred to in this chapter in light of the data analysis that occurred simultaneously to the preparation of the final report. This final report *Learning for all: Investing people's*

*knowledge and skills to promote development: World Bank Group Education Strategy Executive Summary* is also referenced, but the process of synthesizing the Indian context to the World Bank strategies requires the references to the planning and draft versions of the report as well.

# REFERENCES


Aggarwal, M. (2010, March 30). Plugging the skills gap. *India Together*. Retrieved from http://www.indiatogether.org/2010/mar/eco-skills.htm

Alexander, R. (2000). *Culture and pedagogy: International comparisons in primary education*. Malden, MA: Blackwell.

Anaparra, D. (2005, December 7). A few chapters short. *India Together*. Retrieved from http://www.indiatogether.org/2005/dec/edu-ncf2005.htm

Azim Premji Foundation. *Home page*. (n.d.). Retrieved from http://www.azimpremjifoundation.org/home.html

Baily, S. (2007). Options for urban young adults: Debating the relevance of nonformal education in India. In M. Boucouvalas (Ed.), *Proceedings of the 2007 Commission on International Adult Education pre-conference*. Norfolk, VA: American Association for Adult and Continuing Education.

Baily, S. (2009). Playing catch up: Leveling education for young adolescent students in India. In S. Mertens, V. A. Anfara, Jr. & K. Roney (Eds.), *An international look at educating young adolescents: The handbook of research in middle level education*. Charlotte, NC: International Age Publishing.

Bradley, R. H., & Corwyn, R. F. (2002). Socio-economic status and child development. *Annual Review of Psychology*, *53*, 371–399.

Bray, M. (1998). Financing education in developing Asia: Themes, tensions, and policies. *Educational Research*, *29*, 627–642.

Central Advisory Board on Education (CABE). (2007). *Universalization of primary education*. New Delhi, India: Ministry of Human Resource Development.

Das, J. K., Hall, G., Kapoor, S., & Nikitin, D. (2011). *Indigenous peoples*. Washington, DC: World Bank.

Fershtman, C., Murphy, K. M., & Weiss, Y. (1996). Social status, education and growth. *The Journal of Political Economy*, *104*(1), 108–132.

Government of India, Ministry of Human Resource Development. (2008). *Secondary education*. Retrieved from http://education.nic.in/secedu.asp

Grubb, W. N. (1985). The convergence of educational systems and the role of vocationalism. *Comparative Education Review*, *29*, 526–548.

Hill, S., & Calaux, T. (2011). *Improving access and quality in the Indian educational system*. OECD Economics Department Working Papers no. 885. OECD Publishing, Paris, France.

Jarmul, D. (1987). *A Peace Corps guide to literacy, adult learning, and nonformal education*. Washington, DC: Peace Corps.

Joshi, R. (2001). DPEP and primary education. *Economic and Political Weekly*, *36*(12), 1051–1052.

Kingdon, G. G. (1996). The quality and efficiency of private and public education: A case-study of urban India. *Oxford Bulletin of Economics and Statistics*, *58*(1), 57–82.

Kingdon, G. G. (2007). The progress of school education in India. *Oxford Review of Economic Policy*, *23*, 168–195.

Kumar, K. (2004). Quality of education at the beginning of the 21st century: Lessons from India. Paper commissioned for the EFA Global Monitoring Report 2005, The Quality Imperative. UNESCO, Paris, France.

Kumar, K., Priyam, M., & Saxena, S. (2001). Looking beyond the smokescreen: DPEP and primary education in India. *Economic and Political Weekly*, *36*(7), 560–568.

Lall, M. (2005). *The challenges for India's education system*. London, UK: The Royal Institute of International Affairs.

Mahajan-Bansal, N., & Prasad, S. (2010, April 9). The education crisis in India is much more serious than can be solved by calling in foreign universities. *Business India*. Retrieved from http://www.in.com/news/business/fullstory-the-education-crisis-in-india-is-much-more-serious-than-can-be-solved-by-calling-in-foreign-universities-13461865-in-1.html

Mehta, A. (2003). Universalisation of secondary education? Can it be achieved in the near future? *Journal of Educational Planning and Administration*, *17*(4), 507–528.

Nambissan, G. B. (1996). Equity in education? Schooling of Dalit children in India. *Economic and Political Weekly*, *31*(16/17), 1011–1024.

National Council for Educational Research and Training. (2005). *National Curriculum Framework, 2005*. New Delhi, India: NCERT.

Pandey, R. (2000). *Going to scale with education reform: India's DPEP: 1995–1999*. Washington, DC: World Bank.

Pandey, S. (2006). Para-teacher scheme and quality education for all in India: Policy perspectives and challenges for school effectiveness. *Journal of Education for Teaching*, *32*(3), 319–334.

Prabhu, N. (2003, July 23). DPEP has little impact in North Karnataka. *The Hindu*. Retrieved from http://www.hinduonnet.com/2003/07/23/stories/2003072304190400.htm

Rao, N., Cheng, K. M., & Narain, K. (2003). Primary schooling in China and India: Understanding how socio-contextual factors moderate the role of the state. *International Review of Education/Internationale Zeitschrift f*, *49*(1), 153–176.

Rawal, S., & Kingdon, G. (2010). *Akin to my teacher: Does caste, religious or gender distance between student and teacher matter? Some evidence from India*. DoQSS Working Papers. Working Paper No. 10–18 October. University of London, London.

Sadgopal, A. (2005). On the pedagogy of writing a national curriculum framework: Some reflections from an insider. *Social Scientist*, *33*(9/10), 23–36.

Sarkar, T. (2007). *Higher educational reforms for enhancing youth employment opportunity in India: CIPE international essay competition*. Washington, DC: Cener for International Private Enterprise.

Sharma, S. K., & Singh, V. P. (2007). Seventh all India school education survey: A statistical profile on selected parameters of school education. *Journal of Indian Education*, *32*(1), 81–92.

Singh, M. (2000). Combining work and learning in the informal economy: Implications for education, training and skills development. *International Review of Education*, *46*(6), 599–620.

Thapar, R. (2005, September 5). National curriculum framework and the social sciences. *The Hindu*. Retrieved from http://www.hindu.com/2005/09/05/stories/2005090501141000.htm

Trilling, B., & Fadel, C. (2009). *21st century skills: Learning for life in our times*. San Francisco, CA: Jossey-Bass.

UNICEF. (2009). *India Statistics.* Retrieved from http://www.unicef.org/infobycountry/india_statistics.html#67

World Bank. (n.d.) *Education – World Bank Education Strategy 2020 – Draft executive summary.* Available at http://web.worldbank.org/WBSITE/EXTERNAL/TOPICS/EXTEDUCATION/0,,contentMDK:22474207~menuPK:282402~pagePK:210058~piPK:210062~theSitePK:282386,00.html. Retrieved on March 9, 2011.

World Bank. (1997). *Project appraisal document on a proposed credit in the amount of SDR 111.8 million to India for a third primary education project.* Washington, DC: World Bank.

World Bank. (2010a). *Concept note for World Bank education strategy 2020.* Retrieved from http://web.worldbank.org/WBSITE/EXTERNAL/TOPICS/EXTEDUCATION/0,,contentMDK:22474207~menuPK:282402~pagePK:210058~piPK:210062~theSitePK:282386,00.html

World Bank. (2010b). *Report of Phase I external consultations.* Retrieved from http://web.worldbank.org/WBSITE/EXTERNAL/TOPICS/EXTEDUCATION/0,,contentMDK:22474207~menuPK:282402~pagePK:210058~piPK:210062~theSitePK:282386,00.html

World Bank. (2010c). *Learning for all: Investing in people's knowledge and skills to promote development.* Retrieved from http://web.worldbank.org/WBSITE/EXTERNAL/TOPICS/EXTEDUCATION/0,,contentMDK:22474207~menuPK:282402~pagePK:210058~piPK:210062~theSitePK:282386,00.html

World Bank. (2011). *Learning for all: Investing people's knowledge and skills to promote development: World Bank Group Education Strategy Executive Summary.* Washington, DC: The International Bank for Reconstruction and Development/The World Bank.

Wu, K. B., Goldschmidt, P., Boscardim, C. K., & Azam, M. (2007). Girls in India: Poverty, location, and social disparities. In M. Lewis & M. Lockheed (Eds.), *Exclusion, gender, and education: Case studies from the developing world* (pp. 119–143). Washington, DC: Center for Global Development.

# THE WORLD BANK AND EDUCATIONAL REFORM IN INDONESIA

Victor J. Sensenig

## ABSTRACT

*This chapter examines World Bank publications, including publicized reports and widely disseminated policy statements like the World Development Reports, as well as the plans and appraisals of two specific operations in Indonesia. Based on this examination, the author suggests that characterizations which emphasize the Bank's intransigence or celebrate its responsiveness fail to provide a satisfactory description of country-level education policy evolution. The chapter begins with two of the major theoretical frameworks that have been used to study the Bank's work in education. This is followed by a summary of the evolution of the Bank's involvement in education at the international level. The third part of this chapter analyzes two educational reforms that the World Bank has promoted in Indonesia in the last 10 years – programs advancing vocational education and decentralization – and examines how these priorities have been affected by local context and demands and shifts in the global discourse on education. The author concludes that the World Bank's role in the diffusion of education reform is best understood from a world culture perspective but that its interests – and the interests of its primary*

**Education Strategy in the Developing World: Revising the World Bank's Education Policy**
**International Perspectives on Education and Society, Volume 16, 395–421**

**ISSN: 1479-3679/doi:10.1108/S1479-3679(2012)0000016021**

*shareholders – are advanced in particularly opportune moments like democratic transitions.*

## INTRODUCTION

The *World Bank Group Education Strategy 2020* describes its first priority as strengthening education systems. Project inputs that increase educational attainment are not sufficient. Learning outcomes are paramount because "growth, development, and poverty reduction depend on the knowledge and skills that people acquire, not the number of years that they sit in a classroom" (World Bank, 2011b, p. vii). According to the system approach outlined in this report, in order to deliver better learning outcomes more efficiently, "the mechanisms that connect the various parts of the system (specifically, its governance, management, financing rules, and incentive mechanisms) need to be reformed so that functions, authority, and relationships of accountability within the system are clear and aligned with national education goals" (p. 18). A crucial supposition here is that national education goals provide the basis for particular reforms, although this nod to national goals is juxtaposed to the Bank's principal objectives of economic growth and poverty reduction. This chapter is a case study of the World Bank's influence on educational reform in Indonesia. It argues that these national education goals – which Bank boilerplate depicts as the quintessence of local ownership – are neither locally generated nor nationally distinctive. National education goals are highly susceptible to the fashions and orthodoxies of a worldwide model of mass schooling of which the World Bank is a chief proselytizer.

Talk of the accountability of schools always contains an implicit assumption of to whom the schools are accountable, and the *Education Strategy 2020* seems to acknowledge the primacy of national interests. This notion that schools should serve national interests is accompanied by references to countries as partners in improving the performance of education systems. According to the document, "the Bank will focus on helping partner countries build the national capacity to govern and manage education systems" (p. 21). To reinforce this impression, the process of drawing up the document involved a yearlong consultation process, including meetings with government, academic and civil society representatives around the world, and notes from these meetings were posted on the Bank's website. Subtle shifts in rhetoric can also be seen at the Bank's country-level offices where Country

Assistance Strategies have been renamed Country Partnership Strategies. Similar claims have been made of other major Bank reports. According to Joseph Stiglitz (2009), former Chief Economist of the World Bank, the Bank's annual report has traditionally functioned as a summary of "received wisdom" in a few "messages" intended to set the policy agenda for developing countries. Stiglitz describes his attempts to change the concept to one in which the World Bank offered advice but allowed each country to make decisions on its own. The annual report was a way "to begin a global dialogue, a democratic conversation about some of the most contentious issues in development" (p. 140). To Stiglitz, there is a difference between a policy agenda that is externally enforced and a policy framework that offers ideas that national and educational elites may adopt, discard, or debate.

The partnership rhetoric of the *Education Strategy 2020* has roots in the World Bank's 1999 Comprehensive Development Framework (CDF). Shepherded to the fore of Bank policy by reform-minded president James Wolfensohn, this framework proposed that "when countries 'own' reforms, governments and their citizens are more committed to seeing them through" (World Bank, 2011a). Countries receiving loans were to be given more control. The CDF reflects the recognition that conditionality had generally failed as the Bank's main instrument and needed to be replaced by policy advice and a proposal-based approach to supporting projects.

Significant national ownership of World Bank policy would be a remarkable turn of events, a marked departure from the agency's institutional charter. Several scholars of the Bank's work have noted how little it has evolved ideologically from its inception. Although it has periodically shifted its focus and brooks substantial internal dissent (Yi-chong & Weller, 2009), the World Bank has maintained consistent mantras. These mantras include the beliefs "that economic development reduces poverty, that private business promotes economic growth, and that having fewer centralized public services promotes private business" (Collins, 2011, p. 65). As Philip Jones (2006) argues in his seminal analysis, "Despite its proven dexterity, the World Bank functions within relatively firm parameters, the institution's banking character being their most powerful determinant" (p. 242). Richard Peet's (2009) conclusion is even less tempered: "neoliberal Washington Consensus policies prevail, despite protests, critique, proven failure, supposed reform, and so on" (p. 165).

This chapter considers the case of the World Bank's recent policy and programs in Indonesia. The resulting picture suggests that celebration of a new era of responsiveness to national and local interests is premature. My argument is essentially that the Bank's claims about increasing collaboration with government and civil society partners do not go much beyond rhetoric. However, the case of Indonesia also does not fully justify the caricature of the World Bank as a neoliberal supervillain. The visions and strategies for Indonesian schools that the Bank promotes have not been generated at the local level but adhere instead to world-cultural principles. The chapter begins with two theoretical frameworks that have been used to explain the Bank's work in education. I then summarize the evolution of the Bank's involvement in education at the international level, arguing that human capital theory has guided the Bank's education programs from the beginning and that it has not substantially deviated from this theory's assumptions. I give a brief historical overview of the Bank's relationship with the Indonesian government. Finally, I analyze two educational reforms that the World Bank has promoted in Indonesia in the last 10 years – projects advancing vocational training and school-based management – and examine how these priorities have been affected by national interests and shifts in the global discourse on education.

## THEORETICAL PERSPECTIVES

This section outlines two theoretical perspectives that can be used to explain the operation of a global scale institution like the World Bank – world-systems theory and world culture theory. World-systems theory makes two central claims. First, it emphasizes that the modern world system must be understood as a whole system. The smallest human interaction networks, such as a household's daily routines, are embedded in an intersocietal system of trade and information flows. As Chase-Dunn (2007) explains, "the world system is all the people of the earth and all their cultural, economic, and political institutions and the interactions and connections among them" (p. 1060). Second, the theory describes the world system as a hierarchical structure determined by capitalist accumulation. Societies can be located in this stratified system based on whether they are "economically, culturally, and militarily dominant core societies" or "dependent peripheral and semiperipheral regions" (p. 1060). Core societies compete in the modern world system through the exploitation of peripheral peoples.

In world-systems theory, the diffusion of educational reform follows channels delved by economic and political interests. The dominant educational models emanate from the core to the periphery through institutions like the World Bank that are primarily controlled by core societies. The World Bank group is owned by 185 members with voting based on numbers of shares owned; the five largest shareholders are the United States, Japan, Germany, France, and the United Kingdom. The Bank is thus an important tool in the imposition of wealthy nations' agendas on the poor, the primary objectives being the production of better workers, and increased productivity. Because it advances "sensible" development policies that are primarily geared toward the creation of friendly sites for private investment, the World Bank's education portfolio is "a window on what global capital has to say about economic and social policy" (Jones, 2004, p. 189).

Critiques of the World Bank's work in education that draw on the core/periphery framework of world-systems theory have focused on the Bank's model of reform and model of learning. According to Spring (2009), the Bank promotes a purely instrumental concept of literacy in which students learn to function in modern society and manipulate information, but are not permitted political empowerment or even enjoyment (p. 45). He argues that the Bank uses terms associated with progressive education, like "learner-centered instruction" and "learning by doing," while retaining a rigid focus on preparation for a knowledge economy. Others contend that Bank education policy neglects the important role schools have in nurturing democratic practices and politics. Torres (2009) argues that a top-down reform model constitutes external determination and disallows participation and representation: "The banking education heralded by the World Bank will never be the appropriate cognitive and political resource for citizenship and democratic politics" (p. 40). To Torres, education should be an act of freedom, involving the construction of "a theoretical and methodological perspective that is always suspicious of any scientific relationship as concealing relationships of domination" (p. 42).

World culture theory concurs with world-systems theory in conceiving of the world as a single place. The essential difference is that world culture theory is less interested in the overt coercive strategies of wealthier nations than in the institutional trends that they initiate. These trends catalyze the spread of worldwide cultural principles, the ideas that people all over the globe begin to take for granted. These ideas include the stimulation of consciousness of being part of a global whole and the ideology of human equality that underpins campaigns like Education for All. These worldwide constructs define individual and collective identities. In world culture theory, nation-states are ritualized actors, deriving their legitimacy from the universally applicable models provided by the world culture and adopting rational organizational forms (Boli & Thomas, 1997).

School systems exemplify how the purposes of an institution come to be known and taken for granted. After a normative, institutionalized model of mass schooling developed in the West, the model spread along with state formation in the twentieth century. New states relied on mass schooling to forge links to an "imagined community" and turn individuals into citizens (Ramirez & Ventresca, 1992). Public systems of education came to be seen as necessary components of modern democratic societies. As a consequence, modern school curricula do not conform to national patterns but rather to standardized models, which are adopted regardless of a nation's level of economic development or form of government (Benavot, Cha, Kamens, Meyer, & Wong, 1991). In sum, as Baker and LeTendre (2005) argue, "education as an institution has become a global enterprise ... The same global ideas, demands, and expectations filter into nations, greatly shaping their schools in union with school all over the world" (p. 3). This view counters the idea that schools are primarily national enterprises with distinctive features that depend on the needs of particular nations. Instead, the similarities across national education systems derive from the spread of a Western mass schooling concept that educational planners around the world have diligently adapted.

The expansion of mass schooling across the world coincided with a proliferation of global organizations that promoted educational expansion and reforms, all sharing a common educational ideology. In world culture theory, international organizations like the World Bank help to spread the sets of scripts that are used by national education systems. According to Boli and Thomas (1997), "In mobilizing around and elaborating world-cultural principles, INGOS lobby, criticize, and convince states to act on those principles" (p. 187). From this perspective, the World Bank is a major contributor to national development logics and pro-education discourse. In studying the Bank's work in particular countries using this approach, we would expect to see the Bank primarily responsive to standards of rationality rather than the strategies of domination emphasized by world-systems theory.

## METHODS

This study takes an historical organizational approach to understand the actions of an organization over a period of time in a particular context. In terms of the single case designs advocated by Yin (1994), the case of the World Bank in Indonesia is not "critical," capable of definitively testing competing theories. Nor is it necessarily "unique," meriting description because of its rarity. I would argue that it is "revelatory," illuminating a situation that may prove typical of other cases and offering a wealth of largely unexamined data.

The study relies primarily on document analysis of three major types of documents. First, it analyzes policy documents that deal with grand strategies at the global level, like the annual World Development Reports and the *Education Strategy 2020*. These documents primarily reflect the World Bank's attempts to bolster its status as a development agency that relies on "the quality of its thinking as much as on its financial leverage and power to influence and shape governmental and intergovernmental thinking about development issues" (Jones, 2006, p. 10). In contrast, country-level policy documents attempt to cultivate bank–borrower relationships, indicating what an acceptable loan application would contain and generally defining "sound" policy. Third, this study considers research reports commissioned by the World Bank. These fall along the Bank's "policy-research axis" as part of an attempt to summon evidence for particular approaches in order to convert borrowers or others in the Bank to particular lines of thinking (Jones, 2006, p. 11). Finally, I analyze documents that offer details about approved programs. These reports provide rationales for the projects, anticipate outcomes, and detail the amounts and recipients of the loans. All of these documents are publicly accessible, most of them through the World Bank's website.

The data were analyzed inductively. The documents were coded to identify recurring themes, first in a process of open coding and then in a process of sorting by major topical themes. I paid particular attention to several emerging categories: (1) the Bank's claims about collaboration and partnership, (2) statements about the purposes of education, such as human capital creation, (3) rationales for implemented programs or future policy directions, and (4) depictions of local or national needs and demands.

World Bank policy documents rank among the blandest of human creations. The clear limitations of this study's reliance on policy papers and policy-oriented research must be acknowledged, particularly the lack of triangulation, which would build the case for the study's internal validity. For this reason, I include consideration of the extensive secondary literature on the Bank's history and workings, though the Bank's own documents are of main interest. As the World Bank has aspired to expand its influence from the leverage enabled by loan covenants to a larger influence on national policies and international thinking about education, its forays into the world of ideas grow more important. Lending activities are only part of the institution's work and must be considered next to the "body of rhetoric, policy analysis, research, and publications through which the Bank has attempted to influence and shape prevailing climates of opinion about educational development" (Jones, 2006, p. 244). Because the World Bank has increasingly seen itself as a source of reliable ideas about education and education's relationship to development, its presentation of itself and the nature of its ideas deserve investigation.

## EDUCATIONAL EVOLUTION OR IDEOLOGICAL CONSISTENCY?

The World Bank's purposes and rationales relating to education have evolved, and a historical perspective is imperative if we are to understand its work in a bounded context. The story of the Bank's educational evolution begins with a critical shift in the model that characterized the diffusion of modern education systems in the middle of the twentieth century. In the original modern model, traditional religious education was displaced by the educational agenda of nation-states. This agenda was initially maintained through colonial education, as when the Dutch opened up Western education to indigenous people in Indonesia at the beginning of the twentieth century, offering elites an alternative to traditional *pesantren* education (Vickers, 2005). Newly independent nations sustained the modern model through bilateral assistance by former colonizers.

After World War II and the elevation of education to a human right by the United Nations, a "postcolonial centralized model" ushered in an era of state-led development, and the international education community focused on training the staff of national education ministries and building schools (Williams & Cummings, 2005). Organizations like UNESCO, formed in 1946, assumed that developing countries' education systems needed funding, materials, technical consultation, and a rational orientation to planning. The World Bank originally followed the UNESCO approach. Beginning with the allocation of funds for the construction of secondary schools in Tunisia in 1962, the Bank's initial education projects embraced human capital theory as their rationale. This theory's core idea is Theodore Schultz's (1960) conceptualization of useful skills and knowledge as a form of capital acquired through deliberate investment. Gary Becker (1964) built on the theory by arguing that differences in productivity across countries reflect differences in two kinds of human capital, accumulated knowledge and good health. Using this theoretical framework, the World Bank invested in projects that treated schooling primarily as preparation for the job market. It particularly promoted vocational specialization, filling gaps in the labor force by training people for farms, factories, and companies in strategic sectors.

Concern about "bloated" national bureaucracies led the World Bank to favor decentralized models in the 1980s, seeking greater efficiency through local control and looking to markets to take over former functions of the state (Williams & Cummings, 2005). In brief, decentralization involved the "delegation of authority for the control and governance aspects of education to another organization, generally at a lower level in the hierarchy of size" (McGinn, 1992, p. 164). Baker and LeTendre (2005) call this transfer of decision-making authority from national to subnational units the "devolution revolution." They observe the World Bank's abrupt turn from advocating centralized educational authority to making decentralization a condition for loans. The decentralized model in education was promoted as the means to achieve several desirable outcomes, including increased efficiency in the provision of public services, improved school performance, and strengthened democracy through more local decision making.

In the most recent stage of its educational evolution, the Bank has begun reimagining itself as a "knowledge bank" that dispenses knowledge and not mainly funding. In this model, the Bank would scale back its lending operations in favor of research production and economic analysis as well as efforts to disseminate policy advice and technical assistance. Country ownership is an important piece of this model. Countries are depicted as bearing much of the responsibility for creating their own goals, and the Bank is only there to dispense advice. The "knowledge bank" model explicitly contrasts with Truman's vision, expressed in his 1949 inaugural address, of sharing "the fruits of existing knowledge by exporting and building capital goods and infrastructure abroad without necessarily transferring the knowledge itself" (Morduch, 2008, p. 379).

Truman's vision has been jettisoned, but does the knowledge bank model represent a fresh incarnation of the Bank, capable of engaging in technical work and unaffected by political pressures or ideology? Morduch concludes that "both knowledge creation and knowledge sharing are likely to be driven in part by bureaucratic and professional incentives, not just by the pure pursuit of relevant information" (p. 391). Bureaucratic forces dictate that replication of what's been done before is more efficient and less risky than innovative work. At another level, what counts as knowledge at the Bank has been confined by strict parameters. The pendulum swings between centralized and decentralized models and the knowledge bank transformation are not as revolutionary as they seem. As Collins (2011) argues, "the apparent shift in language (and allocated funds) within the World Bank may not have impacted the deep roots of the institution's ideological consciousness" (p. 87).

The 2007 *World Development Report: Development and the Next Generation* is among the most important recent policy statements on education and provides evidence of how exclusive and entrenched the human capital approach is in the Bank's educational imagination. Human capital theory holds that "economics is at the core of modern life," making the most crucial question, "Why do some economies grow faster than others?" (Keeley, 2007, p. 26).

The theory envisions time spent in school as the acquisition of a form of capital and defines education as an investment with long-term economic returns. At the same time, the rapid evolution of the workplace requires the continuing investment of lifelong learning. Education, it is argued, supports the creation of wealth by preparing workers for higher-skilled, better-paying jobs, but economic growth also enables people to go to and stay in school.

The 2007 report argues that the well-being of youth between the ages 12 and 24 depends on "a solid foundation of human capital acquired before adolescence – an application of the principles of investment models long recognized in economics" (World Bank, 2006, p. 10). The report's innovation is its depiction of the young person as the potential investor, rather than governments or families. It proposes policies that expand opportunities for young people, including enriched preschool, universal lower secondary schooling in academic subjects, and the alignment of the upper secondary curriculum with the skills demanded by the labor market. Most interestingly, a second set of proposals focuses on young people's capabilities. These capabilities are determined by "access to information, command over real resources, and the ability to process and act on information" (p. 16). According to the report, schools have a critical role in developing the skills that enable young people to process information and make good decisions.

This emphasis on capabilities draws on the capability approach associated with the work of economist and philosopher Amartya Sen. Sen's theory critiques assessments of human well-being in terms of commodities and standard of living. It also critiques educational ideas about distribution that focus on the kinds of inputs necessary for desired outcomes like economic growth. Instead, education should equalize capabilities – what people are able to do and be – rather than focusing on resources as the intrinsic end

(Walker & Unterhalter, 2007). Well-being, in Sen's approach, is based on achieved functionings, and a large literature exists around compiling lists of basic functionings. One list includes functionings like "being able to use the senses, to imagine, think, and reason – and to do these things in a 'truly human' way" (Wolff & de-Shalit, 2007, p. 39).

The capability approach emphasizes complex outcomes and a highly expanded notion of agency in which people believe that their actions and contributions count and that structures can be contested. The 2007 *World Development Report* appropriates elements of the capability approach that align with the human capital framework. The human capital framework requires the assumption of a well-informed investor, able to weigh costs and benefits as well as discount the future and assess risk. In the Bank's report, the point of informing youth is to influence their decisions regarding investment in human capital, a much narrower frame than that envisioned in the capability approach. There is a vital difference between equalizing capabilities and enabling more efficient cost–benefit calculations.

The World Bank has responded to criticism by attempting to reform its coercive tendencies and taking on a more dispassionate, knowledge-producing role. However, its commitment to a model of education as human capital creation has not been altered. Coercion may be recast as persuasion, but the conversion of the masses is still the point. In the new Bank, "Policies in effect became projects, with investment in economic policy-making infrastructure replacing investment in physical infrastructure" (Gilbert & Vines, 2000, p. 22).

## EDUCATION AND THE BANK'S NATIONAL STRATEGY

The question of whether or not the World Bank has determined to share control of its education policy requires consideration of change over time. This section analyzes the World Bank's evolving relationship with the Indonesian government between the New Order (1965–1998) and the *Reformasi* period following the resignation of Suharto in 1998. This change from authoritarian to democratic government opened a window for genuine national ownership in contrast to the relatively hollow decentralization efforts of the previous decades.

The fourth largest country in the world, Indonesia also has the fourth largest education system with over 50 million students and 2.5 million teachers. Since the 1970s, Indonesia has achieved enrollment rates of 90 percent in primary school, 60 percent at the junior secondary level, and 40 percent at the noncompulsory senior secondary level (Arze del Granado, Fengler, Ragatz, & Yavuz, 2007). In the last decade, education has entered the World Bank's core agenda in Indonesia, and major projects have attempted to extend access to the approximately 300,000 primary-age children still out of school, increase junior secondary enrollment, improve teacher quality, and provide early childhood education for children of poverty.

Basic education was an early and sustained priority of Suharto's New Order government. Sukarno, the nation's first president, opened schools to the vast majority of Indonesian young people who had not been schooled under Dutch administration, but the steepest enrollment increases occurred under Suharto. By the early 1990s, the nearly universal primary school enrollment led to Indonesia's placement in the "high range among developing countries" (World Bank, 1992). Under the New Order, economic growth justified disregard for civil rights, and foreign loans made it possible for the New Order regime to circumvent the formation of a strong domestic tax base that might have held them accountable (Collins, 2007).

The World Bank supported Suharto's New Order government from its origin in the anti-communist mass killings in 1964–1965 and in the face of its chart-topping corruption. (Transparency International estimated that the Suharto family embezzled $15–35 billion, roughly three times the total of the runner-ups, Ferdinand Marcos of the Philippines and Mobutu Sese Seko of Zaire (Denny, 2004).) The Bank's relationship with the Suharto government was cemented by the establishment of a Resident Mission in 1968, and lending spiked in the 1970s as Suharto stocked the government with US-trained economists who became known as the Berkeley Mafia (Woods, 2006). Bank support for the regime in the form of loans and advice was rationalized by the material advancement that many Indonesians experienced during Suharto's three decades.

In an authoritarian political context, the Bank pursued educational decentralization but without the rhetoric of following the government's lead. In his ethnographic study of the ambitious Local Content Curriculum reform, Bjork (2005) details the implementation of one Indonesia's many decentralization projects in the 1980s and 1990s. Encouraging the development of a curriculum more closely connected to local conditions, policymakers imagined that teachers would try new courses and methods and that parents and communities would participate in their schools. Bjork (2005) finds that efforts to decentralize education failed to decrease the power of central authorities or increase the autonomy of Indonesian teachers and principals. The Ministry of Education and Culture attempted to append this reform to an existing core, in particular a culture of education that for decades has made individual initiative a threat to job security. Many teachers had been killed in the military-orchestrated killings of the mid-sixties, and as public employees, educators pledged loyalty to the state and devoted teaching efforts to transmitting the Suharto government's directives and inculcating the state ideology, *Pancasila* (Levinson & Sutton, 2008). The promises of decentralization in the absence of a democratic government were too good be true.

After Indonesia held free elections in 1999, for the first time since 1955, and held direct presidential elections in 2004, the government faced the question of how decision-making power was to be concentrated or dispersed. Beginning with the Local Government Law in 2001, the central government began ceding power and financial control to provincial and local governments, while retaining jurisdiction over such matters as defense, foreign affairs, and monetary policy. By most accounts, state institutions have remained thoroughly corrupt, and the diffusion of power has as often resulted in elite capture as in the participation of citizens or the provision of vital services. Fair and predictable institutions are crucial to democratic rule of law, but the nation's central institutions suffer from its incomplete democratic consolidation, which requires not only competitive elections but also the enforcement of institutional rules by staff and state elite (Davidson, 2010).

Despite these ongoing challenges, the Bank's country-level policy has noticeably shifted in response to Indonesia's democratization. The 2003 Country Assistance Strategy frames the struggle against corruption as challenge to the Bank's own operations:

> Our entire success will be judged by the contribution that our programs are seen to make towards greater transparency and accountability ... Since the crisis, the Bank has responded to the triple threat of corruption by scaling back our lending, while seeking to build a capacity to act as a catalyst for anti-corruption reforms, cultivating partnerships to promote good governance, and strengthening the team's own capacity for mitigating corruption risks to our projects. (World Bank, 2003, p. 13)

The strategy expresses a clear sense of ownership of Bank programs, and its central concern is that corruption could keep them from meeting their objectives.

On the other hand, the current Country Partnership Strategy turns the emphasis from direct corruption prevention to institutional effectiveness. All World Bank support is viewed through an "institutional lens" in which the key to improved development outcomes is the accountability and capacity of critical institutions in both the private and public sectors. According to the latest strategy, "successful institutional change in a large, diverse, dynamic and democratic middle-income country such as Indonesia needs to be government-initiated and -led, and may initially have to be limited in scope and to specific areas" (World Bank, 2008a, p. 14). Because the Indonesian government is now accountable to its citizens and has developed coherent reform priorities, the World Bank agrees to be guided by it. As the introduction to this chapter shows, these themes are also at the heart of the *Education Strategy 2020*.

A second shift in country-level policy can be glimpsed in the commissioned policy research. These policy-research working papers are disseminated with the caveat that the findings "do not necessarily represent the view of the World Bank," but they can give a reasonable sense of how policy-research concerns shift. The first, entitled *Poverty, Education, and Health in Indonesia: Who Benefits from Public Spending?* and released in 2001, assesses the extent to which the poor have benefited from the expansion of educational services. Education is addressed primarily as a poverty reduction strategy, effective in enhancing the main asset of the poor, their labor. The study finds a pro-poor distribution of education at the primary level, partly because poor families have more children and so use more of the public resources for primary education. The distribution becomes very regressive by the senior secondary level where the richest quintile assumes three times the expenditures of the poorest quintile. The paper argues that senior secondary enrollment could be increased with additional spending. It highlights the problem of class disparities in enrollment and culminates with the proposal that primary and junior secondary enrollment could be expanded through reductions in the rich-favoring senior secondary subsidies (Lanjouw, Pradhan, Saadah, Sayed, & Sparrow, 2001).

A 2007 report, *Investing in Indonesia's Education: Allocation, Equity, and Efficiency of Public Expenditures*, acknowledges substantial increases in education expenditures and greater equality in enrollment rates, but its main concern is quality:

> The quality of schooling in Indonesia is low and education infrastructure is deteriorating. Some important determinants of education quality that need to be addressed include the level of teacher qualification, the structure of teacher compensation, classroom quality, teacher attendance rates, and class size. (Arze del Granado et al., 2007, p. 3)

Additional spending aimed at increasing enrollment, even for poor students, is inadequate. Low-quality schooling does not prepare people to work in the sectors with the most growth potential. Instead, the report imagines that the Bank can assert a much broader influence on policies that would improve educational quality and learning outcomes, including incentives for teachers to work in understaffed remote regions, attend classes, and obtain certification. This report reflects the shifting focus of the Bank's country office to quality rather than access, a shift that makes even more pressing the question of whose goals for education are being pursued. While a newly democratic government in Indonesia seems to have extended the World Bank's reach in Indonesian education policy, this reach does not necessarily entail openness to Indonesian leadership.

## LIFE SKILLS EDUCATION FOR EMPLOYMENT AND ENTREPRENEURSHIP

The Life Skills Education for Employment and Entrepreneurship (LSE3) project, approved by the World Bank's board in 2010, focuses on nonformal education, specifically scholarships for poor youth to receive training in marketable skills from accredited private providers. The project proposal highlights two problems. First, the drop-out rates of Indonesian young people are very high – 27 percent by the end of primary school and 80 percent by the end of secondary school. Second, despite consistent economic growth of 5–6 percent since the recession in 1997–1998, youth unemployment and underemployment remain high with youth making up two-thirds of the 8.1 percent of population that was unemployed in 2009 (World Bank, 2010c).

The LSE3 program proposes to provide poor youth with a "second chance" by giving them skills training demanded by the labor market. This single intervention is purported to create jobs, encourage economic growth, and reduce poverty. According to the project description, its main task is "linking unemployed youth with private training providers who train, certify, and match them, referring to a prior labor needs analysis ... to domestic and overseas jobs in either the formal or informal sectors" (p. 2). These links will be created by giving poor youth scholarships to accredited training providers. Outside of formal employment, young entrepreneurs will receive training and financial support as they develop their own businesses.

In addition to providing scholarships, the program has more sweeping institutional ambitions, envisioning "the development of a national, standardized technical and vocational education and training system" (p. 3). Currently, incoming senior secondary students choose between distinct vocational and general tracks. About 75 percent of secondary students follow the general track, choosing between majors in language, social science, and natural science. Vocational schools offer a wide variety of majors, including technical and industrial arts, business management, agriculture, and tourism, and generally cost more than public general schools (Newhouse & Suryadarma, 2009). According to the Bank's LSE3 project description, the government of Indonesia needs to be helped to "improve systems that identify and channel disadvantaged and willing youth to training opportunities" (p. 3).

The Bank's project description is very explicit in its alignment with the Country Partnership Strategy's claim that lasting institutional change requires that programs be initiated and led by the government. In the project description's words, "the proposed project reflects the shared priorities and strategies of the government of Indonesia and the Bank on addressing unemployment and training issues" (p. 3). In particular, it describes the program as collaboration with Indonesia's Ministry of National Education and in line with the government's Medium Term Development Plan for economic growth and poverty reduction. In fact, the Indonesian government has been very enthusiastic about expanding vocational education. In its 2006 education strategy, the Ministry of National Education set a target of a 50:50 ratio by 2010 and a 70:30 vocational to general ratio in 2015 (Ministry of National Education, 2006). Although these targets are respectively unmet and unattainable, the government's preoccupation with vocational education has real consequences as general high schools are not constructed or are converted to vocational schools (Newhouse & Suryadarma, 2009). Plans for expanding vocational schooling have also been supported by UNESCO (2008) and the Asian Development Bank (2008), which provided $80 million for a 20 percent vocational schooling expansion. LSE3 seems to be proof of the Bank's increased responsiveness to national initiatives.

This evidence for Bank acquiescence to Indonesian government priorities is substantially qualified when viewed beside contemporaneous World Bank-commissioned research on the issue of vocational education in the country. These findings have been highly critical of investment in vocational education. Newhouse and Suryadarma (2009) observe that while the majority of vocational programs prepare students for technical occupations, jobs have been shifting from the industrial to the service sector since the 1997 regional crisis. They find that the benefits of vocational education, such as lower unemployment and higher wages, are experienced early but not sustained and that vocational graduates ultimately face a large wage penalty and no advantage in maintaining formal employment in their forties. In sum, "vocational graduates' specific skills may enable them to work immediately at a market wage after graduation, while general graduates need to be trained further by the firms that employ them. Over time, however, general graduates may find it easier to upgrade their skills to cater to employers' demands" (p. 19). Chen (2009) implicates the vocational education systems with processes of social stratification. Highly educated parents in Indonesia are more likely to choose general over vocational schools for their children, while vocational schools draw students with the lowest test scores and from lowest income households. Chen finds that vocational school attendance confers no labor market advantage and lowers academic achievement, resulting in a lower likelihood of attending college. The study concludes that the primary effect of vocational schooling is depressed cognitive skills development. A subsequent summary report, *Education, Training, and Labor Market Outcomes for Youth in Indonesia*, draws on these studies to caution against the government's proposed expansion of vocational schools. The recommendation is not subtle:

> Do not plan supply-driven expansions of vocational schools, but focus on broadening the skill base and improving quality: While the correct mix of general and vocational education is hard to determine empirically, there is significant evidence to argue against a large supply-driven expansion of vocational schools. (World Bank, 2010a, p. 41)

These conclusions contradict the purposes of the LSE3 project, which was approved in the same year, revealing a striking degree of independence between project planning and policy research in the Bank's operations. But what explains the Bank's ambivalence on the issue?

World-systems theory readily explains the Bank's openness to the markedly class-based framework for education advanced by the LSE3 project. According to the project description, everybody benefits – employers and students, especially poor students who can increase their earning potential – but the program is susceptible to critiques searching for domination of the periphery. First, the project description refers to the likelihood of overseas jobs. The highly volatile capital flows in the region mean that specifically trained workers are envisioned as uprooted, mobile populations, which has serious consequences for communities who send a large percentage of young people to vocational programs. Because the

"LSE3 requires that training providers receiving support already have firm job orders to be filled" (p. 2), the skills in which these young people receive training are not guaranteed to be of lasting value as industries will evolve and become obsolete. The time lag between training and placement may mean that training is no longer in demand when students graduate or that particular industries have shifted location. Second, the formalization of different tracks may also exacerbate inequality, relegating a substantial proportion of young people to training at low skill levels. If the job market demands limited skills, the curriculum becomes less demanding and less cognitively beneficial.

However, the theory is less useful to understanding the Bank's research-based reservations. As world culture theory would suggest, these cautions against the expansion of vocational schooling reflect the defunct condition of vocationalism at the world cultural level. Although human capital theory remains its lens for understanding the purposes of education, the World Bank now wholly subscribes to the mass schooling model, devoting its efforts to formal education for as many children as possible and for ever longer periods of time. Benavot (1983) observes that up to World War II, vocational education was central to the educational policies of international agencies. Subsequent decades saw a worldwide decline of secondary vocational education, which he attributes to changes in global ideological currents that idealized multi-dimensional schooling and delegitimized narrow vocational training.

The vocational training dimension of the LSE3 project does not signal a renewed interest in vocationalism. The project plans underscore the fact that the project targets young people who have already dropped out of formal schooling. Further, the Bank's research literature does not embrace the national government's more sweeping ambition to expand vocational education relative to general education. In fact, Bank research publications caution against this policy as infringement on general education, and this Bank-endorsed critique of vocational education is a much more powerful influence than an actual LSE3 loan.

## BOS-KITA

Since 2000, Indonesia's National Ministry of Education has embraced a vigorous decentralization agenda, closing its provincial offices and instituting a school-based management program. One consequence of decentralization, as in other cases around the world, has been increasing disparity in per student spending between schools and regions (Toi, 2010), likely due to the diminished equalizing capacity of a central ministry. The BOS program (Bantuan Operasional Sekolah, or School Operations Fund) is one solution to the increase in school funding differences. In 2002, the Indonesian government initiated school-based management policies, inviting school personnel and parents to participate in decision making in school committees. This local decision making became more momentous in 2005, when the BOS program began to provide block grants directly to schools using a per-pupil formula. The fund's main purpose was to ease operating costs for schools and reduce school fees. Registration, uniform, book, and tuition fees are typical at public schools despite a constitutional commitment to free education. All schools are eligible for the funds, including private and religious schools.

As with the LSE3 program, the World Bank characterized its eventual financing of BOS as support for a government led and already successful Indonesian program. Guided by the 2008 Country Partnership Strategy, the Bank's BOS-KITA program offered $1.1 billion in IBRD loans in order to scale up the BOS program. Its support does come with certain "enhancements" of the government's operations. The Bank's assessment lists several components of BOS that it finds particularly urgent: provision of teaching materials and books to improve teaching methods, support for teachers' continuous professional training, and the recruitment of more specialized teachers to teach subjects such as computer training and local content (World Bank, 2008b, p. 7). The Bank also noted its approval of attempts to increase community involvement by requiring that funds be managed by parental and school committees and that records of the use of funds be posted on school notice boards.

Notably, Bank documents also praise the role of community oversight in discouraging the misuse of funds, citing the state auditor's report that a small fraction of BOS funds did not meet guidelines in 2008. Of the more than a billion dollars eventually disbursed, only $996,000 had not been used appropriately, less than 0.1 percent of the total (World Bank, 2010b, p. 2). This estimate is undoubtedly low, and criticisms of the program are common in the Indonesian media. In one typical insinuation of corruption, a rat wearing a tie scampers across the BOS logo, rupiah notes escaping from its briefcase. Nevertheless, the primary complaints about the program have revolved around the perception that the program would more quickly eliminate school fees, a campaign promise of current president Susilo Bambang Yudhoyono (Darmaningtyas, 2011).

World-systems theory is hard-pressed to explain how the Bank's support for a program like BOS is in its hegemonic interests. The program involves not only formal means for communities to get involved in schools through school committees but also distributes funds to be used at their discretion. World culture theory's account of the spread of educational ideologies is much more useful in this case. The BOS-KITA program's ideas about decentralized management reflect a global ideological trend in institutional culture. The administrative philosophy of decentralization is essentially one more component of the educational improvement kit that international agencies specialize in disseminating. As Baker and LeTendre (2005) observe, "Pressure from these agencies to adopt certain forms of educational administration, such as decentralized forms of authority, often drives national reform for economically marginalized nations" (p. 137). However, idiosyncratic national responses to this "worldwide love affair with devolution" result in many mixed models of centralized and decentralized administration.

In Indonesia's case, the educational policymakers of the Ministry of Education and Culture did not just accept this idea as a necessary precondition for loans but as a rational strategy to improve the quality of teaching and learning and increase democratic participation. The BOS-KITA program is one of the World Bank's flagships in the demonstration that the Bank is following Indonesia's lead, but once again this story has some twists. The Bank's claim of acquiescence to national ownership is complicated by the fact that the government embrace of school-based management is rooted in research produced by the Bank, particularly research on the pedagogical success of autonomous schools in Central America. These studies, based in El Salvador (Jimenez & Sawada, 1999) and El Salvador, Guatemala, Honduras, and Nicaragua (Di Gropello, 2006), look at various effects of school-based management reforms and conclude that the main benefits are community empowerment, greater teacher effort and autonomy, and some improvement in student outcomes like attendance. A great part of the influence of the Bank is not direct lobbying efforts but its role in producing evidence-based research and transporting models across national boundaries.

## CONCLUSION

Have we have reached "the end of development education" and entered an era in which all countries borrow and donate ideas about education (Heyneman, 1999, p. 142)? Has the World Bank determined to take a more collaborative approach and rely on national ownership of reforms? This study of the implementation of World Bank policy in Indonesia suggests that reports of the birth of a more sensitive, more collaborative Bank have been exaggerated. The realities of poverty in Western nations and the heterogeneity of the "Third World" may have blurred the boundaries between developed and developing societies, but the direction of ideas and influence has not significantly shifted.

This is not a new argument. Joel Samoff, in particular, has made it forcefully based on his research on the work of the World Bank and other aid agencies in Africa. He argues that international financial institutions have replaced powerful nations as the "principal enforcers of global dictates" (2007, p. 53). The Bank's terminology has evolved. Talk of "effective governance" gives way to "national ownership" and "poverty reduction." To Samoff, these are rhetorical fig leaves:

> On examination, though, we find the same thinking about the requisites for development and many of the same imposed conditions. Subtly insinuated in a rhetoric of partnership and development cooperation, these precepts for progress become difficult to discern and even more difficult to challenge. Wearing the cloak of science and resting on the staff of research, this orientation dismisses alternative perspectives as political and nonscientific. (p. 55)

The rhetoric of collaboration is accompanied by reinforcement of particular conceptions of education, cementing potentially controversial assertions as conventional wisdom. The technical advice that the Bank dispenses can be stamped with the insignia of "local ownership" with little meaningful adoption of more participatory or inclusive policies. From this world-systems perspective, the wolf is wearing Grandmother's bonnet, but the perceptive observer can still note the size of its teeth.

Because it is a bank and guided primarily by macroeconomic concerns, the World Bank is interested in those aspects of education that are "bankable." As Heyneman (1999) argues, because World Bank assistance usually goes through a country's ministry of finance, the purposes of programs are macroeconomic. The measure of an educational proposal is what it portends for economic growth: "Technical rationales – that it is good for education – are not enough. Rationales in an environment of resource scarcity must meet criteria of a different kind – why good education is a higher priority than a good hospital or a good road. This distinguishes education in the World Bank from education in agencies with a more specialized focus" (p. 133).

In other words, the Bank does not approach its work in education with wide-ranging questions about processes of teaching and learning, let alone questions of human well-being and happiness. The Bank's work in education follows the same thinking as its investments in railroads, highways, and power plants in its first quarter century. As Mason and Asher (1973) argue in their history, "It was the availability of financing for such undertakings that stimulated philosophizing about the vital role of economic infrastructure in the development process, rather than the reverse" (p. 152). In education, human capital theory is highly useful to the Bank because it legitimates its involvement in education not because an economic model and tools of banking and finance work so well to enhance human development and learning.

In line with world-systems theory, the Bank attempts to align government policy with its ideas about education, particularly its human capital rationales. Its financial operations, including tools like loan covenants, are the means to ensure governments' conformity. Bank policy papers like *Policies and Strategies for Education* (1995) depict education as a sector ripe for privatization with little concern for educational processes, and subsequent rhetorical softening has not altered these fundamental parameters.

But this is a tale of two theories, and the second theory suggests a much more subtle and pervasive kind of influence is at work than the coercion of conditionality. The Bank's ideas about education and education reform are embedded in prevailing sets of ideas about schooling that transcend the interests of powerful governments. The world culture perspective effectively theorizes what is perhaps the most striking aspect of the Bank's interventions in Indonesia: the inexorable march of national isomorphism. The programs created by the Indonesian government and the enhancements proposed by the World Bank draw from the same the research substratum. The ideas about what works are quite clearly not generated at the national level, but drawn from a body of research to which the World Bank is a major contributor. Studies of how interventions worked in particular countries or regions are exported, and the policies are adopted elsewhere, regardless of national idiosyncrasies.

As a result, policy shifts in Indonesia have been affected more by world society priorities than by local demands. The World Bank makes tremendous contributions to the definitions of reality that national systems of education come to accept, a process by which INGOs can "unobtrusively foster intellectual, technical, and economic rationalization that is so thoroughly institutionalized that they are hardly seen as actors" (Boli & Thomas, 1997, p. 187). This influence in creating "reality" may be as important as the Bank's overt policy influence through lending criteria. The power of its instruments of leverage can easily be overestimated given the ease with which borrowers ignore covenants, but the Bank is much more powerful as a disseminator of ideas about education.

Despite its claims, the Bank's research on education is not geared toward country-specific advice, let alone advice that is regionally sensitive or attuned to the staggering cultural diversity of the Indonesian archipelago. Claims of following the lead of the national government remain unfounded. However, even efforts to promote local ownership by gearing policies to meet national education goals, as opposed to the goals of the core countries who "own" the Bank, would not necessarily result in significant local educational reform. National education goals are drafted from the same scripts that INGOs like the Bank have been promulgating for decades and which have been adopted along with all the other trappings of legitimate statehood. Reform initiatives need to be built upon local needs rather than the world-culture perspectives.

What would real local ownership look like? One revision of world culture theory has been attempted by culturalists, who accept much of the theory, but add emphasis on local variability. A surface isomorphism may obscure actual divergent organizational structures and processes (Anderson-Levitt, 2003). Spring (2009) describes this process as "a superstructure composed of global flows and networks within which their influence is determined by the interpretation, adaptation, or rejection by local educators" (p. 7). Culturalists emphasize both the powerful presence of local culture and the agency of educators and administrators in transforming global models.

Anthropologist Ronald Lukens-Bull's (2005) study of Islamic boarding schools (*pesantren*) provides an example of the culturalist model. The *pesantren* in the study is overseen by the Indonesian Department of Religious Affairs, and approximately 20–25 percent of Indonesian primary- and secondary-level students attend *pesantren*-based schools. The *pesantren* community rejects the ideas that modernization involves Westernization and that tradition and modernity are antagonistic, as imagined by fundamentalists. In making an Islamic modernity, they adopt Western technology and institutions but underpin these changes with core Islamic values and insistence on the all importance of salvation. Modernity is thus dangerous but malleable, capable of destroying traditional values but open to the insertion of Islamic values of self-sufficiency, simplicity, and selflessness. These *pesantren* appropriate certain materials of modernity while attempting to sidestep those effects deemed harmful, like materialism and social inequities.

As Lukens-Bull's study makes clear, the idea of local ownership of schooling does not require the search for pristine systems of traditional education, unsullied by the influences of the world culture of schooling.

Even by the mid-twentieth century, *pesantren* had begun to adopt modern curricula. He observes that at the high school level, these schools "aspire to deliver both the pre-twentieth century *pesantren* curriculum and the newer government curriculum with the hope that the graduating alumni have the religious knowledge and morality of a religious leader as well as the basic education needed to pursue further education at the college level" (p. 18). The example does suggest that a real commitment to local ownership would require the World Bank to displace its human capital approach, permitting religious and traditional values to inform the purposes of education. The human capital perspective enlists education for economic growth and increased earnings, and the perspective is so powerful in the Bank's work in education because it is exclusive and pervasive. Local ownership would entail an almost unimaginable alteration at the Bank's ideological core in order to accommodate visions of education that are decidedly not bankable.

## REFERENCES


Anderson-Levitt, K. M. (2003). A world culture of schooling?. In K. M. Anderson-Levitt (Ed.), *Local meanings, global schooling: Anthropology and world culture theory* (pp. 1–6). New York, NY: Palgrave Macmillan.

Arze del Granado, F.J., Fengler, W., Ragatz, A., & Yavuz, E. (2007). *Investing in Indonesia's education: Allocation, equity and efficiency of public expenditure*. Policy Research Working Paper no. 4329. The World Bank, Washington, DC.

Asian Development Bank. (2008). *Vocational Education Strengthening Project: Indonesia*. Retrieved from http://www.adb.org/Projects/project.asp?id = 33409

Baker, D., & LeTendre, G. K. (2005). *National differences, global similarities: World culture and the future of schooling*. Palo Alto, CA: Stanford University Press.

Becker, G. (1964). *Human capital*. New York, NY: Columbia University Press.

Benavot, A. (1983). The rise and decline of vocational education. *Sociology of Education, 56*(2), 63–76.

Benavot, A., Cha, Y., Kamens, D., Meyer, J. W., & Wong, S. (1991). Knowledge for the masses: World models and national curricula, 1920–1986. *American Sociological Review, 56*(1), 85–100.

Bjork, C. (2005). *Indonesian education: Teachers, schools, and central bureaucracy*. New York, NY: Routledge.

Boli, J., & Thomas, G. M. (1997). World culture in the world polity: A century of international non-governmental organization. *American Sociological Review, 62*(2), 171–190.

Chase-Dunn, C. (2007). Dependency and world-systems theories. In G. Ritzer (Ed.), *The Blackwell encyclopedia of sociology* (pp. 1060–1062). New York, NY: Wiley-Blackwell.

Chen, D. (2009). *Vocational schooling, labor market outcomes, and college entry*. Policy Research Working Papers Series 4814. The World Bank, Washington, DC.

Collins, C. S. (2011). *Higher education and global poverty: University partnerships and the World Bank in developing countries*. Amherst, NY: Cambria Press.

Collins, E. F. (2007). *Indonesia betrayed: How development fails*. Honolulu: University of Hawai'i Press.

Darmaningtyas. (2011, March 22). *BOS selalu bermasalah (BOS continues to have problems)*. *Tempo Interactif*. Retrieved from http://www.tempointeraktif.com/hg/kolom/2011/03/22/kol,20110322-344,id.html

Davidson, J. S. (2010). Dilemmas of democratic consolidation in Indonesia. In W. Case (Ed.), *Contemporary authoritarianism in Southeast Asia: Structures, institutions and agency* (pp. 125–142). New York, NY: Routledge.

Denny, C. (2004, March 26). Suharto, Marcos and Mobutu head corruption table with $50bn scams. *The Guardian*. Retrieved from http://www.guardian.co.uk/world/2004/mar/26/indonesia.philippines

Di Gropello, E. (2006). *A comparative analysis of school-based management in Central America*. World Bank Working Paper no. 72. The World Bank, Washington, DC.

Gilbert, C. L., & Vines, D. (2000). The World Bank: An overview of some major issues. In C. L. Gilbert & D. Vines (Eds.), *The World Bank: Structure and policies* (pp. 10–36). New York, NY: Cambridge University Press.

Heyneman, S. P. (1999). Development aid in education: A personal view. In K. King & L. Buchert (Eds.), *Changing international aid to education: Global patterns and national contexts* (pp. 132–146). Paris: UNESCO.

Jimenez, E., & Sawada, Y. (1999). Do community-managed schools work? An evaluation of El Salvador's EDUCO program. *The World Bank Economic Review*, *13*(3), 415–441.

Jones, P. W. (2004). Taking the credit: Financing and policy linkages in the education portfolio of the World Bank. In G. Steiner-Khamsi (Ed.), *The global politics of educational borrowing and lending* (pp. 188–200). New York, NY: Teachers College Press.

Jones, P. W. (2006). *World Bank financing of education: Lending, learning and development* (2nd ed). New York, NY: Routledge.

Keeley, B. (2007). *Human capital: How what you know shapes your life*. Paris: Organization for Economic Co-operation and Development.

Lanjouw, P., Pradhan, M., Saadah, F., Sayed, H., & Sparrow, R. A. (2001). *Poverty, education, and health in Indonesia: Who benefits from public spending?* World Bank Policy Research Working Paper no. 2739. The World Bank, Washington, DC.

Levinson, B. A. U., & Sutton, M. (2008). Civic education reform for democracy: U.S. models in Mexico and Indonesia. In E. D. Stevick & B. A. U. Levinson (Eds.), *Advancing democracy through education? U.S. influence abroad and domestic practices* (pp. 129–157). Charlotte, NC: Information Age Publishing.

Lukens-Bull, R. (2005). *A peaceful jihad: Negotiating identity and modernity in Muslim Java*. New York, NY: Palgrave Macmillan.

Mason, E. S., & Asher, R. E. (1973). *The World Bank since Bretton Woods*. Washington, DC: Brookings Institution.

McGinn, N. F. (1992). Reforming educational governance: Centralization/decentralization. In R. F. Arnove (Ed.), *Emergent issues in education* (pp. 163–172). Ithaca, NY: State University of New York Press.

Ministry of National Education. (2006). *Rencana Strategis Departemen Pendidikan National Tahun 2005–2009 (Strategic Plan of the Ministry of National Education, 2005–2009)*. Jakarta: Ministry of National Education.

Morduch, J. (2008). The knowledge bank. In W. Easterly (Ed.), *Reinventing foreign aid* (pp. 377–397). Cambridge, MA: MIT Press.

Newhouse, D., & Suryadarma, D. (2009). *The value of vocational education: High school type and labor market outcomes in Indonesia*. Policy Research Working Papers Series 5035. The World Bank, Washington, DC.

Peet, R. (2009). *Unholy trinities: The IMF, World Bank, and WTO* (2nd ed). London: Zed Books.

Ramirez, F. O., & Ventresca, M. J. (1992). Building the institution of mass schooling: Isomorphism in the modern world. In B. Fuller & R. Rubinson (Eds.), *The political construction of education: The state, school expansion, and economic change* (pp. 47–59). New York, NY: Praeger.

Samoff, J. (2007). Institutionalizing international influence. In R. F. Arnove & C. A. Torres (Eds.), *Comparative education: The dialectic of the global and the local* (pp. 47–77). Lanham, MD: Rowman & Littlefield.

Schultz, T. (1960). Capital formation by education. *Journal of Political Economy*, *68*(6), 571–586.

Spring, J. (2009). *Globalization of education: An introduction*. New York, NY: Routledge.

Stiglitz, J. (2009). The World Development Report: Development theory and policy. In S. Yusuf (Ed.), *Development economics through the decades: A critical look at thirty years of the World Development Report* (pp. 139–151). Washington, DC: The World Bank.

Toi, A. (2010). An empirical study of the effects of decentralization in Indonesian junior secondary education. *Educational Research for Policy and Practice*, *9*, 107–125.

Torres, C. A. (2009). *Education and neoliberal globalization*. New York, NY: Routledge.

UNESCO. (2008). *Scientific, technical and vocational education for girls: Schools and learning centres as community catalysts for poverty reduction and empowerment of girls*. Retrieved from http://portal.unesco.org/geography/en/ev.php-URL_ID=9875&URL_DO=DO_TOPIC&URL_SECTION=201.html

Vickers, A. (2005). *A history of modern Indonesia*. New York, NY: Cambridge University Press.

Walker, M., & Unterhalter, E. (2007). The capability approach: Its potential for work in education. In M. Walker & E. Unterhalter (Eds.), *Amartya Sen's capability approach and social justice in education* (pp. 1–18). New York, NY: Palgrave Macmillan.

Williams, J. H., & Cummings, W. K. (2005). *Policy-making for education reform in developing countries: Contexts and processes*. Lanham, MD: Scarecrow Education.

Wolff, J., & de-Shalit, A. (2007). *Disadvantage*. New York, NY: Oxford University Press.

Woods, N. (2006). *The globalizers: The IMF, the World Bank, and their borrowers*. Ithaca, NY: Cornell University Press.

World Bank. (1992). *Indonesia: Primary Education Quality Improvement Project*. Jakarta: The World Bank.

World Bank. (2003). *Indonesia Country Assistance Strategy (2004–2008)*. Jakarta: The World Bank.

World Bank. (2006). *World development report 2007: Development and the next generation*. Washington, DC: The World Bank.

World Bank. (2008a). *Indonesia Country Partnership Strategy (2009–2012)*. Jakarta: The World Bank.

World Bank. (2008b). *Project appraisal document: School operational assistance-knowledge improvement for transparency and accountability*. Jakarta: The World Bank.

World Bank. (2010a). *Education, training, and labor market outcomes for youth in Indonesia*. Report No. 54170-ID. The World Bank, Jakarta.

World Bank. (2010b). *BOS-Frequently asked questions for policymakers*. Retrieved from http://www-wds.worldbank.org/external/default/WDSContentServer/WDSP/IB/2010/12/23/000356161_20101223032924/Rendered/PDF/586230WP0BOS0FAQ1Eng0BOX353808B01PUBLIC1.pdf

World Bank. (2010c). *Project information document: Life skills education for employment and entrepreneurship*. Jakarta: The World Bank.

World Bank. (2011a). *Comprehensive development framework*. Retrieved from http://go.worldbank.org/N2NDBE5QL0

World Bank. (2011b). *World Bank Group Education Strategy 2020, Learning for All: Investing in People's Knowledge and Skills to Promote Development*. Washington, DC: The World Bank.

Yi-chong, X., & Weller, P. (2009). *Inside the World Bank: Exploding the myth of a monolithic Bank*. New York, NY: Palgrave Macmillan.

Yin, R. K. (1994). *Case study research: Design and methods* (2nd ed). Thousand Oaks, CA: Sage.

# INCREASING THE FLOW OF STUDENTS, WASHING OUT QUALITY: WORLD BANK POLICY EFFECTS IN TANZANIAN SECONDARY SCHOOLS

Donna C. Tonini

## ABSTRACT

*The purpose of this chapter is to highlight the dichotomous nature of two World Bank educational goals and examine how enrollment growth became prioritized over quality in Tanzania. Nestled within the theoretical framework of developmental discourse, the chapter begins with a historical review of World Bank educational policy, exploring Tanzania's lending relationship with the Bank. The chapter next evaluates the new World Bank 2020 educational strategy using the Tanzanian context to draw attention to policy strengths and weaknesses. Finally, using current research regarding World Bank policy in Tanzania, this chapter explores the implications of the new strategy on the next installment of Tanzania's SEDP policy. By locating the intersections of these policies, one may gauge a better understanding as to why the past trend of flooding Tanzania's classrooms with students has had the effect of eroding educational quality.*

**Education Strategy in the Developing World: Revising the World Bank's Education Policy**
**International Perspectives on Education and Society, Volume 16, 423–450**

**ISSN: 1479-3679/doi:10.1108/S1479-3679(2012)0000016022**

# INTRODUCTION

The rainy season in the rural region of Manyara, Tanzania, is fraught with unexpected deluges, turning the local dirt roads into muddy lakes that are all but impassable. As we traveled to visit a new secondary school to conduct research in the area in 2008, our vehicle hit one such washed out road, becoming nearly engulfed in the floodwaters. Our skillful driver managed to guide his taxi safely across, delivering us to the school in time for our interviews. The purpose of this visit was to collect qualitative data to glean insight into the impact of government educational policy on the local stakeholders, such as the schools, the teachers, the students, and their parents. The particular policy in question was phase one of Tanzania's Secondary Educational Development Plan (SEDP I), which was in effect from 2005 to 2009,[1] and funded by the World Bank from 2005 to 2007. The World Bank's first two objectives for the SEDP I included: (1) increase the proportion of the relevant age group completing secondary education and (2) improve learning outcomes of students, especially for girls (World Bank, 2008a, p. ii). Although the dual focus on educational access and quality was admirable on paper, the actual outcome of the policy revealed the challenges of accomplishing both objectives, as highlighted by our interviewees.

According to one of the headmistresses at this particular secondary school, somehow educational quality had been sacrificed for greater enrollment:

> I am saying that the education that we are having, especially [in] most of the community schools, is just quantity. Most numbers of students are going to these schools with a large number of enrollment, but the real sense is that the quality is not good – there is poor quality. You cannot have good quality if you don't have enough teachers, you don't have enough teaching and learning materials, you don't have laboratories for these science projects, you don't have libraries; those things add quality. (H. M. Baraka, personal communication, April 11, 2008)[2]

As explained by this headmistress, despite the Bank's commitment to ameliorating educational access and quality, somehow the access goal of raising the enrollment of age-appropriate cohorts surpassed that of increasing the educational inputs necessary to improve learning outcomes. These two worthwhile objectives had unfortunately become conflictual.

The purpose of this chapter is to highlight the dichotomous nature of these two World Bank educational goals and examine how enrollment growth became prioritized over quality in Tanzania. Nestled within the theoretical framework of developmental discourse, the chapter begins with a historical review of World Bank educational policy, exploring Tanzania's lending relationship with the Bank. The chapter next evaluates the new World Bank 2020 educational strategy using the Tanzanian context to draw attention to policy strengths and weaknesses. Finally, using current research regarding World Bank policy in Tanzania, this chapter explores the implications of the new strategy on the next installment of Tanzania's SEDP policy. By locating the intersections of these policies, we may gauge a better understanding as to why the flooding of Tanzania's classrooms with students has had the effect of eroding educational quality, much like the impact of rainy season on the local roadways.

## THEORETICAL FRAMEWORK

To understand the influence of World Bank policy on the large enrollment streams and receding educational resources in secondary schools in Tanzania, Escobar's (1995) model of developmental discourse will serve as a framework to glean insight into how educational policy is constructed by the Bank and interpreted by aid recipients. Employing Escobar's premise that institutions such as the World Bank are systems of knowledge production highlights the role of power relations within educational policy development and discourse. In a Foucauldian sense, this knowledge as power perspective will be helpful in grounding some of the historical developments in World Bank educational policy. The analysis will be augmented by multilateral aid evaluations by Samoff (2009, 2007), Mitchell (2002), Heyneman (2003), and Degnbol-Martinussen and Engberg-Pedersen (1999), to further outline how the World Bank's loan priorities influence aid to developing countries. Using development discourse theory heightens awareness of the possible impact of discursive power permeating aid flows and how this institutional authority erodes the agency of aid recipients in devising their own educational policies.

## METHODOLOGY AND DATA SOURCES

This analysis employs the country of Tanzania as a case study to evaluate past World Bank educational policy as well as the Bank's new 2020 strategy. This technique allows us to understand how World Bank policy has affected Tanzania's ability to develop and implement its secondary education plan in the midst of surging enrollment and diminishing resources. The case study approach is also bolstered by educational policy analyses conducted on relevant World Bank and Tanzanian government documents.

In order to explore this research topic, between 2005 and 2008 I reviewed a large body of literature that looked at access to schooling issues in terms of demand for education and the supply of schooling in developing world contexts. I also performed in-depth analyses of the World Bank's loan agreements with Tanzania. This data was triangulated through research conducted over nine months in Tanzania in 2008 with Ministry of Education officials, school staff, parents, and students. The study was situated in eight secondary schools within the Kilimanjaro and Manyara regions, and utilized both questionnaires and interviews to determine how educational policy was impacting both the access and quality of secondary education. The study participants, including over 200 parents, approximately 100 students and around 40 school staff members were selected nonrandomly, using both quota and convenience sampling at each school site.[3] Although this chapter provides insufficient space to review this work in depth, key pieces of scholarship and pertinent interview data are used to inform the investigation herein. The analysis of qualitative interview data gives voice to the local stakeholders of secondary education in Tanzania, and lends credence to the allegory of rising tides of student enrollment and ebbing educational resources.

## RESULTS

The difficulties of balancing educational access and quality goals are not unknown to the World Bank. In the Bank's Action Plan for Africa (2005), they state:

> The magnitude of the projected increase in demand poses a major challenge regarding the resources required to expand places without diluting the quality of services and the reforms needed to manage costs and ensure equitable distribution of the burden of financing. (p.41)

Despite their awareness of the hardships of pursuing these two very disparate objectives, within the past loan agreements with Tanzania, both goals were prioritized without adequate provisions regarding how resources may be allocated equitably between them to achieve policy success on both fronts. Nor was proper attention paid to the need to shore up educational resources to sustain educational quality amidst swelling student enrollments (MoEVT, 2010). By favoring the more easily achieved objective of raising enrollment, both the World Bank and the government of Tanzania lost sight of the need to maintain quality, opening the floodgates for unlimited student enrollment while at the same time eroding the existing educational infrastructure (MoEVT, 2010). By evaluating the World Bank's new strategy and linking it to the secondary education development plan in Tanzania, this chapter will highlight the intersections necessary for policy success, and what further elements will promote sustainability in the future and prevent educational development from becoming a washout.

## A BRIEF HISTORY OF WORLD BANK EDUCATION POLICY IN TANZANIA THROUGH THE LENS OF DEVELOPMENT DISCOURSE

In 1995, Columbian scholar and University of Massachusetts professor Arturo Escobar emerged at the forefront of a new wave of postcolonial and poststructural development critique. Influenced by Foucault's (1972) notions of "discourse" as a collection of rationalized statements and privileged knowledge supported and validated by experts and transformed into a system of power, Escobar posited that development, with its own unique set of discourses and discursive practices, constituted a new language of power (1995). From this premise, Escobar constructed a matrix which highlights the creation of development discourse within the institutions of development, and traces how this discourse evolves into a new social construction of reality (Peet & Hartwick, 1999).

As discourse stems from power relations within knowledge systems that determine what may be included in the canon and who may contribute (Ball, 1990, as cited within Vavrus & Seghers, 2010), development discourse originates in both academic institutions and large development organizations such as the World Bank, from which flow the dominant ideas and representations which fuel the discourses (Peet & Hartwick, 1999). Institutions such as the World Bank often perpetuate this power through the construction and articulation of knowledge and the assumptions used to define development problems and solutions. Escobar (1995) argues that the discourse production and the centers of discourse revolve around First World institutions and are thus anchored by Western ideals. The World Bank technicians and experts, socialized and educated in Western economic approaches and thus predisposed to neoliberal theory and capitalist ideology, have "monopolized the power of speech" (p. 100) producing a hegemony of development discourse, and a Western construction of economic principles which provided the West with a "mode of seeing and a way of organizing the world" (Mitchell, 2002, p. 272). By modeling their own economic, societal, and cultural norms and behaviors they "reproduce forms of discourse that contribute to the social and cultural domination effected through forms of representation" (Escobar, 1995, p. 95).

At the intersection of these institutions and the discourse created was power, driven by modernization theories which viewed the West as the epicenter of progress with the role of bringing modernity to backwards countries on the periphery, the post–World War II initiative to reconstruct and urbanize the world in the image of the West, and vast capital flows to invest in development projects (Peet & Hartwick, 1999). This power was exercised through the construction, accumulation, and implementation of knowledge, comprising a new form of global domination (Peet & Hartwick, 1999). The development machine thus enforced the global hierarchy already in place between the First World and Third World, solidifying the former's position of supremacy in relation to the latter. With these positions of power firmly entrenched, it facilitated the ease in which these First World development discourses were spread throughout the Third World and accepted as global truths. For example, the portrayal of the "under-nourished African child" in Western media shows the patronizing position of the First World over the Third World, revealing unequal power relations (Escobar, 1995, p. 103). "The infantilization of the third world was integral" to the notion of development as salvation (p. 30).

The interests and ideologies of the First World thus perpetuate Western supremacy as they represent the dominant development discourse. These representations enframe the world in Western categories, capturing "social imaginaries and constructed identities" (Peet & Hartwick, 1999, p. 146). According to Escobar (1995), development institutions succumb to a "colonization of reality," whereas "certain representations become dominant and shape indelibly the ways in which reality is imagined and acted upon" (p. 5). Escobar proposes that this "enframing" occurs according to a Western set of experiences and expectations, which allows development technicians to set themselves apart from the beneficiaries of aid, as if they are "visitor[s] at an exhibition" (p. 7). In addition, Escobar also posits that the process of enframing produces discourses that formulate identities and construct categories which label developing societies as "poor," "underdeveloped," and "Third World," according to a Western view of the world (p. 4). It is this notion of separating oneself from "questions of power and inequality" and the social and political context of the situation that allows one to see "reality" in a new form (Mitchell, 2002, p. 242). It is also with this new detached perspective that Escobar (1995) asks us to view the realm of development as an "encompassing cultural space" in which exists the commonly accepted idea of development as a necessary advancement of society in order to achieve peace and abundance on a global scale (p. 4). Thus, development is seen as a new "regime of representation," dictated by Western constructs of history and ideology (p. 6).

Escobar (1995) suggests that these pre-conceived images represent "more as a sign of power over the Third World than a truth about it" (p. 9). In other words, the discourse of development "has created an extremely efficient apparatus for producing knowledge about, and the exercise of power over, the Third World" (p. 9). Escobar's main goal is to bring into focus the "forms of knowledge" that support development, while isolating the "system of power that regulates its practice" and identifying the "forms of subjectivity" by which "people come to recognize themselves as developed or underdeveloped" (p. 10).

The "knowledge systems" of which Escobar (1995) speaks chiefly use First World constructs of history, economics, and social order to define modernity, and disqualify any views that are not of the West (p. 13). Thus, the identity construction of the Third World as lesser-developed is based on Western interpretations of "abnormalities" such as poverty and hunger which were then problematized, prompting new interventions such as economic development, also built under Western guises (pp. 13, 30, 44). Within this new "space" of development, the discourse redefined reality – gleaned from Western observations, modes of inquiry, cataloguing of problems, and intervention proposals (p. 42).

Escobar (1995) argues that development discourse is not just an ideology but practices which have become embedded in the way Third World peoples experience social and economic life. It is through implementation and practice that development discourses are deployed top-down from aid institutions to the local level in developing countries. Nations which receive aid are governed by the institutional processes of development, and these practices and their resulting discourses influence and permeate varying levels of social relations between the different actors engaged in development such as aid agencies, which control the flow of capital, and government entities, which are "conditioned by the need to obtain funding" (p. 111). Such interactions between government and World Bank staff are "structured by World Bank routines" (p. 111), thus contributing to the institutionalization and incorporation of both development practice and discourse.

Furthermore, Escobar (1995) postulates that development discourse deconstructs various social ills in developing nations as problems to be solved by professionals who generally hail from Western nations, and who portray themselves as possessing high level skills and knowledge in the areas pertaining to these issues. Mitchell (2002) explains that the West categorizes itself as having a "monopoly of expertise," which in its view differentiates it from the non-West, where it considers such technology and management skills to be lacking (p. 211). Samoff's (2007) example of the World Bank as an institution which inherently views its advice as more important than its funding highlights these embedded assumptions regarding the relevance and necessity of their expertise. The way in which these institutions and professionals define problems and develop the discourse surrounding them helps to further crystallize the development practices and technologies "as a mechanism of social production" through which development is perpetually continued and advanced (Escobar, 1995, p. 89).

Thus, it is critical to understand how the recipients of aid and their problems are defined and portrayed by development professionals, which can be divorced from the actual context in which these recipients exist. "This work of abstraction is a necessary condition for development to work in the process of describing, inquiring into, interpreting, and designing treatments for their clients or beneficiaries" (Escobar, 1995, p. 111). This process of structuring and abstraction tends to take place at the international and national levels, but cascades down to the ground, where the actual work takes place. "The local level must reproduce the world as the top sees it" (p. 111), and typically, the top views these pre-defined issues as problems to be solved through development. Samoff (2009) explains that "because it is negotiated with and generally provided to governments, aid helps leaders ignore [the] alternative voices and critics," that may serve to challenge or resist these development visions of the West (p. 4). As such, a new "social construction of reality" is formulated and perpetuated via the discourses incorporated through the institutionalization and professionalization of the development field (Peet & Hartwick, 1999, p. 146.) Continually subjected to these new forms of power and control, people's ability to define their own lives and take care of themselves was deeply eroded, as people's identities became further intertwined with the Westernized development constructs (Escobar, 1995). One such mechanism that uses development discourse to reify these new social realities is policy.

## EDUCATION POLICY DEVELOPMENT VIA THE WORLD BANK

Although constructing educational policy is usually a sovereign matter, the involvement of international financial institutions forces a country to consider external interests in addition to domestic concerns. The World Bank is a multilateral organization that commands great influence over the governments and policies of debtor nations by imposing strict economic conditionalities in exchange for loans and other forms of aid. According to Samoff (2009), the World Bank is highly influential in both managing aid, *and* the education agendas of its aid recipients. Countries whose situations are financially dire enough to warrant requesting such assistance usually find themselves in the position of manifesting the mantras of the World Bank into their own policy stances. In the spirit of Escobar, examining policy discourse helps determine if the policies developed out of these conditional agreements are written for those who will be affected by the policy, or for those who have effected the policy.

Tanzania is one such country that struggled with the dilemma of poverty and under-development after its independence in 1961. As a "Highly Indebted Poor Country,"[4] it has shared a lengthy relationship with the International Monetary Fund (IMF) and the World Bank, implementing conditional terms known as Structural Adjustment Policies in return for loan disbursements and other resources. These stringent structural reforms are negotiated between the IMF and World Bank and the debtor country in order to stabilize a nation's economy. Often the fiscally austere measures result in budget cuts aimed at reducing government spending and budget deficits. As these budget cuts are typically made within the "softer" social sector of the economy, usually education, health care, and other social welfare programs are the hardest hit (Logan & Mengisteab, 1993).

In the early 1980s, an economic crisis and a change in presidency prompted Tanzania to seek IMF and World Bank assistance, resulting in its first Structural Adjustment Program in 1986, with additional agreements signed in 1987, 1991, and 1996 (IMF, 1999). Under the guidance of the IMF, Tanzania enacted a broad range of economic liberalization policies in an attempt to install a more free-market economy (Weissman, 2000). In the quest to curtail government spending, sharp cost reductions were sought within the social sector, especially in the areas of education and health care. To make up for this loss of government funding, cost sharing programs were introduced to help pay for services that were previously free (Vavrus, 2003). In the education sector, these "cost recovery" programs involved direct payments by students and their parents, otherwise known as "school fees." The government's argument for school fees centered on maintaining educational quality in light of diminishing resources (Ministry of Education and Culture [MoEC], 1995). Yet, as more cost-sharing initiatives were introduced by the government, educational inequities became more pronounced as poorer households were forced to spend a larger percentage of their resources on education than richer households (World Bank, 1999). Thus, in the Tanzanian context, school fees are an excellent example of the dichotomy that often exists between achieving educational access and quality goals simultaneously. As the Government of Tanzania aligned itself to the development rhetoric of cost sharing and quality within its education strategy, the poor were disenfranchised from schooling opportunities.

As an example of the transition of development discourse into educational policy in Tanzania, two important documents were drafted alongside this conditional aid that mandated first the presence, and later the absence, of school fees in conjunction with World Bank and IMF policy dictates. The first document, which sanctioned the institution of school fees, was the Education and Training Policy paper, implemented in 1995. Authorizing the subsequent removal of school fees was the Poverty Reduction Strategy Paper, written in 2001, with the policy enacted in January of 2002. A brief review of these documents will shed light on Tanzania's motivations regarding the enactment of two opposing financial strategies, written merely six years apart, in pursuit of increasing enrollment while maintaining quality.

The aforementioned policy which established a basis for cost sharing was the Education and Training Policy (1995), written by Tanzania's Department of Education, formerly known as the Ministry of Education and Culture (MoEC). Set up as a social sector policy under the auspices of the IMF and the World Bank, this document outlines the aims and objectives of education in regards to both access and quality goals (IMF, 1999). Taking into account the government's declining fiscal resources, the policy proposes a method of cost sharing between the government and private households, in regard to the financing of both education and vocational training.

The pursuit of cost recovery measures via charging fees for infrastructure provision has been espoused by the World Bank since the 1970s (World Bank, 1994). In the 1980s, the idea of cost recovery was more actively promoted within the education sector, focusing on higher and secondary education (World Bank, 1987), as well as worker training (World Bank, 1995). However, a study at the World Bank claimed that as "education could be viewed in the same way as any other commodity," lesser developed countries with supply constraints at the primary and secondary levels of schooling could implement user charges at these basic levels of education without a negative effect on enrollment (Mingat & Tan, 1986, p. 274). This premise underscored the educational development policies in Malawi, where the study was based, with the resulting ideology carrying through to the policies of other fellow lesser developed countries, such as the Education and Training Policy in Tanzania (Mingat & Tan, 1986).

Analyzing the policy discourse, the Tanzanian government admits that "it increasingly became apparent that the government did not have enough resources to continue financing free education, hence the re-introduction of school fees and direct costs in primary and secondary schools ..." (MoEC, 1995, p. 90). The government follows up this pressing statement with a plea for cost sharing. Instead of flatly stating that fees and other contributions toward education will be imposed, the government uses the term "cost sharing," which implies that the responsibility for education should be dutifully shared between the government and society. Since sharing insinuates mutual interests and assumes participation, the government is better positioned to ask for scarce resources from its citizenry, in the name of "partnership" with the nation. As this policy is directed toward "communities, parents, local government authorities, individuals, NGOs and donor agencies," in a call to "collaborate with the Government in realizing the objectives of this Policy," it appears as if the Tanzanian government is appealing for help (MoEC, 1995, Foreword). Thus, the discourse of the document effectively conveys the needs of the government in a way that is more imploring of its people as well as externally interested parties, as opposed to being demanding. At the same time, the Tanzanian government gives the appearance of continued commitment to economic recovery, by following the recommended tenets laid out in its Structural Adjustment Program.

Employing Escobar's model, the notion of utilizing cost recovery programs for basic public services is an example of the World Bank – an institution imbued with great power and financial resources – employing Western economic theory to solve the problem of insufficient educational supply as defined in a First World context, but applied to a Third World country. Samoff (2009) emphasizes that "the adoption, localization, and internalization of key constructs may be the most powerful form of external control" employed by the World Bank (p. 14). The Tanzanian government appears to have internalized the discourse of cost sharing, which is heavily dispersed throughout the Education and Training Policy, despite the fact that the majority of its citizenry live on less than two dollars a day (World Bank, 2008b). As the policy recognizes the support provided by donor agencies, it is understandable as to why this development terminology would be used in the hopes of securing further educational project funding.

However, despite the World Bank rhetoric claiming that poor families are willing to share schooling costs, evidence exists that shows that even if quality was maintained, access to education is compromised. Samoff (1996) critiques the notion of cost recovery, claiming the poor are merely paying more out of their own pockets for educational services, making education cost prohibitive. Heyneman (2003) points to the inequality already inherent in the education budgets of developing countries, calling attention to the fact that privileged families are better equipped to pay for public education than their poorer fellows. Degnbol-Martinussen and Engberg-Pedersen (1999) highlight this contradiction between ideology and praxis, as the World Bank pledges improved access for poorer students yet in practice their support of privatization and market forces allows those with more financial resources better access to education. As Tanzania's enrollment growth at the primary school level was stagnant during the years the Education and Training policy was in force, it is apparent that the World Bank's premise of lack of supply creating its own demand did not hold true in the Tanzanian context, reducing the flow of equitable educational resources to all (Tonini, 2010).

In response to mounting criticism that cost sharing plans increased social inequities that excluded the poor from critical social services such as education and health care, in the late 1990s, the IMF and World Bank refocused their efforts on reducing poverty in lesser developed countries (Cooksey, 2004). In addition to a change in rhetoric, the international financial institutions also intended to shift responsibility, by providing more freedom to the developing countries in formulating their policies (Dembele, 2004). Hence, the advent of the World Bank's Poverty Reduction Strategy Papers, and support for the abolition of fees within the social sector, in regards to education and health care.

In 2001, the World Bank approved an adjustment credit towards a Primary Education Development Program to "support efforts by the Government of Tanzania to improve education quality, expand school access, and increase school retention at the primary level" (World Bank, 2001). This aid was in response to the IMF's' initiative to reduce the debt level of Heavily Indebted Poor Countries. One of the key requirements Tanzania needed to accomplish was the completion of a Poverty Reduction Strategy Paper, which would outline their major goals in regard to decreasing their rate of poverty. Embedded within that policy document is Tanzania's objective to remove school fees, in efforts to both improve school access and quality, and achieve reductions in its level of poverty. Thus, as a result of the Poverty Reduction Strategy Paper, primary school fees were abolished in 2002.

Reviewing the discourse regarding the Poverty Reduction Strategy policy's audience, the document opens with a layout of all involved parties, listing international stakeholders first, and domestic stakeholders, including "representatives of the poor, civil society and the private sector" as second (United Republic of Tanzania, 2001, p. 2). The order connotes importance, indicating for whom this document is written. In addition, the document repeatedly stresses the patronage of its donors, with statements such as the "document has benefited from comments by the World Bank and IMF missions," conveying an overall tone of partnership (United Republic of Tanzania, 2001, p. 3). Thus, it is feasible that the Poverty Reduction Strategy Paper was intended more for the international donor community, and was written to demonstrate that Tanzania was abiding by the rules laid out by the World Bank (Tonini, 2010; Vavrus & Seghers, 2010). In fact, the Tanzanian government has been criticized for "preparing its PRSP [Poverty Reduction Strategy Paper] with more input from foreign creditors and donors than from its own citizens" (Weissman, 2000, p. 1). As Tanzania relies heavily on donor aid to support its budget, the motivation to heed input from its creditors is apparently stronger than its incentive to listen to its citizens (Weissman, 2000). The last listed stakeholder of the Poverty Reduction Strategy Paper is the government of Tanzania itself, which implies that it may consider itself to bear the least amount of responsibility for the process. In looking at the roles that each stakeholder will play, it is interesting to note that both the international community and the domestic stakeholders have action items on their plate in regards to fulfilling their commitment to Tanzania's poverty reduction goals, while the government of Tanzania is only responsible for "reviews." The big picture overall communicates the limited role of Tanzania's government in regard to its own policy document, emphasizing instead the need for outside help and authority to ensure policy success. Perhaps this approach effectively conveys need, but there also appears to be a submerged theme of encouraging donors to provide as much aid as possible. Thus, although the policy ownership concept championed by the Poverty Reduction Strategy Paper was supported in theory, apparently in practice, it was merely another aid-procuring, conditional agreement to Tanzania.

The policy shift against school fees, albeit striking, should not be surprising as the ideological change was fostered by the World Bank, and backed up with promises of debt forgiveness. The policy's overt attention to its donor audience highlights the power relations inherent in Tanzania's relationship to the World Bank, despite the "stakeholder" discourse used to designate other involved parties. Thus, the prioritization of the World Bank's goals is not unexpected. Using the lens of Escobar again, enframing poverty as a problem to be solved and devising the Poverty Reduction

Strategy Paper as the solution allowed the World Bank to professionalize the development process by employing experts to assist in the crafting of policy drafts, further incorporating their discourse within practice.

In regard to policy impact, the total enrollment figures for primary education show that the removal of school fees in 2002 increased enrollment by 22 percent from 2001, rising to 34 percent in 2003 and 44 percent in 2004, respectively (Davidson, 2004). Yet, according to Sumra (2003) of HakiElimu, one of Tanzania's foremost education NGOs, the quality of schooling was poor, as a result of budgetary allocations to school expansion over improvements in teaching and learning. Therefore, although everyone had access to primary education, Sumra argued that not everyone had access to quality education (2003). Thus, school fees were removed, satisfying the requirements of the Poverty Reduction Strategy Paper; yet without adequate provisions for schooling inputs, quality once again was in question. As Heyneman (2003) reminds us, since the relevance of a project to Bank lending requirements takes precedence, there is "little incentive to question the reasoning on which the lending depended" (p. 320). Degnbol-Martinussen and Engberg-Pedersen (1999) also note that the Bank's priorities have often focused more on making new loans, rather than determining the efficacy and outcome of old ones. As paradigm shifts within the Bank's lending apparatus may have served to increase loans, through the Poverty Reduction Strategy Paper the business of poverty became more institutionalized.

In sum, the Structural Adjustment Policies fostered by the IMF and World Bank appeared to be the driving force behind the drafting of documents such as the Education and Training Policy, which promoted user fees within the social sector. With the need for donor funding and loans at a critical level, the Government of Tanzania reacted to the fiscally austere conditionalities set forth by the international financial institutions by setting up financially stringent cost-sharing measures of their own. Yet, as enrollment levels dropped, it became quickly apparent that the economic ideals championed by those indoctrinated in Western ideologies[5] and envisioned by the conditionalities were not so readily adaptable within a Third World context (UNICEF, 2001). Plus, with world criticism mounting over these international financial institutions' records in regards to exacerbating the deteriorating situation of the poor, the IMF and World Bank needed to better manage its public face. Hence, the advent of the Poverty Reduction Strategy plans, which served up many of the same loan conditionalities, but with the overarching goal of poverty reduction, as opposed to economic revitalization. In the same vein as Escobar, Ferguson (1990) explains there is a "complex relation between the intentionality of planning and the strategic intelligibility of outcomes" (p. 20).

Thus, the Government of Tanzania advocated for user fee removal, in order to comply with the IMF and World Bank's new poverty alleviation theme. In comparing the Education and Training Policy and the Poverty Reduction Strategy Paper, one discovers that despite the differences in educational financing recommendations, both the intended audiences and the fundamental ambitions have generally remained the same. It was the uneven ebb and flow of enrollment levels that changed, at the expense of equitable access to quality – a trend that would replicate itself on the secondary level too.

## SECONDARY EDUCATION POLICY AND WORLD BANK INFLUENCE

The SEDP I was a five-year plan for secondary education in Tanzania that followed in the footsteps of its predecessor, the Primary Education Development Program, in regards to focusing on expanded access and quality education for all students. The main objectives of the SEDP I were to: improve access and increase overall transition rates to the secondary level from primary school, raise secondary school completion rates, and promote educational quality and equity, among other administrative goals (MoEC, 2004). The SEDP I was to be implemented in three phases of five years each, with its first phase starting in 2004 and ending in 2009. The first phase was primarily supported by a three-year financial package from the World Bank, which included a Structural Adjustment Credit[6] of $123.6 million, and a grant of $26.4 million, with the first disbursement in May 2005 and the last distribution in December 2007. The Government of Tanzania was expected to provide the rest of the necessary funding. The World Bank's access and quality objectives were similar to those listed in the SEDP I, but prioritized differently: (i) Increase the proportion of the relevant age group completing secondary education and (ii) improve learning outcomes of students, especially among girls (World Bank, 2008a, p. ii). Of these goals, the World Bank (2008a) verified that Tanzania achieved, and in fact exceeded, the original 2007 target increases regarding their secondary enrollment and transition rates. There were no improvements to learning outcomes reported, although surprisingly, the World Bank (2008a) disclosed that they did not expect progress until the first phase of the SEDP I was well past completion.

Although it is laudable that Tanzania was able to not only increase but exceed the enrollment targets laid out by the World Bank, it is important to note that it was the only SEDP I goal reached within the tenets of the loan agreement. However, as the World Bank still released each of the three loan tranches in accordance with its disbursement plan, in a sense, it was prioritizing the educational access goal over the quality improvement goal. "In other words, the World Bank was rewarding Tanzania for filling their secondary school classrooms with students, rather than focusing on the educational inputs that provide a quality learning experience to those students" (Tonini, forthcoming). Thus, Tanzania had more motivation to continue building classrooms and filling those with pupils rather than the inputs necessary to engender a quality educational experience, as it was apparent that their financial reward was tied to the singular focus of access.

Escobar's (1995) model is useful in explaining how Tanzania's original SEDP I goal of improving educational quality was undermined at the expense of increasing secondary school enrollment rates. As the World Bank was in a position of power as sole lender for the first three years of the SEDP I, the government of Tanzania was understandably subordinate to its agenda. Degnbol-Martinussen and Engberg-Pedersen (1999) remind us that the World Bank has great impact on lesser developed countries not only through loans, policy advice, and procedural assistance, but also pressure. Thus taken together, the World Bank's financial role in Tanzania's secondary education program, the discourse embedded in defining the goals and developing the policy, and the technical expertise provided which entrenched development doctrine via practice, all influenced the policy-making practices of the Tanzanian government, making the social reality constructed by the World Bank their own. As Heyneman (2003) points out, financing educational policy is only part of the World Bank mandate – the value inherent in effecting that policy change is just as important. As the World Bank was engaged in a results-oriented theme during SEDP I (World Bank, 2011), and increasing the flow of students in and out of the classroom in Tanzania proved to be an easier goal to reach than improving the educational inputs that those students were receiving, policy efforts became more focused on access, to the detriment of quality, prompting a new policy avenue for the next phase of the SEDP – yet still influenced by the World Bank.

## THE FUTURE OF WORLD BANK POLICY – THE 2020 PLAN IN TANZANIA

The new World Bank educational strategy is an approach called "Learning For All" which takes a "country-level" focus on reforms to a nation's educational system by "moving simply beyond providing inputs" such as buildings or textbooks to strengthening school governance and management to ensure efficient usage of schooling inputs and promote learning outcomes (World Bank, 2011, pp. 1, 5, 6). The 2020 Plan also proposes building the capacity of a nation's education system in order to increase the effectiveness of government resources and financing for schooling (2011). The segue from "Education for All" to "Learning for All" recognizes the fact that education should be more broadly defined to reflect a lifelong process of knowledge and skills acquisition in a variety of settings in a more global environment. The new World Bank strategy is commendable for taking a more holistic approach to learning, employing the view of American education reformer John Dewey that life experience is central to the education process (Dewey, 1938).

By taking a wider view of the field of education and having a more microlevel, country-specific approach to education development and lending, the World Bank has the potential for more project success through stronger partnerships. Additionally, although the World Bank's attention to aid financing has always been part of its mandate, it is reassuring to see the Bank focus on government financing, and maximizing the reach and effectiveness of government resources, as a country's ability to fund their own educational projects is the key to their sustainability. Evoking Escobar (1995), reducing Tanzania's reliance on foreign aid flows also lessens the power dynamics between them and the World Bank, allowing them to become better agents in their own development.

Ideally, in the Tanzanian context, such an approach would be positive as the broader definition of education allows World Bank projects wider scope as both formal and informal learning environments are included and validated as educational opportunities. As such, the value of education moves beyond the purely academic to skills acquisition and labor force readiness, which will be beneficial to Tanzanians who need to transform abilities and knowledge into employment. Furthermore, due to the strengthened focus on country-specific needs, the quality and relevance of World Bank projects to Tanzania should increase. Finally, of great importance is the Bank's commitment to assist Tanzania in bolstering their ability to finance their own education system, as they have had difficulty doing so in the past. Despite its agreement with the World Bank to provide financing for the SEDP I beyond the $150 million pledged by the Bank, the Government of Tanzania was unable to fulfill its secondary education funding commitments, relying instead on other donors, local communities and the parents to fill the gaps (Tonini, 2010). One of the secondary school headmasters interviewed acknowledged the financial shortcomings of their government's efforts:

> There is a big gap between the amount given by the central government and the actual amount required for the completion of a classroom or a teachers' house. Because the government expects that the other stakeholders in the SEDP, which includes the local government, which includes the various donors, the parents and the community as a whole, will cover up the gaps that exist so that the houses will be completed. (H. M. Mpya, personal communication, May 7, 2008)

Thus, as the first three years of the SEDP I were nearly 100 percent financed by the World Bank,[7] it is critical to ensure that Tanzania has enough of its own resources and funding in place to guarantee sustainability of its education programs. The more support Tanzania can lend its own education sector, the quicker the country can end its dependence on foreign aid. Yet, despite the positive direction of the World Bank's new strategy, the experience vocalized earlier by the school headmaster indicates that achieving financial self-sustainability is not without challenges. Although the World Bank's 2020 strategy uses a multisectoral approach to address issues such as tackling corruption and promoting accountability in governance, recognizing that the success of the education sector is linked to other factors, the Bank does not explain how government budgets will be enabled to maintain expenditure levels without donor assistance. Most countries need a large tax base in order to provide wide-scale sustained investment in social services. Lacking national wealth, in order to maintain social programs such as the SEDP, a country needs access to other resources, either in the form of financial aid from donors or in the form of cost-sharing plans with its citizenry. As demonstrated by the earlier examination of education sector policies, Tanzania has traditionally sought its education funding through both aid agencies and user fees – a trajectory that is not sustainable in the long run. The World Bank's lack of consideration regarding this financing scenario is troubling, and merits further attention within its policies.

The World Bank 2020 strategy is not without additional faults. First, although the Bank is correct in stating that a sole focus on educational inputs will lead to limited success, it should not assume that concentrating funding on educational inputs is not without value. For example, according to the Ministry of Education, building infrastructure is not considered as learning inputs in Tanzania, and in fact commands its own funding mechanism called the Development Grant which is dedicated to school construction and includes new classrooms, teachers' houses, and the rehabilitation of old classrooms (Tonini, 2010). This distinction is important as the classification of a school in Tanzania is based upon the presence of a mere building (Tonini, 2010), exclusive of the learning inputs necessary to ensure a quality educational experience. As building materials and labor are generally found locally, classroom construction is actually one of the easier components to add when creating or revitalizing a school. Since the Tanzanian government considers a school to be merely a constructed building, it is easier to increase enrollment numbers once a classroom is erected. This problem was highlighted in the earlier quote of the Headmistress from the Baraka School, who alluded to the fact that secondary education in Tanzania was more focused on increasing the enrollment numbers than enhancing quality. The following quote from one of the students at Baraka highlights the issues regarding lack of student access to resources:

> We only see books when the teacher is teaching and that is in the teacher's hands. Mostly the ones with books are the ones who bought them on their own, and for us who are not able we don't get them. (S. I. Baraka12, personal communication, April 14, 2008)

As actual educational inputs are gravely lacking in Tanzania due to the fact that enrollment growth outpaced the schools' ability to resource their classrooms, it is important to continue focusing funding on books, teachers, materials and the like to increase the quality of schooling in Tanzania.

Additionally, although the World Bank (2011) proposes being more country-specific in its new approach, it is still using problematic categories by classifying nations into "low-income countries", "middle-income countries" and the like (p. 55). These groupings indicate that the Bank still approaches developing countries from a collective perspective rather than a collection of sovereign nations, blurring the different social, cultural, and economic contexts for individual countries. For example, one of the World Bank's (2011) listed objectives is "expand the supply of high-quality basic education," which once again combines access and quality goals without differentiated attention to either (p.58). As demonstrated within the Tanzanian context, it is important to separate these goals and establish individual achievables with separate funding mechanisms, or else one goal, such as quality, may be diminished at the expense of the other goal. In addition, one of the highlighted objectives for middle-income countries is to "enhance the quality and relevance of the education system so as to improve its links with the labor market and the school-to-work transition," which according to many of the students interviewed in Tanzania, is a worthwhile goal for a low-income country too (World Bank, 2011, p. 58). Considering these critiques, an individual country approach is necessary for policy success in the future.

Finally, although the World Bank's new definition of "education system," which "consists of all parties who participate in the provision, financing, regulation, and use of learning services" is applicable to Tanzania, it does not recognize the primary financial player in the SEDP I – the World Bank itself (2011, p. 29). As was mentioned earlier, Tanzania was nearly 100 percent reliant on the World Bank to provide funding to the SEDP I (Tonini, 2010). Therefore, it is important for the World Bank to stay steadfast in its commitment to support a country's government in providing its own funding to maintain sustainability of educational programs. As Escobar (1995) would qualify, development discourse allows the Bank to more easily classify borrowers into simplified categories rather than maintain their individual country characteristics. However, if the Bank can unpack these categories and construct more individualized financial policy approaches towards these nations as opposed to seeing them through a singular lens, the Bank will garner more policy success in the future. A quick review of the second phase of Tanzania's SEDP II through the lens of the 2020 plan will help demonstrate how the new World Bank strategy will help or hinder their new secondary education policy.

## THE SECONDARY EDUCATION DEVELOPMENT PLAN PHASE II

The document outlining the second phase of Tanzania's SEDP II, written by the Ministry of Education and Vocational Training (MoEVT), is quite frank in outlining the successes and failures of its predecessor, the SEDP I. It opens by calling attention to the fact that the enrollment targets for the SEDP I exceeded expectations in regards to expanding access to secondary education throughout Tanzania (Ministry of Education and Vocational Training [MoEVT], 2010). Yet, the document also declares that as the goal to enhance educational quality faltered under SEDP I, quality improvement takes precedence in SEDP II:

> However, it is becoming increasingly evident that demand for secondary education which led to increase in the construction of schools and consequent increase in the number of students has created a bigger constraint on the provision of quality secondary education. While in practice access precedes quality and we should be proud of what has been achieved in this area, it is crucial that the two should be tackled together if one is to get value for money invested in education. Therefore, a priority is given to the improvement of the quality and relevance of education provided. (MoEVT, 2010, p. 18)

The SEDP II further details the need to improve quality in schooling, increase pass rates, hire more teachers, remedy the deficit of learning inputs, provide more teacher training, especially in science and mathematics, raise transition rates, instill more quality control at the school management level, and expand access even further for poor learners.

It is interesting to note that within the SEDP II, Tanzania reflects on their lending relationship with the World Bank, admitting that as the World Bank loan program ended, the government's ability to finance the SEDP I was adversely affected, especially as it related to funding for poor students. The Tanzanian government also acknowledged that their success in providing financing for the SEDP I fell short, revealing the fact that the secondary schools were forced to request contributions from the students, their parents and communities in order to aid in school construction as well as buy basic schooling necessities. It is apparent that Tanzania's Ministry of Education drafted the SEDP II with this experience in mind, as demonstrated by their outlook regarding participants in the SEDP II.

As in the Primary Education Development Plan, the SEDP II lists all the pertinent stakeholders regarding secondary education planning, but this time, the development partners are listed last. This new order indicates a departure from Tanzania's original position of prioritizing the donors first within educational policy. In other words, Tanzania still expects funding from development partners, but the tone is different as the implied intention conveyed by the discourse is to become more reliant on national government and local community resources rather than establish dependency on external funders. For example, the SEDP I document proclaims that the plan will be "financed" by "loans and grants from development partners" (MoEC, 2004, p. viii), whereas the same section in the SEDP II states the plan will merely be "implemented" by "development partners" (MoEVT, 2010, p. viii). In addition, regarding the education budget, the SEDP I highlights the quest for funding, declaring "The Government will continue to work with Development Partners in education so as to find means and ways of increasing SEDP funds for both recurrent and development expenditures" (MoEC, 2004, p. 20). The SEDP II document, however, appears to convey a stronger sense of government accountability, pronouncing that:

> The Government, in collaboration with Development Partners, Non-State Actors and communities, will continue to mobilize resources to address the key areas, strategies, and targets outlined SEDP II. The Government reaffirms its commitment to continue focusing resource allocation to [the] secondary education sub sector. (MoEVT, 2010, p. 55)

In fact, the verbiage of the SEDP II takes a refreshingly responsible approach regarding their financial strategy, stating that they will closely monitor the SEDP II implementation, and if it goes off target the education ministry will adjust budget accordingly[8] – which is a very different tactic from attempting to secure new loans. As the SEDP II has only been in force for a few months it is not yet possible to match the stated intent to the outcome of this policy. Thus, it is difficult to determine if the new tone and diction are examples of a more independent policy direction or hollow development rhetoric aimed once again at its donors in attempts of garnering further support – aid that was already forthcoming.

As Tanzania launched the SEDP II in the spring of 2010, it did so with renewed financial support from the World Bank, with their funding plan effective July 2010 and an annual review scheduled for July 2011 (World Bank, 2010). Using similar lending parameters from the SEDP I, the World Bank Project proposed a new credit within their Proposed Project Appraisal on the SEDP II,[9] with the development objective "to improve the quality of secondary education with a focus on underserved areas" (World Bank, 2010, p. x). The Bank outlines four components in the project:

> (i) upgrading existing schools infrastructure (IDA US$78.3 million; GoT [Government of Tanzania] US$192.2 million); (ii) improving the equitable provision of teachers and quality of teaching in mathematics, sciences, and languages (IDA US$27.1 million); (iii) ensuring adequate financing to secondary schools and improving utilization of resources (IDA US$37.8 million; GoT US$127.1 million); and (iv) providing capacity building and technical assistance to implement reforms (IDA US$6.8 million). (World Bank, 2010, p. x)

From outward appearances, it seems that the highlighted goals and objectives of the World Bank are now more closely aligned with those of the SEDP II than they were for the SEDP I. The discourse alludes to a renewed focus on improving quality within existing schools, while also mitigating the problem of uncontrolled secondary school growth of the SEDP I era. Each achievable listed above supports the World Bank's 2020 mission on "Learning for All," as the objectives focus on maximizing educational opportunities for learners. Also, in regards to financing, the World Bank's project proposal appears to have been influenced by its 2020 plan because as a development partner, it is apparent that the Bank is taking a stronger role in the support of the Tanzanian government's educational plan as opposed to just providing funding in accordance with its own goals.

As an example, within the objectives listed above, the Bank clearly delineates the financial responsibility to be borne by the Bank, and also the share to be shouldered by the Government of Tanzania. This division of financial labor indicates that both the Bank and the Tanzanian Government are individually fiscally accountable to the success of the SEDP II. If both parties hold true to this agreement, in performance as well as in spirit, it is highly possible that the SEDP II might not only face success, but sustainability. Viewed through the lens of Escobar's (1995) development discourse model, it is clear that there is still a hierarchical financial relationship between Tanzania and the World Bank. It is also possible that the development discourse in the SEDP II merely rationalizes the policy as an intervention (Ferguson, 1990). However, alluding to the discourse in their above quote regarding their ownership of previous policy failings, Tanzania may have learned from its earlier mistakes regarding its dependence on the Bank for both funding and policy direction, and this awareness has engendered new agency, giving them both voice and choice in future policy matters.

## CONCLUSION

The beginning of this chapter introduced the government of Tanzania and the World Bank as key actors in the construction and implementation of the SEDP, a policy which orchestrates fifteen years of secondary school development in Tanzania, focusing on improving both access to schooling and the quality of the learning experience. Conducted in three phases of five years each, the SEDP I ran from 2005 to 2009, with the recently enacted SEDP II running from 2010 to 2015. Through discourse analysis informed by the writings of Arturo Escobar (1995), policy reviews of the SEDP I and SEDP II and qualitative interviews with school staff who were impacted by the policies, the triangulated data revealed that both the World Bank and the government of Tanzania more actively pursued the easier objective of raising enrollment, losing sight of the goal to improve quality. The answer to why both actors pushed enrollment over quality lies within the data. First of all, increasing access to secondary school was an objective both listed in Tanzania's SEDP I policy, written by the Ministry of Education, and validated by the World Bank agreement, which funds the SEDP I. Similar to Mitchell's (2002) description of the legitimization of development in Egypt, this SEDP I goal received validation not only through the policy discourses that described it, but secondly, also via the monetary flows that occurred as this goal was achieved. Keeping in mind that the quality goals had not yet been reached but the World Bank kept releasing its loan tranches, it is comprehensible that the Government of Tanzania would interpret such payments as approval of their enrollment-raising aggressive school-building plan, despite the fact that the uncontrolled growth in student enrollment was eroding the existing educational infrastructure – and the quality goal. One secondary school parent offered evidence that there was a price to pay for such rapid expansion: "schools are built in each ward but the schools do not have enough teachers, laboratories, and books so generally standard of education has been lowered" (P. I. Babati1 (1-3), personal communication, April 24, 2008). Samoff (2009) reminds us "that aid dependence also influences how education itself is conceived" (p.12), and as Tanzania became dependent on the World Bank to fund its secondary education policy, it became apparent that schooling in Tanzania was being defined more as "Education for All" rather than "Learning for All."

Although the SEDP II, the next phase of the Secondary Education Development policy was the planned follow-up to the SEDP I, there is more to link the two documents together than natural succession. That connection, once again, can be found in the development discourse of the World Bank's newest education strategy, the 2020 Plan. As was aforementioned, the World Bank 2020 Plan shifts the core of its education strategy from a primary focus on access, encompassed in its previous theme of "Education for All," to "Learning for All" which recognizes that the value of education is derived not from being merely present in an educational facility, but being exposed to a quality learning experience. Highlighting the past with an eye to the future, the Bank admits that "projects have been most successful in getting and keeping children in school and improving educational equity, but they have lagged in improving learning and employment outcomes" (2011, p. 50). The SEDP II captures the essence of this transition, proclaiming first the access and equity successes of the SEDP I, but also admitting to the shortcomings of the SEDP I: "Poor performance in secondary education examinations ..."; "Acute shortages of teachers ..."; "Inequalities in learning environments ..."; "Insufficient infrastructure ..."; "Poor teaching approaches in the classroom ..." (MoEVT, 2010, p. vi, vii). In the same vein as Escobar, Samoff offers an explanation for the similarities in discourse, positing "The most obvious manifestation of aid dependence, first, is the external specification of education objectives and content" (2009, p. 12). As the World Bank 2020 Plan claims that "Gains in access to education have turned attention to the challenge of improving education quality and accelerating learning" (2011, p. 2), and the SEDP II embraces "improvement of quality and relevance" as one of its top educational goals (2010, p. vi), the influences of the World Bank are clear, embedded and internalized within Tanzania's national policy process, revealing the power of development discourse when backed by donor dollars.

The purpose of this chapter was to highlight the connections between World Bank rhetoric and educational policy development using Tanzania as a case study in which to observe and understand how power relations between a donor and a developing country serves to influence domestic policy in an arena once reserved for the sovereign nation. By using Escobar's (1995) model of development, this chapter calls attention to how development verbiage more firmly entrenches the donor/recipient power structure, and the effects this dependence has on educational policy development. By looking at Tanzania's primary and secondary education development plans and their struggles concerning their quest for increased educational access and quality, this piece provides insight regarding how a developing nation might negotiate this hierarchy to achieve their domestic priorities. Although this development relationship scenario is still playing out between Tanzania and the World Bank within the scope of SEDP II, it is hoped that future research will determine that the rising tide of enrollment in Tanzania was met by an equally high surge in quality.

## NOTES

1. Tanzania's second phase of the Secondary Educational Development Plan (SEDP II) is in effect from 2010 to 2015.

2. The names of all schools have been changed to maintain anonymity. In addition, all interviewees are anonymous, identified only by a code that differentiates between each of the schools used as interview sites, and whether the recipient was a student, teacher, headmaster or headmistress, parent or ministry official. Please see Tonini (2010) for further explanation of the coding table used for all schools and interviewees.

3. Please refer to Tonini (2010) for a more detailed description of the study.

4. In 1999, Tanzania was denoted as a Highly Indebted Poor Country (HIPC) as part of the HIPC initiative, which is a program jointly developed by the World Bank and the IMF to work towards debt reduction and macroeconomic reform as part of an overall poverty alleviation strategy (Tonini, 2010, p. 20).

5. Samoff (2009) makes the point that oftentimes Western economic agendas are articulated and supported by African nationals who are schooled in the theories and principles of Western economics. He terms this phenomenon as "the institutionalization of international influence" (p. 18).

6. The International Development Association (IDA) is the department of the World Bank that helps the world's poorest countries, and complements the Bank's other lending arm – the International Bank for Reconstruction and Development (IBRD) – which serves middle-income countries with capital investment and advisory services. IDA lends money (known as credits) on concessional terms. This

means that IDA credits have no interest charge and repayments are stretched over 35–40 years, including a 10-year grace period. IDA also provides grants to countries at risk of debt distress. Source: World Bank (n.d.). International Development Association (IDA). Retrieved from http://go.worldbank.org/55TJCXJ4D0. Accessed on September 20, 2009.

7. See Tonini (2010), Chart 3 for supporting data. Chart 3, titled "Percentage of Ministry's SEDP Budget Funded by Donor Aid" uses the Ministry of Education's SEDP I budget and expenditure data from 2005 – 2009 to determine the amount of funding provided for SEDP I from the World Bank, other donors, and the Ministry of Education itself.

8. See the annexes of the SEDP II document for a detailed description of the different proposed budget scenarios (MoEVT, 2010).

9. Of note, the "Proposed Project Appraisal on the SEDP II" is the funding commitment document authored by the World Bank (2010), and is completely separate from the SEDP II policy document, which is written by Tanzania's Ministry of Education and Vocational Training (2010).

## REFERENCES

Cooksey, B. (2004). Tanzania: Can PRS succeed where SAP failed? HakiElimu Working Paper Series, 04(3).

Davidson, E. (2004). The progress of the Primary Education Development Plan (PEDP) in Tanzania: 2002–2004. HakiElimu Working Paper Series, 2004(2).

Degnbol-Martinussen, J., & Engberg-Pedersen, P. (1999). *Aid – Understanding international development cooperation*. London: Zed Books.

Dembele, M. D. (2004). The International Monetary Fund and World Bank in Africa. Retrieved from http://spip.red.m2014.net/article.php3?id_article=62. Accessed on August 2, 2005.

Dewey, J. (1938). *Experience and education*. New York: Collier Books.

Escobar, A. (1995). *Encountering development: The making and unmaking of the Third World*. Princeton: Princeton University Press.

Ferguson, J. (1990). *The anti-politics machine: "Development," depoliticization, and bureaucratic power in Lesotho*. Cambridge: Cambridge University Press.

Foucault, M. (1972). *The Archaeology of Knowledge*. Trans. A. M. Sheridan Smith. New York: Harper & Row.

Heyneman, S. P. (2003). The history and problems in the making of education policy at the World Bank 1960–2000. *International Journal of Educational Development*, *23*, 315–337.

IMF. (1999). Tanzania: Enhanced structural adjustment facility policy framework paper, 1998/99–2000/01. IMF: Washington DC. Retrieved from http://www.imf.org/external/np/pfp/1999/tanzania/index.htm. Accessed on August 20, 2005.

Logan, I. B., & Mengisteab, K. (1993). IMF-World Bank adjustment and structural transformation in sub-Saharan Africa. *Economic Geography*, *69*(1), 1–24.

Mingat, A., & Tan, J. (1986). Expanding education through user charges: What can be achieved in Malawi and other LDCs? *Economics of Education Review*, *5*(3), 273–286.

Ministry of Education and Culture [MoEC]. (1995). *Education and training policy*. Dar es Salaam. Retrieved from http://www.tzonline.org/pdf/educationandtraining.pdf. Accessed on May 25, 2005.

Ministry of Education and Vocational Training [MoEVT]. (2010). Education sector development programme: Secondary education development programme II (July 2010–June 2015). Retrieved from http://www.moe.go.tz/PDF/SEDP%20II-%20FINAL%20DRAFT%20-%2023%20JUNE%202010.pdf. Accessed on March 14, 2011.

Mitchell, T. (2002). *Rule of experts: Egypt, techno-politics, modernity*. Berkeley, CA: University of California Press.

MoEC. (2004). Education sector development programme: Secondary education development plan, 2004–2009. Retrieved from http://www.tzonline.org/pdf/educationsectordevelopmentprogramme2009.pdf. Accessed on December 7, 2005.

Peet, R., & Hartwick, E. (1999). *Theories of development*. New York: Guilford Press.

Samoff, J. (1996). African education and development: Crisis, Triumphalism, research, loss of vision. *Alberta Journal of Educational Research*, *42*(2), 121–147.

Samoff, J. (2007). Education quality: The disabilities of aid. *International Review of Education*, *53*, 485–507.

Samoff, J. (2009). The fast track to planned dependence: Education aid to Africa. Paper presented at the International Political Science Association XXI World Congress, Santiago, Chile, July 12–16.

Sumra, S. (2003). Implementation of the Primary Education Development Plan: Voices from the community. HakiElimu Working Paper Series, 2003 (7).

Tonini, D. (forthcoming). The impact of access investments on quality: Evaluating costs and constituencies in Tanzania. *Society of International Education* (7), 1–15.

Tonini, D. (2010). The wide divide between policies and impacts: Examining government influence over parental educational choice in Tanzania. Doctoral Dissertation. Teachers College, Columbia University, Columbia.

UNICEF. (2001). Situation analysis of children in Tanzania 2001. Government of Tanzania. Retrieved from http://www.tzonline.org/pdf/situationanalysisofchildren.PDF. Accessed on August 20, 2005.

United Republic of Tanzania. (2001). *Poverty reduction strategy paper: Progress report 2000/01*. Dar es Salaam. Retrieved from http://www.imf.org/external/np/prsp/2001/tza/01/081401.pdf. Accessed on May 24, 2005.

Vavrus, F. (2003). *Desire and decline: Schooling amid crisis in Tanzania*. New York: Peter Lang.

Vavrus, F., & Seghers, M. (2010). Critical discourse analysis in comparative education: A discursive study of "partnership" in Tanzania's poverty reduction policies. *Comparative Education Review*, *54*(1), 77–103.

Weissman, R. (2000). Structural Adjustment Program (SAP) alert on IMF and World Bank lending to Tanzania. Stop IMF Digest, 1(69). Retrieved from http://www.hartford-hwp.com/archives/36/347.html. Accessed on August 7, 2005.

World Bank. (1987). World Development Report. World Bank and Oxford University Press, New York.

World Bank. (1994). World Development Report. World Bank and Oxford University Press, New York.

World Bank. (1995). World Development Report. World Bank and Oxford University Press, New York.

World Bank. (1999). *Tanzania: Social sector review*. Washington, DC: The World Bank.

World Bank. (2001, October 10). Tanzania: World Bank approves primary education project. Retrieved from http://web.worldbank.org/WBSITE/EXTERNAL/COUNTRIES/AFRICAEXT/TANZANIAEXTN/0,contentMDK:20012776~menuPK:287355~pagePK:141137~piPK:141127~theSitePK:258799,00.html. Accessed on May 24, 2005.

World Bank. (2005). *Meeting the challenge of Africa's development: A World Bank Group Action Plan*. Washington, DC: The World Bank.

World Bank. (2008a). Implementation Completion and Results Report (IDA-39150 IDA-H0930) on a credit in the amount of SDR 82.7 million (US$ 123.6 million equivalent) and a grant of SDR 17.7 million (US$ 26.4 million) to the United Republic of Tanzania for the Secondary Education Development Program. Washington, DC: The World Bank.

World Bank. (2008b). World Development Index. Retrieved from http://siteresources.worldbank.org/DATASTATISTICS/Resources/GNIPC.pdf. Accessed on October 13, 2009.

World Bank. (2010). *Project appraisal document on a proposed credit in the amount of SDR 98.8 Million (US$150 Million equivalent) to the United Republic of Tanzania for a Secondary Education Development Program II APL 1 Project*. Washington, DC: The World Bank.

World Bank. (2011). *World Bank Group Education Strategy 2020*. Washington, DC: The World Bank.

# ABOUT THE AUTHORS

**Richard Allington** is professor of education at the University of Tennessee. Richard is a past president of the International Reading Association and the Literacy Research Association. He has been principal investigator on a number of research projects funded by the United States Office of Educational Research and Improvement, the Office of Special Education and Rehabilitation, and the National Institutes of Health. He is the author of over 150 articles and several books.

**Robert F. Arnove**, past president and honorary fellow of the Comparative and International Education Society, is chancellor's professor emeritus of educational leadership and policy studies, Indiana University, Bloomington. He has written extensively on the promise and limitations of educational reform movements as well as the workings of international financial and technical assistance agencies.

**Supriya Baily** is assistant professor at George Mason University, researches issues around gender, youth, nonformal education, and teacher's perceptions of international students. She has spent 15 years working in international women, peace and justice, and children's organizations. She is beginning to have a number of publications in print, and is coeditor of a soon to be released book: *Internationalizing Teacher Education in the United States.*

**Sarah Beardmore** is an education development policy specialist with RESULTS Educational Fund where she manages a multicountry advocacy campaign to achieve Education for All. She has a master of science in political sociology from the London School of Economics, and over 10 years of experience in policy research and advocacy to promote human rights and equity.

**Tammy Boyd** is assistant professor of higher education and policy studies at the University of Central Florida. Her current research interests are international education policy, the use of education as a tool of national development, and the anthropology of education, particularly the experience of colonized/marginalized populations in the public education system, including postsecondary education.

**Christopher S. Collins** is assistant professor of education at the University of Hawaii at Mānoa. His research interests include the role of education related poverty reduction, land-grant extension, and social rates of return to higher education. He recently published *Higher Education and Global Poverty: University Partnerships and the World Bank in Developing Countries* (Cambria Press, 2011). In 2009 he earned a Ph.D. in higher education and organizational change with the "Best Dissertation Award" from the Graduate School of Education at UCLA.

**Chijioke J. Evoh** works for the New York City department of education. He holds a doctorate in public and urban policy from the New School University. He has done consultant work for UNICEF and ILO in macroeconomic policy, ICT-skill development and employment generation for youths. He is the author and coauthor of various book chapters and journal articles on ICTs and educational development in the developing countries.

**D. Brent Edwards, Jr.** is Ph.D. candidate in the International Education Policy program at the University of Maryland, College Park. During the 2011–2012 academic year he is on Fulbright in El Salvador collecting data for his dissertation, which focuses on the involvement and interaction of international, national, and local level actors in processes of education policy formation. His other research interests include decentralization and participation in development and education governance.

**Rachael Gabriel** is assistant professor in curriculum and instruction at the University of Connecticut. She holds Ph.D. in education from the University of Tennessee, as well as graduate certificates in both quantitative and qualitative research methods in education and a reading specialist license. Her research focuses on education policy, teacher development and evaluation, discourse analysis in education and policy settings, and interventions for struggling readers.

**Stephen P. Heyneman** received his Ph.D. in comparative education from the University of Chicago in 1976. He served the World Bank for 22 years. In July 2000 he was appointed professor of international education policy at Vanderbilt University. Current interests include the effect of higher education on social cohesion, the international trade in education services, and the economic and social cost to higher education corruption.

**Devin Joshi** is assistant professor in the Josef Korbel School of International Studies at the University of Denver where he teaches courses on political and human development in Asia. His articles and reviews have appeared in *Contemporary South Asia, Economic and Political Weekly, International Studies Review, Journal of Education Policy, Perspectives on Global Development and Technology*, and the *Taiwan Journal of Democracy*.

**Steven J. Klees** is professor of international education policy at the University of Maryland. His work examines the political economy of education and development with specific research interests in globalization, neoliberalism, and education; the role of aid agencies; education, human rights, and social justice; the education of disadvantaged populations; the role of class, gender, and race in reproducing and challenging educational and social inequality; and alternative approaches to education and development.

**Owen G. McGrath** has worked for many years in educational technology at the University of California (UC) Berkeley. He has led development and implementation efforts for multimedia courseware, collaboration tools, and community source software such as Sakai. Previously, he was also a research consultant at the Carnegie Foundation for the Advancement of Teaching. He has a Ph.D. in Education from UC Berkeley and bachelor's degrees in english and computer science.

**Francine Menashy** is post-doctoral research fellow at the Comparative, International and Development Education Centre of the University of Toronto/Ontario Institute for Studies in Education. Her research focuses on international education policies and private sector engagement in education. Her work has been published in such journals as *Globalisation, Societies and Education, the McGill Journal of Education*, and *the Journal of Educational Thought*.

**John Middleton** has over 30 years of experience in education development and project operations in sub-Saharan Africa and South Asia, and has now retired from the World Bank where he worked in various roles since 1986. He holds a doctorate in educational planning from Harvard University and has conducted policy research on vocational and technical education and training, education management, and reform and ICT for development learning.

**Karen Mundy** is associate professor and Canada research chair at the Ontario Institute for Studies in Education of the University of Toronto. Her award winning research has focused on the politics of international education assistance in the developing world, educational reform in Africa, the role of civil society advocacy in educational systems, and the issue of global education in North American schools. Her recent research, published in more than two dozen journal articles and book chapters and in her five edited volumes, is concentrated on the evolution of global efforts to ensure "education for all"; the role of the World Bank in education; and civil society activism in Africa. Dr. Mundy has been a consultant for, or carried out sponsored research for, such organizations as UNICEF, UNESCO, Hewlett Foundation, the World Bank, Mastercard Foundation, the Canadian International Development Agency, the Open Society Institute, UNESCO, and USAID. She is also the founder and cochair of the Canadian Global Campaign for Education, a coalition of NGOs, teachers unions, and universities committed to advancing education for all.

**Tom Owens** is currently the director of the Center for Educational Research and Development in the College of Education at The University of Central Florida. He received his Ph.D. in international/intercultural development education from The Florida State University and has worked in Latin America and the Middle East.

**Victor J. Sensenig** is doctoral candidate in education policy at Penn State University. He previously worked on education projects with the relief and service agency Mennonite Central Committee in Central Java, Indonesia. His current research focuses on reading education policy and the distribution of print access.

**M. Najeeb Shafiq** is assistant professor at the University of Pittsburgh's Department of administrative and policy studies, and Department of Economics (secondary appointment). He uses advanced quantitative methods to explore educational topics in developing countries and the United States. Dr. Shafiq received his Ph.D. in economics and education from Columbia University and previously held appointments at the World Bank and Indiana University, Bloomington.

**William Smith** is doctoral student at Penn State University pursuing a dual-degree in education theory and policy and comparative international education. His research has focused on mapping out the connection between education and economic development, with particular interest paid to how international finance institutions impact educational equity. He has interned for Namlo International and carried out consultant work with the Global Campaign for Education.

**Nelly P. Stromquist** is professor of international education policy in the College of Education at the University of Maryland. She specializes in issues related to international development education and gender. Her research interests focus on the dynamics among educational policies and practices, gender relations, and social change. She has written several books and numerous articles. Her most recent books include editing *The Professoriate in the Age of Globalization* and writing *Feminist Organizations and Social Transformation in Latin America.*

**Donna C. Tonini** received her Ed.D. in international educational development with a specialization in finance and planning from Teachers College, Columbia University in 2010. Her research evaluates how current educational policy in Tanzania addresses access to quality schooling, and impacts the local constituents. She also holds an MBA in international business from Bentley University, and has worked for USAID on development projects in Africa and the Caribbean.

**Athena Vongalis-Macrow** began researching and writing about global education in 1998. Since then she has produced a number of publications and reports on education policy and international education. She currently teaches in global education policy and continues to research education policy, education leadership, and gender in leadership at Deakin University in Burwood, Australia.

**Alexander W. Wiseman** is associate professor of comparative and international education in the College of Education at Lehigh University. Dr. Wiseman conducts educational research using large international datasets on math and science education, information and communication technology (ICT), teacher preparation, professional development, and curriculum, as well as school principal's instructional leadership activity, and is the author of many research-to-practice articles and books.

# AUTHOR INDEX

# SUBJECT INDEX

Printed and bound by CPI Group (UK) Ltd, Croydon, CR0 4YY

16/06/2026

14900974-0003